JOHANNINE STUDIES

Frank Pack

JOHANNINE STUDIES

Essays in Honor of Frank Pack

James E. Priest, Editor

Editorial Consultants

W. Royce Clark   Ronald L. Tyler

Pepperdine University Press
Malibu, California
1989

Copyright © 1989
James E. Priest

All rights in this book are reserved. No part of the book may be reproduced in any manner whatsoever without written permission of copyright owner except brief quotations embodied in critical articles or reviews.

For information address
Pepperdine University Press
Malibu, California

Library of Congress Cataloging-in-Publication Data

Johannine studies.

"Bibliography of Frank Pack": p.
Includes indexes.
1. Bible. N.T. John — Criticism, interpretation, etc. 2. Bible. N.T. Revelation — Criticism, interpretation, etc. 3. Pack, Frank, 1916-   . I. Pack, Frank, 1916-   . II. Priest, James Eugene, 1923- III. Clark, W. Royce. IV. Tyler, Ronald, L.
BS2615.2.J58   1989   226'.506   88-25501
ISBN 0-932612-20-2

Set up, printed, and bound by
Gospel Teachers Publications,
Dallas, Texas, U.S.A.

Dust Cover Design
Bill Henegar
Assistant Vice President for Creative Services
Pepperdine University, Malibu, California

Table of Contents

An Open Letter to Frank Pack (James E. Priest) viii
Biography of Frank Pack (J.P. Sanders) ix
Bibliography of Frank Pack (Elizabeth N. Whatley) xiii
Essay Writers.. xxii
Bread of Life in *Joseph and Aseneth* and in John 6
   (Randall D. Chesnutt)... 1
The Fourth Gospel and Christology in Modern Dogmatic and
   Systematic Theology (W. Royce Clark) 17
Johannine Christology During the Reformation (Dan G. Danner) 36
Origen's Demonology (Everett Ferguson).......................... 54
Interpersonal Relationships in the Gospel of John (John C. Free)...... 67
Missions and the Servants of God (John 5) (Evertt W. Huffard)....... 84
The Semitic Background of the Gospel of John (Jack P. Lewis) 97
Metaphors and an Obligational Norm for Ministry in the Fourth
   Gospel (Stuart L. Love) 111
John 3:14-15: The Raised Serpent in the Wilderness: The Johannine
   Use of an Old Testament Account (Rick M. Marrs).............. 132
Counseling from the Gospel of John (Carl Mitchell) 148
The Theology of the Signs in the Gospel of John
   (Thomas H. Olbricht).. 171
Contemporary Apocalyptic Scholarship and the Revelation
   (James E. Priest) 182
The Source and Function of Isaiah 6:9-10 in John 12:40
   (Ronald L. Tyler) 205
Archeology and the Origins of the Fourth Gospel: Gabbatha
   (John F. Wilson) 221
The Old Testament and the Book of Revelation (John T. Willis) 231
Bibliography 240
Indexes.. 263
   Hebrew Bible 264
   New Testament.. 267
   Apocrypha.. 280

Jewish Ancient Writings 280
Non-Jewish Ancient Writings 282
Key Words, Subjects, and Places 286
Persons.. 294
    Biblical 294
    Authors 296
    Editors.. 303
    Translators 306
    Others 308

An Open Letter to Frank Pack

It is traditional to have a preface in a book. In this case, it seems too impersonal. Permit me to explain why.

In the spring of 1954, I was working for Texaco in Port Arthur, Texas, and serving the South Park Church of Christ in Beaumont, Texas, as a deacon. As was your custom, you were traveling away from Abilene Christian College that summer, preaching in various cities. You came to Beaumont. As I sat in the audience from night to night and listened to your preaching, you changed my life.

By late summer of 1954, my family and I were working with a little church in the town of Woodville, located in East Texas. I was happy to be preaching. When you came to the nearby town of Jasper, I took a car load of friends to hear you preach. Again, you changed my life. As I listened to your erudition, eloquence, and mastery of Scripture, I realized how much more education and training I needed to be a responsible steward of God's Word.

One year later my family and I moved to Cross Plains near Abilene, Texas. While preaching for the church in Cross Plains, I had the privilege of attending Abilene Christian College. As I sat in your classes, the world of the Bible and the significance of God's Word opened up to me. Again, you changed my life.

Nine years later, I was preaching in Baltimore, Maryland, and attending Johns Hopkins University. You came to Washington, D.C., to deliver a series of lectures. I attended. We had a pleasant visit after your lecture. You invited me to join the Religion Faculty at Pepperdine University where you were then serving as Professor of Religion and Chairman of the Religion Division. I accepted. Again, you changed my life.

The past 25 years of close association with you have been wonderful. True, they have often been blurred with activity. There have been relentless demands. At times, the daily schedule has been hectic and harried. The classrooms have often been crowded. Administrative responsibilities have emerged. Also, in our ministerial work with area churches through all these years there have been lessons to prepare, marriages to perform, funerals to conduct, sermons to preach, counseling to give, *ad infinitum*.

You have been a stabilizing, sustaining influence for me through these years. Your presence, your handshake, your smile, have always been an encouragement. You have always been near to bolster and strengthen. Our conversations have stimulated; our struggles with tough questions have sharpened my wits. How you have, indeed, changed my life! I have seen Jesus in you. Because of you, I have often been motivated to walk more diligently in His footsteps.

So you can see why it is not appropriate to call this a preface.

It has been a gratifying privilege and pleasure to work with esteemed colleagues in preparing this volume in you honor. For us, it has been a labor of love. We all regard you highly for what you have done and for what you are. And, when we think of you, we realize what a tremendously positive impact your lovely wife Della has had upon your life and upon all those who have known her as we have. We salute both of you.

Fraternally,

James E. Priest
Editor

Biography of Frank Pack

J.P. Sanders

Frank Pack was born in Memphis, Tennessee, on March 27, 1916. His parents are Walter and Mary Gibson Pack. Frank was the eldest of three boys — Charles, Dwight, and Joe. Frank attended the public schools of Memphis and graduated from Memphis Technical High School as salutatorian of the graduating class. He, together with his parents, began attending the Harbert Avenue Church which became the Union Avenue Church of Christ in Memphis.

John Allen Hudson was the preacher then and was followed by G.C. Brewer. Frank's parents were baptized in the summer of 1926 when N.B. Hardeman was conducting a gospel meeting. Later the same year, Frank became a Christian under the preaching of Horace W. Busby of Fort Worth, Texas. Hudson, Hardeman, Brewer, and Busby were well known and distinguished names in the church. Consequently, Frank heard the gospel from able and powerful preachers.

Even before he became a Christian, Frank had decided that he wanted to become a preacher. He entered David Lipscomb College in the fall of 1932. He had been encouraged to go to a Christian school by G.C. Brewer, who preached for the Union Avenue Church where the Pack family attended. Brewer was a graduate of Lipscomb when it was known as the Nashville Bible School. He was a strong supporter of Christian education. I.C. Finley also encouraged Frank to go to Lipscomb. Frank came to know the Finleys as a result of visiting his grandfather Gibson in the summers. Finley was a member of the Lipscomb board and an elder of the Reid Avenue congregation where Frank attended with his grandfather. The entire Finley family became a dynamic influence in Frank's life.

At Lipscomb Frank distinguished himself as a student and as a campus leader. He was active in both debate and drama, in which he had several leading roles. While a freshman, he won the Founder's Day Oratorical Award and in 1934 became president of the debate club.

While at Lipscomb, Frank had the opportunity of studying under a number of well-known and distinguished Bible teachers, such as H. Leo Boles, the beloved Sam Pittman, E.H. Ijams, and Hall L. Calhoun, minister of the Central Church of Nashville, who served as a part-time faculty member. He was, no doubt, the most distinguished Biblical scholar the church had at that time. During this period, Frank made a number of friendships destined to remain friends and later be colleagues in Christian higher education. Chief among them were Howard A. White and M. Norvel Young.

In July of 1932, before entering Lipscomb in the fall, Frank preached his first sermon at the Reid Avenue Church of Christ. Throughout his three years at Lipscomb, he regularly filled monthly preaching appointments. Frank was interested in people and entered into meaningful friendship relationships with many of the members of his congregation. Some of these friendships remain warm to this day, and he continues to hold gospel meetings for congregations where he preached while a student at Lipscomb.

On leaving Lipscomb, Frank was asked to serve as minister for the St. Elmo congregation in Chattanooga, Tennessee. During the first year of his ministry, he enrolled in the University of Chattanooga and completed his bachelor of arts degree. He wanted to continue his education and decided to enroll in Vanderbilt University to work on the master's degree in sociology. He continued to preach for the St. Elmo Church three Sundays each month, and on the fourth, he preached for the Grace Avenue Church in Nashville. He completed work on the M.A. degree and graduated in 1939; he continued preaching for the St. Elmo Church in Chattanooga until 1940.

For the next four years he taught sociology and Bible at David Lipscomb College and preached for the Grace Avenue Church of Christ. Frank did all of his work with fairness and intelligence. Just as he was recognized as a superior preacher, even though young, the administration of the college soon came to appreciate not only his scholarship, but also his skill as a communicator. He mediated the truth of God's word to his students with skill and effectiveness. He caught their attention and held their interest as only a superior teacher can. Through his ability, his scholarship, and effectiveness, he won the respect of the school's administration and his colleagues, and; through his Christian devotion, he won their admiration.

The desire for further training called Frank to go to the University of Southern California, where he enrolled in the speech department in February of 1945. He had long had an interest in speech and drama, and he felt this would be a great background as well as a material help in his preaching. The dean of the School of Speech was Dr. Immel, and Frank enrolled in one of his classes. Dr. Immel suffered a heart attack and died before the term was out. With the passing of Dr. Immel, the glamour of the drama department vanished for Frank.

Under the encouragement of Dr. W.B. West, Jr., and other friends, Frank decided to major in New Testament studies. This was, after all, where his real heart interest lay. Dr. Titus, professor of New Testament in the Graduate School of Religion at USC, was delighted to have Frank as a graduate student and encouraged him. While Frank was taking a class under Dr. Titus, Titus recognized his ability and encouraged him to do his work in his division. Frank's good work, and Dr. Titus' appreciation of it, eventually led to Frank's receiving the Phi Beta Kappa key.

Dr. Titus was also the chairman of Frank's dissertation graduate committee. His dissertation was entitled "The Methodology of Origen as a Textual Critic in Arriving at the Text of the New Testament." His dissertation emphasized the fact that Origen's textual work should be seen as part of his attitude toward the Scriptures as a whole. During the years of graduate study, Frank preached for the church in Burbank (1945-1949), and served on the faculty of Pepperdine College (1945-1949). He was awarded the Ph.D. degree in 1948.

But scholarship was not the only thing that interested Frank while a graduate student from 1945 to 1948. In the late summer of 1946, he met Della Carlton. She was a native of Kansas, and after teaching two years in that state, she decided to move to Los Angeles to be with her family. She was teaching in San Marino when Frank met her. Frank was introduced to Della by their mutual friends, the George Beal family. Frank fell in love with Della immediately. They were engaged in December and were married the following June, 1947. The Packs believe, and their friends concur, their marriage was really made in heaven. A great marriage is the result of two great persons, each of whom is concerned with the building unto himself or herself the kind of personality characteristics revealed in the person of Jesus. The Packs have that kind of marriage. They have so built their lives together that their marriage has become a role model for hundreds of young people who have known them.

Frank accepted the invitation of Abilene Christian College to join their faculty in 1949, and held that post until 1963. At Abilene, he soon gained the reputation of being a superior teacher. He was popular among students for his interesting and exciting classes. Highly regarded by his colleagues for his erudite scholarship, he was asked to take the post of dean of the college. But while pondering that offer, he received an invitation to return to Pepperdine. He faced a difficult decision but elected to come to Pepperdine, motivated by his feeling that he was needed at Pepperdine to help make the school what George Pepperdine wanted it to become. He became chairman of the Religion Division and was soon appointed to become dean of the Graduate School. He introduced uniformity of admission requirements and graduation requirements among the various divisions as graduate dean, and helped to restore the confidence of many church people in the integrity of the college. After a number of years of service, to show appreciation for his distinctive and superior work, the school appointed him "Distinguished Professor of Religion." Until his retirement from Pepperdine, he was the only distinguished professor Pepperdine University ever had.

While at Abilene, Frank preached regularly for the Northside Church (1950-1958); and, after coming to Pepperdine, he has preached for the Culver-Palms Church since 1964, during which time the congregation has experienced tremendous growth both in membership and in Christian maturity.

Whatever else he has done, he has always been a preacher of the gospel since he preached his first sermon in 1932. His preaching is distinctly Biblical. Since the key to any literature is the language in which it is written, Frank's knowledge of both Hebrew and Greek provide him an excellent tool for studying the Scriptures. Not only the texts of his sermons, but all Scriptures used in his preaching, are carefully examined in the original languages. Consequently, his exegesis is sound, and his sermons are true to their Biblical sources.

Frank is the author of nine books and over 300 journal articles. He holds membership in the Phi Beta Kappa, Phi Kappa Phi, Pi Gamma Mu, and Alpha Chi. He is a member of the Society of Biblical Literature, the American Society of Church History, and the Evangelical Theological Society. He is listed in *Who's Who in America* and *Who's Who in Religion*.

[These and other facts about Frank Pack may be found in an excellent unpublished M.A. thesis in the Payson Library of Pepperdine University written by Elizabeth N. Whatley entitled *Frank Pack: Preacher, Scholar and Writer*.]

Bibliography of Frank Pack

(Compiled by Elizabeth N. Whatley)

A. Books

Lessons in Church History. Tennessee: Cole Printing Co., 1940.
Sermons of Frank Pack. Abilene, Texas: Biblical Research Press (Great Preachers of Today, v. 5, ed. J.D. Thomas), 1963.
Revelation, Part 1, Chapters 1-11. Austin, Texas: R.B. Sweet Co., Inc., 1965.
Revelation, Part 2, Chapters 12-22. Austin, Texas: R.B. Sweet Co., Inc., 1965.
Preaching to Modern Man. Co-author with Prentice Meador, Jr., Abilene, Texas: Biblical Research Press, 1969.
Tongues and the Holy Spirit. Abilene, Texas: Biblical Research Press (Way of Life Series, ed. J.D. Thomas), 1972.
The Gospel According to John: Part 1, 1-10:42. Austin, Texas: R.B. Sweet Co., Inc., 1975.
The Gospel According to John: Part 2, 11:1-21:25. Austin, Texas: R.B. Sweet Co., Inc., 1977.
The Message of the New Testament, The Revelation, Parts I and II. Abilene, Texas: Biblical Research Press, 1984.

B. Published Works: Chapters in Books

Godhead

"God and Human Suffering," in *Abilene Christian College Bible Lectures*, ed. Reuel Lemmons, (Austin: Firm Foundation Publishing House, 1958), pp. 128-142.
"The Revelation of God in Christ," in *The Inspiration and Authority of the Bible*, ed. B.C. Goodpasteur, (Nashville: Gospel Advocate Company, 1971), pp. 141-155.
"The Story of Redemption — Old Testament," in *My Best Book*, ed. W. Stanley Mooneyham, [Gastonia: Good Will Publishers, Inc., (The Master Library, v. 10), 1968], between pp. 360-361.
"The Story of Redemption — New Testament," in *My Best Book*, ed. W. Stanley Mooneyham, [Gastonia: Good Will Publishers, Inc., (The Master Library, v. 10), 1968], between pp. 266-267.

Christian Evidences

"Forward," *Sacredness and Authority of the Bible*, by Bill Paterson, (Dallas: Gospel Teachers Publications, 1984).

"The Inspiration of the Scripture," in *Abilene Christian College Bible Lectures*, ed. J.D. Thomas, (Abilene: ACC Students Exchange, 1964) pp. 30-46.

"The Inspiration of the Scriptures," in *Pillars of Faith*, ed. by H.O. Wilson and Morris Womack (Grand Rapids: Baker Book House, 1973), pp. 175-185.

Church

"The Church and the Times," in *Abilene Christian College Bible Lectures*, ed. Reuel Lemmons, (Austin: Firm Foundation Publishing House, 1950), pp. 61-79.

"The Mission of the Church: Helping Those in Need," in *Harding College Lectureship*, ed. Reuel Lemmons, (Austin: Firm Foundation Publishing House, 1959), pp. 147-162.

"Overcoming Problems in Worship," in *Abilene Christian College Bible Lectures*, ed. Reuel Lemmons, (Austin: Firm Foundation Publishing House, 1954), pp. 114-129.

Educational

"Preparing the Missionary," in *Abilene Christian College Bible Lectures*, ed. Reuel Lemmons, (Austin: Firm Foundation Publishing House, 1959), pp. 115-136.

"Reviving Daily Teaching," in *Arizona Bible Lectures*, 2nd., ed. John Young, (Phoenix: Highway House, 1964).

Exegetical/Textual

"Blood"; "Script"; "Joy"; "Sergius Paulus"; "Epistles, Spurious"; "Doxologies." Articles in *The Wycliffe Bible Encyclopedia*, ed. Charles F. Pfeiffer, (Chicago: Moody Press, 1962).

"Exegesis of Revelation 20:1-6," in *Abilene Christian University Bible Lectures*, ed. Carl Brecheen, (Abilene, Texas: ACU Bookstore, 1980), pp. 153-168.

"Septuagint," in *The New Smith's Bible Dictionary*, ed. by Reuel Lemmons, (Garden City: Doubleday & Company, Inc., 1966), pp. 346-348.

"New Testament Textual Criticism," in *Biblical Interpretation*, ed. by Furman Kearley, (Grand Rapids: Baker Book House, 1986), pp. 214-225.

Practical Christian Living

"The Living Word for Living Man," in *Harding College Lectureship*, (Austin, Texas: Firm Foundation Publishing House, 1962), p. 142.

"The Power of Prayer," in *Great Sermons*, (Austin, Texas: R.B. Sweet & Co., Inc., 1967), pp. 142-149.

"The Role of the Christian Journal: The Editor's Responsibilities," in *Abilene Christian College Bible Lectures*, ed. J.D. Thomas, (Abilene, Texas: ACU Bookstore, 1968), pp. 466-471.

"First They Gave Themselves," in *Harding University Lectures*, ed. Reuel Lemmons, (Austin, Texas: Firm Foundation Publishing House, 1980), pp. 367-375.

Textual

"Acts 17:31: The Final Judgement," in *Lubbock Christian College Lectures*, (Lubbock, Texas: Lubbock Christian College, 1972), pp. 29-37.

"Grace in Galatians," in *Harding University Lectures*, ed. Eddie Cloer, (Delight, Arkansas, Gospel Light Publishing Co., 1984), pp. 18-25.

"Romans," in *Fort Worth Christian College Lectures*, (Fort Worth, Texas: FWCC Bookstore, 1962), pp. 99-114.

C. Periodicals: Articles In

Book Reviews

Bales, James D., *Communism: Its Faith and Fallacies*, reviewed in *Restoration Quarterly* VI:3 (1962) 105-106.

"Books to Challenge Christian Thinking," reviewed in *20th Century Christian* XXV (February, 1963) 27-28.

"Books to Challenge Christian Thinking," reviewed in *20th Century Christian* XXV (May, 1963) 13-14.

Bruce, F.F., *Commentary on the Book of Acts*, reviewed in *Restoration Quarterly* I:3 (1957) 143-144.

Bruce, F.F., *The Acts of the Apostles*, reviewed in *Restoration Quarterly* I:3 (1957) 144.

Buttrick, George A. (ed.), *The Interpreter's Dictionary of the Bible*, reviewed in *Restoration Quarterly* VI:3 (1962) 151-155.

Feinberg, Charles L., *Millennialism: The Two Major Views*, reviewed in *Journal of the Evangelical Theological Society* XXIV (Dec., 1981) 343-344.

Gaster, Theodor Herzl, *The Dead Sea Scrolls in English Translation*, reviewed in *Restoration Quarterly* I:3 (1957) 142.

Pack, Frank, "An Evaluation of the Revised Standard Version, Catholic Edition," *Restoration Quarterly* IX:1 (1966) 21-30.

Tillich, Paul, *Perspectives on 19th and 20th Century Protestant Theology*, reviewed in *Restoration Quarterly* XII:1 (1959) 55-56.

Warren, Thomas B., *Have Atheists Proved There Is No God — A Review*, reviewed in *Gospel Advocate* CXIII (Feb., 8), 86-87.

Christian Education

"Discipleship on the Campus." *Mission* I (August 1967) 47-50.

"Every Teacher Teaching Christ by Precept and Example (1)." *Gospel Advocate* XCIX (Nov. 14, 1957) 726-730.

"Every Teacher Teaching Christ by Precept and Example (2)." *Gospel Advocate* XCIX (Dec. 12, 1957) 792-795.
"How Christian Schools Can Help." *20th Century Christian* XV (May, 1953) 11-12.
"Soldiers of Courage." *Gospel Advocate* CV (Nov. 7, 1963) 713.
"Some Great Things Are Happening." *Firm Foundation* LXXXVII (Nov. 2, 1971) 695.
"Some Great Things Are Happening." *Gospel Advocate* CXIII (Nov. 18, 1971) 726.
"Teaching the Bible and Religion at Pepperdine." *Firm Foundation* LXXXV (Oct. 28, 1969) 678.
"That We May Serve More." *Gospel Advocate"* CVI (Nov. 19, 1964) 740-741.
"Training the Teacher." *Gospel Advocate* XCIX (May 2, 1957) 279-280.
"Twenty-Five Years of Teaching in Christian Colleges." *Gospel Advocate* CVIII (March 17, 1966) 169-170.

Christian Evidences

"Archeological Confirmations of the Bible." *Gospel Advocate* XCIV (Dec. 4, 1952) 790-791.
"The Bible Is Inspired of God." *Power for Today* 1 (Oct., 1955) 39.
"Can an Educated Person Believe in Virgin Birth?" *20th Century Christian* XXI (Dec., 1958) 28-30.
"The Christ of the Gospels? A Response." *Mission* II (April, 1969) 13-16.
"The Early Church Shows and Shares the Loving Christ." *20th Century Christian* XXXII (April, 1970) 35-41.
"General Texts on Inspiration." *Gospel Advocate* XCV (Jan. 29, 1953) 56.
"How Do We Know the Bible Is Inspired?" *Gospel Advocate* CXI (Jan. 23, 1969) 61-63.
"How The Bible Was Written." *20th Century Christian* XIV (Nov., 1951) 7-9.
"The Meaning of Revelation (No. 1)." *Gospel Advocate* XXCIV (Nov. 6, 1952) 713.
"The Meaning of Inspiration (No. 2)." *Gospel Advocate,* XCIV (Dec. 11, 1952) 803-804.
"The Offense of the Cross." *20th Century Christian* XV (Aug., 1953) 14-16.
"The Resurrection in Early Preaching." *20th Century Christian* XXV (April, 1963) 8-9.
"Was Peter Ever in Rome? The Biblical Evidence." *Gospel Advocate* XCVII (April 28, 1955) 321, 335-336.
"Why We Believe the Bible." *Gospel Advocate* XCVII (July 14, 1955) 592, 594).

Church

"Build on Jesus," *Power for Today* XX (April 17, 1973) 50.
"How To Enter The Church," *Gospel Advocate* CII (March 24, 1960) 185-187.

"I Will Build My Church," *Gospel Advocate* CIV (Oct. 4, 1962) 631-633.
"Jesus and the Kingdom," *Gospel Advocate* CIV (July 12, 1962) 433, 441, 443.
"The Church and the Alcohol Problem," *20th Century Christian* XV (Jan., 1953) 24-30.
"The Church as Jesus Saw It (No. 2)," *Gospel Advocate* CVI (Jan. 4, 1962) 4-5.
"The Nature of the Kingdom in Jesus' Teaching," *Gospel Advocate* CIV (Sept. 13, 1962) 586-587.
"The Plea of the Church," *20th Century Christian* XXVII (Jan., 1965) 18-19.
"Who Sets the Standards?" *20th Century Christian* XXII (Oct., 1959) 3-4.

Apologetics

"Modernism Views Jesus (No. 1)," *Gospel Advocate* XCIII (Aug. 9, 1951) 502-503.
"Modernism Views Jesus (No. 2)," *Gospel Advocate* XCIII (Sept. 13, 1951) 580-582.
"Modernism Views Jesus (No. 3)," *Gospel Advocate* XCIII (Oct. 4, 1951) 630-631.
"Modernist Conceptions of Paul (No. 1)," *Gospel Advocate* XCIII (Oct. 22, 1951) 675-678.
"Modernist Conceptions of Paul (No. 2)," *Gospel Advocate* XCIII (Nov. 1, 1951) 694-695.
"Mysticism — Why Its Appeal?" *Gospel Advocate* CXX (March 2, 1978) 129, 135.
"Pentecostalism and Neo-Pentecostalism," *Alternative* II (April, 1976) 1.
"Some Modern Views on Infant Baptism," *Restoration Quarterly* I:4 (1957) 220-225.
"The Significance of Vatican Council II," *Gospel Advocate* (Sept. 6, 1962) 568-569.
"What is Modernism? (No. 1)," *Gospel Advocate* XCIII (June 28, 1951) 402-403.
"What is Modernism? (No. 2)," *Gospel Advocate* XCIII (July 26, 1951) 469-470.

Exegetical/Textual

"The Contributions of Textual Criticism to the Interpretation of the New Testament." *Restoration Quarterly* V:4 (1961) 179-192.
"Drawn by God." *Gospel Advocate* CXXV (Oct. 20, 1983) 616, 619.
"The Importance of Proper Bible Study (No. 1)." *Gospel Advocate* XCV (Sept. 10, 1953) 569, 583-584.
"An Interesting Textual Study of Second Timothy." *Gospel Advocate* CV (Sept. 5, 1963) 564-565.
"Problems in the Translation of the Gospel of John." *Restoration Quarterly* XVI:3-4 (1973) 209-218.
"Qualifications and Requirements of Proper Bible Study." *Gospel Advocate* XCV (Sept. 24, 1953) 612-613.

"Tools of Bible Study: Archeology." *Gospel Advocate* XCV (Dec. 3, 1953) 812-813.

"Tools of Bible Study: Bible Dictionaries and Encyclopedias." *Gospel Advocate* XCV (Nov. 19, 1953) 777-778.

"Tools of Bible Study: Bible Geographies and Atlases." *Gospel Advocate* XCV (Nov. 19, 1953) 777-778.

"Tools of Bible Study: Commentaries." *Gospel Advocate* XCVI (April 22, 1954) 308-310.

"Tools of Bible Study: Greek Grammars and Lexicons." *Gospel Advocate* XCVI (Jan. 7, 1954) 11-13.

"Tools of Bible Study: Modern Speech Versions of the Bible." *Gospel Advocate* XCVI (Feb. 18, 1954) 132-134.

"Tools of Bible Study: Hebrew Grammars and Lexicons." *Gospel Advocate* XCV (Dec. 3, 1953) 857-858.

"Tools of Bible Study: Reference Bibles and Their Uses." *Gospel Advocate* XCV (Oct. 8, 1953) 655-656.

"The Western Text of Acts." *Restoration Quarterly* IV:4 (1960) 220-234.

"The Word 'Church'," *Gospel Advocate* CIII (Dec. 14, 1961) 785, 791-792.

Godhead

"Baptism and Faith," *20th Century Christian* XLI (June, 1979) 9-11.

"Confession of Faith in Christ," *20th Century Christian* XIV (May, 1952) 17, 22.

"The Father's Love for His Son," *Gospel Advocate* CIII (Jan. 5, 1961) 2, 6-7.

"God and His People: The Vineyard," *Gospel Advocate* CIII (May 4, 1961) 277-278.

"God Speaks Through His Son: The Supreme Revelation," *20th Century Christian* XXV (Sept., 1963) 17-18.

"He Is Coming Again," *20th Century Christian* XXVI (July, 1964) 22-24.

"The Holy Spirit: What or Who?," *20th Century Christian* XXIX (Nov., 1966) 5.

"Jesus' Example in Baptism," *20th Century Christian* XVIII (Dec., 1955) 6-7.

"Justified (Saved) By Faith," *20th Century Christian* XLIV (Feb., 1982) 24-26.

"The Living Christ: My Heart," *20th Century Christian* XIX (Dec., 1956) 22-24.

"The New Birth," *Power For Today* XXIII (Jan., 1977) 11.

"Our Father Who Art In Heaven . . . ," *20th Century Christian* XIV (March, 1952) 20-23.

"Repent and Be Converted," *20th Century Christian* XXXV March, 1973) 16-17.

"Saved by Grace," *Gospel Advocate* XCIX (July 18, 1957) 449.

"The Seven-Fold Oneness Christ Desires," *20th Century Christian* XVII (Nov., 1954) 18-19.

"The Triumphal Procession in Christ 2 Corinthians 2:14," *Gospel Advocate* CXXXII (July 10, 1980) 401, 434.

History

" 'A Celebration of Heritage' Observed," *Firm Foundation* CI (March 2, 1982) 131.
"A Valuable Book," *Gospel Advocate* XCVI (Sept. 16, 1954) 729-739.
"Amos Lincoln Cassius: Pioneer Black Leader," *Discipliana* XLIII (Summer, 1983) 25.
"An Unprecedented Accomplishment," *Firm Foundation* XCVI (May 22, 1979) 323.
"Difficult Places," *Gospel Advocate* CVI (June 25, 1964) 401, 406-407.
"Federal Court Declares Transcendental Meditation a Religion," *Firm Foundation* XCVI (Oct. 23, 1979) 682.
" 'Historical Perspectives' Part I," *Image* I (Nov. 15, 1985) 16-17.
" 'Historical Perspectives' Part II," *Image* I (Dec. 15, 1985) 10-13.
"One Hundred Years Ago: 1959," *Gospel Advocate* CI (Nov. 19, 1959) 737, 745.
"One Hundred Years Since Westcott and Hort: 1881-1981," *Restoration Quarterly* XXVI:2 (1983) 65-79.
"Over A Century of Service," *Gospel Advocate* CIX (June 15, 1967) 373-374.
"Ten Million Readers," *Gospel Advocate* XCVII (Dec. 8) 1110.

Men Honored

"Another Elder Honored," *Gospel Advocate* CX (Feb. 15, 1968) 99-100.
"Glenn L. Wallace Honored," *Gospel Advocate* CXVII (Nov. 27, 1975) 756.
"Gus Nichols, A Great Man of God," *Gospel Advocate* CXIII (March 25, 1976) 199.
"Honor To Whom Honor is Due . . . Three Christian Educators Honored," *Gospel Advocate* CVII (July 15, 1965) 449, 458.
"Recent Celebrations," *Gospel Advocate* CXXI (March 22, 1976) 183.
"To a Great Elder," *Gospel Advocate* CVIII (Nov. 10, 1966) 714-715.

Practical Christian Living

"A Comradeship Through Prayer," *20th Century Christian* XII (Aug., 1950) 23.
"A Modern Challenge," *20th Century Christian* XXIV (Feb., 1962) 12-13.
"Biblical Standards of Morality," *20th Century Christian* XXVII (Jan., 1965) 28-29.
"Christians Must be Peacemakers," *20th Century Christian* XI (April, 1949) 26-28.
"Confess Your Faults," *20th Century Christian* XI (July, 1949) 3-7.
"Confess Your Faults," *20th Century Christian* XIII (Dec., 1950) 22-25.
"Confessing Our Faults," *Firm Foundation*, LXXI (Sept. 28, 1954) 8.
"Cultivate the Fine Art of Good Cheer," *20th Century Christian* XXIII (Nov., 1960) 28-29.
"Do You Take Your Vows Seriously?" *20th Century Christian* XV (Oct., 1952) 3-5.
"Faith and Works," *20th Century Christian* XXI (Aug., 1959) 14-16.

"Faith and Works," *Power For Today* XXVII (Nov. 2, 1981) 41.
"God Is the Audience," *20th Century Christian* XXVII (Nov. 2, 1964) 30-32.
"God's Call to Change," *Gospel Advocate* CXII (Oct. 15, 1970) 668-669.
"God's Wise Little People," *20th Century Christian* XIX (May, 1957) 15-16.
"Hannah the Prayerful Mother," *20th Century Christian* XLII (Jan., 1980) 29-30.
"Has Your Life Style Changed?" *Power For Today* XXI (Sept. 30, 1975) 33.
"I Met A Man!" *Power For Today* XIX (Oct. 21, 1973) 53.
"My Stewardship of Talent," *20th Century Christian* XX (June, 1958) 6-7.
"Nurture the New Christian," *20th Century Christian* XIII (Nov., 1950) 33-34.
"Our Light Afflictions," *20th Century Christian* XXVII (March, 1965) 16-17.
"Peace Be Still," *20th Century Christian* XXIV (Nov., 1961) 16-17.
"Radiant Faith and Courage," Co-author with Della Pack, *20th Century Christian* XXXVI (Aug., 1974) 9-10.
"Respect of Persons," *20th Century Christian* XXIII (April, 1961) 14-15.
"Shall We Glorify Violence?" *20th Century Christian* XXX (Sept., 1968) 16-17.
"She Hath Done What She Could," *20th Century Christian* XLVC (Sept., 1983) 23-24.
"Some Reassuring Experiences," *Firm Foundation* XVC (Nov. 5, 1967) 712.
"Spiritual Food for the Soul," *Gospel Advocate*, C (Oct. 30, 1958) 693-695.
"The 25th Anniversary of Repeal . . . ," *20th Century Christian* XXI (Feb., 1959) 11-12.
"The Central Purpose of Life," *Gospel Advocate* CVII (April 15, 1965) 237.
"The Good News of Rest," *Power For Today* III (May 11, 1957) 13.
"The Lord Weighs the Heart," *20th Century Christian* XLI (April, 1979) 20.
"Three Looks . . . 'Lift Up Your Eyes and Look,' " *20th Century Christian* XIII (Jan., 1951) 13-14.
"Turning Many to God," *Power For Today*, I (Jan. 3, 1955) 5.
"Understanding Adults," *Firm Foundation*, LXXII (Nov. 8, 1955) 733.
"Vacation Time Again," *Gospel Advocate* XCVIII (June 21, 1956) 561.
"Watch And Pray," *Power For Today* XXVII (Sept. 10, 1981) 80.
"We Pray With the Psalmist," *Power For Today* XV (Jan. 25, 1969) 29.
"What Do Ye More Than Others?" *Gospel Advocate* XCIX (Aug. 8, 1957) 497.
"What Is Faith?" *20th Century Christian* XXXVII (July, 1975) 24.
"What Is Wrong With Gambling?" *20th Century Christian* XII (March, 1950) 20-23.
"What Is Your Faith?" *20th Century Christian* XX (Dec., 1957) 5-25.
"What Is Your Role in This Drama?" *20th Century Christian* XIII (June, 1950) 3.
"Why Couldn't This Happen Among Us?" *Gospel Advocate* CI (Nov. 5, 1959) 705, 714.
"Work and Word," *Gospel Advocate* CXII (March 5, 1970) 155.
"Yield Not to Temptation," *20th Century Christian* XIII (Aug., 1950) 34-36.

"Your Most Important Outside Reading — The Bible," *20th Century Christian* XXVII (Aug., 1965) 9.

Textual Studies

"A Study of Romans 8:28," *Restoration Quarterly* XXII:1-2 (1979) 44-53.

"God and His People: The Potter and the Clay," *Gospel Advocate* (Nov. 24, 1960) 746-747.

"God's Fruitful Word," *Gospel Advocate* CI (July 23, 1959) 468-470.

"Keep the Door of My Lips," *Gospel Advocate* XCVI (Sept. 23, 1954) 746-747.

"A Man's Sinfulness and God's Righteousness, Romans 1-3," *20th Century Christian* XLVI (Feb., 1986) 4-6.

"The Power of God's Word," *Gospel Advocate* CI (July 23, 1958) 468.

"The Power of God's Word," *Gospel Advocate* CI (June 11, 1959) 370.

"The Sheep of His Pasture," *Gospel Advocate* CII (Dec. 1, 1960) 759, 761-762.

"The Uniform Lesson — January 4, 1942" *Gospel Advocate* LXXXIII (Dec. 25, 1941) 1237.

"Thy Word Is a Lamp Unto My Feet," *Gospel Advocate* C (Oct. 2, 1958) 625, 634.

Worship

"Breaking Bread Each Lord's Day," *20th Century Christian* XV (June, 1953) 9-10.

"Do You Really Worship God?" *20th Century Christian* XIV (June, 1952) 16-18.

"Lord's Supper," *Power For Today* XXIII (Feb., 1977) 39.

"This Day Belongs to God," *Gospel Advocate* XCIX (Sept. 5, 1957) 562-563.

"What Does Worship Mean to You?" *Gospel Advocate* CV (May 16, 1963) 306.

"Worship," *20th Century Christian* XXXV (March, 1973) 22-23.

"Worship in Spirit and Truth," *Firm Foundation* LXXXI (April 21, 1964) 245.

"Worship: What Is It?" *20th Century Christian* XX (Feb., 1958) 21-22.

Essay Writers

Randall D. Chesnutt, Assoc. Prof. of Rel., Pepperdine U.; Ph.D., Duke U.; Th.M., Duke Divinity Sch.; M.Th., M.A., Harding Grad. Sch. of Rel.; B.A., Alabama Christian Sch. of Rel. Memberships: Soc. of Bib. Lit., Catholic Bib. Ass'n. Exp. of Pub.: "The Social Setting and Purpose of Joseph and Aseneth," *Journal for the Study of the Pseudepigrapha* 1 (1988) in press; *Conversion in 'Joseph and Aseneth'* (Sheffield: JSOT in press.

W. Royce Clark, Prof. of Rel., Pepperdine U.; Ph.D., U. of Iowa; M.A., B.A., Abilene Christian U., J.D., Pepperdine U. School of Law. Memberships: American Academy of Religion; Society of Biblical Literature; Society of Christian Ethics; Society for Buddhist Christian Dialogue. Exp. of Pub.: A rev. of John F. Wilson's *Religion: A Preface* (Prentice-Hall, 1988); "The Example of Christ and Voluntary Active Euthanasia," *Journal of Religion and Health* (Winter, 1986).

Dan G. Danner, Prof. of Theol., U. of Portland; Ph.D., U. of Iowa; M.A., B.A., Abilene Christian U. Memberships: American Academy of Religion, American Society of Church History, American Society of Reformation Research, American Association of University Professors. Exp. of Pub.: Articles in *Church History, Journal of the American Academy of Religion, Sixteenth Century Journal.*

Everett Ferguson, Prof., Col. of Biblical Studies, Abilene Christian U.; Ph.D., S.T.B., Harvard U.; M.A., B.A., Abilene Christian U. Memberships: American Society of Church History, Society of Biblical Literature, Ecclesiastical History Society (Great Britain), North American Patristic Society, Association internationale d'études patristiques. Exp. of Pub.: *Early Christians Speak* (ACU Press, 1987); *Backgrounds of Early Christianity* (Eerdmans, 1987).

John C. Free, Director of Health and Counseling, Pepperdine U.; Ph.D., Fuller Graduate School of Psychology; M.A., B.A., Pepperdine U.

Everett W. Huffard, Assoc. Dean; Assoc. Prof. of Missiology, Harding Grad. School of Rel.; Ph.D., HUGSR, M.Th., M.A., Fuller Theol. Seminary. Memberships: American Society of Missiology, Association of Evangelical Professors of Missions, Association for Theological Field Education. Exp. of Pub.: *Deciding to Grow: Church Growth Perspectives From 2 Corinthians* (Quality, 1983).

Jack P. Lewis, Prof. of Bible, Harding Grad. School of Rel.; Ph.D., Hebrew Union Col.; Ph.D., Harvard U.; S.T.B., Harvard Divinity School; B.A., Abilene Christian U. Memberships: Evangelical Theo. Society, American Academy of Rel., Society of Biblical Literature, Nat'l. Association of

Prof. of Hebrew. Exp. of Pub.: *The Minor Prophets* (Baker); *The Interpretation of Noah and the Flood in Jewish and Christian Literature* (E.J. Brill, Leiden); *Archaeological Backgrounds of Bible People* (Baker).

Stuart L. Love, Asst. Dean of Seaver Col., Pepperdine U.; Assoc. Prof. of Rel., Pepperdine U.; S.T.D., San Francisco Theol. Seminary; S.T.B., M.S., B.A., Abilene Christian U. Memberships: SBL, AAR, Ass'n. for Theol. Field Ed, Nat'l. Academic Advising Assoc. Exp. of Pub.: *Good News for Marriage*, co-author with Mark and D'Esta Love (DMS Communications, 1987); "Women's Roles in Certain Second Testament Passages: A Macrosociological View," *Biblical Theology Bulletin* XVII (April, 1987).

Rick R. Marrs, Assoc. Prof. of Rel., Pepperdine U.; Ph.D., Johns Hopkins U.; M. Div., B.A., Abilene Christian U. Memberships: Society of Biblical Literature, Catholic Biblical Association. Exp. of Pub.: "A Cry from the Depths (Ps. 130)," *Zeitschrift für die alttestamentliche Wissenschaft* 100 (1988). "Psalms 122, 3.4: A New Reading," *Biblica* 68 (1987). "Micah and the Task of Ministry," *Restoration Quarterly* 30 (1988).

Carl G. Mitchell, Dir. and Prof. in Residence, Florence, Italy, Pepperdine U.; Ph.D., U. of Southern California; M.A., B.A., Pepperdine U. Memberships: California license of Marriage, Family and Child Counselor, clinical member of American Psychological Ass'n., member, American Psychological Ass'n. Exp. of Pub.: Italian publications on Christian Evidences and Christian Psychology.

Thomas H. Olbricht, Chair, Rel. Div., Prof. of Rel., Pepperdine U.; Ph.D., U. of Iowa; S.T.B., Harvard Divinity School; M.A., U. of Iowa; B.S., Northern Illinois U. Memberships: Society of Biblical Literature; American Academy of Rel., Speech Communication Assn. Exp. of Pub.: *He Loves Forever* (Sweet, 1980); *The Message of Ephesians and Colossians* (ACU Press, 1983).

James E. Priest, Prof. of Rel., Pepperdine U.; Ph.D., St. Mary's U.; M.A., Johns Hopkins U.; M.S., Abilene Christian U.; B.A., U. of Colorado. Memberships: Society of Biblical Literature; Biblical Archaeology Society; Nat'l. Assoc. of Prof. of Christian Education, Evangelical Theol. Soc. Exp. of Pub.: *Governmental and Judicial Ethics in the Bible and Rabbinic Literature* (KTAV-Pepperdine, 1980); "Gen. 9:6 — A Study of Bloodshed in Bible and Talmud," *Journal of the Evangelical Theological Society* 31:2 (June, 1988).

Ronald L. Tyler, Prof. of Rel., Pepperdine U.; Ph.D., Baylor U.; M.A., B.A., Eastern New Mexico University. Memberships: Society of Biblical Literature, American Academy of Religion, Catholic Biblical Association.

John F. Wilson, Dean of Seaver Col., Pepperdine U.; Prof. of Rel.; Ph.D., U. of Iowa; M.A., B.A., Harding U. Memberships: American Academy of Rel., Society of Biblical Literature; American Schools of Oriental Research (assoc. Trustee). Exp. of Pub.: *Religion: A Preface*, 2nd ed., (Printice-Hall, 1988); co-author, *Discovering the Bible: Archeologists Look at Scripture*, ed. Tim Dowley (Marshall Pickering/Eerdmans, 1986).

John T. Willis, Prof. of Bible, Abilene Christian U.; Ph.D., Vanderbilt U.; M.A., B.A., Abilene Christian U. Memberships: Society of Biblical Literature; American Academy of Rel.; Inter. Org. for the Study of the O.T. Exp. of Pub.: *Isaiah* in The Living Word Commentary (Sweet); translator of *A Rigid Scrutiny* by Ivan Engnell (Vanderbilt U. Press).

Bread of Life in Joseph and Aseneth and in John 6[1]

Randall D. Chesnutt

The New Testament writing to which Frank Pack has devoted more of his study than to any other (the Gospel of John) and the apocryphal work on which my recent research has centered (the Jewish romance *Joseph and Aseneth*) have one very interesting expression in common — "bread of life." Far from commonplace, this terminology is quite distinctive of the two writings mentioned; of the now vast corpus of extant Jewish works earlier than or roughly contemporaneous with the emergence of the New Testament writings, only *Joseph and Aseneth* shares with John 6 the exact expression *artos (tēs) zoēs*, "bread of life."[2] Moreover, the similarity is not merely verbal. In both places the claim is made that the one who eats the life-giving food will not die but will live forever; both envision this attainment of life as a present reality; and both reflect the influence not only of the narrative about the manna in Exodus but also of later Biblical and post-Biblical amplification of the manna tradition.[3]

In spite of these and other similarities, the relationship between the bread-of-life terminology in *Joseph and Aseneth* and that in John 6 has not been

---

[1]It is a pleasure to dedicate this study to Frank Pack. For his pioneering efforts within Churches of Christ to bridge the gap between the academy and the Church, between Biblical scholarship and Christian ministry, I have the greatest admiration. In the very task of bringing historical-critical methodology to bear on the interpretation of Scripture within the context of universities affiliated with the Church of Christ, contributors to this volume are warming by a fire kindled by Frank Pack and a very small handful of other Christian educators whose labors we must not fail to appreciate.

[2]Since bread is often a symbol of the Torah in rabbinic literature, and since the Torah is designated by such terms as "Torah of life" and "tree of life," H. Strack and P. Billerbeck, *Kommentar zum Neuen Testament aus Talmud und Midrasch*, 4 vols. (Munich: Beck, 1922-28), vol. 2, pp. 482f., speculate that the Torah was also called "bread of life." However, the expression is not actually attested in the rabbinic sources.

[3]Here, and throughout this study, the term "post-Biblical" is used with reference to Judaism of the period after the *Hebrew* Scriptures (the Old Testament) but not necessarily after the *Christian* Scriptures (which of course include the New Testament). This usage, though quite standard among specialists in Judaic studies, admittedly is a potentially misleading one. However, "post-Biblical Judaism" is no more problematic than other common designations for the same phenomenon, such as "Intertestamental Judaism," "Second Temple Judaism," and the increasingly popular but nebulous "Early Judaism."

extensively investigated. Several have noted the common element and the need to investigate it thoroughly, but discussions of possible affinities are found only in a very few works which provide little more than terse and preliminary remarks within discussions of larger topics.[4] In view of the scant attention devoted to the subject, the purpose of the present study is to explore briefly this small plot of relatively uncharted common ground between the Fourth Gospel and *Joseph and Aseneth*. The basic question to be resolved is whether there is sufficient affinity of thought between the two usages of the bread-of-life motif to shed light on either or both of them.

Two factors account for the neglect of the topic to be investigated here. The first is the very late date and Christian character assigned to *Joseph and Aseneth* by several influential early interpreters. Most influential was P. Batiffol, who, in his introduction to the *editio princeps* in 1889-90, assigned the apocryphon to a Christian author of the fifth century A.D.[5] So prevalent was this view, or slight variations of it, that *Joseph and Aseneth* was not included in the collections of Jewish pseudepigrapha by E. Kautzch[6] and R.H. Charles[7] and was rarely cited by or even known to New Testament scholars prior to the middle of the twentieth century.[8] However, the solid current consensus that *Joseph and Aseneth* is Jewish and not Christian in its

---

[4] See C. Burchard, *Untersuchungen zu Joseph and Aseneth; Überlieferung-Ortsbestimmung*, Wissenschaftliche Untersuchungen zum Neuen Testament 8 (Tübingen: Mohr, 1965), p. 130; R. Schnackenburg, "Das Brot des Lebens," *Tradition und Glaube: Das frühe Christentum in seiner Umwelt. Festgabe für K.G. Kuhn*, eds. J. Jeremias, H.W. Kuhn, and H. Stegemann (Göttingen: Vandenhoeck und Ruprecht, 1971), pp. 335-42; idem, *Das Johannesevangelium*, 3 vols. (Herders Theologischer Kommentar zum Neuen Testament (Freiberg: Herder, 1965-75), vol. 2, pp. 57f. (ET: *The Gospel According to St. John*, 3 vols., trans. K. Smyth *et al.* (New York: Seabury Press, 1980-82), vol. 2, p. 44]; S. Légasse, "Le pain de la vie," *Bulletin de littérature ecclésiastique* 83 (1982) 248-51; and most recently C. Burchard, "The Importance of Joseph and Aseneth for the Study of the New Testament: A General Survey and a Fresh Look at the Lord's Supper," *New Testament Studies* 33 (1987) 119-21.

[5] *Le Livre de la Prière d'Aseneth*. Studia Patristica: Études d'ancienne littérature chrétienne 1-2 (Paris: Leroux, 1889-90), pp. 7-18,30-37 This view was popularized in the introduction to the first English translation by E.W. Brooks, *Joseph and Asenath*, Translations of Early Documents, Series 2 (London: SPCK, 1918).

[6] *Die Apokryphen und Pseudepigraphen des Alten Testaments*, 2 vols. (Tübingen: Mohr, 1900).

[7] *The Apocrypha and Pseudepigrapha of the Old Testament in English*, 2 vols. (Oxford: Clarendon, 1913).

[8] *Joseph and Aseneth* seems to have made its debut in the study of the New Testament and Christian origins in 1952. In that year G.D. Kilpatrick, "The Last Supper," *Expository Times* 64 (1952) 4-8, suggested that the meal of the bread and cup in *Joseph and Aseneth* is important for understanding the origins of the Lord's Supper.

earliest attainable form[9] and that it dates between 100 B.C. and A.D. 115[10] means that this apocryphon is indeed significant for the study of early Judaism and Christian origins and that its usage of bread-of-life terminology should not be overlooked in research on John 6.

A second factor which no doubt has been a deterrent to the exploration of our topic is the uncertainty surrounding the enigmatic passages on the bread, cup, and ointment in which the expression "bread of life" occurs in *Joseph and Aseneth* (8.5-7; 8.9; 15.5; 16.16; 19.5; 21.21). As we shall see, these passages have evoked widely divergent interpretations and claims regarding history-of-religions analogies. A phenomenon so problematic in its own right naturally has not commended itself as helpful for illuminating John 6. In view of this difficulty it is appropriate to begin with a brief examination of the bread-cup-ointment passages in *Joseph and Aseneth* as a basis for comparison with John 6.

Bread, Cup, and Ointment in *Joseph and Aseneth*

In the text of *Joseph and Aseneth* edited by C. Burchard,[11] the triad "bread of life," "cup of immortality," and "ointment of incorruption" appears three

---

[9]See especially the arguments in Burchard, *Untersuchungen*, pp. 91-99. The view that the work has unmistakable Christian elements even in its earliest known form (e.g., T. Holtz, "Christliche Interpolationen in 'Joseph und Aseneth,' " *New Testament Studies* 14 [1968] 482-97; and H.F.D. Sparks, "Joseph and Aseneth: Introduction," in *The Apocryphal Old Testament*, ed. H.F.D. Sparks [Oxford: Clarendon Press, 1984], p. 469) is now very much in the minority.

[10]Because of the strong probability that the work was composed in Egypt, the *terminus ante quem* of A.D. 115 is established by the pogrom of A.D. 115-17 in which Egyptian Jewry was reduced to virtual oblivion. The extensive dependence of *Joseph and Aseneth* on various parts of the Septuagint indicates a *terminus post quem* of c. 100 B.C. A date in the first century B.C. is favored by J.J. Collins, *Between Athens and Jerusalem: Jewish Identity in the Hellenistic Diaspora* (New York: Crossroad, 1983), p. 91; and by the present writer in "Joseph and Aseneth," *Anchor Bible Dictionary* (Garden City, N.Y.: Doubleday, in press). C. Burchard, "Joseph and Aseneth," *The Old Testament Pseudepigrapha*, 2 vols., ed. J.H. Charlesworth (Garden City, N.Y.: Doubleday, 1983-85), vol. 2, pp. 187f., is reticent to suggest anything more specific than a date of composition between c. 100 B.C. and A.D. 115.

[11]"Ein vorläufiger griechischer Text von Joseph und Aseneth," *Dielheimer Blätter zum Alten Testament* 14 (1979) 2-53; supplemented in idem, "Verbesserungen zum vorläufigen Text von Joseph und Aseneth," *Dielheimer Blätter zum Alten Testament* 16 (1982) 37-39. The priority of this long version is argued quite convincingly in idem, "Zum Text von 'Joseph und Aseneth,' " *Journal for the Study of Judaism* 1 (1970) 3-34, and is assumed by most modern interpreters. However, in the absence of an edition of the long text which is both more recent than Batiffol's and more accessible than the recondite journal in which Burchard's preliminary edition appears, some continue to depend by default on the short recension published by M. Philonenko, *Joseph et Aséneth: Introduction, texte critique, traduction et notes*, Studia postbiblica 13 (Leiden: Brill, 1968). In Philonenko's text the number of passages employing the expression "bread of life" is reduced to three (8.5; 8.11; 15.4).

times (8.5-7; 15.5; 16.16), and the dyad "bread of life" and "cup of blessing" or "cup of immortality" is used three other times (8.9; 19.5; 21.21). These formulaic expressions have most commonly been supposed to reflect some sort of sacred meal, and on this assumption analogies have been drawn with a broad spectrum of other phenomena, including the sacred meals of the Qumran sectarians,[12] the Therapeutae,[13] the mystical Jewish circles posited by E.R. Goodenough,[14] the mystery religions (especially the cult of Isis)[15] and the early Christians.[16] Indeed, it is precisely on the basis of the supposed sacred meal in *Joseph and Aseneth* that most claims regarding the history-of-religions affinities of the work have been made. A minority view is that the reference is not to a ritual meal at all but to the everyday Jewish meal, which itself had a solemn religious character, or to the entire Jewish way of life.[17]

Elsewhere I have argued that it is the sociological rather than the ritual dimension of conversion to Judaism that is central in *Joseph and Aseneth*, and therefore that it is more difficult than many have supposed to extrapolate the ritual formalities of conversion for purposes of history-of-religions comparisons.[18] The Judaism reflected in *Joseph and Aseneth* existed in dynamic tension with gentiles and struggled to maintain a distinctive Jewish identity. Table fellowship and intermarriage with gentiles, including the marriage of a convert to Judaism and a born Jew, were live issues. Conversion to Judaism carried the possibility of ostracism from family and former gentile associates. Considerable discord seems also to have existed within the Jewish community

---

[12] K.G. Kuhn, "The Lord's Supper and the Communal Meal at Qumran," *The Scrolls and the New Testament*, ed. K. Stendahl (New York: Harper and Brothers, 1957), pp. 73-77; W. Nauck, *Die Tradition und der Charakter des ersten Johannesbriefs*, Wissenschaftliche Untersuchungen zum Neuen Testament 3 (Tübingen: Mohr, 1957), pp. 169-71; and more recently R.T. Beckwith, "The Solar Calendar of Joseph and Asenath: A Suggestion," *Journal for the Study of Judaism* 15 (1984) 90-111.

[13] Kuhn, "The Lord's Supper and the Communal Meal at Qumran," pp. 75-77; and M. Delcor, "Un roman d'amour d'origine thérapeute: Le Livre de Joseph et Asénath," *Bulletin de littérature ecclesiastique* 63 (1962) 3-27.

[14] Philonenko, *Joseph et Aséneth*, p. 98.

[15] Kilpatrick, *Expository Times* 64 (1952) 4-8; M. Philonenko, "Initiation et mystère dans Joseph et Asénath," *Initiation*, ed. C.J. Bleeker, Supplements to Numen, Studies in the History of Religions 10 (Leiden: Brill, 1965), pp. 147-53; idem, *Joseph et Asénath, passim*; idem; "Un mystère juif?" *Mystères et syncrétismes*, Etudes d'histoire des religions 2 (Paris: Geuthner, 1975), pp. 65-70; and most recently H.C. Kee, "The Socio-Cultural Setting of Joseph and Aseneth," *New Testament Studies* 29 (1983) 394-413.

[16] E.g., Holtz, *New Testament Studies* 14 (1968) 482-97; and Sparks, "Joseph and Aseneth: Introduction," *The Apocryphal Old Testament*, p. 469.

[17] So especially J. Jeremias, "The Last Supper," *Expository Times* 64 (1952) 91f.; Burchard, *Untersuchungen*, pp. 121-33; Schnackenburg, "Das Brot des Lebens," pp. 335-42; and more recently, with some modifications, D. Sänger, *Antikes Judentum und die Mysterien: Religionsgeschichtliche Untersuchungen zu Joseph und Aseneth*, Wissenschaftliche Untersuchungen zum Neuen Testament 2.5 (Tübingen: Mohr, 1980), pp. 167-90; Collins, *Between Athens and Jerusalem*, pp. 213f.; and Burchard, *New Testament Studies* 33 (1987) 109-17.

[18] "The Social Setting and Purpose of Joseph and Aseneth," *Journal for the Study of the Pseudepigrapha*, forthcoming in April, 1988.

regarding the relative status of the convert. It is within the context of this determinative social matrix that Aseneth's conversion is narrated and the bread-cup-ointment passages appear. Only with great peril to the understanding of these passages can this basic fact be ignored and hasty comparisons drawn with other texts and phenomena where the underlying concerns are quite different.

The literary and social context and function of the bread-of-life language in *Joseph and Aseneth* may be illustrated by reference to two of the passages in which the expression appears: 8.5-7 and 16.15f. In the first of these, Aseneth meets Joseph and comes forth to kiss him, but Joseph spurns her because, in his words,

> It is not proper for a man who worships God, who blesses with his mouth the living God and eats blessed bread of life and drinks a blessed cup of immortality and is anointed with blessed ointment of incorruption, to kiss a strange woman, who blesses with her mouth dead and dumb idols and eats from their table bread of strangling and drinks from their libation a cup of deceit and is anointed with ointment of destruction. Rather, the man who worships God will kiss his mother and the sister born of his mother and the sister from his tribe and kinsfolk and the wife who shares his bed, who bless with their mouths the living God. Likewise, it is not proper for a woman who worships God to kiss a strange man, because this is an abomination before the Lord God (8.5-7).[19]

Here the obvious function of the meal language is to distinguish the *theosebēs*, or "worshiper of God" (the Jew), from the idolatrous gentile, and to justify the social separation which the former must maintain from the latter. A fourfold series of antitheses expressed in relative clauses specifies the differences between the two classes of people. That the social concerns reflected here are not merely literary but are real ones in the author's community is decisively confirmed by the last sentence of the above quotation, which goes beyond the previous interdiction and envisions a situation not called for by anything in the story line itself. This generalization from the specific case at hand to a related situation not represented in the narrative betrays an interest in clarifying Jewish self-identity and appropriate Jewish conduct in a gentile environment. The contaminating effect of association with idolatry, including especially physical intimacy and intermarriage with gentiles, was a matter of grave concern to the author. Closely related is the concern for the maintenance of table fellowship in separation from gentiles and from the pollution of idols — a concern which is explicit in 7.1 and at least implicit in the repeated use of meal terminology in 8.5-7 and elsewhere to express the essence of the Jewish way of life *vis-à-vis* gentile existence.

The scene in *Joseph and Aseneth* 16 in which Aseneth eats from a mysterious honeycomb betrays another of the major concerns of the work — to

---

[19]This and all subsequent quotations of *Joseph and Aseneth* are my own translation of Burchard's provisional Greek text; see p. 3, n. 11 above.

enhance the status of the convert within the Jewish community and to establish the propriety of marriage between a convert to Judaism and a born Jew. D. Sänger correctly perceives that the visit of the "man from heaven" in chapters 14-17 is not the cause nor the occasion of Aseneth's conversion but functions to provide heavenly ratification of a conversion that has already taken place and to articulate the benefits of conversion to the true God and membership in the elect people of God.[20] The detailed narrative of this heavenly endorsement of Aseneth's conversion and marriage to Joseph and her full acceptance as one of the people of God by God's own chief angel is only one of numerous indications in *Joseph and Aseneth* that there existed in the Jewish community behind the document considerable dissension centering on the perception of the gentile convert, the relative status of the convert within the Jewish community, and especially on the propriety of marriage between a convert to Judaism and a born Jew.[21] It is within such a literary and social context that the language of "bread of life" is used in *Joseph and Aseneth* 16.16. By having Aseneth eat from the mysterious honeycomb — and we shall return to the significant point that she partakes of *honey*, and not of *bread, cup*, or *oil* — the author places this convert on a par with the Jew by birth, and indeed with the angels of God, who are said to eat the same immortal food. Aseneth's eating of the honey and her full participation in the blessings of life and immortality symbolized by the honey, all at the direct command of God's chief angel, function as proof that this convert is worthy to be received fully into the community of Israel and to be married to the revered patriarch.

The explanation that "all the angels of God . . . and all the chosen ones of God and all the sons of the Most High" eat from the same honeycomb (16.14) suggests that a continual feeding of the people of God is in view and that any ritual practice underlying the scene is not exclusively initiatory in character. Similarly, since it is *Joseph*, not *Aseneth*, who is characterized in 8.5 as one who eats bread of life, drinks a cup of immortality, and is anointed with ointment of incorruption, J.J. Collins is right that what this language describes "is evidently not, or at least not only, an initiation ritual. Rather, it is the habitual practice of the pious."[22] Moreover, in chap. 16 the miraculous appearance and disappearance of the comb, the strange marking of the

---

[20]"Bekehrung und Exodus: Traditionshintergrund von 'Joseph und Aseneth,' " *Journal for the Study of Judaism* 10 (1979) 29f.; and idem, *Antikes Judentum und die Mysterien*, pp. 156f., 182.

[21]Other indications of such tensions are discussed at length in my aforementioned article in *Journal for the Study of the Pseudepigrapha*, forthcoming in April, 1988.

[22]*Between Athens and Jerusalem*, p. 213. The same can be argued from 21.21, if Burchard's edition of this textually-corrupt section can be trusted. In 21.13f. Aseneth expresses the whole of her former pagan life in terms of eating and drinking from the table of idols. It is reasonable to suppose, therefore, that when she balances this in 21.21 with a reference to eating and drinking the bread of life and cup of wisdom, this latter eating and drinking also represent an entire way of life which stands over against heathen conduct — the life *more judaico*.

comb, and the mysterious appearance and behavior of millions of bees dressed in royal attire make it unlikely that any repeatable ritual is reflected here at all. If traces of an actual cultic meal are present in this enigmatic episode, they are so interwoven into the literary fabric of the narrative that their particular form and significance are no longer recoverable.

In addition to the above considerations of literary context and function, which suggest that the bread-cup-ointment passages do not refer only, or even primarily, to a cultic meal involving these elements, one further fact renders it unlikely that this language refers to a specific ritual at all. It is an extremely important but often overlooked fact that Aseneth never actually receives any bread, cup, or ointment anywhere in the narrative. Instead she eats a piece of honeycomb and is then told by the man from heaven: "Behold, you have eaten bread of life, drunk a cup of immortality, and been anointed with ointment of incorruption" (16.16; see also 19.5). The explicit equation of eating the honey with eating the bread, drinking the cup, and being anointed with the ointment makes it highly unlikely that allusion to a fixed ritual form is intended in either half of the equation.[23] Rather, both express the privileged status to which Aseneth has been elevated by virtue of her conversion.

Even though it is unlikely that the formulaic references to food, drink, and ointment, reflect a special ritual, and even if it is the representative function of this language to express life as a Jew which stands out in *Joseph and Aseneth*, it probably is not without significance that the particular acts chosen as representative are eating, drinking, and anointing. This triad echoes the Old Testament formula "grain, wine, and oil," and, like that formula, summarizes the staples of life. It provides a representative expression for the Jewish way of life *vis-à-vis* gentile existence. The proper acquisition, preparation, and use of these staple commodities according to Jewish tradition, including the proper blessings said over them, stands over against the defiling food, drink, and oil of the gentile world.[24] This repeated use of meal terminology to contrast Jewish and gentile existence combines with the explicit

---

[23]Similarly, G. Delling, "Die Kunst des Gestaltens in 'Joseph und Aseneth,'" *Novum Testamentum* 26 (1984) 23, concludes from this equation that the eating, drinking, and being anointed do not denote something separate but mean the same thing as the eating of the honeycomb. For similar reasons it is unlikely that the threefold kiss by which Joseph is said to have imparted to Aseneth a spirit of life, a spirit of wisdom, and a spirit of truth (19.10f.) represents an established ritual. Sänger, *Antikes Judentum und die Mysterien*, pp. 165f., 206f., correctly observes that these kisses conferred upon Aseneth nothing substantially different from what she already possessed. The variety of actions to which the same or similar effects are attributed tends to devalue the fixed ritual character of any one of them and to highlight what is common to them all — the symbolic expression of the blessings which Aseneth came to enjoy as a result of converting to Judaism.

[24]A possible objection to this line of interpretation lies in the inclusion of the oil of anointing in the triadic formula. Burchard, *Untersuchungen*, p. 128, sees this as the Achilles' heel in all attempts to interpret the formula. Oil was of course used in meals, but there is little if any evidence that an *anointing* played a part in Jewish

concern expressed in 7.1 for the maintenance of table fellowship in separation from gentiles and from the pollution of idols to suggest that great significance was attached to meals and to table fellowship in the Jewish community behind *Joseph and Aseneth*. J. Jeremias rightly emphasizes the solemnity attached even to the "ordinary" daily Jewish meal where a blessing is pronounced.[25] That Jews sometimes contrasted their blessed daily meals with pagan sacrifices is clear from Sibylline Oracles 4.24-30, and the prayer in Didache 9.3f. seems to rest upon a Jewish tradition in which everyday food was considered to be a heavenly gift conferring life and wisdom.[26] It seems most likely that this high evaluation of the daily meal and the concern for the maintenance of purity in table fellowship is what gave rise to the use of meal language as a representative expression for life as a Jew.

In summary, the possibility cannot be excluded that the bread-cup-ointment passages in *Joseph and Aseneth* echo some otherwise unattested Jewish ritual meal. However, there is little in the document itself to suggest this, and in any case the nature and form of such a meal would be irrecoverable. On the other hand, if we cannot discern a special ritual meal in *Joseph and Aseneth*, neither should we conclude that the language is merely literary and symbolic. While the language of eating, drinking, and being anointed expresses the whole Jewish way of life, it grows out of and represents something very concrete in the Jewish community — the effort to maintain a distinctively Jewish way of life in precisely those areas in which susceptibility to gentile impurity was considered to be the greatest, namely, food, drink, and oil contaminated by association with idolatry. So representative of Jewish identity in a gentile environment is the peculiarly Jewish use of these three items that the entire life *more judaico* comes to be expressed in a triad or dyad

---

meals. Jeremias, *Expository Times* 64 (1952) 91, cites only the anointing of the guest before the meal mentioned in Luke 7:46, and Collins, *Between Athens and Jerusalem*, p. 214, mentions only a few rabbinic references to the use of oil for cleaning the hands after a meal. However, as the Biblical triad of grain, wine, and oil itself attests, oil was a staple commodity in Jewish tradition and throughout the ancient Near East. It served the basic human needs for light, heat, nourishment, medicine, condiments, and perfume, and it figured prominently also in sacrifice and ritual, including the anointing of persons and vessels of special distinction. Moreover, as is well documented in Jewish sources, oil was regarded as especially susceptible to impurity, and pagan oil was regularly associated with idolatrous rites. Therefore, in view of the author's apparent concern to maintain a distinctive Jewish self-identity *vis-à-vis* gentiles and to show that the openness to gentile converts is no concession to pagan idolatry and its corrupting effect, it is not surprising to find oil ranked alongside food and drink in a triadic formula in which the uniquely Jewish use of the staple commodities of life is set over against their usage outside Judaism and employed as an expression for the entire life *more judaico*. For a discussion of the uses and perception of oil in ancient Judaism, see S.B. Hoenig, "Oil and Pagan Defilement," *Jewish Quarterly Review* 61 (1970-71) 63-75.

[25] *Expository Times* 64 (1952) 91f.

[26] On the traditio-historical study of the liturgical material in Didache 9 and 10 and its Jewish antecedents, see J.W. Riggs, "From Gracious Table to Sacramental Elements: The Tradition History of Didache 9 and 10," *Second Century* 4 (1984) 83-101, and the works cited there. Also worthy of note in connection with our topic is the fact that Didache 18.5f. mentions oil along with bread and wine as provisions needed by traveling prophets.

so formulaic that it has been assumed — probably mistakenly and certainly too readily — to be a liturgical formula referring to a special ritual meal.

Comparisons with John 6

Formal differences between the bread-of-life theme in John 6 and that in *Joseph and Aseneth* are readily apparent. The stereotyped triadic and dyadic formulas in which the expression "bread of life" occurs intermittently in *Joseph and Aseneth* have no formal counterpart in John 6, where the expression rather represents the central theme of one sustained discourse. Theological differences are equally conspicuous. The Christological focus of the bread-of-life discourse in John 6 stands in marked contrast to the absence of any Christological or messianic thrust in *Joseph and Aseneth*. However, allowance must be made for the fact that borrowed imagery is inevitably filtered through the mind of the borrower and reshaped in the process. As is well known to students of New Testament Christology, early Christians regularly transferred to Jesus those attributes which had been ascribed in Jewish tradition to such non-messianic entities as Wisdom and Torah. Thus the absence of any Christological thrust in the bread-of-life conception in *Joseph and Aseneth* does not militate against the possibility that this conception lies behind the bread-of-life discourse in John 6. Neither do the differences in literary genre, the anti-Jewish polemic of John 6 versus the strongly Jewish character of *Joseph and Aseneth*, nor the other obvious dissimilarities between the two writings exclude the possibility of some affinity of thought between them in their use of the expression "bread of life." The issue must rather be decided on the basis of whether there are, in addition to the expected differences, sufficient similarities of thought or language to suggest some sort of connection. To these similarities we now turn.

The most obvious point of similarity between the bread in *Joseph and Aseneth* and the bread in John 6 is that which is expressed in the genitival qualifier *zōes* (or *tēs zoēs*), "of life." In both cases the explanation is provided that the partaker of the bread of life will not die but will live forever. The honeycomb which is equated with the bread-cup-ointment triad in *Joseph and Aseneth* is said to be "the comb of life, and everyone who eats of it will not die for ever and ever" (16.14). In very similar language, the bread of life in John 6:50f. is said to be such that "a person may eat of it and not die . . . if anyone eats of this bread, he will live for ever." In *Joseph and Aseneth* 16.14 the honeycomb is said to be the "spirit of life," and once again in similar language John 6:63 declares the words of Jesus to be "spirit and life." Thus the works being compared both use the metaphor of eating bread to symbolize that which is considered to be of ultimate importance and most expressive of the identity of the people of God, and for both the result of this "eating" is unending participation in the divine life.

A further similarity lies in the fact that in both the Fourth Gospel and *Joseph and Aseneth*, this sharing in the divine life is not merely, nor even primarily, an eschatological experience, but has a decidedly "realized" character. The tension between present and future in the eschatology of the Fourth Gospel is a matter of long-standing discussion which need not detain us here. There clearly are elements of futuristic and apocalyptic eschatology in John; in the bread-of-life discourse itself the refrain "and I will raise him up in the last day" appears with slight variations four times (vv. 39, 40, 44, 54). Neither R. Bultmann's view that these elements were added by an ecclesiastical redactor,[27] nor the more common view that they are mere remnants of pre-Johannine beliefs which the evangelist failed to discard but also failed to integrate into his thought,[28] does justice to the text. Rather, John shares the *already-but-not-yet* tension which pervades early Christian thought in general and which is traceable to Jesus himself.[29] Nevertheless, it certainly is true that Johannine eschatology is predominantly "realized" in character. The "life" envisioned in John 6, as elsewhere in the Fourth Gospel, is a present possibility for the believer even if a future consummation is awaited: "the one who believes *has* (*echei*, present tense) eternal life" (6:47).

Similarly, the divine life in which Aseneth comes to participate upon her conversion to the God of Israel is expressed in terms which emphasize the blessings *presently* accruing to those who worship God. Following her repentance Aseneth is assured by the man from heaven that her name is written in the book of the living in heaven and will never be erased (15.4). She is told further that in turning to the God of Israel she has eaten honey from the "comb of life" which is made from the dew of the "roses of life" and imbued with the "spirit of life" (16.14). She has partaken of the same food as that eaten by the angels of God in paradise and thus shares in their immortality (16.14). She has eaten "bread of life," drunk a "cup of immortality," and been anointed with "ointment of incorruption" (16.16). As a result, she will not die but possesses untiring vitality and unfailing beauty (16.16). Her present participation in the divine life is symbolized by the radiant garments which she puts on at the command of her heavenly visitor (14.12-15.2; 15.10; 18.12f.) and by the glorious transformation of her physical appearance (18.10f.; 19.4; 20.6f.). The description of Aseneth's blessed new status borders at times on an ascription of angelic status to her (18.9-11; 20.6f.), and this language is only one of several indications that the author considers the

---

[27] *Theology of the New Testament* 2 vols., trans. K. Grobel (New York: Charles Scribner's Sons, 1955), vol. 2, p. 39; and idem, *The Gospel of John: A Commentary*, trans. G.R. Beasley-Murray (Oxford: Blackwell, 1971), pp. 218-20.

[28] E.g., E. Käsemann, *The Testament of Jesus*, trans. G. Krodel (Philadelphia: Fortress, 1968), p. 14; and M.E. Boismard, "L'évolution du thème eschatologique dans les traditions johanniques," *Revue Biblique* 68 (1961) 507-24.

[29] See, among many other studies, W.G. Kümmel, "Futurische und praesentlische Eschatologie in ältesten Urchristentum," *New Testament Studies* 5 (January 1959) 113-26; idem, *Promise and Fulfillment: The Eschatological Message of Jesus*, trans. D.M. Barton, Studies in Biblical Theology 23 (London: SCM Press LTD, 1961); G. Bornkamm, *Jesus of Nazareth*, trans. I. and F. McLusky and J.M. Robinson (New York: Harper and Row, 1960), pp. 90-95; O. Cullmann, *Christ and Time: The Primitive Christian Conception of Time and History*, trans. F.V. Filson (Philadelphia: Westminster, 1950); and idem, *Salvation in History*, trans. S.G. Sowers (New York: Harper and Row, 1967).

people of God already in this life to be leading an angelic sort of existence characterized especially by immortality. That the soteriology of *Joseph and Aseneth* is not exclusively *here and now* may be seen from the references to a place of rest prepared by God (8.9; 15.7; 22.13) — clearly a heavenly and eschatological concept even if nothing is said about when and how this new existence will be brought about. Nevertheless, in *Joseph and Aseneth*, as in John 6, the emphasis is on *zoē* "life," as a present possession of the participant in the bread of life.

Moreover, in *Joseph and Aseneth* this participation in the divine life is couched in dualistic language which sets life over against death, knowledge against ignorance, light against darkness, and truth against error — antitheses very prominent also in the Fourth Gospel. Thus, for example, Joseph begins his prayer for Aseneth's conversion with an address of God as the creator "who gave life to all things, and called them from darkness to light and from error to truth and from death to life" (8.9).[30] The conception of conversion as passage from death to life which is expressed here and elsewhere in *Joseph and Aseneth* is not unlike that expressed by Jesus according to John 5:24f.:

> Truly, truly, I say to you, the one who hears my word and believes in the one who sent me has eternal life, and he does not come into judgment but has passed out of death into life. Truly, truly, I say to you, the hour is coming, and now is, when those who are dead will hear the voice of the son of God, and those who hear will live.

The expression "bread of life" is itself part of a dualistic contrast in both *Joseph and Aseneth* and John 6; in the latter the life-giving bread supplied by the Son of man is set over against food which perishes (6:27; the verb used is *apollumi*), just as in *Joseph and Aseneth* the "bread of life" and the other incorruptible elements in the triadic formula are set over against the food, drink, and ointment of destruction (*apoleia*).

The bread imagery in both *Joseph and Aseneth* and John 6 is based in part on the tradition of God's provision of manna for the children of Israel during their sojourn in the wilderness. This connection is explicit in the case of John 6, where the crowd's request that Jesus produce manna or an equivalent sign (6:30f.) probably reflects the expectation that in the last days God or the

---

[30]That God's activity in conversion as well as creation is envisioned here is suggested not only by the centrality of the former theme in *Joseph and Aseneth*, but especially by the phrase "from error to truth," which is hardly applicable to the physical creation. Similarly, in her own confession and prayer Aseneth appeals to God to resolve her predicament on the basis that he is the giver of life, the creator of being out of non-being (12.1f.); God's salvific activity is conceived as analogous to his creative activity. Creation language in which conversion is represented as transition from death to life is found also in 15.5,12; 20.7; and 27.10.

Messiah would renew the gift of manna.[31] In the discourse itself Jesus declares his teaching and himself to be the *real* bread from heaven, in explicit contrast to the manna eaten by the fathers in the wilderness (6:32f., 48-51). P. Borgen has shown that even the literary form and midrashic technique of the bread-of-life discourse are heavily influenced by post-Biblical reflection on the manna tradition. Not only does the discourse reflect a number of specific haggadic traditions regarding manna; in its very exegetical method and its overall form it follows a fairly well-defined homiletic pattern attested in expositions of the manna miracle both in Philo and in Palestinian midrashim.[32]

The influence of the manna theme is far less explicit in *Joseph and Aseneth* — a fact no doubt to be explained by the author's desire to avoid the anachronism of having manna present in the patriarchal context in which the story is set. Nevertheless, *Joseph and Aseneth* does echo certain traditions regarding manna. The contrast drawn in both *Joseph and Aseneth* and John 6 between the bread of life and perishable food is similar to Philo's distinction between the heavenly manna and things that are perishable.[33] The equation of the bread of life with the honeycomb in *Joseph and Aseneth* 16.15f. is reminiscent of the statement in Exodus 16:31 and in various post-Biblical sources that the manna tasted like honey.[34] The life-giving properties attributed to this honey in *Joseph and Aseneth* 16 are the properties attributed elsewhere in Jewish tradition to the Torah,[35] which, as we shall see below, was sometimes represented symbolically by manna. The explanation in *Joseph and Aseneth* 16.14 that the honeycomb from which Aseneth ate is also the food of the angels of God in paradise recalls the tradition, attested at least as early as the

---

[31] 2 Baruch 29.8; Sibylline Oracles, frag. 3.46-49. The rabbinic references cited by Strack and Billerbeck, *Kommentar*, vol. 2, p. 481f., including Mekilta on Exodus 16:25,33, and Midrash Rabbah on Ecclesiastes 1:9, are considerably later than the Fourth Gospel, but the passages from 2 Baruch and the Sibylline Oracles demonstrate that the tradition existed much earlier.

[32] P. Borgen, *Bread from Heaven: An Exegetical Study of the Concept of Manna in the Gospel of John and the Writings of Philo*, Supplements to Novum Testamentum 10 (Leiden: Brill, 1965). This thesis has been clarified and defended recently in idem, *Philo, John and Paul: New Perspectives on Judaism and Early Christianity*, Brown Judaic Studies 131 (Atlanta: Scholars Press, 1987), pp. 121-29 and 131-44. Less convincing are the arguments of B. Gärtner, *John 6 and the Jewish Passover* (Lund: Gleerup, 1959); A. Guilding, *The Fourth Gospel and Jewish Worship: A Study of the Relation of St. John's Gospel to the Ancient Jewish Lectionary System* (Oxford: Clarendon, 1960), pp. 58-68; and E.J. Kilmartin, "Liturgical Influence on John 6," *Catholic Biblical Quarterly* 22 (1960) 183-91, that the form and content of the discourse in John 6 were determined largely by the Passover synagogue lectionary and the Passover Haggadah. Even though these claims are exaggerated, the heavy influence of manna and Passover traditions on John 6 is certain.

[33] See Borgen, *Bread from Heaven*, pp. 131f.

[34] Josephus, *Antiquities* 3.1.6; Codex Neofiti I; see also Sibylline Oracles, frag. 3.34f., 46-49.

[35] E.g., Mekilta on Exodus 15:26: "The words of the Torah which I have given you are life unto you." See further Strack and Billerbeck, *Kommentar*, vol. 2, pp. 482f.; and Borgen, *Bread from Heaven*, pp. 148f.

Septuagint, that the manna was the food of the angels.[36] For these reasons manna was an especially appropriate symbol of that participation in angelic immortality which is the soteriological ideal in *Joseph and Aseneth*.

An obvious difference in the two uses of the manna tradition is that *Joseph and Aseneth* builds *favorably* on that tradition, whereas John 6 *contrasts* Jesus, the true bread of life, with manna. Nevertheless, it is significant that both draw on the same set of traditions to define the identity of the people of God, and the difference is only the expected Christian reevaluation and reformulation of inherited Jewish traditions in light of the Christ event. In the Hebrew Bible itself a distinction is drawn between the manna as physical nourishment and the power of God's revelation to provide spiritual nourishment (Deuteronomy 8:3). R. Brown correctly notes that in John 6 Jesus goes far beyond this background in speaking not only of his revelation but also of *himself* as the bread from heaven,[37] but the fact remains that the symbolism in John 6 builds upon a tradition begun in the Hebrew Bible and developed in post-Biblical Judaism in which manna symbolizes something more than mere physical nourishment.[38] *Joseph and Aseneth* therefore lies on the same trajectory of manna traditions which arrives at its Christian terminus in the Christology of the bread-of-life discourse.

The widespread Jewish use of bread (and sometimes of manna) as a symbol of the Torah[39] lies behind the concept of the bread of life in both John 6 and *Joseph and Aseneth*. That such symbolism is intended in John 6, and there-

---

[36] In the Massoretic text of Psalm 78:24f., manna is described as "the bread of the powerful beings" (*'abbîrîm*). The Septuagint translates *'abbîrîm* as *angeloi*, thus making clear that in eating manna "man ate the bread of angels." The same idea is explicit in Wisdom of Solomon 16.20-23, Pseudo-Philo *Liber Antiquitatum Biblicarum* 19.5, and at least implicit in the Palestinian Targum on Psalm 78.25, which speaks of the manna as "food which came down from the dwelling of angels." According to the Babylonian Talmud, Yoma 75b, Akiba considered the manna to be the food of angels, but the sages came to the consensus that this was not the case since according to Deuteronomy 9:18 angels neither eat nor drink. See further L. Ginzburg, *The Legends of the Jews*, 7 vols., trans. H. Szold et al (Philadelphia: Jewish Publication Society, 1910-38), vol. 5, p. 236.

[37] *The Gospel According to John*, 2 vols., Anchor Bible (Garden City, N.Y.: Doubleday, 1966-70), vol. 1, p. 266.

[38] On the history of the manna tradition and its midrashic adaptation, see B.J. Malina, *The Palestinian Manna Tradition: The Manna Tradition in the Palestinian Targums and Its Relationship to the New Testament Writings*, Arbeiten zur Geschichte des späteren Judentums und des Urchristentums 7 (Leiden: Brill, 1968).

[39] Such symbolism is implied already in Deuteronomy 8:3, as we have seen. The representation of the word of God as bread is especially well attested in the Wisdom tradition (e.g., Proverbs 9:5; Psalm 119:103; Sirach 15:3; 24:21-23; and Wisdom of Solomon 16:26). The gift of the Torah and the gift of manna are closely related in Nehemiah 9:13-15, 20. Philo equates manna with Wisdom and therefore implicitly also with Torah (*Ouis Rerum Divinarum Heres* 39). For numerous rabbinic references to the Torah as bread, see Strack and Billerbeck, *Kommentar*, vol. 2, p. 483f., and vol. 3, p. 302. See also H. Odeberg, *The Fourth Gospel* (Uppsala: Almquist and Wiksells, 1929), pp. 239-45, 255.

fore that the contrast between the manna and the true bread from heaven implies a contrast between the Torah and the teaching and person of Jesus (as in 1:17), has been argued frequently and convincingly.[40] It is less obvious, but quite likely, that the imagery in *Joseph and Aseneth* also was influenced by a tradition in which the eating of bread was symbolic of Torah observance. *Joseph and Aseneth* obviously lacks the kind of extensive regulations regarding food and agriculture that dominate rabbinic halakah, but in her soliloquies and prayer Aseneth does confess to having been lawless (*anomeō*, 12.4) and to having committed "sins" (*hamartiai*) and "lawless deeds" (*anomiai*, e.g., 11.17; 12.3), and she places a premium on the observance of the commandments (*entolai*) and ordinances (*prostagmata*) of God (12.2). Moreover, as we have seen, a crucial feature of Jewish self-definition in *Joseph and Aseneth* is the avoidance of the defilement of idolatry in the contexts of meals and marriage — concerns not unlike those which dominated the Torah-centered circles known to us from rabbinic literature. It seems likely, therefore, that in *Joseph and Aseneth* the metaphorical usage of "eating bread of life" to express the avoidance of gentile impurity in table fellowship, and more generally to express the entire life *more judaico*, was influenced by the traditional use of bread as a symbol of Torah.

If the traditional use of bread and manna to symbolize Torah is in fact reflected in both John 6 and *Joseph and Aseneth*, the two represent quite divergent conclusions on the efficacy of Torah observance. As we have seen, *Joseph and Aseneth* is quite emphatic that in living the life *more judaico* one attains blessed life and immortality; to live faithfully as a Jew is to share the divine food and hence the immortality of the angels in paradise. In John 6, on the other hand, Jesus is contrasted with the manna (and hence with the Torah) precisely on the basis of the *inability* of the latter to give life:

> Jesus then said to them, "Truly, truly I say to you, it was not Moses who gave you the bread from heaven; my Father gives you the true bread from heaven. For the bread of God is that which comes down from heaven, and gives life to the world" (6:32f.).

> "I am the bread of life. Your fathers ate the manna in the wilderness, and they died. This is the bread which comes down from heaven, that a man may eat of it and not die. I am the living bread which came down from heaven; if any one eats of this bread, he will live forever" (6:48-51b).

---

[40]E.g., C.K. Barrett, *The Gospel According to St. John*, 2nd ed. (Philadelphia: Westminster, 1978), p. 291, maintains that in the description of Jesus as the bread from heaven who gives life to the world (John 6:33), the life-giving function of the Torah has been transferred to Jesus. See, among many other studies, S. Pancaro, *The Law in the Fourth Gospel: The Torah and the Gospel, Moses and Jesus, Judaism and Christianity According to John*, Supplements to Novum Testamentum 42 (Leiden: Brill, 1975), esp. pp. 452-72; W. Meeks, *The Prophet-King: Moses Traditions and the Johannine Christology*, Supplements to Novum Testamentum 14 (Leiden: Brill, 1967); and T.F. Glasson *Moses in the Fourth Gospel*, Studies in Biblical Theology 40 (Naperville, Ill.: Allenson, 1963).

In view of this difference, it may be suggested that the element in *Joseph and Aseneth* which compares most favorably with John 6 lies not in that which the latter designates "bread of life," but precisely in that which the bread-of-life discourse polemicizes *against*, namely, the idea that life is attainable through Torah observance. *Joseph and Aseneth* does not define the Jewish way of life primarily in terms of the observance of Torah, but it does, as we have seen, employ a traditional symbol of the Torah to express the Jewish way of life more generally in terms of a monotheistic faith concerned to maintain separation from gentiles and from the corruption of idolatry. It also employs as most expressive of Jewish identity the eating of sacred food, by which is meant either a special sacred meal or, more likely, the everyday eating of food and generally the everyday conduct of life in separation from the contaminating influences of an idolatrous gentile environment.

The bread-of-life discourse, as if composed to counter such ideas, emphasizes that life *cannot* be attained through any sort of Jewish legal piety. The same metaphor of "eating bread" is used, but the "eating" that leads to life is equated with the act of faith in Christ rather than with the ordering of life according to Jewish traditions. A "bread of life" is espoused, but the predicate is declared to be appropriate only for Jesus, not for the Torah. Jesus alone is the bearer of divine life; he is the *true* bread from heaven; life is attainable only through faith in him. The Christian identity articulated here is expressed most concretely, though not only, in the sacred Christian meal,[41] just as in *Joseph and Aseneth* the literal act of eating represents the most concrete and definitive, though not the only, expression of Jewish piety. In view of this it is reasonable to suggest that *Joseph and Aseneth* witnesses to a type of Judaism which forms a part of the backdrop for the bread-of-life discourse. The milieu of *Joseph and Aseneth* was of course very different from that of Jesus and John, but the use of related traditions in these cases to work out the identity of the people of God suggests that the motif of the bread of life in *Joseph and Aseneth* provides at least one part of the grid against which the motifs in John 6 should be compared.

Conclusion

This study has uncovered no evidence that *Joseph and Aseneth* exerted direct influence on the bread-of-life discourse in John 6. Certainly the use of the expression "bread of life" in both places is inadequate grounds for claiming such a direct connection; the independent coining of this expression in the two places is not at all surprising in view of the traditions which they share regarding the life-giving properties ascribed to manna and Torah. The similarities which we have noted in the use and development of these shared

---

[41]Without entering here into the complex and much-debated issue of the extent to which the Lord's Supper is in view in John 6, we may safely assume that at least in vv. 51c-58, early Christian readers could hardly have failed to see such an allusion.

traditions, while significant for interpreting both writings, lack the specificity needed to demonstrate direct influence of one upon the other.

This conclusion does not mean that *Joseph and Aseneth* has no bearing on the interpretation of the bread of life in John 6. At the very least, *Joseph and Aseneth* witnesses to a type of Judaism which has important elements in common with the Jewish backdrop of the bread-of-life discourse. Without implying that *Joseph and Aseneth* itself influenced either Jesus or John, it is fair to conclude that this apocryphon is one of many witnesses to the varieties of Jewish thought which did influence the discourse in John 6 and which should therefore be taken into account in attempts to reconstruct the Jewish milieu of that discourse. More specifically, certain ideas in *Joseph and Aseneth* — including the dualism, the manna traditions, the Torah symbolism, and the metaphor of eating bread as an expression of Jewish identity — seem to lie on the same Jewish trajectories as those which receive Christian application and development in John 6. The common dependence on these traditions not only suggests the importance of *Joseph and Aseneth* for the study of John 6 and of the New Testament in general; it also adds another link in the chain of arguments for the essential Jewishness of the Johannine portrait of Jesus.[42]

---

[42]I regret not being able to take into account B. Lindars, " 'Joseph and Asenath' and the Eucharist," *Scripture: Meaning and Method, Essays Presented to A.T. Hanson for His Seventieth Birthday*, ed. B.P. Thompson (Hull: Hull University Press, 1987), pp. 181-99, which appeared after the present study was completed. However, nothing in Lindars' article necessitates changes in the present study, and in fact some of Lindars' conclusions correspond closely to those expressed above. For example, with regard to the bread, cup, and ointment in *Joseph and Aseneth*, Lindars writes (pp. 194f.): "The meal references do not relate to a particular meal, nor to rites of initiation. The common meal, whether in the home or in a special group, is central to religious self-definition, and may thus be used as a symbol of the religion as a whole which is professed by the participants. By the same token it can be used to denote differentiation from pagan religion, which also has its meals effecting social definition."

The Fourth Gospel and Christology in Modern Dogmatic and Systematic Theology

W. Royce Clark

Introduction

During the past two centuries, ironically while Biblical scholarship was becoming convinced that the Fourth Gospel was less reliable than the synoptic gospels for reconstructing a historical picture of Jesus, systematic theology persisted in using the Fourth Gospel and even often *preferred* it. From Friedrich Schleiermacher (1768-1834) to the present, many Christian theologians have found the Fourth Gospel more compatible and fruitful in eludicating the Christian faith than the synoptics.[1]

At first glance, one might suppose the reason for this was some dogmatic bias or ignorance of historical critical studies. This suggestion collapses, however, upon a closer look at the method of theologians such as Friedrich Schleiermacher, Alfred Loisy, Karl Barth, Paul Tillich, Karl Rahner, Hans Küng, and Edward Schillebeeckx, to mention only a few.[2] Or one might

---

[1]Early in the nineteenth century, the historical accuracy of "John's" gospel was challenged particularly by Karl Bretschneider. *Probabilia de evangelii et epistolarum Ioannis Apostoli indole et origine cruditorum iudiciis modeste subjecit* (Leipzig, 1820). By the end of that century, critical Biblical studies had become convinced generally that the Fourth Gospel could not be used to reconstruct the historical Jesus and his message.

This historical judgment reached its climax in dogmatic theology in the work of Adolph von Harnack, but was rejected by the most influential Protestant theologians of the twentieth century, Karl Barth and Paul Tillich. Harnack was, in fact, first countered by the Catholic theologian, Alfred Loisy, *L'Evangile et l'Eglise*, (1903), but Loisy was excommunicated shortly thereafter (1907) and had little influence on subsequent Catholic theology, despite the fact that his insights could have supplied a point of continuity between past and present — namely, by his understanding of the "work" of Christ in the church — that would have alleviated the fear of historical relativism the church so much feared.

[2]Even the rigorously historically-oriented theology and Christology of Wolfhart Pannenberg is able to make use of the Fourth Gospel in the development of Christology once the proleptic event of Jesus' resurrection is established by the earliest traditions and documents of the Christian faith. For Pannenberg, the openness beyond any given that is present in interpretation, as grounded in the interpretation of Jesus' resurrection, establishes the continuity and eliminates relativity by virtue of that power of the future which elicits the openness being none other than God.

argue that their continued usage of the Fourth Gospel was from a fear that historical criticism was going to dislodge faith, so the Fourth Gospel was used as a bastion against such incursions. While it is true that most of these theologians felt that historical verification is not the equivalent of Christian faith, even this answer does not appear to be the real reason.

Finally, one might think that the reason for this continued usage of the Fourth Gospel or even preference for it, especially among Protestant theologians, was to remain faithful to the continuity of the historical theology of the church. That is, a Lutheran theologian would naturally embrace the Fourth Gospel because of the position taken by Luther,[3] and others similarly in different communions. But this explanation also quickly breaks down. Protestant theologians after Schleiermacher began to realize that the synoptic gospels are not just historical facts, nor does the Fourth Gospel's apparent explanation of "who" Jesus was and "why" he did what he did in any way really distinguish it from the synoptics. Further, positions taken by Loisy, Küng, and Schillebeeckx have been considered by the church as embracing at best only a fragile or questionable continuity with its official position.

Therefore, it may be that the most logical explanation is simply that the concerns of the theologians were of a wider nature than those of the Biblical scholars. That is, they felt a need not merely to explain what something once meant and how it related to the present Christian message and experience, but in order to facilitate the latter, they were concerned to develop a systematic hermeneutic and epistemology which could include an awareness of significant historical change without being swallowed by historical relativism.

That is, the theologians seemed to be driven by the concerns of: (1) reconstructing a probable historical picture of the "Jesus" behind the gospels; (2) determining the relation any such probable picture has to Christian faith, and, in turn, to Christological assertions; which, in turn, necessitates (3) defining an inherently logical position on the question of historical diversity, pluralism, or the evolution of the thought, practices and structures involved in Christian history and life itself.

Obviously, it is highly unlikely that the problems encountered in these three broad areas could be resolved by mere reference to the Fourth Gospel or some new insight furnished either by the Fourth Gospel or by the entire Christian scriptures for that matter. These necessitate a formulation of methodological procedures which could be derived at best only from an awareness of the larger hermeneutical difficulties or the general problem of interpretation and the relativity of historical knowledge — an awareness that has been discovered significantly *only in the last two centuries*.[4]

---

[3]Luther, of course, had insisted that the synoptic gospels only gave facts about Jesus, whereas the Fourth Gospel informs us of who he was, what he did, and why he did it.

[4]The modern discussion of hermeneutic in systematic theology and the philosophy undergirding it usually looks back to F. Schleiermacher's *Hermeneutik* (1810 and years following), see Friedrich D.E. Schleiermacher, *Hermeneutik*, ed. Heinz Kimmerle (Heidelberg: Carl Winter, Universitatsverlag, 1959), and *Dialektik*

So the theologians preferring the Fourth Gospel have not done so because they felt its writer had consciously articulated the answer to hermeneutical problems of which he could not even have been aware. But the Fourth Gospel was thought to possess other characteristics which were more compatible with this broader interpretive and theological quest than the more limited synoptic gospels.

Opinions as to what these particular characteristics or elements were have differed from theologian to theologian. Importantly, though, all three of the concerns mentioned above were usually worked out interdependently so as to produce a somewhat logical position as well as to provide a conceptual continuity for the two millennia of Christian history and theology.[5]

(1818 and years following), see Schleiermacher, *Dialektik*, ed. Rudolf Odebrecht (Darmstadt: Wissenschaftliche Buchgesellschaft, 1976), as the beginning point of the study in its real breadth. Hans Georg Gadamer posits Schleiermacher's hermeneutic as an advance over earlier hermeneutic in the fact that it (1) rejected any dogmatic determination, whether based upon scripture or the classics; and it (2) supplemented the purely grammatical hermeneutic with a "psychological" hermeneutic. Gadamer, however, faults Schleiermacher with (1) still being too preoccupied with the Biblical texts to develop a hermeneutic that would furnish a method that would be universally applicable to all the human sciences; (2) focusing so narrowly on knowing the author better than he knew himself that it ends up more concerned with the creative act (art) and the individual thought or text than it is with the truth of the object of the text and; (3) the universality Schleiermacher sought for his hermeneutic — based upon his presupposition that "all individuality is a manifestation of universal life so that the reader can both identify with and feel the alien aspect of the author's thought — fails to the degree that he considered understanding a text from the past no more difficult than any other kind of understanding. Gadamer, *Truth and Method*, (New York: The Seabury Press, 1975), pp. 153-173.

[5]While history has been important to most of the Christian theologians of the nineteenth and twentieth centuries, the *relativity* of the historical has been continually addressed, with a variety of answers supplied. For example, for Schleiermacher, the truth of the Christian message was in the Christ's power to awaken one's God-consciousness in any generation, even as in the first, and his person can best be known from the *Fourth Gospel*. The awareness of this truth comes when one realizes that his or her experience of redemption through the Spirit in the Word corresponds to what the early Christians experienced. This did not mean that "experience" became Schleiermacher's "norm" for theology, as Tillich often accused him, but rather that "experience" was correlated with and corroborated by historical tradition, an approach that Tillich at other times said was very similar to his method of correlation.

For Hegel, the Spirit (Geist) was the power not simply in the church to give a certainty or continuity for believers, but was the driving force of history itself, thereby giving meaning to history rather than allowing it to fall into relativity. He insisted against Schleiermacher that by his conception of the Spirit, he retained reflection in the Christian faith rather than abandoning it for some supposed "immediacy." And in his earliest theological writings, *The Positivity of the Christian Religion* and *The Spirit of Christianity and Its Fate*, the *Fourth Gospel* supplied Hegel with proof that humans share the divine nature with God, which, of course, eliminates the relativity of history. "Spirit" was likewise the answer Strauss supplied, while criticizing Kant, Schleiermacher, and Hegel. For him, the certainty for the Christian was not to be found in any of the gospels, and definitely not in either literal-supranatural or

The theological hermeneutical problems are still being clarified from hermeneutical concerns in philosophy and critical theory in literature. But to understand the necessary breadth of the scope in which these theologians have utilized the Fourth Gospel to address the three concerns listed above, we turn briefly in a bit more depth to the work of Friedrich Schleiermacher.

---

rational or naturalistic interpretations of even the synoptics. It was rather in the "idea" behind the Christology or Messianic myth. "Christ," therefore, is an idea supplied by God's Spirit, of the full realization of divinity, not just by one person, but rather the whole of humanity. While Kierkegaard reacted against Hegel's historical gnosticism as he saw it, he too found a certainty despite the radically different gospel pictures, but he referred to that certainty as "faith," supplied by the Absolute in the moment of relation. This enabled one to move above mere historical judgments.

Although nineteenth century Biblical studies made acceptance of the Fourth Gospel's historical accuracy difficult, theology had tended to find in the Spirit or faith a certainty and continuity between the ancient church and the present Christian experience. So it was not any wonder that in the twentieth century Barth and Tillich took their cue from theology in its hermeneutical quest rather than from historical-Biblical studies. As close as they were even to Bultmann theologically who also *preferred the Fourth Gospel*, they found themselves unable to accept his answer to historical relativity as mere "decision," as they saw it.

That is, Tillich argued that Bultmann spoke of God's accosting demand but failed to indicate where the power could be found by which one could meet that demand. Barth's and Tillich's reasons for not rejecting the picture supplied by the *Fourth Gospel* varied, but were certainly centered upon the following convictions: (1) no absolute historical certainty about past events can be attained, no matter which gospel or which data are utilized; (2) since historical relativity cannot be overcome by more data or facts, only faith can grant certainty; (3) faith, as commitment to God rather than certainty of propositions, is accessible to all as a gift of God, whereas historical scrutinizing is limited to very few scholars, and is therefore a subtle form of works-righteousness, manipulation of God, or self-salvation. But this did not allow the whole Christian faith to lapse into relativity because they both found a point of continuity in some form of analogy that connected the past with the present: for Barth, an *analogia fidei*; for Tillich, an *analogia imaginis*, a continuity of *power*.

Further, the Logos in the *Fourth Gospel* supplied Tillich not only with the idea of objective reason as a part of the structure of being, but with the necessity of revelation due to the dead-end of reason's quest. It also gave to Tillich a key to seeing a Gestalt for the biblical picture of New Being in Jesus rather than being bogged down in separate and often conflicting details of the various gospels.

In Roman Catholic theology, the same Logos furnished Rahner with ground for an, "Incarnation" which is real but not a necessity forced upon God, and through which humans could therefore legitimately hear God's address. And back at the turn of the century, although Loisy was aware of the historical problems of the *Fourth Gospel*, and although he for the most part did not use it in reconstructing his picture of Jesus, his understanding was that even in the synoptics one does not get behind the "work" of the church. Thus the "work" of the Christ through the church became the point of continuity which gave validity *even to the Fourth Gospel*, a gospel which Loisy explained as necessary for the church to survive.

Present Catholic theology, though not brandishing Loisy's name or work, shows somewhat the same awareness. So in the work of Schillebeeckx and Küng, one finds the point of continuity between past and present Christian experience the power of Christ in one's life, which is defined as one's "suffering for others" or renouncing one's rights to help others. Küng refers to this as the "human face" of God — the key and "vocational" *continuity* supplied as much by the *Fourth Gospel* as by the others.

Schleiermacher and the Fourth Gospel

Prior to the nineteenth century, systematic theology, which should be more properly still called only "dogmatic" theology,[6] had fairly gone its way, oblivious to the advances in historical-critical Biblical studies as well as the implications of current epistemology. This was to be expected just as Biblical theology had been determined totally by dogmatics. Many of the nineteenth century theologians and biblical scholars, however, became aware not simply of historical-critical method for ancient documents, but were also cognizant of the fact of change or development in history in general.

Theology[7] took a quantum leap forward with Schleiermacher's combination of: (1) a historical-critical examination of the scriptures;[8] (2) the new Kantian epistemology;[9] and (3) a devotion to the church's present under-

---

[6]"Dogmatic" in the sense that the teaching of the church determined the way the content of any text was to be understood, Schleiermacher had sketched what would be required for a "philosophical theology" or "systematic theology" rather than merely a "dogmatic theology" in his *Kurze Darstellung des Theologischen Studiums*, ed. Heinrich Scholz, (Leipzig: 1910; Hildesheim: G. Olms, 1961), Eng. trans. *Brief Outline on The Study of Theology*, tr. T.N. Tice, Richmond: John Knox, 1966), (hereafter referred to as KD, with p. first in German, then Eng.). But he felt that in light of Kant's critique of reason, there was as yet no philosophical theology presently available.

[7]By the categories Schleiermacher solidified in his *Kurze Darstellung*, his monumental work, *Der Christliche Glaube*, Siebente Auflage, ed. Martin Redeker (Berlin: Walter de Gruyter & Co., 1960), Eng. trans. *The Christian Faith*, tr. H.R. Mackintosh & J.S. Stewart (Edinburgh: T. & T. Clark, 1928) (hereafter cited as CG, with p. in German, then Eng.) was "dogmatic" theology in that it was based upon most recent Protestant creeds. Yet because of his prolegomena by which religion, the church, the essence of Christianity, and other things received their definitions through "propositions" "borrowed" from anciliary fields of study, the work is obviously also a "systematic" or "philosophical" theology to the degree these definitions informed the following content.

[8]Among most of the astute critical historians in the church at the time, it was still largely assumed that the Fourth Gospel was written by an immediate disciple of Jesus.

[9]While he accepted Kant's distinction between theoretical and practical reason, between phenomena and noumena, and Kant's rejection of knowing the *Ding an sich*, Schleiermacher rejected Kant's answer that "religion" was to be found in morality. Although both men believed in "Christ," another crucial difference between them related to the idea of Christ being the *Urbild* or archetype. Kant utilized the Johannine Logos to reinforce the concept of universal moral duty. But he went further to insist that it is an archetype (*Urbild*) of the moral that is within reason but must not be thought to have been embodied in any single historical individual. Immanuel Kant, *Die Religion innerhalb der Grenzen der blossen Vernunft* (1793), pp. 61-62, Eng. trans. *Religion Within the Limits of Reason Alone*, Tr. T.M. Greene & H. Hudson (New York: Harper, 1960), pp. 54-56. Schleiermacher, on the other hand, utilized the Fourth Gospel to reinforce his understanding that the *Urbild* was fully historically realized in Jesus of Nazareth. But it is not an archetype of externals or even morality. Rather, he was the archetype of humanity *only* as regards his God-consciousness or relation to God and the way that informed his thought and action. To think otherwise, would be to eliminate all traces of humanity from Christ.

standing of the essence of the gospel, which was found in its most recent definitive creed — which is the way he defined "dogmatics."[10]

Schleiermacher's View of the Gospels

Schleiermacher was far ahead of his day in his understanding and appropriation of the gospel material in reconstructing a probable historical picture of Jesus, of relating this to Christological assertions in general, and to historical development or the pluralism and apparent relativity of life in general. Whereas most theologians in his day regarded all four gospels of fairly equal weight for the construction of the picture of Jesus and thus for Christian theology, Schleiermacher emphasized: (1) the general fragmentary and biased nature of the gospels for a purely historical reconstruction; (2) the paucity of genuine source material from opponents of Christianity that could be used in such a reconstruction; (3) the ruthless historical demand laid upon Christian theologians to examine every possible source, including apocryphal gospels; and (4) the radical and irreconcilable differences between the synoptics and the Fourth Gospel.

More importantly than even these insights, he showed a keen awareness of the long period of oral tradition lying behind the various gospels. He formulated general principles for redaction and tendency criticism,[11] approximately a century ahead of the general acceptance of such methods among Biblical scholars. His understanding of the complexity and method of incorporation of each pericope by the synoptists enabled him to see that although they appeared to be in considerable agreement, the picture that could be reconstructed through a critical use of them was not as historically credible as that supplied by the author of the Fourth Gospel.[12]

Not only were the synoptics "more aggregates of individual narratives than continuous presentations,"[13] but until the reasons or rules could be discovered

---

[10]Karl Barth criticized Schleiermacher for avoiding the truth question by (1) admitting in his "dogmatics" that in his description of God, humanity, and the world, he really was only discussing "states of mind" rather than the *Ding an sich*, and (2) defining "dogmatics" as description of the present belief of the church. Barth, *Protestant Thought: from Rousseau to Ritschl*, (New York: Simon & Schuster, 1969), pp. 306-354, tr. Brian Cozens from eleven chapters of *Die Protestantische Theologie im 19, Jahrhundert* (Evangelischer Verlag A.G., Zollikon, Zurich, 1952). But this criticism unfairly overlooked the normative objective element of the Spirit or the impress of Christ which Schleiermacher saw as common to all Christians. Rather than not focus on the question of truth, as even Gadamer accused Schleiermacher, Schleiermacher was convinced that the truth is God, encountered objectively by Christians via the Spirit. Admittedly this metaphysical dimension makes his hermeneutic to that degree inapplicable to *other* sciences, but that alone does not prove it incorrect if there be such a thing as God or Spirit.

[11]Schleiermacher, *Das Leben Jesu* (Berlin: Georg Reimer, 1864), pp. 37-46, Eng. trans. *The Life of Jesus*, ed. Jack C. Verheyden (Philadelphia: Fortress Press, 1975), pp. 36-44, (hereafter cited LJ with pages first in German, then English).

[12]LJ, pp. 37-44 (ET, 36-44).

[13]LJ, p. 40 (ET, 39).

to explain why each of the synoptists combined individual "narratives" (pericopes) in his own peculiar way, no chronology of the development of the traditions could be ascertained.[14] Since, as a matter of fact, the historian will naturally seek to reconstruct a *single* picture from the comparison of the synoptists,[15] Schleiermacher thought it was an accurate assessment of the situation to say that we have only "two sources" for reconstructing the life of Jesus: the source of the three synoptics, and source of the Fourth Gospel. And the first is more difficult to recover by the "aggregative" nature of the synoptics.

Another important consideration for him were the credentials of the writers of these materials. He admitted that the church very early on attributed only the first and fourth gospels to two of the immediate disciples of Jesus: Matthew and John. Historical evaluation naturally prefers eyewitnesses where possible. When one compares these two, however, the radical differences between the locality or geographical situations and the temporal durations attributed to Jesus' ministry are irreconcilable. Since Matthew, however, unlike John, was considered a mere aggregation of separate discourses and events without any real coherence,[16] one would naturally have to prefer John's picture where they differed so radically.

Schleiermacher emphasized that regarding these sources, the Gospel of John had always given him the impression of being a "coherent, comprehensive presentation" of Jesus' life. But even so, he acknowledged that it had too many inherent gaps — even skipping entirely over Jesus' life prior to his public ministry — to be an adequate source. He concluded:

> Therefore it is undeniable that we cannot achieve a connected presentation of the life of Jesus. We must limit our task in accordance with the material at our disposal. Consequently the only question remaining is: How far can we unite the reports that we have in order to form an outline by which we wish to proceed?[17]

Two examples, then, will illustrate his method of reconstruction. First, regarding the question of whether Jesus was born in Jerusalem or Bethlehem or was raised in Bethlehem or Nazareth, Schleiermacher, upon close exami-

---

[14]LJ, p. 40 (ET, 39).

[15]Schleiermacher was familiar with the synoptic parallels of Wilhelm M.L. de Wette and Friedrich Lucke, *Synopsis evangeliorum Matthaei, Marci, et Lucae cum Parallelis Joannis pericopis* (Berlin, 1818), see Schleiermacher, LJ, pp. 38-39 (ET, 37-38).

[16]That is, this lack of a coherent plan or evident rationale for the document was perceived by its use of pericopes found in the other synoptic gospels, which were in fact utilized differently or interpreted differently by the various writers. One could generalize that according to the evident methodology of Schleiermacher's, John's credibility came primarily from the fact of the radical dissimilarity of any other gospel, for had there been another gospel that incorporated a number of pericopes also found in John, yet utilized or seen differently in any way, it would have had to have been judged as the synoptics, as a mere aggregation of otherwise disconnected narratives.

[17]LJ, p. 44 (ET, 43).

nation of the two evangelists, found them in hopeless contradiction. Since the synoptics are only "aggregations of individual accounts," whereas the Fourth Gospel is a "connected narrative" or one which gives a coherent or whole picture, the Fourth Gospel must be preferred.[18] That does not indict Matthew and Luke for falsifying a story. They did the best they could with what was at their disposal in light of the absence of any extant authentic reports of Jesus' birth. But since references to the birth or life of Jesus in Bethlehem or Nazareth are missing from John, and the latter is a coherent whole, the only conclusion is that the question of Christ's birthplace or the place he was raised "has no essential place in the gospel narrative."[19]

Other narratives related to Jesus' birth were just as problemmatic. The slaughter of children in Bethlehem, and Jesus' flight to Egypt are typical. Schleiermacher, after intensive examination, concluded that these are best explained as "facts" of some kind rather than some mere production on the basis of the Messianic idea in the Old Testament passages. That is, nothing in the Old Testament necessitated either of these stories, despite the evangelists' mistaken notion that it did. Nevertheless, Schleiermacher continued,

> You see how skeptically I go to work. If we cannot recognize any original authentic source and it is improbable that the narrative as it stands has come from immediate eyewitnesses, then we are obliged, because we are engaged in a piece of historical research, to place no weight on the difference between canonical and apocryphal writings. On the contrary we must presuppose as possible that these narratives have an apocryphal character because they are based on such a definite tendency.[20]

More specifically, Schleiermacher argued that had the events occurred in the unambiguous way the evangelists describe, then even though Jesus did not begin his public ministry until years later, people would have drug up those earlier incidents and identified him immediately with these Messianic happenings.

> But there is no trace of any such identification at the time of Christ's public appearance. Consequently the birth stories must have been restricted to a very narrow circle and must later acci-

---

[18]LJ, pp. 51-58 (ET, 49-55).

[19]LJ, p. 58 (ET, 56) Schleiermacher, as historian as well as theologian, demanded some evident or at least logical link between the events and their reporting in the gospels. So if the evangelists were not eyewitnesses of Jesus' birth and youth, what is the source of the information? He thought it incredible to suppose that Jesus sat around describing his childhood days and the circumstances of his birth to his disciples. What about Mary, his mother? Schleiermacher conceded that it is possible she could have supplied information to some later disciples. But a single source such as that would not explain the grossly different pictures the gospels present with such an apparently simple matter as the manner and place of birth. So when neither John nor Mark give birth accounts of Jesus, they simply have no essential place in the gospel narratives (*Geschichtschreibung*).

[20]LJ, p. 69 (ET, 66).

dentally have come again to light, and these events had nothing to do with the appearance of Christ or the origin of faith in him.[21]

Time and again, then, Schleiermacher noted that the accounts of the synoptists contradict the Gospel of John. Sometimes the contradiction can be worked out; other times it cannot so John is preferred. For example, only Luke mentions Jesus' trial before Herod. The only way this trial could be explained, yet omitted by John, who was an eyewitness at Jesus' trials before Annas and Pilate, is by positing the possibility that when John said that Pilate called Christ into the praetorium, from that point his actions could not be traced by John, so Pilate might have sent him out another exit to go see Herod. Otherwise, it is inconceivable why only Luke mentions it.[22]

The contradictory statements made about Jesus' resurrection pose the same problem. Here, Schleiermacher repeated that sometimes a way of resolving them can be found, but other times it cannot, and then John must be followed.[23] At other times, it is not just the absence of the pericope in John but either (1) the total incongruity of the picture, or (2) the lack of connection such a pericope has to the Messianic dignity,[24] that caused Schleiermacher not to accept it as required by the faith. Examples of this are the stories of the rending of the veil of the temple and the resurrection of the bodies from tombs at the time of Jesus' crucifixion, the bribing of the guard, and the words of despair assigned mistakenly to Christ on the cross, "My God, my God, why has thou forsaken me?"[25]

The Relation of the Reconstructed Picture to Christological Assertions

With Schleiermacher's reference to "faith in him," we have moved from a mere historical reconstruction to *Christology*. Of course, the Christology is based upon the *actual history of Jesus*, his person and work, but it is corroborated by the power of Christ in the life of the present believer. What one has

---

[21]LJ p. 71 (ET, 68).

[22]LJ, pp. 435-436 (ET, 408).

[23]"I know no rule to set up except this: The Gospel of John is an account by an eyewitness, and the whole Gospel was written by one man. The first three Gospels are compilations of many accounts that earlier stood by themselves. If the individual sections of the different Gospels are examined, we find differences which are genuine contradictions, and they can only be hypothetically reconciled, not wholly." LJ, p. 461 (ET, 433).

[24]As, for example, the way he sees the doctrine of the virgin birth of Christ.

[25]LJ, pp. 441-460 (ET, 411-431). On the issue of the words from the cross he insists "Some claim that such a state of abandonment by God was a necessary part of the plan of redemption. I admit gladly that I do not believe that. It contains an untruth, for if such a one had been abandoned by God he would have to be an untruth. He was an object of divine favor and must always have been that." He explains further that Christ was quoting Ps. 22 not to identify himself with the opening verses of despair, but directing attention to it as a whole, which ends quite triumphantly LJ, p. 451 (ET, 423).

to believe in the present is therefore no more than what the early disciples had to believe about this Jesus, but it must be as much. What this means is that he insists that the faith of the early Christians was grounded on their actual *historical* experience with Jesus — the "being of God" in Jesus, or his potent God-consciousness which redeemed or transformed their ineffective God-consciousness. That is, Christology must trace itself back to the actual way he *affected them in history*. This guards against the alternative of Christology merely being faith in faith.[26]

If, conversely, Christology were grounded in something like his virgin birth or his crucifixion and resurrection, it would be possible to think that the Christian faith is based merely upon an *idea* of something supranatural or an *image* rather than *real event*. People could have been overwhelmed by the enthusiastic preaching of such fantastic things, so that their faith was rooted in *ideas* which were in no way corroborated either by historical evidence about Jesus nor by one's personal experience. This is the reason, for example, that Schleiermacher insisted that faith in the resurrection, ascension, and future judgment by Jesus is *not essential* to the Christian faith — that is, because Jesus had redeemed people or had disciples who believed in him *prior to* those alleged events and whose belief was *independent* of any such events ever occurring.[27] He wrote:

> Belief in these facts, accordingly, is no independent element in the original faith in Christ, of such a kind that we could not accept Him as Redeemer or recognize the being of God in Him, if we did not know that He had risen from the dead and ascended to heaven, or if He had not promised that He would return for judgment, Further, this belief is not to be derived from those original elements; we cannot conclude that because God was in Christ He must have risen from the dead and ascended into heaven, or that

---

[26]Ironically, Wolfhart Pannenberg has faulted Schleiermacher's Christology, even more so than Barth's as being a mere "faith in faith." He argues that Schleiermacher determined the content of his Christology from inferences from soteriology, and did not mind thereby neglecting the actual Jesus. *Jesus — God and Man* (Philadelphia: Westminster Press, 1968), pp. 25, 48. But such a caricature overlooks the fact that Schleiermacher believed the gospel accounts that represented Jesus as saving or redeeming people during his lifetime by the actual encounter they had with him. Since for Pannenberg, Jesus became the "Son of God" *retroactively* only from his *resurrection*, Pannenberg's explanation seems less historically verifiable and intelligible than Schleiermacher's. Neither one is a mere "faith in faith," though.

[27]CG, II, pp, 82-89 (ET, 417-424). Among other arguments, he insists that the *Fourth Gospel* does not "adduce the visible ascension as a proof of the higher dignity of Christ." CG II, p. 83 (ET, 418). And when he analyzes the belief in Jesus' role in the coming judgment, he notes that the idea of Christ's return to judge is only "an accidental form for the satisfaction of the longing to be united with Christ." Such judgment, he insists, "implies nothing greater in the person of Christ than already we ascribe to Him apart from this; and in any case it does not really belong to the work of redemption itself, [and redemption is the essence of Christianity] since of course *those who believe do not come into judgment*." CG, II, p. 83, (ET, 419) emph. added. The latter statement shows again his dependence upon the *Fourth Gospel*.

because He was essentially sinless He must come again to act as Judge. Rather they are accepted only because they are found in the Scriptures; and all that can be required of any Protestant Christian is that he shall believe them in so far as they seem to him to be adequately attested. Here the sacred writers are to be regarded only as reporters; accordingly, belief in these statements belongs, immediately and originally, rather to the doctrine of Scripture than to the doctrine of the Person of Christ. Yet an indirect connexion with that doctrine is not to be denied to such belief, in so far, that is, as our judgment about the disciples as original reporters reacts upon our judgment about the Redeemer.[28]

This, to Schleiermacher, assures us that the faith is based on the actual Jesus and actual influence he exercised rather than upon supposed events which were unintentionally misconstrued, exaggerated, or simply concocted from Messianic ideas. He was historically astute enough to know that a religion's sacred scriptures are not totally immune to the latter. Thus faith ultimately has to lie in the *historical Christ* rather than even the Scriptures.

We can further elucidate his *Christological method* by looking more closely at his treatment of Jesus' "virgin birth." He found this idea superfluous for faith as well as insufficiently attested historically. He stressed that

---

[28]Schleiermacher qualified this even further, insisting that if one, in order to avoid having to believe in Jesus' literal resurrection, believed that the disciples were *deceived*, taking an inward experience as a literal external resurrection, that would be unacceptable because of what it would imply about the disciples' judgment, as well as Jesus' judgment in selecting them. CG, II, 84-85 (ET, 420). However, he insisted that the "disciples recognized in Him the *Son of God without having the faintest premonition of His resurrection and ascension*, and we too may say the same of ourselves; moreover neither the spiritual presence which He promised nor all that He said about His enduring influence upon those who remained behind is mediated through either of these two facts. This may well depend upon His sitting at the right hand of God — by which, however, since the expression may be strictly an impossible one, we must understand simply the peculiar and incomparable dignity of Christ, raised above all conflict — but not upon a visible resurrection or ascension, since of course Christ could have been raised to glory even without these intermediate steps, and if so, it is impossible to see in what relation both these can stand to the redeeming efficacy of Christ." CG, II, p. 82 (ET, 418) (emphasis added). Strauss rightly perceived that the church would be incapable of distinguishing what Schleiermacher called the "doctrine of Scripture" (which has finite elements in it) from the "doctrine of Christ," so that Schleiermacher's treatment of Jesus' resurrection would be an offense to the church. In LJ, however, Schleiermacher's acceptance of the resurrection is more obvious; he finds John's account the only credible one, and Jesus' explanation there the extent of our knowledge of his state of mind. He concludes that by so accepting John's picture of the resurrection appearances, etc., the only element that remains incomprehensible is the resurrection itself, to which he responds, "the same thing is true of Christ's whole appearance upon earth. His coming was a miraculous act, but all that followed it was wholly natural." (aber so ist es mit der ganzen Erscheinung Christi auf Erden, das Erste ist ein wunderbarer Akt, aber das folgende ist ein vollkommen Naturliches gewesen) LJ, p. 474 (ET, 445).

from the standpoint of faith, there are two legitimate concerns involved: (1) that Scripture contain the truth; and (2) that "nothing sinful entered into the origin of the life of Christ."[29] But the mere absence of the physical influence of Joseph does not suffice to break the chain of hereditary sin; for that would have necessitated a dissolution of any physical connection, even Mary's. Thus, Schleiermacher concluded:

> The indwelling of the divine in him cannot rest only on the proposition, viewed in and for itself, that Christ was begotten without the cooperation of a man, but rather on a positive, divine act. Therefore the divine act must also have availed to make Christ free from all connection with hereditary sin, regardless of the physical influence which must have played its part if his life was to be truly a human one. We can therefore discuss this question without having to fear a disadvantage for the Christian faith, even if we have to say that it cannot be maintained that the narrative of the supernatural conception of Christ is a wholly historically founded statement.[30]

Schleiermacher's historical criticism was rigorous, but one could hardly accuse his *historical method* thus far of being arbitrary or inconsistent, especially since the first thorough-going rejection of Johannine authorship had appeared only in 1820 by Karl Bretschneider, and was directly opposed by Schleiermacher's lectures on the *Life of Jesus*. Perhaps the distinction he drew between the coherence of John vis-à-vis the piecemeal compilation by the synoptists could be considered his basic move to validate *Christological assertions* by connecting them with the reconstructed historical picture. He deplored the fact that so many scholars were viewing the synoptics as earlier than the Fourth Gospel and therefore more accurate.[31] This not only left them in a chaotic mess because of the inaccessibleness of the synoptists' particular selection and disparate use of various pericopes; but more importantly, it virtually *left Christology without any foundation* since the synoptists provided almost nothing in the way of a universally applicable picture of *Jesus' awareness of his own person*. They rather focused on his

---

[29] LJ, p. 62 (ET, 59).

[30] LJ, p. 61 (ET, 59). In *The Christian Faith*, the idea of the supernatural conception is made more explicit as the absolute uniqueness in history of the appearance of this completely potent God-consciousness, which Schleiermacher thinks of as a "*wundarbare Erscheinung*"! But this uniqueness is corroborated by the effect that God-consciousness of Jesus has on him or her through the Spirit, whereas a uniqueness of a virgin birth would have appeared for Schleiermacher as setting up a barrier for faith rather than being corroborated from present experience. That is, it is both "inadvisable" as well as "superfluous" to set up a doctrine of the "virgin birth," since (1) it focuses too much on something pertaining to a "purely scientific character"; (2) it feeds into other positions about Mary or about sex that are totally unwarranted; CG, I, pp. 68-69 (ET, 406-407).

[31] He insisted that one cannot simply assume that John makes up discourses to ascribe to Christ. One would instead have to prove this. LJ, pp. 277-278 (ET, 259-260).

teaching about the coming Kingdom of God, presented in light of the Jewish theocracy, thereby lacking universalizable analogies from which sufficient Christological grounds could be obtained.[32]

In fact, Schleiermacher argued, since no convincing reason can be given for the assertion of some that John concocted these discourses and then ascribed them to Jesus, "what John represents as the content of the discourses of Christ must have been what Christ really said."[33] Among other reasons, Schleiermacher reached this conclusion because he held that John was the only one of the circle of Jesus' disciples who communicated his account directly in written form. The synoptics, on the other hand, are "only end results of a process of oral transmission," a process that consisted of rather unplanned incorporation of certain traditions as well as failures to gain access to other narratives (e.g. the apostles who reported the discourses orally would probably have suppressed those things that might easily be misconstrued).[34]

So as Schleiermacher saw it, one appears to have a choice between reconstructing the life of Jesus, and therefore *grounding Christology* on the synoptists' rather fortuitous collection of pericopes which in themselves only indirectly tell us what Jesus thought of himself, or reconstructing that life from the Gospel of John which seems planned, reasonable, and trustworthy, giving us a credible picture of *Jesus' self-consciousness*.

Or, even more to the point, Schleiermacher argued that to reconstruct a biography of a person, it is not enough to lay hold on disconnected events of his or her life, even if one could recover every single event. These externals themselves provide only the framework. The person is discovered only to the degree that we find behind these events a *unity of the person* driven by a *constant inner force*, an identity that remains throughout the variety of confrontation with externals and through the historical changes encountered even with the person's own being itself.[35]

That is, the explanation for one's responses to the externals cannot be adequately given by pointing merely to the externals, but rather to the inner directing force and identity known to the person as himself or herself. No one would accept a biography written of himself or herself that explained his or her character strictly by reciting otherwise perceptible unattached externals, historical episodes or narratives. This would either open up the possibility that such externals could elicit similar responses from others, so people could be exactly alike, or would make one's character totally fortuitous, depending upon the convergence of unique combinations of externals, denying free will

---

[32]LJ, pp. 275-276 (ET, 257-258). Of course, a mere report of Jesus' self-consciousness is not absolute evidence *per se* as to who he really is. But the indirect pointers of Jesus' self-consciousness in the synoptics and the conflicting pictures these gave of his Messianic dignity, could not supply the ground for Christology that was needed. That is, the church's later picture of Christ has to find justification somehow even in *his own self-consciousness*. This was supplied coherently only in the *Gospel of John*.

[33]LJ, p. 280 (ET, 262).
[34]LJ, pp. 278-280 (ET, 260-262).
[35]LJ, pp. 5-7 (ET, 6-7).

and real human uniqueness. Schleiermacher opted instead for the *unity and uniqueness* of the person that is somehow preserved through any kind or number of external stimuli.

This is the "tendency" involved in Schleiermacher's "psychological" hermeneutic approach which proves that his hermeneutic was *not* merely some romanticistic empathizing nor purely subjective idealism. The biography[36] demands distinguishing the particular unity of one individual from the unity of all others, and this requires being able to form an *image* of the whole person[37] that is coherent enough that one can calculate to a degree how the person would respond to externals which he or she, in fact, did *not* encounter. Without this ability to calculate, one really does not know the person.[38]

On the other hand, Schleiermacher insisted that this abstraction of the inner unity of Christ or his "disposition," must be derived *only* from the most graphic picture possible — which meant seeing him entirely within the *particular circumstances of his own time*. So he was not giving any license to attempts to view Jesus *in the present* under the circumstances of his life. These attempts *impose foreign circumstances* on him or our picture of him.

The only proper method is instead to utilize *only* the circumstances of *his own time*, and to try to penetrate to what is exemplary in his, which is found in *his actual disposition*, which, in turn, we find articulated in his "maxims." Since the "maxims" transcend the particular circumstances of Jesus, by their

---

[36] Admittedly, of course, the various gospels are not "biographies," not even the *Fourth Gospel*. As Schleiermacher wrote, "John is ruled by a definite point of view throughout but it is not a coherent biography (*zusammenhängenden Lebensbeschreibung*), for many of the moments necessary for a biography (*Bigraphie*) are entirely lacking in his Gospel," *Hermeneutik und Kritik mit Besonderer Beziehung auf das Neue Testament*, ed. F. Lucke (Berlin, G. Reimer, 1838), 223-224. See also LJ, 169 (ET, 159): "For those, however, who undertake the task of viewing the life of Jesus in its continuity, the Evangelist John is just as unsatisfactory as the others." Nevertheless, John's superiority to the other evangelists is that while they do not present his life as a unity, John does. John's "tendency" Schleiermacher describes with the following: "The author wishes to make understandable the disaster in Christ's destiny together with the authentic nature of his activity, while — regarding the matter from John's own standpoint — the two conflicted with one another. Everyone who had, like John, won through to faith, had to expect that Christ would be recognized by all in the same way, and the catastrophe had therefore to be viewed in general as something that appeared unexpectedly. However, he wishes to make it comprehensible, and consequently everything is set forth in order to give a clear picture, in the first place of the actual nature of Christ's activity, and in the second place of the development of his relationship to the people and to the authorities among the people, and to make both comprehensible side by side with one another." LJ, pp. 168-169, (ET, 159).

[37] The idea of uncovering the "whole" person corresponds to Schleiermacher's general emphasis that understanding of parts or individual requires including the whole. So, e.g., a typical aphorism of his was "Jedes Verstehen des Einzelnen ist bedingt durch ein Verstehen des Ganzen." *Hermeneutic*, p. 46. This corresponds to his conception of religion being an immediate self-consciousness or consciousness of the Whole or Totality which was so important in the *Reden*.

[38] LJ, p. 15 (ET, 16).

assistance we can *apply this disposition* to *our own circumstances*.[39] The degree to which this knowledge of his inner nature or disposition was acquired by either the earliest disciples or by any subsequent disciples, it must have been due to *Christ's own initiative* or his disclosure. Therefore it was "his work," rather than a disciple manipulating the facts or "standing higher" than Jesus, as Schleiermacher puts it.[40] As *Christ's "work,"* this knowledge through the Spirit, as well as the experience of redemption through the Spirit, gives *objective continuity* to the Christian community and its theology, as it continues to manifest itself through the Word.

Or, put slightly differently, if one cannot be removed hypothetically from his or her individual existence or specific time and place, and placed into another, then knowledge of such person would "have no practical value, for he ceases to have exemplary character."[41] But, if by the impetus of one's own life, the person "exercises an influence which extends beyond his people and his age," or the more universalizable his exemplary character, the greater the dignity of the person.[42]

For Christ to carry Messianic dignity, his exemplary character must be *universally intelligible and affective*. This means that we must have a knowledge of his inner person that is separate from any if not every actual external stimuli, a picture of the whole Christ. When one understands this, it is quite clear why Schleiermacher argued that there are *no single events* in Jesus' life and no unique combination of them that in themselves prove his dignity or his "sinlessness" or absolutely-potent God-consciousness.[43] That can be proven only as his Spirit operates on our spirit in a direct confrontation through the community he founded,[44] his whole unique person influencing us. Again, to think otherwise, would lay one open to the possibility of basing faith only upon reports of some types of events that easily catch the imagination or are supranatural if not wholly mythological.

This corresponds with Schleiermacher's explanation of the beginning of a religion. He articulated a "positive-individual"[45] explanation of Christianity and religion in general, as opposed to Hegel's "historical-evolutionary" schema. The new religion was to be attributed not to externals nor to some quality that all humans have. Rather, a new religion begins by a specific occasion or moment in which the actual inner direction of an individual impacts others decisively. That which is universalizable or the *maxim* of the

---

[39]LJ, pp. 15-16 (ET, 16-17).
[40]LJ p. 17 (ET, 18).
[41]LJ p.10 (ET, 11).
[42]LJ, pp. 10-12 (ET, 12-13).
[43]CG, II, p. 34 (ET, 377).
[44]Schleiermacher finds no credible possible answer to Christology and to the image of "Christ" as the Vorbild and Urbild except that ideality was embodied fully in Jesus of Nazareth, and by his power of redemption, he passed on that redemption through the corporate or church life he established. Anything less would have given a less than ideal image since it would have originated with humans whose God-consciousness is so weak that it is almost non-existent. CG, II, pp. 34-37 (ET, 378-380).
[45]CG, I, pp. 64-71 (ET, 44-52).

whole person's behavior and *particularly his words*, creates his dignity as he influences others.

This alone, accounts for a new religion. And this alone explains the birth of Christianity, according to Schleiermacher. It did not simply evolve naturally from the causal externals. To hold such would be to make Christ unnecessary since anyone else could have responded in the same way to those externals.[46] So Schleiermacher insisted that he detested the notion that Judaism was the "forerunner" of Christianity.[47]

From Christological Assertion to the Issue of Historical Development and Diversity

To the contrary, Christianity came from the positive impetus of a particular individual named Jesus of Nazareth, at a particular time. His very appearance, or especially the historic reality of his "absolutely-potent God-consciousness" was "eine wunderbare Erscheinung"[48] — by which Schleiermacher meant that it was *absolutely unique* in the history of the world. By his using "miracle" in this way — as something never before encountered in the history of the world,[49] rather than as commonly understood as a suspension or breach of natural law — the historical claim could not be dislodged merely by scientific objections or later rationalism or critical studies. Especially would this be true if one's *present experience* of redemption has as its *only* possible explanation the impetus *begun* by this *historical Christ*.

That is, Christ's person and work would not be intelligible to humans if it were absolutely supranatural or suprarational. But it would not be archtypal and exemplary if it were only natural and rational.[50] So the key, as we have already seen, is that the person of Christ must be discovered in his absolute uniqueness, which is the natural concern of a biography. But although he apparently influenced all ages and places or was totally universalizable in his influence, he nevertheless was still a concrete person subject to the general conditions of his age.

So Christ was both natural and supranatural, both fully man and fully God. Although he developed as any normal human being would, his birth was marked with his potential capacity for the absolutely-potent God-con-

---

[46]LJ, pp. 13-14 (ET, 14-15).

[47]*On Religion, Speeches to Its Cultured Despisers*, tr. John Oman (New York: Harper & Brothers, Pub., 1958), p. 238. In fact, Schleiermacher was consistent in his position, so the Jewish background was minimized as an explanation of Jesus' potent God-consciousness, and the Old Testament or Jewish Bible he held as superfluous to the Christian faith. CG, I, pp. 83-85, II, pp. 36-37 (ET, 60-62; 379-380).

[48]CG, II, pp. 38 (ET, 381).

[49]CG, II, pp. 37-39 (ET, 380-382). See especially his definition of "miracle" as a new beginning spiritually that cannot in anyway be explained by what preceded it. CG, I, pp. 99-101 (ET, 71-73).

[50]CG, I, pp. 86-94 (ET, 62-68). See also on miracles attributed to Jesus, CG, II, pp. 115-118 (ET, 448-450).

sciousness which then matured naturally and informed every moment of his life.⁵¹ Schleiermacher warned that to minimize this natural development would tend toward the most common heresy in the church, docetism. To minimize the supranatural or absolutely unique appearance of his personal unity would put one in danger of the Ebionite heresy.⁵²

As already noted, Schleiermacher contended that one does not come to this Christological conviction by simply isolating some specific incidents in Christ's life. No single event or combination of them are sufficient.⁵³ That would be again to revert too much to dependence upon externals to discover the unity of the person, a method he discounted. But by the presentation of a whole picture of Christ, as in the Gospel of John, one's experience of redemption corroborates the professed unity or dignity ascribed to that person.

If this be true — that the redemptive experience of each Christian in all subsequent generations was *historically derived* from this *original historical event* of the absolutely-potent God-consciousness of Jesus of Nazareth, and that each person redeemed was and is aware of this — then this impress of Christ or his Spirit is the *same* for all subsequent generations.⁵⁴ What this means is that no generation has an advantage on any other as regards redemption through Jesus of Nazareth. In fact, if any generation suffered a disadvantage, it was the original one since (1) while Jesus' original disciples were still with him, changing circumstances made any abstract universalizing of him or any formulation of his inner character virtually impossible;⁵⁵ and (2) the most likely time for influences foreign to Jesus' dignity to enter the

---

⁵¹CG, II, pp. 34-48 (ET, 377-389).

⁵²LJ, pp. 24-37 (ET, 24-36); CG, II, pp. 34-48 (ET, 377-389). Ironically, despite Schleiermacher's ruthlessly objective historical method, his dogmatics tend more toward docetism than the Ebionite heresy merely by the positing of potent God-consciousness in Jesus from birth, something totally unknown among all other humans. This is the "Achilles' heel" that D.F. Strauss attacked, namely, how could one present a credible "scientific" picture by positing one member of a species reaching absolute perfection in total isolation from every other member of that species? David F. Strauss, *The Life of Jesus Critically Examined*, tr. George Eliot (Philadelphia; Fortress Press, 1972), pp. 768-773. Schleiermacher, however, had even already anticipated that criticism, but he reminded his readers (1) that by "ideality" (Urbildlichkeit) he meant *only Christ's God-consciousness," not some ideal of art or skill* postulated from a society; (2) if this ideality is not admitted as actually existing in Christ, then the human species must at least bear or will bear a hope of passing beyond Christ, which means the end of the Christian faith; and (3) to deny this actual ideality in Christ is to relegate the human species to a status lower than animals, for the latter realize their ideal *en toto*, and since humans differ by virtue of their free will, their realization of the ideality must occur in a single person rather than the totality. So to argue that Christ was not it would be to assert that it does not exist, CG, I, pp. 34-37 (ET, 378-379). Strauss, of course, believed that it does exist, but exists not in an individual life but in the whole human species' self-conception and progression toward perfection of its own ideal image, the "Christ."

⁵³Note 42 *supra*.

⁵⁴CG, II, pp. 248-278 (ET, 560-585).

⁵⁵LJ, p. 17 (ET, 18).

stream of the Christian community were in its beginning stages when it had been as of yet incapable of formulating thoroughly the full meaning of Christ.[56]

So the historical encounter of the earliest disciples — the redemption they experienced in Jesus of Nazareth, by his awakening their ineffective God-consciousness — was normative for all time, but not in a heteronomous way. Its normative status was simply corroborated by the redemptive experience of all subsequent disciples. Thus the essence of Christianity was present in the very origins of the religion. But because the experience of subsequent Christians is the same, though in a historically-derivative way, it would not be transcended, contradicted, or outgrown by any amount of later historical-critical studies.

That is, the immediate experience of redemption through one's response to the Spirit through the Word, corroborates the claims of the original Christians about this Jesus. The further the Christian church progresses, the more reflection via this Spirit removes from it any foreign element that contradicts the essence or power of Christ. This is not due to some inherent power of evolution or development nor to the autonomous human reason so exalted by the Enlightenment, but rather to God's Spirit and its continuing effect through Christ's *continuous* historical power.[57]

The implications of this continuous divine power or the possibility of transcending historical relativity are many. To give one example, regarding the Christian scriptures particularly, it has to be recognized that the canonization did not occur at the impulse of the apostles. Further, history shows that different documents accepted in certain localities were later rejected by the universal church, and *vice versa*. The relativity of history might very well take its toll just by the process of canonization for those who fail to distinguish a genuine and potent continuity between the apostolic and post-apostolic ages. For Schleiermacher, the answer, of course, as in the case of true doctrine versus heresy, is the Spirit. The Spirit is the community Spirit as the Spirit of Christ, and "is gradually increasing in the Church."[58] This means that just because the canon has formerly been agreed on "is no guarantee that

---

[56]CG, I, pp. 125-134 (ET, 94-101).

[57]CG, II, pp. 284-309 (ET, 591-611). When Gerhard Spiegler faults Schleiermacher with failing to create a "public theology," insisting that Schleiermacher's position in his *Dialektik* contradicts his position in his systematic theology, he seems to overlook three things: (1) Schleiermacher never contended that the *specific* understanding of the Christian is public; (2) there appears to be no particular reason why the source of the "co-inhering polarity" by which everything *in* the cosmos is relative could not be the same as the "Woher" of Schleiermacher's theology without this relativizing God; and (3) the experience one has with God is immediate and therefore always prior to and transcendent to any subsequent conceptualization of it. See Spiegler, "Theological Tensions in Schleiermacher's Dialectic," *Schleiermacher as Contemporary*, ed. Robert W. Funk, (New York: Herder & Herder, 1970), pp. 13-26.

[58]CG, II, pp. 298-299 (ET, 603). This is true based upon the idea of sanctification (via the Spirit) of the individuals within the church.

its limits have been irrevocably fixed." Rather, the canon must stand under continual scrutiny even as the church is under obligation to take care in assigning "different grades of normative authority" to different portions of Scripture.[59]

While this process of continual canonization or continual interpretation may sound like the Christian faith is simply swallowed up by relativity, Schleiermacher was convinced otherwise. To the contrary, it left the *human* element as *relative* — which included the human element in the church, the Scripture, the apostles, and even Jesus — and it marked the Absolute as One: God, manifest in Christ through the Spirit and Word — the one upon whom we are "absolutely dependent."[60]

Conclusion

With this final observation, we can see how Schleiermacher's whole system reinforced his basic definition of religion as the "feeling of absolute dependence" or "being in relation to God." We have seen how the Fourth Gospel was not only acceptable but very useful in assisting Schleiermacher in the construction of this Christology, a Christology he felt that would survive historical criticism and historical relativity just as surely as it fostered historical inquiry. His theological insights, in fact, may well survive even after his understanding of the Fourth Gospel had dated itself.

Some of his insights placed him far ahead of his day and even rather avante garde today; other views or aspects of his method have now been outgrown. But the significance of his work was in the attempt to produce a coherent whole, a logical explanation that would address the three problems we originally delineated — to establish a Christology on the most likely historical reconstruction of the life of Christ, and in the process to develop a hermeneutic that would both ground the Christology as well as provide a point of continuity by which understanding is not swallowed up by historical relativity. If his efforts did not satisfy everybody, they were nevertheless sincerely Christian, scholarly, and consistent. And his awareness of historical change would have made him the first to suggest that although our generation may use some of his insights, it will necessarily have to move on in the continual interdependence of Biblical scholarship and theology as we pursue the truth of the Christian faith for our generation.

---

[59]CG, II pp. 297-299 (ET, 602-603).

[60]This is not, of course, to suggest that for Schleiermacher the absolute is ever attained as historical-conceptual knowledge. Here the polarities of his *Dialektik* reinforce the difference between the certainty one reaches by understanding and the certainty Schleiermacher equates with Gefuhl. But the relationship of the Christian to God is not relative. In Schleiermacher's words, "Our union with Him [Christ], accordingly, although it never attains more than relative manifestation, is yet recognized by God as absolute and eternal, and is affirmed as such in our faith." CG, I, p. 124 (ET, 455).

Johannine Christology During the Reformation

Dan G. Danner

Johannine Christology during the period of the Reformation in the sixteenth century is obviously tied to the polemical character of religious discourse of the time. No reformer, with the possible exception of John Calvin, approached the Gospel of John the way a modern exegete would with higher and lower critical concerns. To be sure, there were several separate theological treatises, of varying type and quality, which were written by important reformers during the sixteenth century. Yet each of these was hewn out of the hardbed of controversy. In addition to earlier sermons, Martin Luther preached a series of sermons on John's Gospel during the 1530s. Huldrich Zwingli had previously dealt with the Gospel of John in both sermons and exegetical works as early as 1524-25. Martin Bucer published a commentary on John after the Berne disputation in 1528 which was later revised. Johannes Oecolampadius wrote *Annotations on the Gospel of John* in 1533. Heinrich Bullinger wrote a commentary on John's Gospel in 1543. Philip Melanchthon wrote an exposition on John during the Lutheran reformation, and not a few Anabaptists, including Menno Simons, penned treatises on certain topics which indirectly reflected their understanding of Johannine Christology. Second and third generation reformers also wrote exegetical works on the Gospel of John; Calvin's commentary appeared in 1553, and Faustus Socinus wrote an *Explanation of the Prologue of the Gospel of John* before he died in 1604.

Thus the perimeters of our study are the polemical sermons that Luther delivered in the absence of the parish pastor in Wittenberg, Johannes Bugenhagen, beginning in 1530, and the anti-trinitarian controversy which surrounded the life and career of Socinus at the close of the sixteenth century in Poland. It will be necessary, of course, to delve into earlier manifestations of Johannine Christology as they become important to focalize certain theological developments. Initially, however, it should be instructive to see the larger picture of the Reformation and its corollary theological development, especially as it came to relate to the Christological emphases adumbrated by key theologians.

Overview

Roman Catholic remonstrance following Luther's break with the Church of Rome clearly tried to discredit his orthodoxy, rooting his heretical tendencies in his doctrine of Jesus Christ. These were unsuccessful because Luther was clearly in the mainstream of orthodox thought. He believed that his view of Christ reflected the views of the ancient ecumenical councils and their respective creedal formulas, particularly the councils of Nicea and Chalcedon. He never tired of making this clear, and his writings were replete with citations and references to the church's ancient creeds. Actually, Luther's Christology was based on his theology of the cross, for without a Christ who was both divine and human, a Christ who was one with the Father, Luther's understanding of salvation would have made little sense. And, he did not understand that he was developing any new doctrine; the doctrine implicit in the theology of the cross was time-honored. It was the doctrine one could read in the Gospels, in Paul, in the fathers of the church, such as Augustine, and it was the doctrine that had been established and worked out through the painful vicissitudes of theological controversy during the first four centuries of Christian history.

What brought Christological issues to light during the Reformation was actually the controversy over the Lord's Supper. Jaroslav Pelikan is convinced that this controversy precipitated more Christological discussion than any other since the days of the early church.[1] The controversy was polarized between Lutheran and Zwinglian groups, the former advocating a real presence of Christ's body and blood in the eucharist, while the latter viewed Christ's presence as more symbolic and sacramental. Each group claimed adherence to Nicea and Chalcedon, and both groups labeled the other as violator of those principles. Luther called Zwingli "neo-Nestorian." Calvin saw it as inevitable that Luther's view which emphasized that Christ's body was "swallowed up by his divinity" would reduce to a type of "Eutychian" position which had been condemned at Chalcedon.[2]

Etched out in the controversy with Zwingli and Oecolampadius, Luther extrapolated from the orthodox doctrine of the *communicatio idiomatum*. Succinctly put, this doctrine maintained that what could be said of one nature of Christ's person could be said of the other nature. Thus Luther believed that the omnipresence of Christ's divine nature could be ascribed to his entire glorified person, both human and divine. Already in his earthly life and certainly after his glorification the body of Christ was in heaven and on earth at the same time. Thus the phrase, "the right hand of God" was not a place but "the almighty power of God, which at one and the same time can be nowhere and yet must be everywhere."[3] Luther did not see himself basing his belief about Christ's statement, "This is my body," on any kind of rationalistic argument but on the word and promise of Christ. The proper relation

---

[1] Jaroslav Pelikan, *The Christian Tradition: A History of the Development of Doctrine* (Chicago and London: U. of Chicago Press, 1984), IV: 158. Much of the substance of this overview is found in this important contribution to historical theology; its bibliographical references are exceedingly helpful.
[2] Ibid. See John Calvin, *Institutes of the Christian Religion*, ed. by John T. McNeill, trans. by Ford Lewis Battles (Philadelphia: Westminster Press, 1960), 4.17.29.
[3] Pelikan, 160.

of Christ's human and divine natures formed the basis of his doctrine of salvation. Christ took upon himself our humanity to take away the law and its curse, suffering death for us, but because he was God or divine, the power of death could not hold sway over him. Thus the *communicatio idiomatum* was at the heart of Luther's theology of the cross.[4]

The sacramental controversy focused on the interpretation of John 6 and Christ's words, "Unless you eat the flesh of the Son of Man and drink his blood, you have no life in you," and "It is the spirit that gives life, the flesh is of no avail." Huldrich Zwingli, whose liturgy for the Lord's Supper included John 6:47-63, put these two verses together. Most of the reformers agreed that what was being spoken of here in John was faith in Christ. But Luther did not understand the chapter to have anything to do with the Lord's Supper. Bullinger, however, saw matters differently, and Calvin, though more cautious, did use John 6 to explain that the "eating" in the Lord's Supper was something other than "the physical eating by which these crude theologians dream of feeding themselves."[5] Both sides claimed to have Augustine as corroboration of their position.

The opponents of the Anabaptists believed that their biblical hermeneutic would inevitably lead to a denunciation of the early Christian creeds. When Balthasar Hubmaier was faced with such calumnies, he referred to "the confession of the foundation of the universal Christian church" by which he doubtless meant the Nicene and Chalcedonian confessions, and Dirk Philipsz even taught the doctrine of the "filioque." Menno Simons could propound an orthodox summary of the doctrines of the person and work of Christ, and "he opposed Zwinglian Christology on the grounds that it taught 'two sons in Christ,' in some Nestorian fashion."[6] Menno taught that Christ had not taken his flesh from Abraham's seed, nor of Mary's womb, but became human within her womb. Hans Denck gave to one of the chapters of a doctrinal statement the title, "On the Trinity, the Unity, and the Single Threeness of God," but then said nothing about the trinity in the chapter itself.[7]

Luther and Calvin had professed adherence to orthodox dogmas of the trinity and the person of Christ as formulated by Nicea and Chalcedon. Luther transposed the creeds into an exposition on the saving work of Christ and justification of the believer now from the historic treatment of the relation of the Father and the Son. In his interest in the real presence of the Lord's Supper, he elaborated a doctrine of the relationship between the two natures of Christ which matched or exceeded in metaphysical complexity the ancient Alexandrian theology. Calvin had denounced this theology as a denial of the principle of *sola scriptura,* but Calvin had documented from Biblical sources the Nicean dogma more than anyone since patristic times. Both Luther and Calvin disliked the technical language of the early creeds —

---

[4]Ibid., 163.
[5]Ibid., 195.
[6]Ibid., 321.
[7]Ibid., 322.

Luther hated the term *homoousios* and Calvin wanted to see it "buried" — but their conformity to its intent as well as content was unassailable.[8]

Yet the Catholic suspicion of where *sola scriptura* would lead did, in fact, begin to show itself in the views of Michael Servetus and George Blandrata, and later in Fausto Socinus and the Racovian Catechism of 1605. Against such views, Bullinger warned that it was not enough to declare loyalty to the sole authority of scripture, for one was obliged as well to set forth an interpretation of scripture which was simultaneously "native" to the text and "congruous with the articles of the faith." Calvin complained that such views were ignorant of the patristic tradition; but Servetus claimed to be defending "the older traditions of the apostles" and of the earliest church fathers against the later tradition of Nicea, while Socinus complained that the prologue of John's Gospel "has, as far as I know, never until now been correctly expounded by anyone."[9]

Because Anselm's satisfaction theory presupposed, it was thought, the orthodox Chalcedonian dogma of the person of Christ as the God-man, it came to be viewed in the west as the necessary corollary to Chalcedon. Socinus refuted Anselm's theory which he said detracted from "the power and authority, or at any rate from the goodness and mercy of God." Christ was not the "price for our sins" nor did he "placate" the wrath of God. Rather, he "showed and taught the way of salvation," and also "declared" the love of God and "confirmed" it by miracles and his death and resurrection. Thus there was no need for "satisfaction" and no opposition between the justice and mercy of God.[10]

Thus Socinus did not believe in the necessity of seeing Christ as the "Son of God" in the sense that it had been understood in orthodox dogma. Such a phrase was but an appellation and resulted in not a trinitarianism but a tritheism. Servetus said that not one word about "essence," "person" or *homoousios* was to be found in the Bible and in this he was joined by Socinus. In their Biblical arsenal, the unitarians had to view, for example, Philippians 2:5-11 as a passage of adoption: not a "nature" which Christ had but a "power" given to him. He remained subordinate to the Father but he received from the Father "an equality of power" with him. Eventually Christ would surrender this back to the Father. Of course the prologue of John's Gospel was crucial and Socinus devoted a special treatise to this one chapter in his *Explanation of the Prologue of the Gospel of John*. Servetus had identified the Logos as Jesus the human being. So also had Socinus, arguing that the title "the Word" did not refer to his ontological nature but to his office as one who "expounded the evangelical word of his Father." Nothing in the sacred text could be used to contradict the absolute monotheism of the shema. One need not take Christ's words, "I and the Father are one," to be a metaphysical reference, but rather oneness of mind and purpose. So, Servetus believed that the traditional exegesis could use a bit of changing, for "if you take it as

---

[8]Ibid., 323.
[9]Ibid., 324.
[10]Ibid., 325.

your starting point that Christ is the one toward whom all passages of Scripture tend, then everything will be easy," an obvious reference to Luther's kind of Biblical hermeneutic in dealing with the Old Testament.[11]

But there were troublesome passages for the unitarians. John 3:13 ("No one has ascended into heaven but he who descended from heaven, the Son of Man who is in heaven") was viewed as a "trope" by Socinus, but his discussion of the verse was even more suspect: "Christ, after he was born as a man but before he began to undertake the task imposed on him by God his Father, was in heaven, through the plan and action of God, and remained there for some time in order to hear from God himself." The introductory formula of the Lord's Prayer was not intended to indicate who should be worshipped, for when Christ is worshipped so is the Father to whom Christ was subordinate. Thus, regarding Philippians 2, the worship addressed to Christ is to take place "to the glory of God the Father." Because the authority of Christ had been "given" to him by the Father it necessarily followed that "the Son of God, who is Christ, is not eternal" and yet at the same time that "he is to be worshipped." It was therefore possible "to worship Christ for no other reason than that it is obligatory to worship the Father."[12]

Christological expositions, taken only in part from Johannine texts, thus were presented in the sixteenth century within the heated battles of controversy. Nevertheless, it is possible to earmark several key areas of productivity which were to have lasting effect within Protestantism. These areas would be the seminal thought of Luther, and particularly his sermons on the Gospel of John beginning in 1530, the controversy over the eucharist between Luther and Zwingli and how it helped to shape Zwingli's Christology, and Calvin's commentary on John in 1553.

Martin Luther

Luther's exegesis had both continuity and discontinuity with the medieval tradition, the latter demonstrated in the novelty he brought to the exegetical task which culminated in his theology of the cross. It is possible that Luther's first sermon may have been based on the Gospel of John, a Christmas sermon in Latin preached to fellow Augustinian monks in 1514.[13] Luther loved John's Gospel; his favoritism for John over the Synoptics was due to its concentration on the discourses of the Lord rather than on his miracles.

Luther's *German Mass* of 1526 had prescribed that the Gospel of John be the basis of Saturday sermons. It was these Saturday sermons which he delivered in the absence of the parish pastor of Wittenberg, Johannes Bugenhagen. The sermons on John 1-4 cover a period of more than three years, beginning in the summer of 1537. During this time, Luther was embroiled in

---

[11] Ibid., 328.
[12] Ibid., 330.
[13] *Luther's Works: Sermons on the Gospel of St. John Chapters 1-4*, ed. by J. Pelikan (St. Louis: Concordia Publishing House, 1957), 22:ix-xi.

theological conflict and saddled with poor physical and emotional health. He had already preached Saturday sermons on John 6-8 which he had begun in 1530, and at that time his health was bothering him and he was besieged with extra projects and duties. He was ready for Bugenhagen's return even then. Nevertheless, he continued preaching on John during Bugenhagen's protracted absence.[14]

Luther was convinced that the Gospel of John taught the doctrine of the trinity as three distinct persons dwelling in a single essence. The Father begot the Son from eternity and the Holy Spirit proceeds from the Father and the Son. The Father bestowed his "entire divine nature" upon the Son, making him "one together with Him."[15] Luther also was confident that John wrote his Gospel, at least in part, as an answer to the views of Cerinthus. The Word is God, existed before creation, and is totally different from any human word. As God's Word, Christ is a "conversation" God had with himself within his paternal heart. But no one was aware of this until the Word was made flesh.[16] This Word or conversation God has with himself is as complete and perfect as God himself, yet because he is so absorbed in his Word, "He pays no attention to anything else." The Word of God thus became the creator of creation. The Word or Speech of God already was, before the creation of the world, more sublime than anything created or made. Certainly this cannot be known by human reason.[17]

Yet is was clear to Luther that the Word and the Father were distinct, for Christ as the Word was "entirely separate from the Father." Although they were two, the Son remains "the one true God with the Father." The Father speaks, the Son is the spoken. The Word was born of the Father alone. Christ was of the essence or substance of the Father (*hupostasis*), and after his birth from the virgin Mary, he was not only true God but also true man. The Word thus created all things, although Luther called him "co-creator with the Father," for the Father created all things through the Son.[18]

Throughout Luther's treatment of Johannine Christology in these sermons, it is clear that he was dealing with an *article of faith* which must be accepted by the Christian without the test of reason. As we would expect, Luther often applauded the irrational because it flew in the face of human reason and confidence. Christ is the source of offense, "the target of every attack," yet it is he who will have the last word. Luther was certainly fond of using Paul's sense of paradox that the foolish things to human eyes are the very things God has chosen to use in his historic deeds of salvation. In this world the struggle between Christ and the devil will never cease.[19]

---

[14]*Luther's Works: Sermons on the Gospel of St. John Chapters 6-8*, ed. by J. Pelikan (St. Louis: Concordia Publishing House, 1959), 23:xi. It should be pointed out that Luther also preached sermons on John 14-16 during the summer of 1537.
[15]*Luther's Works*, 22:5.
[16]Ibid., 8-9.
[17]Ibid., 11-14.
[18]Ibid., 17-20.
[19]Ibid.

Luther's remarks in the sermons were carefully aimed at heterodox theologians who had challenged the orthodox and catholic position with new-fangled teaching. It is in this context that Arianism becomes the target of rebuke from Luther's invective preaching. It was Arius who taught that Christ was *created*, thereby calling into question his divinity. There were others, such as Kasper Schwenkfeld, who denied that Christ had a humanity akin to ours. But Christ had to be true God and true man; if he were not truly God, what would his death mean for us?

> No, we must have a Savior who is true God and Lord over sin, death, devil and hell. If we permit the devil to topple this stronghold for us, so that we disbelieve His divinity, then his suffering, death, and resurrection profit us nothing.[20]

The Manicheans also got their due from the Wittenberg pulpit. They denied that God could take human form. Luther, however, affirmed that Christ was a "natural man" and assumed human form "from the blood of a woman," "as any other child does from its mother." Christ received everything that a child normally and naturally receives from its mother, except sin. It was the divinity within this humanity which was the "hook concealed under the earthworm" to defeat Satan; Satan swallowed it when Christ died and was buried. With imagery such as this borrowed from the church fathers, especially Augustine, Luther proclaimed that of all the Gospel writers, John was pre-eminent among the apostles "in his powerful portrayal of the deity of Christ the Lord."[21]

The creator Word also continues to preserve creation. "Thus, as we human beings did not create ourselves, so we can do nothing at all to keep ourselves alive for a single moment by our own power."[22] The Son of God draws so close to humanity that he becomes our light. All human, cultural achievements are derived from this light. There is also the light that God grants only to his own, the elect. The light of the world was, of course, Christ, the Word of God. It shone from the beginning of the world, before the flood through Adam, then through the Hebrew patriarchs. Luther speaks of the woman's seed bruising the head of the serpent strictly in Christological terms. Later, the light shone in the prophets of Israel until finally the light of the Lord shone in Christ. "He lit the brightest torch, which shone with unprecedented brilliance." His apostles carried forward the torch, but again scholars, lords and sages despised the light, "'considered it fables, fairy tales, folly and lies of the devil." And, in Luther's day, the papacy and its backers try to keep the light in darkness. The world refuses to see this light, still it shines for the sake of the little flock which is to be illumined by it.[23]

As the Gospel writer introduces the Baptist who bore witness to Christ, Luther takes the opportunity to chastise Francis, Dominic, and others for

---

[20]Ibid., 21-22.
[21]Ibid., 25.
[22]Ibid., 28.
[23]Ibid., 33-35.

bearing witness to themselves and a certain ascetic life-style. He also had words for Anabaptists who deride the written and spoken word in favor of the impartation of the Holy Spirit in some direct way. John the Baptist's oral testimony was necessary to bear witness to the Word of God; external, empirical witness was, in fact, necessary.

Luther used John 1:14 as the occasion to champion Bernard's notion that the incarnation was the stumbling-block that brought the downfall of Lucifer. "God's assumption of human nature and the union of God and man in the person of Christ is comparable to placing a filthy sow at table and chasing away holy and pious people."[24] The devil vanishes when the words, "And the Word became flesh" are uttered. But if faith is lacking there is no power in these words. The mere pronunciation of them brings no magical power. Luther also impugned the views of the Apollinarists who asserted that Christ adopted a human body, but not a human soul. "They were stupid asses," thought Luther, for "flesh" clearly embraces body and soul. Christ therefore took on human flesh "which was mortal and subject to the terrible judgment of God because of the sins of the human race."[25] Like the Manicheans, they reduce Christ to a ghost or phantom.

We become sons and daughters of God by adoption whereas Christ was the Son of God by nature, the one and only "begotten Son." No one is like Christ *by nature*. Adam was not full of grace, but Christ had the grace of God by nature. His words are true. His life was a life of service to humankind. The Synoptics flesh out the details of his life which John narrates only briefly. Luther thought that during his whole life, Christ was consumed with sorrow which prevented him from ever being happy: "And if He had not been crucified, He would have grieved Himself to death over the utter futility of all His efforts with the Jewish people."[26]

Luther used the text of John 3:13 ("No one has ascended into heaven . . . ") to affirm again his traditional ideas about the trinity and the two distinct natures of Christ in the one Son of God; "that God has no other Son than the one born of the Virgin Mary, and that the Son, begotten by the Father before the beginning of the world, lies in the lap of Mother Mary."[27] Against Nestorius, Mary is the mother of God, and Luther consistently supported the orthodox decrees of the early ecumenical councils of the church.

> But if we differentiate two sons in Christ, then it must follow that there are also two persons; this would nullify our redemption and the forgiveness of sin. No, the two natures must be the one Christ. Otherwise no satisfaction could have been rendered for our sins, and nothing would come of our salvation. If Christ were only man, His suffering would have been useless; for no man's suffering has ever been able to overcome my sin and yours, death and the

---

[24] Ibid., 104.
[25] Ibid., 111.
[26] Ibid., 236.
[27] Ibid., 323.

> power of the devil, God's wrath and eternal damnation. Therefore it was necessary for Him to be God, in order to suffer, also true man.[28]

The Father and Mary both had the same Son, the former from eternity and Mary in time. The two natures are separated but there is only one Son. When Christ was born of the virgin Mary, he descended from heaven, "but at the same time remained in heaven." He also ascended into heaven, "but was also in heaven before his ascension." But reason cannot fathom any of this doctrine: "How all this comes to pass, I admit I do not understand."[29] It was an article of faith and reason only gets us lost trying to understand it.

What we attribute to one nature is thus ascribed to the other nature "by virtue of the personal union in Christ." We often differentiate between the two natures, as we might differentiate between the body and soul, yet "we mean to apply to the whole person."

> Oh, dear Lord, You are wandering around on this earth, hanging on the cross, suffering and dying. But how can I make these statements harmonize: that You descended from heaven and ascended again into heaven, that you remain in heaven, and that before this You were in heaven continuously? Can the Son of Man be on earth and the Son of God in heaven? You must answer thus: Our Christian faith makes this harmonize, and so does this text, in which Christ Himself declares: 'As the Son of Man I walk on this earth. I perform My office here; I suffer and die. And although I was born man, I am simultaneously God's Son in heaven. I do not forfeit My divine nature, but I remain in heaven.'[30]

The author of the Gospel of John always links the two natures of deity and humanity together. The attributes of both natures are ascribed and imputed to the whole person of Christ "in the concrete," creating a "communion of properties." One dare not separate the two natures, or divide the one person, therefore, but acknowledge that as John distinguishes between the persons of the Godhead, the Father and Son remain true God.[31]

As we have already indicated, Christ's sermon on "I am the Bread of Life" in John 6 became the hub of debate among Protestants. Luther admitted that there was surely bread and wine on the altar, but that Christ was also present in the supper. Luther did not believe that this chapter in John indicated any basis for a eucharistic theology, but because the Zwinglians treated it so, he was willing to enter the fray and give his own imput. He accused Zwingli of dividing Christ, making only the divinity capable of imparting eternal life. Luther, however, could not divide the two natures, for they were identical in the sense that they were in the one Son. "I am determined to know nothing of

---

[28]Ibid., 324.
[29]Ibid., 325.
[30]Ibid., 329.
[31]Ibid., 352f.

a Son of God who is not also Mary's Son who suffered, the God enveloped in humanity who is one Person. I dare not separate the one from the other and say that the humanity is of no use, but only the divinity."[32] John 6 really refers to the eating, the spiritual eating, of Christ in faith. Just as sugar added to water gives the water a new essence, quality and taste, so divinity added to humanity in the one Son makes it impossible to view Christ like any other human being. "Thus one eats the Godhead in the human nature."[33] The one cannot be separated from the other; the divinity of the Word is intrinsically tied to the humanity of the son of Mary.

Thus Luther accepted the *communicatio idiomatum* in the fullest sense. Zwingli's notion of the *alloeosis*[34] was "the devil's mask," for it robbed the sacrificial death of Christ of its soteriological meaning. All that the Father does in heaven the man Jesus does on earth. Since Christ arose bodily from the grave, his body is present in the sacrament of the Lord's Supper. Luther's theory of the ubiquity of Christ's presence was a logical inference from his Christology. Thus under the visible form of bread and wine are Christ's invisible body and blood. Bread is really eaten, but at the same time so is the spiritual body of Christ. This is not a matter of human imagining but of the real unification of Christ's body with the believer. Only the believer understands this, to be sure, for "this is done by the faith of the heart which discerns this treasure and desires it."[35] Thus the redemptive work of Christ was "coextensive with his entire life," so that when we eat the flesh of Christ, physically and spiritually, "this food is so strong that it transforms us into men who are holy and alive."[36] It made possible the resurrection of the body, and the Lord's Supper united the human being with God who thus communicated his own immortality to us through the saving work of Christ's death and resurrection.[37]

---

[32]*Luther's Works*, 23:102.
[33]Ibid., 120.
[34]See the discussion below.
[35]From Luther's *Large Catechism*, quoted by Reinhold Seeberg, *Textbook of the History of Doctrines*, trans. by Charles E. Hay (Grand Rapids: Baker Book House, 1966), 2 Volumes in 1, p. 328.
[36]*Luther's Works, Companion Volume*, intro. by J. Pelikan (St. Louis: Concordia Publishing House, 1959), p. 187.
[37]Ibid., p. 189.

Huldrich Zwingli and the Eucharistic Controversy

Zwingli's Christology is based on several works which relate directly and indirectly to John's Gospel. His view of the person and work of Christ is quite orthodox, and in this he shared the mainstream with the Christologies of Luther and Calvin. Nevertheless, there are significant nuances within his view. He believed that the divine nature of Christ is more active since the divine nature enters into the human nature but is not absorbed by it. Whereas Luther saw the two natures more dynamically coincident, Zwingli stressed the divine nature. If Luther emphasized God's *revealing*, it was Zwingli who emphasized that it was *God* who was doing the revealing.[38]

It is well known that Zwingli's reform was more in line with Erasmian humanism than its Luther counterpart. He used humanist tools and methods to seek a renewal of Christianity based upon strict adherence to the Scriptures. Luther's application of *sola scriptura* allowed for those things which did not conflict with the Bible; Zwingli looked for direct examples to emulate and doctrinal teachings to restore. Because of this hermeneutical difference, perhaps, Zwingli was suspicious of things of a sensory nature, "for body and spirit are such essentially different things that whichever one you take it cannot be the other."[39] Luther's Christology was more *unitive* and Alexandrian; Zwingli's was more *divisive* and in line with Antiochine tradition. He could not accept the notion of *communicatio idiomatum* to the point of allowing the human nature to become ubiquitous: "If Christ ascended to heaven and sits at the right hand of God, his body cannot be elsewhere."[40] So Christ's body could not be present in the eucharist. Zwingli admitted only the *communicatio naturarum*, and it is only with regard to the *person* of the God-man that one can assert with "alloiosim" that the properties of both natures were alike. This would be akin to making statements about individual persons within the Godhead while maintaining its unity; *alloeosis* is simply a rhetorical device which allows an "interchange," so that in speaking of one nature we may use terms belonging to the other nature. Thus Zwingli carefully discriminated the two natures of Christ.[41]

It was important for Zwingli and the Reformed tradition to maintain the predominance of the infinite, divine nature over the finite, human nature of Christ. As a result, Zwingli's Christology had a definite Nestorian coloring. (an accusation leveled by John Eck and Luther) which could be read as a kind of subordinationism.[42] He developed the details of Christ's earthly life more

---

[38]Gottfried W. Locher, *Zwingli's Thought: New Perspectives* (Leiden: E.J. Brill, 1981), p. 173.

[39]From *On True and False Religion*, quoted in Justo L. Gonzalez, A *History of Christian Thought* (Nashville and New York: Abingdon Press, 1975), III:75.

[40]Gonzalez, 75; cf. G.R. Potter, *Zwingli* (Cambridge: Cambridge U. Press, 1976), p. 200.

[41]Seeberg, p. 321.

[42]Locher, p. 175.

thoroughly than any reformer, but these were interpreted by Zwingli to show Christ's divine nature.

> The Son of the Most High King came clothed in human flesh in order to be the sacrificial lamb . . . and thus render satisfaction to God's inviolate righteousness, so reconciling him to those who, being conscious of their own sins, could never dare to come into the presence of God trusting in their own righteousness.[43]

Such could only be accomplished by a God-man, for "he cannot die according to his human nature." Yet Christ had to be a pure human being, untainted by sin, for otherwise he could not be a savior of *human* beings. Only God can save us, but his human suffering was for our salvation: "Now it does not save us to know how he was crucified, or that he was crucified, but that he was crucified for us, and that he who was crucified is our Lord and our God."[44]

God is really to be found in the human person of Jesus. In his polemic against Eck, Zwingli accused him of "insults and belittlings of the glory and honor of Christ" by denying that the divine nature of Christ could be everywhere, penetrating everything, but the human nature could only be in *one* place. He attempted to keep the tradition of the two natures of Christ so that there was no slippage into monophysitism or docetism. When it is said that Christ is at the "right hand of the Father," the meaning does not point to a place but to the figurative notion that he was equally powerful with the Father.[45] In fact, this expression gave Zwingli the occasion to develop his eucharistic ideas. If Christ had ascended, in his humanity, into heaven, it was there he was until the day of judgment. Thus the body of the risen Christ in heaven could not be eaten in the Lord's Supper. Both transubstantiation and Luther's notion of ubiquity were thereby precluded.[46]

The last pamphlet to come from Zwingli's pen was *Fidei expositio* in 1531. It was sent to Francis I and in it he gave his expositions on a number of issues, showing his orthodoxy on such questions as the doctrine of the trinity and the two natures of Christ. It was here, in his mature thinking, that he wrote that Christ took on human nature in such a way that the divine nature was not lost or changed. Yet, Christ was "truly, properly and naturally man." None of the divine attributes suffer because he took human form. When it is said in the Bible that Christ hungered, it was his human nature so depicted; when it is said that he healed diseases, his divine nature was so depicted.

> In general, I confess that God and man are one Christ, just as one man consists of a soul endowed with reason and a dull body, as Saint Athanasius has taught. He took up human nature into the unity of the hypostasis or person of the Son of God. . . . The person of the eternal Son of God assumed humanity into and by vir-

---

[43]Quoted by Locher, p. 174.
[44]Ibid.
[45]Ibid., p. 177.
[46]Potter, pp. 260-61.

tue of its own power, as holy men of God have truly and clearly shown.[47]

In the same pamphlet he wrote that the material body of Christ "is not eaten literally and in its essence, but only spiritually" in the Lord's Supper. Because Christ took on "all the characteristics and endowments that belong to the nature of the human body," two corollaries follow: one, that the characteristics which are present in our bodies were present in Christ's body, and two, what corporeality there was in Christ's body belongs also to our bodies. Therefore, because his body arose from the dead, so will ours. The resurrected body of Christ in heaven, "in virtue of its character as real body," indicates simply that it cannot be several places any more than ours can. The Lutherans' position, he wrote, maintained that Christ is present everywhere because he was divine. But the issue was his *humanity*, not his divinity, and because the former is finite it is incapable of being everywhere. The two natures of Christ do not sever the unity of Christ's person, and the natures are not confused "as if the divinity had degenerated and been weakened to humanity, or the humanity changed into divinity," an obvious reference to Luther's application of the *communicatio idiomatum*.[48] When Christ said "This is my body," he still had a mortal body. He did not have "two bodies of which one was immortal and exempt from physical sensation, the other mortal." It cannot be, therefore, that we eat his mortal body, with the apostles, while his immortal body sits at the right hand of God.

> To eat the body of Christ spiritually is nothing else than to trust in spirit and heart upon the mercy and goodness of God through Christ, that is, to be sure with unshaken faith that God is going to give us pardon for our sins and the joy of everlasting blessedness on account of his Son, who was made wholly ours, was offered for us, and reconciled the divine righteousness to us.[49]

John Calvin

As has been suggested Calvin followed traditional orthodoxy on matters relating to the trinity and the person and work of Christ. He claimed that Christ had two natures in a single person, so that "he who was the Son of God became the Son of man — not by confusion of substances, but by unity of person." [50] Calvin believed that the first ecumenical councils correctly represented the Biblical testimony regarding the person of Christ. A great deal of Calvin's Christology emerged within his controversial discussions with certain detractors.

---

[47]Ulrich Zwingli, *On Providence and Other Essays*, ed. for Samuel Macauley Jackson by William John Hinke (Durham: The Labyrinth Press, 1983), p. 244.
[48]Ibid., pp. 248-50.
[49]Ibid., p. 252.
[50]*Institutes*, 2.14.1, 2.12.2.

Andreas Osiander had contended that even if Adam had not fallen, Christ would still have become incarnate, and thus the purpose of the incarnation was not the redemption of humankind but the fulfillment of creation, a view shared by many Franciscans during the middle ages as well as Michael Servetus. Calvin's rejection of this view was grounded in his understanding of salvation; his Christology, like Luther's, was intrinsic to his soteriology. Menno Simons and other Anabaptists held that Christ did not have an earthly flesh, but that his body had come down from heaven and taken form in the virgin's womb. Calvin called this a "new Marcionite" notion, his reaction to which helped him to hold emphatically to Christ's humanity and physical descent from Adam.[51]

One of Calvin's most bitter controversies was with Servetus regarding the trinity in 1553. Servetus had claimed that the title "Son of God" meant that Jesus had been begotten in Mary's womb by the Holy Spirit. Before the incarnation Christ was to be called "Word" and only after the incarnation was he properly called a "Son." Servetus thought that Calvin's belief which maintained a discriminate distance between God and humanity was exaggerated. He believed that there was a spark of divinity in each of us; the significant question, for him, was not the union of two opposite natures but how Christ could be called "Son of God" in a special sense not applicable to other beings. Servetus was thus forced to emphasize the *unity* of the two natures in Christ to the point that Calvin accused him of Monophysitism. In reaction, Calvin stressed the *distinction* of the two natures.[52]

Francesco Stancaro had held that Christ is our mediator only through his human nature, probably in refutation of Osiander who taught that Christ mediated only through his divine nature. Against both, Calvin argued that the work of redemption took place through the hypostatic union, and that everything in Christ that had to do with redemption was to be ascribed to the unity of the person and not to one nature or the other. "The significance of this is that toward the end of his life Calvin came to emphasize the *communicatio idiomatum* to a greater degree than he had before. . . ."[53] Earlier, his position had been closer to Zwingli's. He could not accept the *communicatio idiomatum* as an argument for the ubiquity of Christ's presence on the altar. Although the divinity of the second person in the trinity was fully present in Jesus, it was not circumscribed by his humanity, for Christ could not be present in heaven and on several altars at the same time. He was still in heaven while also present in Jesus, and when he was being born from the virgin's womb he was still filling the entire universe.[54] This *extra calvinisticum* certainly leaned heavily in the direction of Antioch rather than Alexandria, but its substance already had been formulated by Zwingli whose Christology was not based as much on soteriology as was Calvin's.[55]

---

[51] Gonzalez, 136.
[52] Ibid., 137.
[53] Ibid.
[54] *Institutes*, 2.13.4.
[55] Gonzalez, 138; Locher, p. 176. Cf. Francois Wendel, *Calvin: the Origins and Development of His Religious Thought* (London: Wm. Collins, 1963), pp. 215f.

It was in 1553, the decisive year of the Servetus affair in Geneva, that Calvin wrote a commentary on the Gospel of John. Calvin saw John's Gospel as different from the other Gospels because it "dwells more largely on the doctrine by which the office of Christ, together with the power of his death and resurrection, is unfolded."[56] Indeed, Calvin believed John should be read first since it opened up the meaning of the other Gospels. In his remarks on John 1:1 and the Logos or "Speech" of God, Calvin inveighed against Servetus and Arianism. The Word was always united with God before the world existed, hidden "before he revealed himself in the external structure of the world."[57] Like so many other reformers, Calvin referred constantly to Augustine's Christology; Christ the Word "was obscurely shadowed out to the Fathers under the Law, and at length was more fully manifested in flesh." Sabellius' views were refuted here also, for the Word was distinct from the Father, being one of the three *hypostases*, "Subsistencies or Persons, in the one simple essence of God." Christ was God in the sense that he shared the same essence with the Father, yet as the Word, Christ was also distinct from the Father. "Now the design of the Evangelist is . . . to show that no sooner was the world created than *the Speech* of God came forth into external operation; for having formerly been incomprehensible in his essence, he then became publically known by the effect of his power."[58]

There are two distinct powers which belong to the Son of God: the first, which is manifested in the structure of the world and the order of nature; and, the second, by which he renews and restores fallen nature. The human being was endued with an extraordinary gift of understanding, and although by his revolt against God he lost the light of understanding, he yet sees and understands, "so that what he naturally possesses from the grace of the Son of God is not entirely destroyed."[59]

In regard to John 1:14, Calvin wrote that the Word or Speech of God became man, taking upon himself flesh. The term "flesh" is not given a Pauline understanding in John, Calvin affirmed, for the meaning was simply that the Word became mortal, "though it marks disdainfully his frail and perishing nature." Apollinarius was wrong, therefore, in believing that Christ was merely clothed with a human body without a soul.

> The plain meaning therefore is, that *the Speech* begotten of God before all ages, and who always dwelt with the Father, *was made man*. On this article of faith there are two things chiefly to be observed. The first is, that two natures were so united in one Person in Christ, that one and the same Christ is true God and true man. The second is, that the unity of person does not hinder the two natures from remaining distinct, so that his Divinity retains

---

[56]John Calvin, *Commentary on the Gospel According to John*, trans. by William Pringle (Grand Rapids: Wm. B. Eerdmans Publishing Co., 1956), I:21.
[57]Ibid., 27.
[58]Ibid., 30.
[59]Ibid., 34.

all that is peculiar to itself, and his humanity holds separately whatever belongs to it.[60]

Various erroneous positions have been witnessed in the church through the ages. Nestorius acknowledged both natures but "imagined two Christs," one who was God and another who was man. Eutyches left Christ with neither of the two natures but imagined that they were mingled together.

> And in the present day, Servetus and the Anabaptists invent a Christ who is confusedly compounded of two natures, as if he were a Divine man. In words, indeed, he acknowledges that Christ is God; but if you admit his raving imaginations, the Divinity is at one time changed into human nature, and at another time, the nature of man is swallowed up by the Divinity.[61]

But the Evangelist refutes both types of error, "for the Son of God began to be man in such a manner that he still continues to be that eternal *Speech* who had no beginning of time."[62]

We have seen how pivotal John 6 was to the debate concerning the Lord's Supper among the reformers. Calvin did not seem too pre-occupied, as was Zwingli, with this chapter in John relating to the eucharist, "To eat Christ" was "an effect or work of faith." So Christ's discourse did not refer to the Lord's Supper "but to the uninterrupted communication *of the flesh of Christ*, which we obtain apart from the use of the Lord's Supper."[63] Yet, Calvin acknowledged that there was nothing said in John 6 "that is not figuratively represented, and actually bestowed on believers, in the Lord's Supper," and that Christ even intended that the communion should be "a seal and confirmation of this sermon." Calvin believed he was again in the good company of Augustine who, Calvin was convinced, showed that "this mystery is symbolically represented, whenever the churches celebrate the Lord's Supper. . . ."[64]

God the Father is a "great distance from us," but Christ's place between the divine and the human allowed him to reveal to us what would have otherwise remained concealed. No one can come to Christ as God if that person "despises him as man." Thus Christ was "clothed not only with our flesh, but with human feelings." Such were, in him, pure and free from sin. There was nothing to prevent Christ from having a natural dread of death, but in his desire to obey God he showed that "the pure will of nature will not of itself rebel against God." Christ was therefore not affected by original sin. Christ had but one battle to fight: to cease from fearing what he naturally feared, as soon as he perceived that the pleasure of God was otherwise. But, on the other hand, because of the sin of Adam, we have two battles, "for we must struggle with the obstinacy of the flesh."[65]

---

[60]Ibid., 45.
[61]Ibid., 46.
[62]Ibid.
[63]Ibid., 265.
[64]Ibid., 266.
[65]Ibid., II:34.

Calvin's Christology could be placed somewhere between Luther's and Zwingli's views. With Luther he could adopt some aspects of the *communicatio idiomatum*, but with Zwingli, he tended not to fuse the two natures together, but to emphasize the importance of nothing being allowed to diminish the divinity or divest it of any of its privileges.[66] Calvin retained the ubiquity of Christ's divine nature, "But he categorically rejected the ubiquity of the body of the Christ, for the same reasons that made him dismiss anything tending towards the deification of man, even in the person of Christ."[67] Locher contends that whereas Luther's Christology belonged to Christmas, Zwingli's belonged to Easter or to the Ascension. It would be more correct to say that Calvin's Christology belonged to Easter and Zwingli's to the the Ascension.[68] The two Reformed theologians were perhaps closer together, but nevertheless quite far apart in what gave impetus to the doctrine of the person and work of Christ.

Conclusion

By way of conclusion, it should be clear from the foregoing what came to be the mainstream of Christological thinking among magisterial Protestants in the sixteenth century. The mainstream was certainly not monolithic, and various nuances held by Lutheran and Reformed theologians provided a healthful dialectic within which to understand the person and work of Christ, as well as other Christian doctrines and practices. That Luther's views could be echoed, to some degree, in England by William Tyndale[69] and Hugh Latimer[70] does not mean that they were unflective of the teachings of Zwingli or Calvin. Nevertheless, it is fair to say that the Reformed or Rhineland theology made a greater impact on English reformers than did Luther. An example of Reformed influence can be seen by a comparison of the views of Bullinger and John Hooper.[71] One may also see similar continuity with the

---

[66]Wendel, pp. 222-23.

[67]Ibid., p. 224.

[68]Locher, p. 177.

[69]See William Tyndale, *A Prologue Upon the Gospel of St. John in Doctrinal Treatises and Introductions to Different Portions of the Holy Scriptures by William Tyndale*, ed. for the Parker Society by Henry Walter (Cambridge: Cambridge U. Press, 1848), p. 482.

[70]*Sermons and Remains of Hugh Latimer*, ed. for the Parker Society by George Elwes Corrie (Cambridge: Cambridge U. Press, 1845), p. 101f.

[71]Cf. *The Decades of Henry Bullinger*, ed. for the Parker Society by Thomas Harding (Cambridge: Cambridge U. Press, 1849), VIII: 12ff, X:238, 270-72, and *A Godly Confession and Protestation of the Christian Faith* (London, 1550), *Later Writings of Bishop Hooper*, ed. for the Parker Society by Charles Nevinson (Cambridge U. Press, 1842), p. 130.

Reformed tradition by an examination of some of the early eucharistic thought of Thomas Cranmer.[72]

Not all of this Christological development was based on the Gospel of John. Yet it would be safe to say that without John's Gospel it doubtless would not have taken the shape that it did. In fact, the Gospel of John was at the heart of the Christology which emerged in sixteenth century Protestant theology.

---

[72]See *An Answer unto a Crafty and Sophistical Cavillation Devised by Stephen Gardner* in *Writings and Disputations of Thomas Cranmer Relative to the Lord's Supper*, ed. for the Parker Society by John Edmund Cox (Cambridge: Cambridge U. Press, 1844), *passim*.

Origen's Demonolgy

Everett Ferguson

Frank Pack's dissertation "Methodology of Origen as a Textual Critic in Arriving at the Text of the New Testament" expressed two of his life-long interests — the Gospel of John and textual criticism. The present paper submitted in his honor takes up the other element in his dissertation: Origen. The purpose will be to survey Origen's response to demonology, which was an important aspect of the world-view of Greeks, Romans, and Jews.[1]

Second-century Christian apologetics had accepted the views shared by the common people and philosophers alike that the demons were objective brings intermediary between the divine and the human. Justin Martyr, for instance, blamed on them all that was opposed to Christianity — pagan religion with its mythology, magic, and sacrificial rituals; moral evils such as murder, war, adultery, and wickedness; persecution; and heresy.[2] Origen, as is shown below, continued this apologetic argument.

---

[1]Everett Ferguson, *Demonology of the Early Christian World* (New York: Edwin Mellen Press, 1984). A fundamental collection of references is found in the article on "Geister (Dämonen)" in Th. Klauser, ed., *Reallexikon für Antike und Christentum* IX (Stuttgart, 1976). For Jewish demonology see K. Kohler, "Demonology," *The Jewish Encyclopedia* IV (New York, 1910), pp. 514-520 and L. Strack and P. Billerbeck, *Kommentar zum Neuen Testament aus Talmud und Midrasch* IV (München, 1961), pp. 501-535. For the Greek background see especially Guy Soury, *La démonologie de Plutarque* (Paris, 1942) with modification by F.E. Brenk, *In Mist Apparelled: Religious Themes in Plutarch's Moralia and Lives* (Leiden, 1977). An interpretation of Origen giving major attention to demons is S. Bettencourt, *Doctrina Ascetica Origenis seu quid docuerit de ratione animae humanae cum daemonibus*, Studia Anselmiana 16 (Rome, 1945). For the spirit world in general according to Origen see Cécile Blanc, "L'angélologie d'Origène," *Studia Patristica* XIV (T. U. 117; Berlin, 1976), pp. 79-109.

[2]Everett Ferguson, "The Demons According to Justin Martyr," in *The Man of the Messianic Reign and Other Essays: A Festschrift in Honor of Dr. Elza Huffard*, ed. Wil C. Goodheer (Wichita Falls: Western Christian Foundation, 1980), pp. 103-112. For the apologists in general see H. Wey, *Die Funktionen der bösen Geister bei den griechischen Apologeten des zweiten Jahrhunderts nach Christus* (Winterthur, 1957). Specialized studies of demonology in early Christian authors include H.J. Schoeps, "Die Dämonologie der Pseudoklementinesn," *Aus frühchristlicher Zeit* (Tübingen, 1950), pp. 38-81; E. Schneweis, *Angels and Demons According to Lactantius* (Washington, 1944); M.P. McHugh, "The Demonology of Saint Ambrose in Light of the Tradition," Wiener Studien, Neue Folge 12 (1978); 205-231: A.C. Baynes, "St. Anthony and the Demons," *Journal of Egyptian Archaeology* 40 (1954): 7-10.

There were other strands of thought in Origen's background. Greek physicians had identified demon possession with mental illness.[3] The association of the word demon with madness or being out of one's mind characterized the usage of the Gospel of John (7:20; 8:48f.,52; 10:20f.). Another interiorization of demons occurred in some Jewish sources (followed by Christians), which attributed to evil spirits the sinful impulses within a person.[4] Clement, Origen's predecessor at Alexandria, said the demons cause sin and testified to the Gnostic appropriation of the idea.[5] Because of sins, spiritual powers rule over human beings.[6] The trend toward psychologizing the demons was carried further by Origen and became almost the exclusive use of demons in monastic literature, as exemplified by another Alexandrian, Athanasius, in his *Life of Antony*.

This brief attempt to situate Origen in relation to both the objective and the subjective strands of thought about demons will introduce a more detailed description of his comments.

Origen repeated the Jewish view,[7] which Christians also adopted, that the heathen gods were demons. "It is then not the idols but the demons living in the idols who are called 'gods,' " he says.[8] An extended discussion in *Contra Celsum* brings out the viewpoint, one which is basic to Origen's demonology:

> It is not only we who say that there are evil daemons, but almost all people who hold that daemons exist. . . . However, in the view of the majority of people who hold that daemons exist, it is only the evil daemons who do not keep the law of God but transgress it. But in our opinion all daemons have fallen from the way of goodness, and previously they were not daemons; for the category of daemons is one of those classes of beings which have fallen away from God. That is why no one who worships God ought to worship daemons.
>
> The worship of the supposed gods is also a worship of daemons. For 'all the gods of the heathen are daemons' (Ps. 95.5, LXX). . . . That is the reason why we have decided to avoid the worship of daemons like a plague. And we maintain that all the supposed worship of gods among the Greeks with altars and images and temples is a worship offered to daemons.[9]

---

[3]Hippocrates, *The Sacred Disease* 1-3; cf. Plutarch, *Lives* 309.
[4]*Testament of Reuben* 2; *Testament of Benjamin* 3:3f.; *Testament of Asher* 6:5; for the personification of vices cf. Hermas, *Mandates* 2:3; 5:2-7; 8:3-7; 10:1; *Similitudes* 6:2; 9:22-23.
[5]*Strom.* II:20.113.
[6]*Ecl. Proph.* 20:1; cf. *Exc. Theod.* 51-52.
[7]Psalms 96:5 LXX; Deuteronomy 32:17; *Jubilees* 1:11; I Corinthians 10:19-21; Rev. 9:20.
[8]*Hom. Num.* XXVII.8. Cf. *C. Cels.* VII.64 and Minucius Felix, *Octavius* 26f. for demons occupying images and temples.
[9]*C. Cels.* VII.69. Quotations from Origen, *Contra Celsum* are taken from the translation by Henry Chadwick (Cambridge, 1953). Cf. VII.65, God, Christ, and angels "are different from all the gods of the heathen who are daemons"; also VIII.13.

Origen adopted the criticisms directed by certain philosophers against the popular religion. This criticism attributed the grosser features of paganism, and indeed all activities which brought the divine into direct contact with human beings (something which philosophers, particularly those influenced by Platonism, deemed unworthy of spiritual being), to the working of demons.[10] These criticisms against the popular religion had already been turned by Christian apologists against paganism as a whole.[11]

For instance, Origen frequently refers to the idea that the demons fed on the sacrifices and so delighted in these because they were dependent on them.[12] Particularly pointed are his remarks in *Exhortation to Martyrdom* 45;

> Some do not consider the truth concerning daemons, namely that if they are to remain in this gross air near the earth they need food from sacrifices and so keep where there is always smoke and blood and incense. . . . Indeed, I think that because of the misdeeds committed by the daemons who work against mankind those who feed them with sacrifices are no less responsible than the daemons who commit wicked deeds. For both the daemons and those who keep them on earth have injured men in like degree, since without the smoke and sacrifices and the food thought to be suited to their bodies the daemons would not be able to subsist.[13]

The demons were said to have given the oracles,[14] and Origen's cynical comment was that "the daemons seem to perform the petitions of those who bring requests to them more because of the sacrifices they offer than because of their virtuous actions."[15] The demons, as immaterial beings having some perception of the future, entered into animals and made possible divination through them.[16]

---

[10] Plato, *Symposium* 202 E-203A; *Epinomis* 984D-985B; Diogenes Laertius VIII.32; Plutarch, *Moralia* 415A-418D; Apuleius, *De Deo Socratis*; cf. Celsus' own use of demon for gods in *C. Cels.* VIII.24ff.

[11] From different standpoints see Wey, *op. cit.* and J. Geffcken, *Zwei griechische Apologeten* (Leipzig, 1907). For the philosophical criticism see H.W. Attridge, "The Philosophical Critique of Religion under the Early Empire," *Aufstieg und Niedergang der römischen Welt. Principat.* II. 16.2 (Berlin, 1978), pp. 45-78.

[12] Cf. the satire in Lucian, *Jup. Trag.* 15, 22; *Icaromenippus* 26f. Porphyry, *De abstinentia* 2.34 assigned the usual sacrifices to demons but spiritual sacrifice to the higher gods.

[13] Translation by Henry Chadwick in *Alexandrian Christianity*, Library of Christian Classics II (London, 1954). Cf. *C. Cels.* III 28f.; 37; IV.32; VII.5; 6; 35; 64, VIII.29f.; 61-63; *De princ.* I.8. 1 (Latin); *Comm. in Matt.* XIII.23. This was a prominent theme in earlier Christian apologetics: Cf. Justin, *Apol.* II, 5; I, 12; Athenagoras, *Leg.* 26f.

[14] *C. Cels.* VII.3; IV.93; VIII.62.

[15] *C. Cels.* VII.6.

[16] *C. Cels.* IV.92. Origen suggested an affinity between the demons "who have fallen from heaven to roam about the grosser bodies on earth" and the wilder animals. See H. Crouzel, *Théologie de l'image de Dieu chez Origène* (Paris, 1955), pp.

Origen seems especially concerned to attribute magic to the demons.

> The truth about daemons is also made clear by those who invoke daemons for what are called love-philtres and spells for producing hatred, or for the prevention of actions, or for countless other such causes. This is done by people who have learnt to invoke daemons by charms and incantations and to induce them to do what they wish. On this account the worship of daemons is foreign to us who worship the supreme God.[17]

Celsus had charged that Christians did miracles by calling on demons[18] and argued that Jesus performed his miracles by sorcery, not by divine power. Origen did not deny the possibility of demon-worked miracles; his approach rather was to appeal to the moral character of those performing the wonders and the moral effects of their works in order to determine which were from God and which from demonic powers:

> What is accomplished by God's power is nothing like what is done by sorcery . . .
>
> If we once agree that it is a corollary from the existence of magic and sorcery, wrought by evil daemons who are enchanted by elaborate spells and obey men who are sorcerers, that wonders done by divine power must also exist among men, then why should we not also examine carefully people who profess to do miracles, and see whether their lives and moral characters, and the results of their miracles, harm men or effect moral reformation? We should know in this way who serves daemons and causes such effects by means of certain spells and enchantments, and who has been on pure and holy ground . . . [19]

Although Origen accepted the reality of magical power, Christians, according to him, were not subject to its influence:

> We affirm that we know by experience that those who worship the supreme God through Jesus according to the way of Christianity, and live according to his gospel, and who use the appointed

---

197-201 for Origen's allegorizing of wild animals in the Bible as demons who attack the inner man; the one who sins takes on the characteristics of these animals. For demons having some perception of the future which they use to lead men astray, cf. Tertullian, *Apol.* 22.

[17] *C. Cels.* VII.69. Cf. VI.45. Other authors who attribute magic to demons include Minucius Felix, *Octavius* 26f.; Tertullian, *Apol.* 23; 35; *De idol.* 9; Hippolytus, *Ref. omn. haer.* IV.28; 35; Lactantius, *Div. inst.* II.17.

[18] *C. Cels.* I.6.

[19] *C. Cels.* II.51. Origen frequently appealed to this moral argument to rebut the charge of Celsus that Jesus was a sorcerer: ibid. I.67; 68; III.28; cf. VI.80; VIII.43. See Henry Chadwick, "The Evidences of Christianity in the Apologetic of Origen," *Studia Patristica* II (Berlin, 1957), pp. 331-339. For demons working miracles see Rev. 16:14. For God working miracles and demons working magic cf. Lactantius, *Div. inst.* IV.15.

prayers continually and in the proper way day and night, are not caught either by magic or by daemons.[20]

It might go without saying, but Origen makes it explicit, that, whereas on the Greek view demons might be either good or bad beings,[21] Christians never used "demon" in a good sense. This was necessary to say because it was an important difference in terminology between Origen and Celsus.

> Celsus fails to notice that the name of daemons is not morally neutral like that of men, among whom some are good and some bad; nor is it good like the name of gods, which is not to be applied to evil daemons or to images or to animals, but by those who know the things of God to beings truly divine and blessed. The name of daemons is always applied to evil powers without the grosser body, and they lead men astray and distract them, and drag them down from God and the world beyond the heavens to earthly things.[22]

In accord with this negative view of demons, Origen shared with early Christian thought in attributing various evils to demons. The demons did not give food, drink, and air to human beings, as Celsus asserted, but brought natural disasters on the earth.

> [The daemons] are responsible for famines, barren vines and fruit trees, and droughts, and also for the pollution of the air, causing damage to the fruits, and sometimes even the death of animals and plague among men. Of all these things daemons are the direct creators; like public executioners, they have received power by a divine appointment to bring about these catastrophes at certain times, either for the conversion of men when they drift towards the flood of evil, or with the object of training the race of rational beings.[23]

They led men astray by teaching false doctrine.[24] The activity most on the minds of early Christian apologists was persecution; this too was attributed to the working of demons.[25] Origen states that those who "condemn Christians

---

[20]*C. Cels.* VI.41.

[21]Origen reflects the Greek usage when he refers to "good daemons" (*C. Cels.* III.37) which were associated with heroes (VII.7 and 9), alludes to the demon of Socrates (VI.8), and quotes Celsus on the *genius* of the emperor (VIII.65). Cf. Tertullian, *Apol.* 32.

[22]*C. Cels.* V. 5. Cf. VIII.31, "the entire race of whom is evil," VIII.39; VII. 69; Clement of Alexandria, *Protrep.* II.40-41.

[23]*C. Cels.* VIII.31f.; cf. I.31; Clement of Alexandria, *Strom.* VI.3. Tertullian had earlier compared the effects of demons upon a person to the way an unseen poison in the breeze can blight crops; he particularly attributed illnesses to the work of demons — *Apol.* 22.

[24]*De princ.* III.3.2-3. Cf. Justin, *Apol.* I, 26; 56; 58; Hippolytus, *Ref. omn. haer.* VI.2 on demons introducing heresy.

[25]From Justin Martyr alone note *Apol.* I, 5; 57; II, 1; 7; 8; 12; *Dial.* 18; 131.

and betray them, and delight in fighting against them, are filled by evil daemons."[26] The demons "have stirred up the emperors, and the Senate, and the local governors everywhere, and even the populace . . . to oppose the Gospel and those who believe in it."[27] This charge was perhaps the more readily made because the demons ("the opposing powers") were generally identified with the "rulers of this world" who stood behind the existing political authorities.[28]

In spite of this malevolent activity of demons, Origen insists that "the word of God is mightier than them all . . . so that it has advanced and won over more souls."[29] Christians are not subject to the demons and are not hurt by them directly. Rather they are guarded and protected by the angels of God.

> The Christian, the real Christian who has submitted himself to God alone and His Logos, would not suffer anything at the hands of daemons, since he is superior to them. . . . For even if daemons are slighted, they are able to do nothing to us who are devoted to the Person that is alone able to help all those who deserve it. He does no less than set His own angels over those whose lives are devoted to Him, that the opposing angels and the so-called ruler of this world who governs them may be unable to do anything against those who are dedicated to God.[30]

Christians do not have to fear the demons because Christ has triumphed over them. At the birth of Jesus "the demons lost their strength and became weak"; the coming of the Magi to worship Jesus indicated their recognition that a superior power had appeared.[31] After the coming and teaching of Jesus souls of believers have freedom from demons.[32] At Jesus' crucifixion in particular the evil powers were defeated.[33] The benefits of Jesus' victory were extended through the preaching of the gospel. "God, who sent Jesus, destroyed the whole conspiracy of daemons, and everywhere in the world in order that men might be converted and reformed He made the gospel of Jesus to be successful."[34] The Christian entered the sphere of safety at his baptism. As the waters of the Red Sea destroyed the army of Pharaoh, so the waters of baptism destroyed the demons:

---

[26] *C. Cels.* VIII.43. Cf. VIII.41; 39; and 69 for discussion of the problem of God not saving Christians from persecution.

[27] *C. Cels.* IV.32; cf. *Hom. in Jesu Nave* IX.10.

[28] *De princ.* III.3.2. See H. Schlier, *Principalities and Powers in the New Testament* (New York, 1961); G.B. Caird, *Principalities and Powers: A Study in Pauline Theology* (Oxford, 1956); G.H.C. MacGregor, "Principalities and Powers: The Cosmic Background of Paul's Thought," *New Testament Studies* I (1954): 17-28.

[29] *C. Cels.* IV.32.

[30] *C. Cels.* VIII.36; cf. VIII.27; 34; VI.41.

[31] *C. Cels.* I.60. For the association of the victory over demons with the incarnation cf. Justin. *Dial.* 45; 78; *Apol.* II, 5; cf. Ignatius, *Eph.* 19.

[32] *Hom. in Jesu Nave* XIV.1.

[33] *Comm. in Matt.* XII.18,40; *Hom. Ex.* VI.8; *Hom. Num.* III.4; XVII.5; *Hom. in Jesu Nave* VIII.3; XIII.4; XV.5. Colossians 2:15 is often cited by Origen in this connection. Cf. J. Daniélou, *Origène* Paris, 1948) pp. 265-67.

[34] *C. Cels.* III.29.

Paul calls that crossing accomplished by Moses in the cloud and the sea a baptism [1 Cor. 10:1-4] in order to bring home to you who were baptized in Christ, in water and the Holy Spirit, that the Egyptians are pursuing you, striving to subject you to them, I mean, the "rulers of this world" and the "spirits of wickedness" to whom you gave your allegiance. They strive to follow you, but you go down into the water, where you are safe, and when you have been purified from all stain of sin, come forth a new man, to sing the new song.[35]

The martyrs especially demonstrated Christ's victory over the evil powers and were themselves conquerors. "The powers of evil suffer defeat by the death of the holy martyrs," Origen affirmed.[36] The martyrs, by sharing in Christ's sufferings shared in his triumph over the "principalities and powers."[37]

A special instance of the Christians' power over demons was the ability to cast them out of a person in whom they had come to dwell.[38] Origen attributed this power to "the name of Jesus,"[39] prayer, and words from the scriptures.[40] Origen knew that the Jews accomplished the same task by invoking "the God of Abraham, the God of Isaac, and the God of Jacob"[41] and that there were pagan accounts of exorcism.[42] In all cases the potency was supposed to reside in the words or formulas recited.[43] Origen contrasted the simplicity of Christian practice with the elaborate incantations and magical procedures in paganism:

> ... the race of daemons which many Christians drive out of people who suffer from them, without any curious magical art or sorcerer's device, but with prayer alone and very simple adjurations and formulas such as the simplest person could use. For generally speaking it is uneducated people who do this kind of work.

---

[35]*Hom. Ex.* V. 5. Cf. VI.3; Cyprian, *Ep.* 75.15. P. Lundberg, *La Typologie baptismale dans l'ancienne église* (Uppsala, 1942), chapter 7; J. Daniélou, *From Shadows to Reality* (Westminster, MD, 1960), pp. 175-201.

[36]*Comm. in Joh.* VI.54 (36). Cf. *C. Cels.* VIII.44; Tertullian, *Apol.* 27.

[37]*Exh. ad mart.* 43. Cf. W. Völker, *Das Vollkommenheitsideal des Origenes* (Tübingen, 1931), pp. 176f.

[38]The earlier apologists had made much of the power of Christians to expel demons by the name of Jesus — Justin, *Apol.* II, 5; *Dial.* 76; Tertullian, *Apol.* 23.

[39]*C. Cels.* VIII.58; I.6, "by the name of Jesus with the recital of the histories about him," with which cf. Justin, *Dial.* 30; 76; 85; *Apol.* II, 6; 8; "by invocation of the name of God" in *Hom. in Jesu Nave* XXIV.1.

[40]*C. Cels.* VII.67.

[41]*C. Cels.* IV.33. Cf. the use of Jewish names for God in the magical papyri, e.g. Paris Magical Papyrus 11.3, 007-3, 085, which is studied by W.L. Knox as an example of "Jewish Liturgical Exorcism" in *Harvard Theological Review* 31 (1938): 191-203. For an account of Jewish exorcism see Josephus, *Ant.* VIII.46-49.

[42]Celsus in *C. Cels.* I.68; VI.39f.; cf. Philostratus, *Vita Apoll.* IV.20; Lucian, *Philopseudes* 16.

[43]The name of Jesus was so potent that Origen claims it was effective when used by those who were not true disciples — *C. Cels.* II.49.

The power of the word of Christ shows the worthlessness and
weakness of the daemons; for it is not necessary to have a wise man
who is competent in the rational proofs of the faith in order that
they should be defeated and yield to expulsion from the soul and
body of a man.[44]

Elsewhere Origen said that Christians did not use adjuration, invocations, or direct address to the impure spirit but only prayer and fasting.[45]

Thus far the material covered may be regarded as standard Christian thought in the first centuries of our era. For the most part Origen's arguments in *Contra Celsum* stand in the mainstream of earlier Christian apologetics; but even here some of his more distinctive emphases stand out. Origen had his own views on some subjects about which early Christians differed, e.g. the origin of demons. He rejected the view of *I Enoch* that demons were the souls of the giants produced by the union of angels with women, pointing out that *I Enoch* was "not generally held to be divine by the churches."[46] He preferred to interpret Genesis 6:1-4 about the "sons of God" marrying the "daughters of men" as referring to souls afflicted with a desire for bodily life.[47]

Origen emphasized that demons were not created evil but became that way through transgression. The thought of a fall of good spiritual beings was certainly not original with Origen,[48] but he integrates it with ideas which were so strongly characteristic of his own religious philosophy that this may serve to introduce his more distinctive approach. Here the key factor was free will, a central element in Origen's thought.[49] He began his discussion of spiritual beings (angels, demons, principalities, powers) in *De principiis* I. 5.3 by raising the question whether some were made incapable of evil, some capable of both virtue and evil, and some incapable of virtue. He laid it down that goodness and wickedness were not part of the essence of the rational powers, for that would mean that God created some things intrinsically evil.

> We conclude then, that the position of every created being is the result of his own work and his own motives, and that the

---

[44]*C. Cels.* VII.4. Cf. I.46; *Hom. in Jesu Nave* XX.1; Ps. Clem., *De virg.* I. 12. For accounts of Christian exorcism see *Acta Pet.* 11; *Acta Thom.* 42-49; 73-81.

[45]*Comm. in Matt* XIII. 7; cf. Irenaeus, *Adv. haer.* II.32.4. Cf. Bettencourt, *op. cit.* (n.1), 44.

[46]*C. Cels.* V.54. The reference is to *I Enoch* 6 and 15; its interpretation was accepted, for example, by Justin, *Apol.* II,5 and Athenagoras, *Leg.* 24f.

[47]*C. Cels.* V.55.

[48]Origen puts the thought that the devil "was formerly an angel, but became an apostate and persuaded as many angels as he could to fall away with him" among the opinions generally held among Christians — *De princ.* pref. 6.

[49]On the origin of evil and importance of free will in Origen's system see H. Koch, *Pronoia and Paideusis* (Berlin, 1932), pp. 96-159. On free will in relation to sin see Georg Teichtweier, *Die Sündenlehre des Origenes* (Regensburg, 1958), pp. 77-85. Cf. also Völker, *op. cit.* (n. 31), pp. 25-44; E. de Faye, *Origène, sa vie, son oeuvre, sa pensée* (Paris, 1928), vol. 3, pp. 179-198; Daniélou, *op. cit.* (n. 27), pp. 203-220, 279-281; B.D. Jackson, "Sources of Origen's Doctrine of Freedom," *Church History* 35 (1966): 13-23).

powers above mentioned which appear as holding sway or exercising authority or dominion over others, have gained this superiority and eminence over those whom they are said to govern or on whom they exercise their authority, not by some privilege of creation but as the reward of merit.[50]

As a corollary the evil powers departed from good of their own free will. The "opposing powers" were at one time "stainless" and dwelt among those who have remained pure, but they became "fugitives."[51] Origen interpreted the "prince of Tyre" in Ezekiel 28 and "Lucifer" in Isaiah 14 as Satan, who had once been among the pure angels, an interpretation which has had a long history in Christianity.[52] The demons were not God's servants any more, but they were "servants of the evil one, the prince of this world, who tries to persuade any whom he can win over to forsake God."[53] Satan is himself called an "evil daemon."[54] The demons, like the Devil whom they serve, have fallen away from goodness. Previously they were not demons, "for the category of daemons is one of those classes of beings which have fallen away from God."[55] Nevertheless, they remained under God's ultimate providential rule; they "have received power by a divine appointment to bring about" evil.[56] They served as "public executioners" to punish the wicked.[57] Even their worst actions were finally subject to God's government of the world.

The demons, as one of their evil works, tempt to sin.[58] "According to the scriptures, the opposing powers and the devil himself are engaged in a struggle with the human race, provoking and inciting men to sin."[59] To commit sin is to be initiated into the cult of demons,[60] and no sin is committed without their collaboration.[61] The victory of Christ on the cross was a foreshadowing of what will be consummated at the second coming;[62] in the meantime the Christian is engaged in a continual combat against the "spiritual hosts of wickedness in heavenly places" (Eph. 6:12 — often cited by Origen in his homilies). The moral application of the Old Testament in Origen's homilies

---

[50] Translations from *De principiis* are taken from G.W. Butterworth, *Origen on First Principles* (London, 1936).

[51] *De princ.* I.5.5.

[52] *De princ.* I.5.4f. Cf. I.8.3; *Comm. in Joh.* II.7. Tertullian offers the same interpretation — *Adv. Marc.* II. 10 — and agrees with Origen in the emphasis on the fall occurring by free will — cf. *Apol.* 22. The classic English statement is John Milton's *Paradise Lost*, esp. I. 34-39, 157-168, 249-263.

[53] *C. Cels.* VIII. 13. Cf. *Hom. in Jesu Nave* XV.5 for a hierarchy of evil beings and *Comm. in Matt.* XI. 1 for a diabolical counterpart to the Trinity.

[54] *C. Cels.* VI.45.

[55] *C. Cels.* VII.69. See at note 4 for the context.

[56] *C. Cels.* VIII.31. See at note 17 for the context.

[57] *C. Cels.* VII.70; cf. VIII.33; Blanc, *op. cit.* (n. 1), p. 107.

[58] Teichtweier, *op. cit.* (n. 43), pp. 102-111, 155-157.

[59] *De princ.* III.2.1. Cf. *C. Cels.* V.5; *Comm. in Matt.* XIII.22f. For earlier Christian statements that the demons cause sin, see Tatian, *Or.* 14; Justin, *Apol.* II, 5.

[60] *Hom. Num.* X.3.

[61] *Hom. Num.* XXVII.8.

[62] *Hom. in Jesu Nave* VIII.4.

frequently employs the motif of fighting against the evil powers.[63] "There is a diabolical race of opposing powers against whom we fight and struggle with great effort during this life."[64] The Christian must slay the demons within himself.[65] He can overcome them by following Jesus and thus will come to dwell in their heavenly realm.[66] The struggle against the demonic forces actually serves a useful purpose:

> If the demons were deprived of free will, the athletes of Christ would have no adversaries; without adversaries they would have no contest; and without a contest they would have neither reward nor victory.[67]

Although Origen attributes the cause of sin to demons, he seems more especially concerned to point out that the demons find their occasion and opportunity in the natural drives and desires of human beings. "We derive the beginnings and what we may call the seeds of sin from those desires which are given to us naturally for our use."[68] So the demons are not the only cause of sin, but they gain their hold on human life because no resistance is offered to them.

> The daemons have been allowed to occupy a place in their minds, a place which intemperance has first laid open, and have then taken complete possession of their intelligence, especially as no thought of the glory of virtue aroused them to resistance.[69]

Human beings in their free will yield to demonic influence.

> It is possible for us, when an evil power has begun to urge us on to a deed of evil, to cast away the wicked suggestions and to resist the low enticements and to do absolutely nothing worthy of blame; and it is possible on the other hand when a divine power has urged us on to better things not to follow its guidance since our faculty of free will is preserved to us in either case.[70]

God provides help to resist temptation.[71] A good angel fights on behalf of the person,[72] and without divine help one could not overcome the opposing powers. But this divine assistance by itself does not guarantee victory. "This

---

[63] *Hom. in Jesu Nave* I.7; VIII.2; XII. 1-2; XV.6; *Sel. In Ps.* 36, *Hom.* II.8. See Bettencourt, *op. cit.* (n. 1), pp. 62-86).
[64] *Hom. in Jesu Nave* I.6.
[65] *Hom. in Jesu Nave* VIII.7. Völker, *op. cit.* (N. 31), pp. 175f.
[66] *Hom. Num.* VII.5.
[67] *Hom. Num.* XIII.7.
[68] *De princ.* III.2.2.
[69] Ibid.
[70] *De princ.* III.2.4.
[71] *Hom. Luc.* 34.4. Although Origen questioned the interpretation of the robbers as demons, he transmitted this interpretation of the parable to his successors — G.J.M. Bartelink, "The démons comme brigands," *Vigiliae Christianae* 21 (1967): 12-24.
[72] *De princ.* III.2.4-5. Origen refers in the passage to *Barnabas* 18 and Hermas, *Mand.* VI.2; *Hom. in Jesu Nave* XV.6 refers to *Testament of Reuben* 2-3 and *Testament of Judah* 16. M. Simonetti, "Due note sul' angelogia origeniana," *Rivista cultura classica e medioevala* 4 (1962): 165-208; Blanc, *op. cit.* (n. 1), pp. 99, 103.

strength, therefore, which is given to us in order that we may be able to conquer, we by the exercise of our free will either use diligently and conquer or feebly and suffer defeat."[73] The purpose of Jesus is to conquer the kingdom of sin in mankind.[74]

Origen moved toward a psychological explanation of the working of demons in the following passage:

> The soul of man, while in the body, can admit different energies, that is, controlling influences, of spirits either good or bad. Now the bad spirits work in two ways; that is, they either take whole and entire possession of the mind, so that they allow those in their power neither to understand nor to think as is the case, for example, with those who are popularly called 'possessed' whom we see to be demented and insane, such as the men who are related in the Gospel to have been healed by the Saviour; or they deprave the soul, while it still thinks and understands, through harmful suggestion by means of different kinds of thoughts and evil inducements, as for example Judas was incited to the crime of the betrayal. . . .
>
> On the other hand a man admits the energy and control of a good spirit when he is moved and incited to what is good and inspired to strive towards things heavenly and divine. . . . From this we learn to discern clearly when the soul is moved by the presence of a spirit of the better kind, namely, when it suffers no mental disturbance or aberration whatsoever as a result of the immediate inspiration and does not lose the free judgment of the will.[75]

There is, according to Origen, for every sin a particular demon. He can speak of the "spirit of fornication . . . the spirit of anger and wrath, the demon of avarice" etc.[76] There is only one spirit for each of the vices, but each has innumerable servants under him to invade different persons.[77]

Some features of Origen's teachings about demons go beyond concurrence with his characteristic emphases and become part of his peculiar teachings. This is notably the case with his view that God's love and disciplinary judgments will persuade even the rebellious spiritual powers to submit to him. In commenting on 1 Corinthians 15:28 Origen says as follows:

---

[73]*De princ.* III.2.3. Cf. *C. Cels.* VIII.36 for one voluntarily in the power of the demons according to whether he chooses to obey them.

[74]*Hom. in Jesu Nave* XV.4-5.

[75]*De princ.* III.3.4. Cf. *Comm. Cant.* III. 15 for demons using base thoughts to destroy virtue in the soul. On sin as a psychological event for Origen, cf. Völker, *op. cit.* (n. 31), p. 42. See notes 4 and 5 and cf. Clement of Alexandria, *Ecl. proph.* 46, "The Passions of the soul are called spirits," but Clement adds, "not spirits of power, since in that case the man under the influence of passion would be a legion of demons."

[76]*Hom. in Jesu Nave* XII.3. Cf. Völker, *op. cit.* pp. 36f.

[77]*Hom. in Jesu Nave* XV.5.

> If therefore that subjection by which the Son is said to be subjected to the Father is taken to be good and salutary, it is a sure and logical consequence that the subjection of his enemies which is said to happen to the Son of God should also be understood to be salutary and useful; so that, just as when the Son is said to be subjected to the Father the perfect restoration of the entire creation is announced, so when his enemies are said to be subjected to the Son of God we are to understand this to involve the salvation of those that have been lost.
>
> But this subjection will be accomplished through certain means and courses of discipline and periods of time; that is, the whole world will not become subject to God by the pressure of some necessity that compels it into subjection, nor by the use of force, but by word, by reason, by teaching, by the exhortation to better things, by the best methods of education.[78]

Much of what Origen says about the demons in an apologetic context can be paralleled from the second-century apologists. Origen seems to be the first, however, to develop the view that the decline of demonic influence in the world is associated with the spread of the gospel. The standpoint seems quite modern, almost rationalist. Whether the change be attributed to the preaching itself, some objective change in reality, the lack of belief any longer in the demons, or whatever factor, Origen points to the end of antiquity in seeing the advance of Christianity as continuing the victory won by the death and resurrection of Christ over the demonic powers. Their defeat was internalized in the moral triumphs of the individual believer, but this was more than a psychological experience, because the demons (although causing psychological experiences) were more than something psychological. The defeat of the demons also had a cosmic significance.

> If by living a chaste and modest life, for example, one has triumphed over a spirit of fornication, it is no more permitted to this spirit who has been conquered by the saint to attack another man. . . . Each spirit conquered by the saints is sent by Christ, the just judge who presides over the struggles of mortals in this life, "into the abyss" or "into the outer darkness" or some such place as it deserves. It follows, then, that since many demons have already suffered defeat, the nations may more readily come to the faith, something which would have been impossible if the legions of demons remained intact as they did formerly.[79]

---

[78] *De princ.* III.5.7-8. Cf. de Faye, *op. cit.* (n. 43), vol. 3, pp. 261f.; E. Ferguson, "Divine Pedagogy: Origen's Use of the Imagery of Education," *Christian Teaching: Studies in Honor of LeMoine G. Lewis* (Abilene, TX, 1981), pp. 357-360.

[79] *Hom. in Jesu Nave* XV.6.

Conversion from sin to God and a life of virtue is a punishment of the demons.[80]

This promise of victory over demonic power was no doubt an important part of the appeal of the Christian faith in the ancient world. We may concur with the judgment of Harnack that deliverance from demons "formed one very powerful method of [Christian] mission and propaganda."[81] And so Origen affirmed the confident stance which Christians took toward the demonic:

> We do not, then, deny that there are many demons upon the earth, but we maintain that they exist and exercise power among the wicked, as a punishment of their wickedness. But they have no power over those who 'Put on the whole armour of God' [Eph. 6:11].[82]

---

[80]*Hom. Num.* XXVII.8: "It seems to me that vengeance is exercised against the demons when a man, attracted by their seductions to the worship of idols but converted by the word of the Savior, renders to God the worship which is due him; by the fact itself of this conversion a vengeance is exercised against the Deceiver. . . . The demons are punished by our reformation and conversion."

[81]Adolf Harnack, *The Mission and Expansion of Christianity*, (New York, 1962 reprint), pp. 125-146.

[82]*C. Cels.* VIII.34.

Interpersonal Relationships in the Gospel of John

John C. Free

Introduction

The study of interpersonal relationships presents useful means for improving our skills of understanding and interpretation. Every message occurs in a socio-cultural and an interpersonal context. The perception of contexts determines in no small part the perception of the message.

The General Context

The larger social/cultural context of the Gospel of John is a combination of Greco-Roman and Jewish/Palestinian components. The more immediate social/cultural context of the gospel narratives was a combination of Judean, Galilean, and Samaritan. The most immediate context of the author was his relationship to his audience, likely late first century churches. Since the location of the author at the time of composition cannot be conclusively established, it is not possible to know with certainty his most immediate social context. A Judean context late in the first century is both possible and likely.[1]

The conventions or rules of interaction in any culture are sometimes stated explicitly (cf. John 4:9b) and at other times must be inferred or derived from other sources. These are the norms by which individuals are socialized in a given culture and which determine what is accepted and expected social

---

[1] I.H. Marshall, "John, Gospel of," in *New Bible Dictionary* [(ed.) J.D. Douglas] (Grand Rapids: Wm. B. Eerdmans, 1962), pp. 649-650. The purpose for questioning the locale of the author is to focus attention on the historical situation in the early churches in order to see if part of the author's purpose may have been to address matters in those churches by calling attention to narratives the early churches would have considered normative. Since several of the New Testament epistles were written to address situations that involved interpersonal relationships in the life of the church, it is not unreasonable to suppose that the authors of the gospels may have been moved in part by similar motives. (This possibility appears to be very likely in the case of the Gospel of Luke which contains a wealth of material on interpersonal relationships.)

behavior.² Just as individual personality characteristics tend to be very stable over time,³ so the rules of interaction which prevail in given cultures also tend to be very stable. It is the differences in these conventions which help set one culture apart from another.

Jews in first century Palestine proclaimed their identity as descendants of Abraham (John 8:33f.) with vigor. Devotion to the law of Moses likely had never been excelled by any of their predecessors. But culturally, they were more than Abraham's offspring. Significant influences had come to bear on their self-understanding and values. Of particular importance was the influence of Greek language, philosophy and culture. Just as the ancestors of first century Jews had accommodated themselves to pagan thought, values and practices, so John's contemporaries had accommodated in varying degrees to the prevailing notions and influences of the Greco-Roman world.

The Hellenization of Judaism brought a syncretism of Jewish ethnic identity, morality, religion, and world view together with elements of Greek culture, traditions, and philosophy, as well as Roman political thought and practice. In some measure it involved the adoption of Greek language, culture and religion in preference to Jewish traditions. In varying proportions the same processes occurred in the somewhat different cultural contexts of both Diaspora and Palestinian Judaism.⁴

A look at the Gospel of John can be used to reveal some of the normative conventions and rules which operated at the time and then to look at the interactions of Jesus to see in what ways Jesus either followed the conventions of the day or set a new standard in personal relationships.

Identities

The study of the formation of identities provides clues to the ways in which relationships function at personal levels. In Western society, identities are primarily individualistic. People understand themselves in terms of internal frames of reference. In many other societies identities take on a more corporate nature. The primary frame of reference for personal identity is external, such as one's place within the community.

The term "solidarity" is sometimes used to describe this phenomenon.⁵ In the Gospel of John there are extensive uses of collectives, names which iden-

---

²Edwin P. Hollander and Raymond G. Hunt, *Current Perspectives in Social Psychology* [3rd ed.] (New York: Oxford University Press, 1975), p. 59. For a fuller discussion of religion and culture, see J. Milton Yinger, *The Scientific Study of Religion* (New York: Macmillan, 1970), pp. 203-211.
³Salvatore Maddi, *Personality Theories: A Comparative Analysis* (Homewood: Dorsey, 1968), p. 10.
⁴John Bright, *A History of Israel* [2nd rev. ed.] (Philadelphia: Westminster Press, 1959), pp. 395ff.
⁵Cf. W.D. Davies, *Paul and the Salvation of Mankind* (London: S.P.C.K., 1965), pp. 83-84. G.F. Moore, *Judaism in the First Centuries of the Christian Era*, Vol. II (Cambridge: Harvard University Press, 1930), pp. 311f. Donald McGavran

tify groups. Often the actual identity of the persons is not considered as important as the groups they represent. Examples include: "the Jews," "priests and Levites from Jerusalem," "disciples," "the Galileans," "the Pharisees," "the dead," "the chief priests," "the officers," "the scribes," "descendants of Abraham," "Samaritans," "disciples of Moses," "some Greeks," and "the authorities."

Likewise, the personal identities of individuals were often presented in connection with their locales of origin, their parentage or other affinities. Examples include: "John *the Baptist*, Andrew *Simon Peter's brother*, Simon *son of John*, Philip *from Bethsaida* — the city of Andrew and Peter, Lazarus *of Bethany* — the village of Mary and Martha, Joseph *of Arimathea* and Jesus, — *the son of Joseph* "whose father and mother we know." In other instances well-known individuals are identified simply by their first names, (Thomas, Caiaphas, Judas, Pilate, etc.).

The question of the identity of John the Baptist (1:19-25) is illustrative. The question was first put to him in simple terms, "Who are you?" The only way in which the delegation which questioned him could understand his identity was in terms of the categories suggested by the names "Christ," "Elijah," or "the prophet." Though he was a unique, perhaps eccentric, individual, they needed to fix his identity with established categories in order to comprehend who he was.

A similar question was put to Jesus later (10:24). Jesus admitted that he was the Messiah when asked directly, but preferred an identity as the Son of the Father (10:30-36: "I and the Father are one . . . I am the Son of God,"). On the other hand, Jesus was apparently comfortable with identifications of himself and others simply as individuals.

Interpersonal and community relationships tended to play a very decisive role in the development of personal identities in the culture of Israel. The questions put to John the Baptist and to Jesus (who are you?) were very important in the minds of those who asked them. They would have been similarly significant to the earliest readers of the Gospel of John.

It is also possible that the rejection of Jesus by the Jews of his time was due to his refusal to measure up to their corporate understanding of the identity and nature of Messiah. It was inconceivable to them that Messiah would not be "one of them" or "part of the establishment" to use a modern term. For the early readers of the gospel who might be enduring persecution, a sense of solidarity with the misunderstood, mistreated Jesus would be a powerful, encouraging, and comforting thought.

The Relationships of the Authorities

The largest body of data about relationships in the Gospel of John concerns persons with authority roles. This was a live issue in the Judean and Galilean

---

writing about contemporary missions discusses the same phenomenon under the rubric of "people consciousness" in *Understanding Church Growth* [rev. ed.] (Grand Rapids: Eerdmans, 1980), pp. 214-216.

communities in the first century (cf. Mt. 22:17-21; Acts 4:13-21). Both civil and religious authorities took themselves with utter seriousness. The ascendance of the Roman emperors presented the Jews with a model of authority which some of them apparently found appealing. The Roman rule was on the one hand powerful and autocratic and on the other benevolent, efficient, and usually responsive to local concerns. Such appeal is particularly apparent in the Sadducees and High Priests, whose positions of power hinged on Roman favor.[6] In his day, Herod the Great had been efficient as a ruler. He had accomplished much, but his rule had never been popular. Upon his death some Pharisees had petitioned Rome for direct rule.[7] Since the deposition of Archelaus in 6 A.D., Judea had been under such rule. In Judea this had apparently provided for greater participation in the political process on the part of the Pharisees and Sadducees. They were reluctant to permit anyone to jeopardize these gains.

The Jews

There are several passages in the gospel in which relationships involving authorities may be observed. In the Gospel of John the term "the Jews" often appears to designate the general Jewish authorities. It is useful to examine their style and tactics and compare these with ways Jesus approached relationships.

The Jewish authorities tended to place *conditions of compliance* on those who were associated with them. When priests and Levites questioned John the Baptist (1:19-23) they were insistent on receiving an answer they could take back to the Jews in Jerusalem (Pharisees) who had sent them. Apparently, the thought of returning empty-handed was unacceptable, perhaps risky. The threat of losing favor with "the Jews" appears to have been a significant motivator for John's interrogators.

The Jewish authorities functioned in a closed circle of authority which they *carefully reserved*. This means that they were very reluctant to share their authority, even if someone undertook a cause that was undeniably just. When Jesus was questioned about driving the money changers from the temple by "the Jews" (2:18-20), they wanted some proof that he was authorized to act. Concern for morality and justice and a zeal for the Lord's house were not sufficient justifications to assume such authority. Hence they called him to account for his action.

The maintenance of political control was a major motivation for Jewish as well as Roman authorities. An early departure of Jesus from Judea to Galilee was connected with a discovery on the part of "the Jews" that Jesus was making more disciples than John the Baptist (4:1). Popular religious movements involving Messianic figures would trigger alarm in the circles of the

---

[6]Samuel Sandmel, *A Jewish Understanding of the New Testament* (Cincinnati: Hebrew Union College Press, 1957), pp. 30-31.

[7]H.L. Ellison, "Pharisees," in *New Bible Dictionary*, [eds. J.D. Douglas, F.F. Bruce, J.I. Packer, R.V.G. Tasker, and D.J. Wiseman] (Grand Rapids: Eerdmans, 1962), p. 981.

Jews who could expect to lose their positions of power if they could not convince the Romans that they were maintaining control.[8]

By the time of Christ, a well developed sectarian party system had developed particularly in Judea.[9] Relations between the sectarian groups had become far more political than fraternal. Political concerns often overrode theological differences. Sectarian agendas also tended to take precedence over justice and evenhanded responses to evidence.

Breaches of sectarian traditions and norms often brought *public confrontation and admonition*. For example, "the Jews" confronted the man who was ill for 38 years whom Jesus had healed on the Sabbath (5:10-16). Their allegation was that the man was doing what was not lawful (carrying his mat on the Sabbath). When he protested that Jesus had so instructed him, their response was to persecute Jesus.

These Jewish authorities *expected unquestioned acceptance* of their judgments. At times this meant that people were not to do their own thinking. At the feast of Tabernacles, Jesus delayed his visit to Jerusalem because "the Jews" sought to kill him and were therefore looking for him (7:1,10-13,15,25-26,32-35,40-52). Likewise, public conversations about him were suppressed for fear of "the Jews." When he did arrive, he taught in the temple, causing amazement on the part of "the Jews" on the one hand, and, on the other hand, an arrest warrant which was not executed because the officers were so taken with the authority of his teaching and the people were divided in their assessment of him. Vs. 48 is particularly interesting, "Have any of the authorities or of the Pharisees believed in him?" This rhetorical question addressed to the officers was designed to make faith in him seem absurd and their failure to arrest him shameful. Divergent thinking was attacked.

Dismissing people as incompetent if they differed from official positions or else *excluding them from the community* were common tactics of the Jews. In a discussion with Jesus about slavery and being children of Abraham (8:48-59) "the Jews" accused Jesus of being a Samaritan with a demon. Their purpose appears to have been to dismiss his logic as coming from a mentally incompetent person. When Jesus maintained his claim calmly, and asserted his preexistance to Abraham, "the Jews" attempted to stone him.

Similarly, the man born blind was brought to the Pharisees for interrogation (9:13-34). His testimony and estimation of Jesus as a prophet created a division among the Pharisees. His assertion that he was blind and had received his sight was not accepted by "the Jews." So his parents were called. They were willing to affirm only that he was their son and had been blind since birth for fear of being put out of the synagogue by "the Jews." When the healed man challenged the incredulity of the Jews, they cast him out as they

---

[8]Sandmel, ibid.

[9]The traditions of the Pharisees are well known. The Sadducees, whose views are not as well known, were nonetheless quite influential. They generally controlled the priesthood and their numbers came largely from the well-to-do of Jerusalem. Other groups were known in the time as well though not mentioned in the gospel, such as the Essenes and Zealots.

had already agreed they would do. For the Pharisees it was a theological dilemma, and for the Jews (perhaps a more inclusive reference) it was a larger practical problem of maintaining control.

Entrapment into acts considered blasphemy were favored tactics of the Jewish authorities. At the feast of dedication (10:22-38) "the Jews" surrounded Jesus and asked him to plainly declare himself to be Messiah. When he indicated that he had already made that claim and that he and the Father were one, "the Jews" again took up stones, threatening to kill him. When Jesus challenged their logic they then tried unsuccessfully to arrest him. Their sectarian thinking permitted a lynch mob mentality to develop among them.

The reaction of the disciples to Jesus' suggestion that they return to Judea (at the death of Lazarus) (11:8-16) was the protest that "the Jews" were but now seeking to stone him and he wants to go there again? This would indicate that the hostile reactions of the Jewish authorities to Jesus was well understood by the disciples and that they tended to take the threat to Jesus as a threat to themselves as well.

It would be a mistake to think that "the Jews" were entirely heartless. They publicly demonstrated their remorse over the death of Lazarus and offered their sympathies to his sisters (11:33-37). But they were at the same time critical of Jesus' failure to prevent the death of Lazarus. Their initial reaction to Jesus' presence was clearly cynical and their purpose was to *inspire doubt where possible.*

The control by Jewish authorities extended over people who dared not think for themselves about the meaning of what they had witnessed. Their beliefs about the meaning of events would be formed by the interpretation of the events they witnessed which those they regarded as authorities provided for them. When some of the same Jews witnessed the resurrection of Lazarus (11:45-53,57) it convinced them that Jesus was the Messiah. However, others of them went to the Pharisees to report it. They appeared unable to form their own judgments of the evidence.

Upon receiving that report, the chief priests and the Pharisees convened the council. Their concern was that allowing Jesus to gather more believers would lead the Romans to destroy both the temple and the nation. The concern which they expressed was not with truth or justice, but with the *avoidance of a political embarrassment.* The response of the chief priests (of the party of the Sadducees) to the resurrection of Lazarus (12:10-11) was to conspire to put him to death and thereby suppress the evidence. This was motivated and designed to control defection from the ranks of the Jews,[10] (likely

---

[10] Though this was from the author's perspective a process that had been at work for some time. Nicodemus, for example, was identified as a ruler of the Jews (3:1-15) who manifested an apparently genuine openness to Jesus and the meaning of the signs which Jesus performed. His visit to Jesus by night may have been motivated by fear of his co-rulers. His questioning of his colleagues (7:50-51) brought him ridicule as a "Galilean." His participation in the burial of Jesus (19:39-40) would indicate that he was willing to make his break with the "official" position of the council known to some of the disciples of Jesus at least.

used in the generic sense of the term) particularly since a great crowd of them had come together. The dimensions of the problem which Jesus was creating for them were clearly growing.

In many situations, the Jewish authorities *employed intermediaries* to deal with problem situations. This was noted in the questioning of John the Baptist and the arrest of Jesus. When he was ready to betray Jesus, Judas (18:3,12) obtained a band of soldiers and their captain and some officers of "the Jews" from the chief priests and Pharisees. The band of soldiers was led by a captain. The officers were likely Jewish police, possibly patterned after the model of the Roman militia.[11] An officer (likely of the same force) struck Jesus when he answered the High Priest in a way he found offensive (18:22).

It appears that the relationship between Pilate and the Jewish authorities was rather finely balanced (18:29-19:16). Their relationship involved *power politics*. The process of placing Jesus on trial before Pilate required formal accusations, which were lacking. So Pilate referred Jesus back to them. He wanted Jesus to be tried by Jewish law. But "the Jews" wanted Pilate to handle the matter since they had only one outcome in mind for Jesus: death.

The claim that Jesus was the King of the Jews was a puzzlement to Pilate, but one about which he showed little concern. At one point there had been a movement in Galilee to make Jesus king, but he did not cooperate with it (6:15). At other times people had referred to Jesus as the King of Israel (1:49, 12:13-15), but this was apparently a fairly isolated phenomenon. As Pilate interrogated Jesus, it is clear that he regarded the Jewish authorities he was dealing with as the legitimate spokemen for the nation as a whole. If Pilate was impressed with Jesus, it was not with his political clout. He likely saw Jesus more accurately as a religious teacher.

The accusations of "the Jews" were not sufficient to lead Pilate to proceed with a criminal condemnation. When Pilate presented Jesus as their King, it may have been a taunt that another Herod-like king was at hand. Both Pharisees and Sadducees wanted no part of a return to the sort of situation they endured under Herod and his son Archelaus. So they affirmed again that "if he let Jesus go, he was no friend of Caesar," and that they had "no king but Caesar" (19:12-15). Pilate finally gave way to their demands when his loyalty to Caesar was questioned. The chief priests clearly revealed their political inclinations when they affirmed, "We have no king but Caesar." "The Jews" would push Pilate on some issues such as their loyalty to Caesar, but on other issues, such as the inscription (19:21-22), would yield when he stood firm.

The Pharisees

There are eleven contexts in the Gospel of John in which are found references to "the Pharisees." In general, the Pharisees were regarded by the

---

[11]The associations around the fire in the courtyard of the priest (18:18) revealed a certain comraderie between the officers of the Jews and the servants of the high priest as well.

author of the gospel as a part of the Jewish authority establishment. The basis of their authority in the public mind was the general perception that they were expert in matters of the law of Moses. In addition to the references cited already, the following are significant.

Mutual accusation was the response of the Pharisees to the triumphal entry (12:19). When the resurrection of Lazarus turned the sentiments of the general public in favor of Jesus, the Pharisees became impatient with each other over their inability to persuade the public that Jesus was another imposter. The problem was rapidly becoming larger than that. Many authorities believed also (12:42-43) but would not confess it for fear the Pharisees would put them out of the synagogue. There are no significant differences between the ways "the Jews" and the ways the Pharisees approached their relationships.

The woman taken in the act of adultery (8:3-11) was brought to Jesus by Pharisees and scribes. Their purpose was to *test* Jesus and to *find cause* for legal action against him. They apparently expected him to contradict the law of Moses. When they could not reply to the conditions which Jesus articulated for executing the woman, they left not as a group, but one by one. They apparently could not openly acknowledge when they had suffered a moral defeat.

The Sadducees

While there are no references to the Sadducees in the Gospel of John, there are some references to the High Priestly family who were known to be Sadducees.[12] They were apparently a relatively small group composed primarily of wealthy aristocrats from Jerusalem.

The High Priest had several who attended him as slaves or servants (18:10,26) which indicates something of his status in the community. Caiaphas, the son-in-law of Annas, had been appointed High Priest about A.D. 18.[13] His cynical comment " . . . it is expedient for you that one man should die for the people, and that the whole nation should not perish" was interpreted by the author of the gospel as a prophecy of the death of Jesus (11:49-52). Personal knowledge of the High Priest provided entry into his courtyard for "a certain disciple" and Peter (18:15-18). If that "certain disciple" was the author of the gospel, then it is possible that there was not just acquaintance but also some feelings of mutual respect between the author and Caiaphas.

After his arrest, Jesus was first interrogated by Annas, father-in-law of Caiaphas (18:19). Annas was the patriarch of the high priestly family and apparently quite influential in political affairs. He had been appointed high priest in A.D. 6 and deposed in A.D. 15 by the Romans for unknown reasons.

---

[12]Joachim Jeremias, *Jerusalem in the time of Jesus*. (Philadelphia: Fortress Press, 1969), pp. 229-232.
[13]D.R. Hall, "Caiaphas," in *New Bible Dictionary*, [eds. J.D. Douglas, F.F. Bruce, J.I. Packer, R.V.G. Tasker, and D.J. Wiseman] (Grand Rapids: Eerdmans, 1962), p. 175.

In the Jewish mind, a high priest held office for life.[14] The author's only comment about Annas is that he questioned Jesus about his disciples and his teaching and that he sent Jesus in bonds to Caiaphas.

Observations. The behaviors of the Jewish and Roman authorities reveal a heavy emphasis on control strategies. These began with benign approaches in the early chapters such as "faint praise," appeals to custom, needs for secrecy, calling for answers to questions presented by a delegation, pretences of reasonableness, statements about lawful action, questions about loyalty, and challenges to personal and vested authority. As the situation became more difficult, the authorities resorted to greater use of pressure and force. These included persecution, loss of social privileges such as access to the synagogue, the issue of orders and warrants, physical force and abuse, destruction of evidence, use of police and military, compromise of due process, conspiracy, and finally execution.

The relationship between the Roman Governor Pilate and the Jewish authorities[15] was delicately balanced if not finely tuned. They were like adversaries who needed each other. There appears to have been a mutual paranoia existing between them. On the one hand, the Romans were officially disliked because of the loss of national autonomy which their presence implied. On the other hand, appeals of loyalty to Caesar could be used as their pretext for wanting Jesus (supposedly a pretender to the throne of David) executed at the hand of the Roman governor in order to maintain control. Another example of the old cliche, "politics makes strange bedfellows."

Similarly, the threat of Roman intervention was used as a reason for suppressing the evidence concerning the resurrection of Lazarus and what that implied about their doctrine of no resurrection. The Gospel of John presents the Jewish authorities as primarily interested in the maintenance of control and as willing to use whatever strategies of rationalization, intimidation, manipulation, suppression, coersion, or force necessary to keep it. The alliance between the Saducees and the Romans made the latter's control of the high priesthood possible.

While these men generally thought of themselves as loyal and true believers, relations among them were often characterized by rivalry, suspicion, characterization, accusation, recrimination, and collusion. Those outside their circles who had to relate to them experienced interrogation, aloofness, pressure to conform, fear, condescension, inconsistency, closedmindedness, intimidation, ruthlessness, callousness, rejection and ostracism. Expediency and efficiency tended to be the dominating principles in these sectarian groups when control was at issue. Parenthetically, it may be noted that similar strategies often characterize sectarian groups arising since that time.

---

[14]D.R. Hall, "Annas," in *New Bible Dictionary*, [eds. J.D. Douglas, F.F. Bruce, J.I. Packer, R.V.G. Tasker, and D.J. Wiseman] (Grand Rapids: Eerdmans, 1962), p. 39.

[15]Comprised of the High Priest, the Council and the leading Pharisees — there is no reference to either Herod the Great or Herod Antipas, tetrarch of Galilee and Perea in the gospel.

Responses of Jesus to the Authorities

John portrays the responses of Jesus to the authorities, Jewish and Roman, as *restrained* and *limited*. His sign for his authority to cleanse the temple (2:19) was a simple affirmation: "destroy this temple and in three days I will raise it up." John indicated that the major thrust of this response was toward the disciples, not the Jews.

When questioned by Nicodemus, Jesus assumed the role of *authoritative teacher*. He spoke of the nature which those in the Kingdom were to take. When Nicodemus revealed that he did not understand, Jesus chided him for being a teacher and not understanding and for being a part of a group that would not receive "our testimony" (3:11). Jesus communicated no special respect for Nicodemus as a ruler or religious authority nor did he attempt to "charm" him into becoming a disciple. The fact that Nicodemus turned out to be a "political moderate/personal sympathizer" did not win for him special treatment by Jesus.

In the face of persecution and threats on his life, Jesus continued to teach and to affirm his identity as the Son and God's identity as His Father (5:15-47). At times his teachings contained elements of *judgment* and *accusation* (5:44). At other times they were enigmatic (6:41-58), which made for difficulty in understanding on the part of those who tended to think concretely (see also 7:32-36).

When the motives of the authorities were to test Jesus and to induce him to incriminate himself Jesus tended to *reaffirm* the Law of Moses, and particularly the intent and spirit of the Law. To the accusers of the adulterous woman, Jesus *encouraged introspection* concurrent with giving permission to execute judgment. His response was to encourage them to do what they proposed to do, if they could say that they were guiltless. Of course, his implication was that they did not have a right to be so judgmental.

When the authorities challenged him to declare, on demand, that he was the Messiah, his response was to turn the tables and *focus on their reluctance to believe*, either his word or his works (10:22-38). Jesus felt they had no right to judge him and acted accordingly. While he did not hide from the Jewish authorities, he tended to appear in Jerusalem only when their efforts to apprehend him were not likely to succeed, when the city was full of people (until his time came).

When Judas, the soldiers, and officers went looking for Jesus in the garden, Jesus *responded with directness*. He identified himself to them as the person for whom they were looking. He also indicated that since it was himself they were seeking, his disciples should not be detained. When questioned by Annas about his disciples and his teaching, he affirmed that he had always acted publicly and that any of his disciples could be asked about his teaching. The thrust of this response was to affirm that his was no secret movement or threat. When struck by an officer, he challenged him to identify what he had said that was wrong. Jesus retained his sense of personal authority in the presence of both political and religious authorities. Such personal authority is not derived from the attributions of others. Rather it stems from a strong sense of personal identity and a strong conviction concerning the truths to which one is committed.

Jesus did not act "impressed" with civil or political authorities. He acted as one who had a right to teach anyone, if that person was willing to learn. In this sense Jesus could be quite intimidating. When questioned by Pilate, Jesus first questioned why Pilate was asking him if he was the King of the Jews. He wanted to know if Pilate had been incited to ask the question. When Jesus was satisfied that Pilate was acting on his own, he affirmed his Kingship (18:33-38), but as not political (of this world). When Pilate affirmed his power over him, Jesus noted that Pilate only had what power had been given to him from above (19:10-22). For Pilate, this may have been a reminder of the tenuousness of his position.

Relationships Between Jesus and His Disciples

Public interactions between adults of the opposite sex had become very formal by the time of Christ. In the period of the patriarchs the cultural rules dictated that women think of themselves as the property of their fathers and husbands. That was a patriarchal society. The law of Moses institutionalized many of those customs, but in addition provided measures of justice. A father could not make his daughter a prostitute and sexual relations between next of kin were prohibited (Lev. 18:6-23,29). A husband could no longer divorce his wife without cause and giving a certificate of divorce (Deut. 24:1-4). These provisions had, over time, tempered the ideas of paternity and absolute rights of fathers and husbands over their possession, although the issues were not finally settled in Jewish minds.[16]

In general, the Old Testament view of women was positive. In the pre-kingdom era a woman (Deborah) emerged as a judge (Judges 4-5). The wisdom literature presents a portrait of a woman who is not only of excellent virtue but with a strong public profile as well (Prov. 31:10f.). The writings of the exilic period portray Esther as a woman of intelligence, influence, authority, and courage even though she had grown up in captivity and was living in Persia (Esther 2-9).

If one takes into consideration the cultural tendencies of the middle east, it is possible to see in the Old Testament a view of women that places them alongside their mates as persons of honor and respect (cf. Gen. 2:18f.).

By the time of the New Testament this had changed somewhat. The honor with which women were treated in the Old Testament had given place to a popularly expressed view that women were suspected of being, by nature, evil.

The intelligence of women was called into question. Their participation in public worship was sharply limited. Their moral qualities were in doubt.

---

[16]An illustration of this principle is readily apparent in the controversy current in the time of Christ over the matter of divorce. See: Jeremias, op cit, p. 370f.

This view, which appears to have originated with the Greek philosophers,[17] was picked up by the Rabbis and readily incorporated into the official teachings of the day. For example, "Rabbi Eliezer says, If any man gives his daughter a knowledge of the Law it is as though he teaches her lechery."[18] The result was an official contempt for women. Public communications between men and women were to be avoided.[19] The disciples were apparently accustomed to this.

Relations Between Jesus and Women

The Gospel of John describes Jesus taking a remarkably different approach to his relations with women. While, on first glance, his verbal response to his mother at the marriage feast in Cana appears to question her propriety (2:4), she knew that he would do something to help. His actions justified her expectation that led her to instruct the servants to do as he said (4:5-10). The quality of the relationship and the interest of Jesus in his mother is most vividly demonstrated in his instruction to her and the beloved disciple while he was on the cross (19:25-27). It was a relationship of mutual respect, concern, and willingness to help.

When Jesus was talking with the woman at Jacob's well near Sychar in Samaria, (4:7-26) both the woman (4:6) and the disciples marvelled (4:27). Jesus not only engaged the woman in casual conversation, but in rather personal dialogue and teaching as well. His disclosures about her personal life, instead of resulting in complete humiliation, eventuated in her exuberant return to the city inviting the residents to "come see a man who told me all that I ever did" (4:29).

The response of Jesus to the woman taken in the act of adultery was at once judicious ("Let him who is without sin among you be the first to throw a stone at her." 8:7), and forgiving ("Has no one condemned you? . . . Neither do I condemn you; go, and do not sin again." 8:10-11).

The responses of Jesus to Mary and Martha, the sisters of Lazarus, were compassionate and defensive of their good intentions. He met their grief with both reassurance and sympathy (11:23-35). When Judas criticized Mary's anointment of the feet of Jesus with pure nard and the wiping of his feet with her hair Jesus rebuked Judas and instructed him to "Let her alone . . . " (12:3-8).

---

[17]See Plato, *Timaeus* 91A, [trans. R.G. Bury] (Cambridge: Harvard University Press, 1954) for example. "According to the most probable report, women are reincarnated men who were evil and cowardly during their first life on earth." Or Aristotle, *Politics* I, 2:12 [trans. H. Rackam] (Cambridge: Harvard University Press, 1954). "The male is by nature superior and the female inferior." These views originated by at least the fifth century B.C. among the Greeks.

[18]*Mishnah, Sotah*, 3:4 as cited in Jeremias, ibid., p. 373.

[19]Jeremias, ibid., p. 360.

Against the Jewish background of contempt for women in general, the relationship between Jesus and Mary Magdalene is remarkable.[20] She was present at his crucifixion (19:25) and at his tomb early on the first day of the week. When she was distressed at the absence of his body, she first notified Peter and "the other disciple." When he called her by name and identified himself to her, she grabbed him and held on. His gentle admonition, "Stop holding me, for I have not yet ascended to the Father . . . " appears to have had an element of amusement coupled with reassurance. His mission for her made her the first visual witness to the disciples of his resurrection.

Surely the impact of these narratives (as well as those in the Gospel of Luke especially) on the women and men of the early church would have been highly instructive. The regard in which Jesus held women was clearly different from the cultural norms of his day. Women were attracted to him and helped by him in a most refreshing way. Dorothy Sayers expressed it concisely.

> A prophet and teacher who never nagged at them, never flattered or coaxed or patronized; who never made arch jokes about them . . . who rebuked without querulousness and praised without condescension; who took their questions and arguments seriously; who never mapped out their sphere for them, never urged them to be feminine or jeered at them for being female, who had no axe to grind and no uneasy male dignity to defend, who took them as he found them and was completely unselfconscious.[21]

Relationships with Individuals

The Gospel of John provides sketches of relationship, which existed between Jesus and a number of individuals. In the context of John's gospel these serve to assert the reality of his humanity, uphold his divinity, and provide a normative example for the gospel's readers. Consider three examples.

Jesus and Peter. The information provided in the gospel about this relationship is brief and descriptive. Upon meeting Simon, Jesus named him Cephas (Peter), meaning "rock" (1:42). When many of the disciples were turning away from the company of Jesus and the apostles, Peter is credited with affirming loyalty to Jesus; "Lord to whom shall we go? You have the words of eternal life; and we have believed, and have come to know, that you are the Holy One of God," (6:68-69).

Chapter 13 describes three interactions between Jesus and Peter. In the first (13:5-11) Jesus washed the feet of the disciples. Peter initially protested

---

[20] According to Luke 8:1-3 she was one from whom he had cast seven evil spirits and who accompanied him and the disciples and helped with their financial support.

[21] Dorothy Sayers, *Are Women Human*, p. 47, as quoted in P.K. Jewett, *Man as Male and Female* (Grand Rapids: Eerdmans, 1975), p. 103.

and then profusely submitted. In the second (13:24) Peter uses and intermediary to get Jesus to reveal the information he wants. In the third (13:36-38) Peter affirms his loyalty and willingness to follow Jesus unto death if needed, only to have Jesus predict his denial before the coming day breaks.

Chapter 18 describes two interactions between Jesus and Peter. In the first (18:10-11) Peter attempts to resist the arrest of Jesus with a blow to the ear of Malchus, a servant of the High Priest, only to have Jesus instruct him to put his sword away. In the second (18:15-27) Peter followed Jesus with "another disciple" to the house of the High Priest where he waited at the gate until the other disciple arranged for Peter to enter. It was at this point that Peter's denials of knowing Jesus began. As he joined the company of officers and soldiers by a fire, his denial continued.

Chapter 20 describes the reaction of Peter to the report of the resurrection of Jesus, but records no interactions between them. Chapter 21 provides a detailed account of the revelation of Jesus to the disciples by the Sea of Tiberias. At daybreak, Jesus called to them about their catch and instructed them to let their nets down on the other side of the boat. When the report was made that it was the Lord, Peter put on his clothes and jumped into the water (probably to swim to shore where Jesus was) while the others came in the boat dragging the fish. When the Lord instructed them to bring some of their fish, Peter is the one who complied, hauling in the nets and counting the fish.

After breakfast, Jesus began asking Peter about his love for the Lord. The question was repeated three times with the author using different terms to describe Jesus' questions and Peter's affirmation of his love. After each of Peter's affirmations of filial love, Jesus instructed him to first "feed my lambs," second, "tend my sheep," and third, "feed my sheep." Then Jesus began to tell Peter about events that would happen in his later years, specifically how he would die. Peter's reaction was to question the Lord about what would befall "the disciple Jesus loved." The Lord's response was authoritative; "If it is my will that he remain until I come, what is that to you? Follow me."

The relationship between Jesus and Peter was characterized by *closeness, personal intensity, the intimacy that comes from self-disclosure, yet marked by very clear boundaries.* Jesus commenced his relationship with Peter by giving him an identity, a name meaning "rock." When Peter attempted to play the hero as Jesus was washing the feet of the disciples, Jesus calmly insisted on compliance as a condition of discipleship and in order to teach the lesson of servanthood. Jesus never abandoned the role of authoritative teacher and Lord in relation to Peter. His will for Peter and his other disciples did not change because of personal feelings or affinities which they tried to develop with Him. Jesus responded to Peter's flattery and affirmations of loyalty by predicting future difficulties for him, to Peter's excesses with calls for simple compliance, to Peter's curiosity with clues he would understand later, to Peter's militarism with an admonition and a rhetorical question, to Peter's denials with a glance (Luke 22:60), to Peter's affirmations of love with questioning of its purity and an instruction to tend to others, and to Peter's concern about fair-play with a reminder that his will and purpose for each disciple is individually tailored, absolute, and not open to question.

While their relationship was close, caring and intimate, there was no inappropriate familiarity. Jesus responded to the personal concerns of Peter for his mother-in-law (cf. Luke 4:38) but He did not allow Peter to dictate his course where his purpose in life was at issue (cf. John 11:7f.). Jesus maintained his autonomy and identity as teacher and Lord.

Jesus and the beloved disciple. There are five references to "the disciple Jesus loved" in the gospel. They appear in the contexts of the last supper (13:23), the crucifixion (19:26), the report of the empty tomb (20:2-10), the fishing trip with Peter (21:7), and the interrogation of Peter by Jesus (21:20). The last reference is followed by a reference to the author (a witness to the events recorded in the gospel — 21:25).

The author's editorial activity in preparing and interpreting the narratives of the gospel is very easy to observe. He inserts numerous definitions, parenthetical and other explanatory statements.[22] In several instances these statements reveal penetrating insight into the mind of Jesus. In 2:24 he reported that Jesus did not trust himself to the people at the Passover feast in Jerusalem who believed in him. In 4:1 is a reference to the Lord's motive for leaving Judea — his knowledge that the Pharisees had heard that Jesus was making and baptizing more disciples than John. 4:6 includes the explanatory phrase "and so Jesus, wearied as he was with his journey . . . " 6:64 stated that Jesus knew from the first who those were that did not believe, and who it was that would betray him.

There are many such statements, some of which are after the fact interpretations, and some of which indicate a relationship of unusual closeness between Jesus and the author of the gospel, and an awareness of the Lord's thoughts and feelings. It was not an exclusive sort of love, as the author points to the love of Jesus for Mary, Martha and Lazarus (11:5). But it was a relationship that allowed the author to see clearly the emotional facet of the Lord's personality (cf. 11:35, 11:38, 12:27, 13:21, 14:9). It was also a relationship that moved the author to record very significant blocks of the Lord's sayings, most of which are not found in the other gospels. No insight is provided, however, into how the relationship may have differed from that between the Lord and other disciples. The author cites no special prerogatives that were his, nor special experiences that were not shared with the other disciples. Taking the Lord's mother into his home may have provided opportunities for developing insight into the mind of the Lord in retrospect. If there was a purpose for that special love, it appears to have only been to further the process of revelation.

Jesus and his family. In general, the gospels provide very limited insight into the relationship between Jesus and his family. Whereas the synoptic nar-

---

[22]See for examples 1:38 "Rabbi" (which means teacher); 1:42 " . . . Cephas" (which means Peter); 1:43 "Now Philip was from Bethsaida, the city of Andrew and Peter;" 2:21 "But he spoke of the temple of his body."

ratives make only one reference to the presence of his family during his ministry (Matthew 12:46-49 and parallels), John mentions her as present at the marriage feast in Cana, in his company as he went to Capernaum (2:3-12), and as present at the crucifixion 19:25-27). 7:2-10 makes a reference to his brothers who are described as unbelieving and critical.

The relationship between Jesus and his younger brothers is a curiosity. We may detect a note of cynicism in their "encouragement." The author did not have a very high view of them. Jesus indicated that the world would not find much in them that it could hate like it did in himself. He apparently felt compelled to hide his intentions and plans from them for fear that their knowledge of his presence in Jerusalem could be precipitous of his falling into the hands of the Jews.

Three observations about these relationships can be made. There was a popular public identification of Jesus as "the son of Joseph, whose mother and father we know" (6:42). But for the author of the gospel, this was secondary to his identity as the one who had come down from the Father (same context). Secondly, the relationship between Jesus and his mother appears to have been characterized by mutual respect and caring, but his concern for his mother did not take precedence over his concern for others or for the fulfillment of his mission. Thirdly, the failure of the brothers of Jesus to believe during his ministry brought no special efforts on the part of Jesus to persuade them. His words to them were designed to show the difference between their understanding and His own.

Jesus' Teachings About Relationships in the Gospel

The example of Jesus as he approached relationships was accompanied by teachings which were included in the gospel. 13:3-17 is the account of the washing of the feet of the disciples. When Peter protested, "You shall never wash my feet" the response of Jesus was "If I do not wash you you have no part in me." This represents one of the few times when Jesus imposed a condition on the disciples for the continuance of the relationship. Interestingly the condition called for submission to the Lord as he assumed the role of a servant. Then he noted that they rightly called him teacher and Lord. If the Lord had set the example of being a servant he had the right to call on them to assume the same role in relationship to each other.[23] Service was to become the hallmark of the disciples.

Jesus taught the disciples to love (agapate) each other (13:34, 15:12,17) using his own love for them as the model. It was given as an unconditional

---

[23]Cf. Luke 22:24 which indicates that in this context there was a dispute over who would be the greatest. Jesus indicated that such concerns were characteristic of relationships among Gentile authorities, but were not to be so among his disciples. The greatest should be as the younger and leaders should be as those who serve.

command. His love had resulted in two outcomes: one, they had become his friends (philoi) instead of his servants, which meant that they had come to understand his own mind and all that the Father had revealed to him, and two, he had chosen and appointed them to "bear fruit" that would abide, which meant that their service in his name would be significant and effective. That sort of love can be commanded and developed as a choice of the will. It means that disciples are to will the good of their brothers and sisters. Commonality of wills, surrendered to the will of God, creates the commonality of friendship, first with Christ and then with brethren. If the command to love was obeyed, the outcome would be the recognition by all men that they were his disciples (13:35).

Jesus called for unity in the relationships of the disciples. It was to derive from their relationship to Jesus and the Father (17:20-26). In this context, "to know" Jesus is equivalent to being "in Jesus" and is on the same order as being "one" as Jesus and the Father are one. 17:3 indicates that eternal life consists in knowing the Father and the Son. There are major implications for personal relationships in these ideas. Eternal life is not to be considered as mainly consisting of existence in a certain sphere or situation, but in relationship to the Father and Son. To the extent that a relationship of knowledge of God based on the revelation of Christ occurs, eternal life becomes a present reality. The proof of their unity was to be the recognition of the world that the Father's love for the disciples is the same as his love for the Son.

The final encounter between Peter and Jesus which the gospel describes is also instructive for personal relationships. As Jesus revealed what he could expect in old age, Peter attempted to shift the focus to the beloved disciple (probably to determine if they were to share a similar fate). Jesus informed Peter that his will for him was specific and not to be judged by criteria such as human fairness. In the fellowship of the disciples the gifts and the call of God were not to be compared or challenged.[24]

Conclusion

The study of interpersonal relationships in the gospel is a study in contrasts of style and tactics. On the one hand, the approaches and strategies of the Jews were oriented toward the maintenance of social control. On the other hand, the approach of Jesus was marked by self-disclosure, teaching, concern for the welfare of people, directness and a strong sense of personal authority. Whereas the Jews had developed traditions that defined social roles and public behavior, Jesus set a new standard by publicly honoring people of both sexes from different backgrounds, by demonstrating an example of leadership by service, and by commanding his disciples to love people as he had loved them. In this gospel the contrast between the typical quality of human relationships in sectarian bodies and the standards set by Jesus for his followers can be seen quite clearly.

---

[24] cf. Romans 12:29.

Missions and the Servants of God (John 5)

Evertt W. Huffard*

Pluralism and The Gospel of John

In December of 1938, the International Missionary Council (IMC) met in Tambaram, a few miles from Midras, India. In preparation for the conference, the IMC had invited Dr. Hendrik Kraemer to write a book. His book, *The Christian Message in a Non-Christian World*, immediately received international attention and became the catalyst for the papers that were presented at the conference. Two particular concerns of Kraemer, who began the conference with a summary of his thesis, involved the historical nature of Christianity in contrast to other religions and the extend to which God might be at work in the lives of non-Christians.

One respondent, Dr. Karl Reichelt, director of a Christian monastery for Buddhists at Tao Fong Shan (Hong Kong), gave such a forceful presentation from the floor that his discussion was drafted into a paper and included in the conference proceedings. He believed that

> the all-embracing activity of Jesus Christ, as well before as after his incarnation, found in the Gospel of St. John, is of the greatest importance with regard to world mission work. . . . I am convinced that a new understanding and a wise application of the missionary thoughts emphasized by the Gospel of St. John also in our times would inaugurate a new and successful epoch, especially in the old culture lands of Asia.[1]

In contemporary missiological jargon, he believed the Gospel of John would be the best source for a contextualized message and development of an ethnictheology within the religious context of China. By applying John's use of the *logos* in the prologue to explain the uniqueness of Christ, he communi-

---

*I first met Frank and Della Pack in 1965 on the street that leads up to the Garden Tomb in Jerusalem. My parents were missionaries in Jerusalem and my mother recognized the Packs as they were walking along the street (she had been a student of Dr. Pack at Pepperdine). Dr. Pack's love for travel has been enriched by an appreciation and love of missionaries. Any tribute to Dr. Pack would be incomplete without some reference to the mission of the church.

[1] Karl Ludvig Reichelt, "The Johannine Approach," in *The Authority of Faith*, Vol. I (New York: International Missionary Council, 1939) 93.

cated the gospel in terms of the Buddhist Tao and attributed anything that is true and good in all nations to Christ as the source. The Buddhists who actually responded to his message called themselves the "friends of the Tao (Logos)." For, according to Reichelt, "Christ is for them the full realization and incarnation of the wonderfully rich Tao-idea, which holds the supreme sway in all the three religions in China (Buddhist included)."[2]

Drawing from twenty years of experience, Reichelt identified four ways in which the Gospel of John served a missiological function for Buddhists: (1) as searchers for the truth and religious experience, it gave them the solution; (2) their difficulty accepting one, personal God was eased by the implications that God created the world through the Logos; (3) the all-embracing paraclete provided a key to understanding the Trinity; and

> (4) The Johannine statement about the new birth, which conditions the entrance into the kingdom of God, gives also a wondrous thrill to many of the pilgrims, who through years of meditation in lonely cells and strenuous pilgrimages to the holy mountains and the great masters have been searching in vain to get that unspeakable experience of "breaking through" for which they are dreaming and longing.[3]

The proceedings of the conference did not include responses to Reichelt, but I would guess that Kraemer and others would have suspected Reichelt of going a little too far. His shift from a soteriological to a christological basis for the Christian message and his bold efforts to contextualize form and meaning could justifiably raise suspicions of potential syncretism.

In August of 1980, Eric Sharpe, an English scholar from Uppsala, gave a lecture at Tao Fong Shan evaluating Reichelt's understanding of the Gospel of John and his methodology.[4] He raised serious questions in both areas and suggested that one needs to begin reading John in its original context before reading it as a Buddhist. If that were done, a Buddhist would more likely reject the gospel as "not addressed to his situation, to the Buddhist tradition, or to any of the infinitely complex ways in which the Buddhist traditions have analyzed the human condition."[5]

Furthermore, he did not believe the gospel could so easily bridge the gulf between two very different worldviews of reality and raised objections to this early example of the "anonymous Christian" perspective.[6] Sharpe argued for

---

[2]Reichelt, 91.
[3]Reichelt, 92.
[4]Eric J. Sharpe, "The 'Johannine Approach' to the Question of Religious Plurality," *Ching Feng* 23 (1980): 117-127.
[5]Sharpe, 123.
[6]Reichelt's "Johannine Approach" is parallel to more recent discussions regarding "anonymous Christians" and Sharpe raises objections to the following assumptions of that position: it assumes every religion has divine revelation and should be left alone to give its "transcendental message" to the world; it assumes Christianity is irrelevant and adherency is maintained more out of loyalty to a heritage than deep personal conviction; and it assumes the mission of the church, if it has one, "may then

the creation of greater tension between the *logos* and the Buddhist worldview. For, he observed, that John

> affirmed equally strongly that faced with the choice between the light of the Logos and the darkness of self-will, human beings have habitually chosen darkness rather than light — a fatal choice which does much to nullify whatever of the light may remain in them . . . between the revelation and the religions of the world there falls the shadow: the Way which is not followed, the Truth which men make into a lie, the Light which is terribly transmuted into darkness."[7]

This example of the role of the Gospel of John in the history of Christian missions could be duplicated in countless other contexts. Historically, missionaries have assumed that the Gospel of John would be the best place in scripture to begin with Muslims. It records more of the words of Christ, making it more compatible to their view of revelation. However, in my experience with Muslims, I found the prologue to be too meaty for their monophysitic theology and 3:16 offensive to their cultural values. This, by no means, discounts of value of the gospel, it only suggests that we find appropriate starting points. The Buddhist and Muslim experiences may be cautions against using the Gospel of John as the initial "kerygma" with audiences that are significantly different from the original audience.

Further study of the issues of pluralism raised by these examples would presuppose a background in world religions, cultural anthropology, contextualization and theology of missions.[8] Since this may be beyond the interest of the reader, I will focus on a few missiological issues from the Gospel of John and, more specifically, the themes of servanthood, witnessing and sending in the fifth chapter.

An Evangelistic Mandate in John

Very few, if any, of the New Testament books were written specifically to non-Christians for the purpose of conversion. The writers of the New Testament fulfilled a prophetic role, calling the church to its divine mission.

---

consist in urging men and women to penetrate to the deepest levels of their own respective traditions, confident that if they look hard enough, there they will find the good, the true, the beautiful and the Real" (125-126). For further discussions of this issue in a missiological context cf., R.J. Schreiter, "The Anonymous Christian and Christology," *Missiology* 6 (1978): 29-52 and W.F. Danker, "The Anonymous Christian and Christology: A Response," *Missiology* 6 (1978) 235-241.

[7]Sharpe 126-7.

[8]For further study of contextualization consult: H.M. Conn, *Eternal Word and Changing Worlds* (Grand Rapids: Zondervan, 1984); B.C.E. Fleming, *Contextualization of Theology: An Evangelical Assessment* (Pasadena: William Carey Library, 1980); C.H. Kraft, *Christianity and Culture* (Maryknoll: Orbis, 1979); and R.J. Schreiter, *Constructing Local Theologies* (Maryknoll: Orbis, 1985).

John does not identify his audience. In fact, the author himself is not specifically identified. It is assumed that the most specific statement of purpose appears in 20:30-31.

> Now Jesus did many other signs in the presence of the disciples, which are not written in this book; but these are written that you may believe that Jesus is the Christ, the Son of God, and that believing you may have life in his name.

The majority of the discussion of the purpose of the book usually concentrates on this single verse. Some scholars assume the book was written to encourage Jewish believers with a christological problem. Advocates of this position would read the passage with an emphasis on the phrase "the Christ."[9] That is, the purpose was to strengthen those Jews who had responded to Christ but through continued tensions with Judaism began to question his identity. John persuades them to continue to accept Jesus as the Messiah and respond accordingly. In fact, this is the only book in the New Testament that uses the term *Messias*, the Hellenized transliteration for the Aramaic term for Messiah.[10] From this perspective, the gospel represents an apologetic or polemic against Jews to support the faith of believers more than an evangelistic tract to reach the unbelieving.

For example, chapter five could be read as a defense of the Christian understanding of the Sabbath and Jesus to a Jewish audience. Thus, Beasley-Murray considers it "a prime example of the missionary apologetic of Christians to Jews" with an appeal to reason.[11] There is further support for this thesis in the fact that Gentiles and unbelievers are not even identified in the book.[12]

This text could also be read with an emphasis on the phrase "that you may believe," giving it an evangelistic objective. Robinson and van Unnik argue that the main purpose of the book was to convert Diaspora Jews.[13] More

---

[9] R.E. Brown, *The Gospel According to John*, Vol. 1, (Garden City: Doubleday, 1966) lxxii.; R. Schnackenburg, *The Gospel According to St. John*, Vol. 2 (New York: Seabury, 1980) 126; G.E. Ladd, *A Theology of the New Testament* (Grand Rapids: Eerdmans, 1974) 237.

[10] But, in each occurrence he translates the term into the Greek *Christos* (Jn. 1:41; 4:25).

[11] G.R. Beasley-Murray, *World Biblical Commentary: John* (Waco: Word, 1987) 80. Also, some argue that this is not an apologetic to unbelievers, otherwise the pluralism of the context of the writing of the book would be more obvious, that is, more specific references to Palestinian Jews, anti-temple Jews, Samaritans, and Hellenistic Jews; cf., D. Senior and C. Stuhmueller, *The Biblical Foundations for Mission* (Maryknoll: Orbis, 1983) 293,281.

[12] Although there is a greater concern for the Samaritans in John than for Gentiles (e.g., Jn. 4). A convincing case is made for the indirect references to the nonbelievers, Gentiles and a more "universalist outlook" in the gospel by R.E. Brown, *The Community of the Beloved Disciple* (New York: Paulist Press, 1979) 55-88.

[13] J.A.T. Robinson, "The Destination and Purpose of St. John's Gospel," *New Testament Studies* 6 (1959-1960) 117-131; more specifically, John was "a mission book which sought to win" visitors of a synagogue in the Diaspora according to W.C. van Unnik, "The Purpose of St. John's Gospel," *Studia Evangelica* I (1959) 410. S.S.

recently, D.A. Carson revived the conclusions of Robinson and van Unnik. Adding a syntactical argument to the case, he identified the major question of John to be: "Who then is the Messiah?"[14]

A textual variant for the tense of the verb "to believe" creates some of the problem in clarifying the purpose. Although the reading is unverifiable due to the condition of the manuscript, Bodmer II (p66) seems to support the original hand of the Codex Sinaiticus as well as Codex Vaticanus in the use of the present subjunctive *pisteuēte*, which could mean "that you may continue to believe." However, the majority of the manuscripts, along with a correction in the Sinaiticus manuscript, use the aorist subjunctive, *pisteusēte*, meaning, "that you might believe."[15] There are instances where the present subjunctive and aorist subjunctive can occur for both conversion and maturation, meaning the purpose of the book should not be determined entirely by the tense of this verb.[16]

We may be tempted to hastily tilt the evidence towards an evangelistic objective because the book itself is known as a "Gospel." Some may also try to impose a rigid dichotomy between conversion and maturation by reading into the text artificial distinctions between the kerygma (gospel) and the didache (maturation). For example, Donald McGavran, in his first book, *Bridges of God*, made a much greater contrast between "discipling" and "perfecting" in Matthew 28:18-20 than is exegetically possible, since the verb "to disciple" is the primary verb in the passage.[17]

Smalley argues the need of a balanced christology as the purpose of the gospel but offers some useful information on the tradition of John as Evangelist and the kerygma in John, in *John: Evangelist and Interpreter* (Exeter: Paternoster Press, 1978) 148, 150-155.

[14]D.A. Carson, "The Purpose of the Fourth Gospel: John 20:31 Reconsidered," *Journal of Biblical Literature* 106 (1987) 642, 645.

[15]The same issue is raised in 19:35 where the manuscript evidence also seems to support the aorist subjunctive: "He who saw it has borne witness . . . that you also may believe," cf., Bruce M. Metzger, *A Textual Commentary on the Greek New Testament* (London: United Bible Society, 1971) 256. Ladd assumes John's main objective was to lead to a proper understanding of Christ because the present tense should imply existing faith that needs further confirmation while the aorist tense would suggest an evangelistic purpose, but D. Guthrie argues that "the work was designed as an evangelistic instrument" because textual support seems stronger for the present tense, in *New Testament Introduction* (Downer's Grove, Ill.; Inter-Varsity Press, 1965) 271. C.F.D. Moule believed John was extremely individualistic and answered the question "What must I do to be saved?" in *Birth of the New Testament* (San Francisco: Harper & Row, 1982) 136. A.C. Winn may be closer to the truth in his observation that the constant use of the second person plural and such metaphors as flock and vine reflect a non-individualistic worldview, in *A Sense of Mission* (Philadelphia: Westminster, 1981), 40-44; missiologists are also hasty to assume an evangelistic purpose, such as J. Verkuyl, *Contemporary Missiology: an Introduction* (Grand Rapids: Eerdmans, 1978) 111; who approaches all of John's writings with the assumption that the first goal was "to bring people to faith in Jesus Christ (20:31)."

[16]1:7; 4:48; 6:29; 11:15; cf., Carson, 640.

[17]D.A. McGavran, *Bridges of God*, (New York: Friendship Press, 1955) 13-16; cf., D.J. Bosch, "The Structure of Mission: An Exposition of Matthew 28:16-20," in

McGavran did not seek to rewrite the text as much as correct the assumption that a decision of faith or baptism was the end of the missionary task of the church. The planting and health of churches were of equal concern. It is also likely that the author of John had a more wholistic goal of producing "true disciples" (8:30-31) who were saved to serve and bear witness to the honor and glory of God. If so, the author may have had a missiological purpose of moving the Johannine community to action in a context of opposition to their christology, more than producing a gospel tract written to convert the Diaspora Jews or Gentiles. In this gospel, the evangelistic mandate under which the Son served the Father was clearly passed on to the disciples.

The Gospel of John begins with a boldly stated christology (1:1-51) followed by a discussion of six signs (or "works") that confirm the Messianic mission of Jesus (2:1-11:57), the preliminaries to the cross (12:1-17:26), the "glorification" (18:1-20:31), and a concluding postscript with the seventh sign and a dialogue with Peter on shepherding God's people (21:1-25).

In the first eleven chapters, John emphasizes the Messianic character of Jesus as King, Prophet, Servant and co-equal with God. The Servant of Yahweh, in the four "servant songs" of Isaiah, is identified as the one who has the support of Yahweh (42:1-4); is honored in the eyes of the Lord, although rejected by his own people (49:1-6); suffers innocently, but would be vindicated (50:4-9); and suffers on his way to glory (52:13-53:12).[18] These themes also appear in John, but parallels between John and Isaiah could not be pressed too far, with only four direct quotations of Isaiah in John (1:23; 6:10; 12:38,40).

Ward Andersen claims that four of the seven signs in John (5:1-9; 6:1-14; 9:1-7; 11:1-44) suggest the image of the Servant of God developed by the prophets, especially Isaiah.[19] Israel had been called to be a Servant of Yahweh to the nations. What began as a national mission decreased to a remnant and then to one man, Jesus Christ, the Son of God. John shows how Jesus fulfilled the eternal will or mission of God with the hope that their response

---

Exploring Church Growth, ed. W.R. Shenk (Grand Rapids; Eerdmans, 1983) 230-233. Due to inevitable overlap, S.S. Smalley cautions against attempts to find sharp distinctions between "preaching" and "teaching" material in the New Testament, p. 152.

[18]For a study of the relationship between the Servant of the Lord and the mission of the Messianic figure see J. Blauw, *The Missionary Nature of the Church* (New York: McGraw-Hill, 1962) 44-54, 149.

[19]W.W. Andersen. "Signs of Jesus' Messiahship: A Biblical-Theological Comparison of the OT Messianic Revelation With the Miracles of John 1-12" (Ph.D. diss., Bob Jones University, 1985) 179-226; for further associations between Isaiah and John see R.E. Brown, *The Gospel According to John*, vol. 1 (Garden City, New York: Doubleday, 1966), ix; D.R. Griffiths, "Deutro-Isaiah and the Fourth Gospel," *Expository Times* 65:355-360; and C.H. Dodd, *The Interpretation of the Fourth Gospel* (Cambridge: Cambridge University Press, 1958) 235ff.

to Christ will move them to become a growing number of witnesses sent from God to reveal his glory.[20]

Due to the missiological implications of the Servant motif, this paper will focus attention on the first of the signs of the Servant in John 5.[21] The chapter begins with the healing of a lame man, followed by a narrative on the honor of God, the resurrection of life, and the witnesses of God.

Let God Be God (5:1-21)

During an unidentified Jewish feast in Jerusalem, Jesus goes to the Pool of Bethesda, beside the Sheep Gate, on the north side of the temple platform. A number of invalids were always there waiting to be healed by mysterious forces that would occasionally move the waters of the pool.[22] Jesus approached a man who had been lame for thirty eight years and asked him if he wanted to be healed. The man did not answer the question, he stated his problem. However, without a statement of faith or identification of Jesus as the Messiah, Jesus simply commands this Jew, on the Sabbath, to "Rise, take up your pallet, and walk" (v. 8). John makes no reference to the reaction of the Jewish authorities to this sign, but gives considerable attention to their objection of this violation of the Sabbath law.[23]

Jesus took the initiative to heal the man and, later that day, to find him in the temple. But the recipient of God's grace proceeded to inform "the Jews"[24] that Jesus was the one who told him to carry his bed on the Sabbath. A monologue between Jesus and "the Jews" follows and further increases the

---

[20] R. Schnackenburg, in *The Gospel According to St. John* Vol. 1 (New York: Herder & Herder, 1968) 163, under the heading of "Church and Mission" concludes: "The Church can finally be recognized in its missionary charge (cf. 17:18; 20:21), especially with regard to non-Jews (cf. 10:16; 11:52; 12:20-24) and in its missionary practice (cf. 4:38), and there is no indication that the evangelist isolates himself and the group to which he belongs from the apostolic mission of the universal Church."

[21] R. Schnackenburg treats ch. 5 and 6 as self contained and considers the body of the gospel to begin with ch. 5, (1980), 1. This chapter may be an unlikely text for developing missiological themes, but beyond the reasons given here for beginning with it, I have had a special interest in further studies in chapters five and eight for contextualization in Muslim evangelism and for my ongoing interest in the themes of honor and glory.

[22] 5:4 is a gloss without support from the earliest and best texts, Metzger, 209, which suggests that an explanation for the gathering of the sick should be found in folk religious practice rather than some action by an angel of God. Jesus demonstrated that God works differently, not as some mysterious and fickle spirit.

[23] John gives an account of Jesus healing two men with long infirmities, one beside the pool on the north and another on the south side of the Temple. The healing of the blind man at the Pool of Siloam (9:1-14) was also on the Sabbath (also 7:22-23; Mt. 12:1-8) and increased the tensions with the temple authorities.

[24] John refers to "the Jews" 71 times and the Pharisees 19 times, but unlike the Synoptics never uses "doctors of the law," "scribes," "ancients," or "Herodians," cf., Schnackenburg, 1968:165. This is probably a reference to a specific group, such as the Pharisees, temple authorities, or those who sought to kill Jesus.

opposition to Jesus. He defends his actions by claiming "My Father is working still, and I am working" (5:17).[25] John explains to his readers that the Jews sought to kill Jesus because he presumed God was his Father, "making himself equal with God" (5:18).[26] Jesus supports this claim with some well known witnesses.

Jesus develops his defense around their understanding of the social relationship between father and son. Because Jesus publicly claimed sonship in this text (5:16-30), it is considered by some to be one of the most profound sections in the gospel.[27] Before probing into the nature of the father-son relationship, allow a brief digression into some possible application of theological themes in this pericope.

First, the gospel flows out of John's observation that Jesus reflected the glory of God, full of grace and truth (1:14). Fascinating examples of that glorious nature appear at every turn of the page. God's grace implies initiative, undeserved blessing. What better example can be given of this divine nature than healing a man without a request, with no commitment on his part, and eventual betrayal to the authorities? Jesus, as God's faithful servant, took the initiative. That is what he was sent to do.

Likewise, at the heart of the mission enterprise rests the willingness of God's people to take the initiative. As Jesus sought and healed the man in need without his request or preliminary obligation, so the task of the Lord's Body today, the church, is to seek opportunities for service and witness.[28] Likewise, in the world, God's servants take the initiative to immerse themselves into the life of a new community, to build relationships and serve people — because our Lord would have done the same.

Secondly, Jesus identifies God as the source of this healing power. Servants of God do not work alone. The faithful engagement in missions requires a partnership with God, who is always at work. He is not an esoteric thought or

---

[25]Contemporary missionaries have less problems with the issue raised by Kraemer in the Tambaram Conference regarding the activity of God. De Ridder, one of the few missiologists that works from a carefully developed Biblical theology of mission, relates this text to Gen. 1:1 and concludes: "One cannot interpret any history — whether of the world or of the church — unless one sees that God is not an absent deity who hides from humankind, but we can know him from what he has made (Rom 1:20). God's deeds, moreover, are not limited to the church but encompass the whole world. God is not only present everywhere, but active everywhere as well." R.R. De Ridder, "The Old Testament Roots of Mission," in *Exploring Church Growth*, ed. W.R. Shenk (Grand Rapids: Eerdmans, 1983) 173.

[26]Rabbinic tradition did not deny God's work on the Sabbath because rain, birth and death are in his power and can occur on the Sabbath, but it was anathema to claim privileges to something given only to God, according to Brown (1966), 217. God could elevate man to himself (Ps. 82:6; Ex. 7:1) but man could not elevate himself, thus Jesus rests his case on witnesses other than himself to confirm his identity and purpose, Beasley-Murray, 75.

[27]Schnackenburg, 1980: 99.

[28]If I could make a personal appeal at this point, I would call for churches to take the initiative to raise up men and women who will go rather than waiting around for some poor family who has been on the fund raising trail for months until a church finally, yet reluctantly, "gets involved" in a mission effort.

passive object of worship, but an active and dynamic partner in the process of reconciliation. In the Old Testament, God is described more by verbs than nouns. Likewise, in this chapter we see the evidence of a God who "works," "loves," "raises the dead," "gives life," and "judges." Thus, the Son does what he sees the Father doing. As God worked with Cornelius before Peter arrived and Lydia before she met Paul, so God works in the lives of the unchurched before the missionary arrives. It will therefore be important to understand the history of those who seek God to determine how God has worked in their lives. In so doing, we find a common point of reference and confirm that God starts with people where they are.

Finally, this text identifies a problem all the monotheists have to struggle with, namely, letting God be God. There is the temptation to confine God to one ethnic or cultural tradition: Hebrew for the Jews, Arabic for the Muslims and Western for Christians. When God is confined to one ethnic setting, the purpose of mission will shift from serving the nations (which requires a worldview broad enough to see humanity through the eyes of God) to preserving our own nation, cultural heritage and religious traditions. When we reach such a point, God's deeds must always be acceptable to our human reasoning and limitations. The binding of God to their culturally confining definition of the Sabbath law destroyed the mystery of the kingdom and blinded the patrons of the temple system to the Messiah. The same can happen with the church today when we fail to accept God as a partner and assume that the task of world evangelism cannot or should not be done because we cannot see beyond our own cultural walls. God's people must acknowledge that their Lord is always at work (Jn. 5:17) and allow for the fact that he may even have "other sheep" (Jn. 10:16) they do no know about. Our task is humble servanthood, modeled after the humble Servant who "can do nothing of his own accord" (Jn. 5:19).

Glorifying God: The Task of Servanthood (5:22-29)

Chapter five presupposes the Son's mission to the world with the expectation of the human response to the unique revelation of the Divine nature.

> The Father judges no one, but has given all judgment to the Son, that all may honor the Son, even as they honor the Father. He who does not honor the Son does not honor the Father who sent him. Truly, truly, I say to you, he who hears my word and believes him who sent me, has eternal life; he does not come into judgment, but has passed from death to life (5:22-24).

John uses two terms for honor in the book as he did for terms like "love" and "sending."[29] In the eastern worldview, the most fundamental value in

---

[29]For the use of *agapaō* and *phileō* in 5:19-20, Pack concludes that: "It is hard in John to distinguish the meaning of these two verbs. This is the only place where *phileō*

the father-son relationship is honor. The prophet Malachi compares the relationship between delinquent Israel and Yahweh to a father with a dishonorable son: "A son honors his father, and a servant his master. If then I am a father, where is my honor?" (Mal. 1:6). It should be no surprise that immediately after Jesus identifies himself as "the Son" for the first time in the Gospel of John (with the possible exception of 3:16) we find a discussion of honor, the "glue" that makes the vertical relationship between father and son functional.

This theme is developed through two common New Testament motifs, both of which are in this text, to describe the relationship between God and man: sonship and servanthood. The quality of both these relationships is directly proportional to the degree to which honor determines motives and behavior. The response of men in society to parents, kings and masters becomes the model for understanding man's relationship with God. The shameful, dishonorable man is the one who does not give *doxa* or *timē* to God.[30] It should be the natural reciprocal response to the one from whom protection and blessing come. Within this social structure, the eldest son has a special obligation to keep the family honor and he does so through a special relationship of unity with his father.

For the 20th century American, the father-son analogy fails to communicate all the nuances the Palestinian peasants or Judean villagers would have grasped. Kenneth Bailey describes the family obligations in his exposition of the parable of the eldest son as seen through the eyes of a Palestinian villager today.

> The older son reflects on the state of affairs and quickly decides not to enter the house. Custom requires his presence. At such a banquet the older son has a special semi-official responsibility. He is expected to move among the guests, offering compliments, making sure everyone has enough to eat, ordering the servants around and, in general, becoming a sort of major-domo of the feast. The custom is widespread all across the Arab world and on into Iran, where in the village the older son stands at the door barefoot to greet the guests. Part of meaning of the custom is the symbolic nature of the gesture, by which the father says,"My older son is your servant."[31]

Although it is too broad a jump from an Arab worldview today to the Galileans or Judeans in the first century, it is even further to the American

---

is used for the love between the Father and Son." Frank Pack, *The Gospel According to John*, Vol. I (Austin: Sweet Publishing, 1975) 88. He also draws the same conclusion in John 21:15-19 and discourages overemphasis on shades of meaning, op. cit., Vol. II, p. 170. For a discussion of *apostellein* and *pempein*, see below.

[30]These themes are also prominent in Paul's letters, such as; "for although they knew God they did not honor (*edoxasan*) him as God or give thanks to him, but they became futile in their thinking and their senseless minds were darkened. Claiming to be wise, they became fools, and exchanged the glory (*doxan*) of the immortal God for images resembling mortal man or birds or animals or reptiles," (Rom. 1:21-23).

[31]K. Bailey, *Poet and Peasant* (Grand Rapids: Eerdmans, 1976), 194.

worldview. We would do well to at least begin within a cultural context where the social structure more closely parallels that of the first century. The continual loss of vertical relationships in a Western society may leave the Bible reader at a loss in understanding the implications of this description Jesus gave of his relationship with God.

When Jesus declared that he was the Son of God (the one and only), the disciples and "the Jews" understood the type of relationship implied. He was not a second or competing god. Father and son are not in competition; the son serves the father. The honor of one is shared with the other. Jesus prayed that the disciples God had given him would see his *doxa* (Jn. 17:24). This honor Jesus would give his disciples was fellowship as sons of God (Jn. 17:22). The only occurrence in John of *timē* with God as the subject is in 12:26: "my father will *timē* the one who serves me."

In the context of chapter 5, Jesus was not setting forth a new principle of father-son relationships, as it may seem to a contemporary western reader, but rather was building on existing cultural values that understood the vertical relationship between father and son.

When accused of demon possession, Jesus responded, "I honor (*timē*) my Father and you dishonor me" (Jn. 8:49). He was not contrasting their ways of worship with his. He was contrasting lifestyles. One was blameless while the other brought shame. Jesus honored God because he kept his word. He concludes, "If I glorify (*doxa*) myself, my glory is nothing; it is my Father who glorifies me, of whom you say that he is your God" (Jn. 8:54). To translate *doxa* in this context as "glory" makes it too easy to shift the meaning away from sin and obedience to some eschatological hope.[32] It should be read as 5:23: "that all may honor (*timē*) the Son, even as they honor the Father."

Jesus was sent on a mission to bring glory and honor to the Father. His task was to do the will of the one who sent him (5:30) because the Jews had not honored God in fulfilling the purposes of their election. Therefore, the glory and honor of God becomes the source and the message of the gospel. The resurrection confirmed the "glorification" (7:39; 21:19) of Christ and became the event to which the disciples bore witness. The resurrection, the will of God, the mission of those he sends are all explained by Jesus as interrelated.

> For I have come down from heaven, not to do my own will, but the will of him who sent me; and this is the will of him who sent me, that I should lose nothing of all that he has given me, but raise it up at the last day. For this is the will of my Father, that every one who sees the Son and believes in him should have eternal life; and I will raise him up at the last day.[33]

---

[32] As argued by Ladd (p. 275) and J. Schneider, "*timē*," in *Theological Dictionary of the New Testament*, [ed. Gerhard Kittel, (trans. and ed. G.W. Bromiley)] (Grand Rapids: Eerdmans, 1972) 8:169-180.

[33] John 6:38-40.

Partnership in Missions (5:30-47)

"To witness" and "to send" are two specific themes in this section that relate to both the task and methodology of the Christian mission and are found throughout the gospel.

Witness and glory are the primary theological themes in this section. In making a defense of his mission to bring eternal life (5:24), Jesus called for a string of witnesses, as if he were in a court of law (resembling the scenes in Isaiah 43 where Yahweh called for witnesses of his love and care for an elect nation that became unfaithful).[34] Jesus did not seek glory for himself (like his opposition, 5:44), but called John the Baptist (5:33-36), the Father (5:36-38), the scriptures (5:39-40), and Moses (5:45-47) as evidence of his mission from God to fulfill his will. If calling God his Father was offensive to "the Jews," then the claim of the divine witness must have been an even greater offense. Jesus attempted to focus attention back to the real issue of his healing the lame man, the sign of God's sending, rather than their Sabbath issue. The climax of the witness is stated in 5:36:

> But the testimony which I have is greater than that of John; for the works which the Father has granted me to accomplish, these very works which I am doing, bear witness that the Father has sent me.

Throughout the gospels, the testimony of Jesus as sent from God motivates a reciprocal response in man of faith in God through Christ.[35] The phrase "him that sent me" or the one "who sent me" occurs so often in John that it becomes another reference to deity.[36] Throughout the gospel, God is identified as the one who sends.[37]

John uses two words for sending in such a way that it is difficult to be sure of the difference in meaning between *apostellein* and *pempein*. These two terms are used to express Jesus' awareness of his mission. Rengstorf argues that *apostellein* is used to denote the authority with which Jesus fulfills his mission and *pempein* to affirm the participation of God in the whole pro-

---

[34]Cf. Beasley-Murray, 77; also D.R. Griffiths, 360, for further similarities between these two accounts; Griffiths notes that in both John and Isaiah 40-66 there is a soteriological sense of Divine righteousness, the authors remain anonymous, there is a monologue by God/Christ, there is a polemical emphasis against unbelieving Jews (for idolatry in one case and against God's Son in the other), and in both "the awareness of a mission of universal scope is more forcibly expressed than in earlier literature with a clearer appreciation of its consummation through suffering (Isa. 42:1-4; 44:3,23; 49:6; 52:13-53:12; 54:5; 55:4-5; Jn. 12:20-36)."

[35]Mt. 10:40; Mk. 9:37; Lk. 9:48; 10:10; Jn. 5:24; 12:44; 13:20.

[36]R.R. De Ridder, *Discipling the Nations* (Grand Rapids: Baker, 1975) 149.

[37]4:34; 5:23-24,37; 6:38-39,44,57; 7:16,18,28-29; 8:16,18,26,29; 19:4; 11:42; 12:49; 13:20; 14:24; 15:21; 16:5; 17:8,21,23,25; cf. A.C. Winn, *A Sense of Mission* (Philadelphia: Westminster, 1981) as a useful source for expository sermons that develop the themes of Jesus, the church, the Christian, and the Holy Spirit as sent from God.

cess.³⁸ As with the other use of similar terms, it may be difficult to make clear distinctions. For example, *pempein* in 5:30,37 and *apostellein* in 5:33,36,38 are both translated "sent" in each instance. With either term, the message is that God initiated the whole process of redemption through Christ and expects mankind to honorably respond to his Son.

The missiological implications of the centrifugal nature of God and the task of human witness creates the standard for any fellowship of God's people who seek to do his will. As John Stott observed, a very precise statement of the mission of the church emerges from this gospel.

> The crucial form in which the Great Commission has been handed down to us (though it is the most neglected because it is the most costly) is the Johannine. Jesus had anticipated it in his prayer in the upper room when he said to the Father: "as thou didst send me into the world, so I have sent them into the world" (Jn. 17:18). Now, probably in the same upper room but after his death and resurrection, he turned his prayer-statement into a commission and said: "As the Father has sent me, even so I send you" (Jn. 20:21). In both of these sentences Jesus did more than draw a vague parallel between his mission and ours. Deliberately and precisely he made his mission the *model* of ours, saying "*as* the Father sent me, *so* I send you." Therefore our understanding of the church's mission must be deduced from our understanding of the Son's.³⁹

---

[38] K.H. Rengstorf, "apostolos," in *Theological Dictionary of the New Testament*, ed. Gerhard Kittel, trans. and ed. G.W. Bromiley, I:404 (Grand Rapids: Eerdmans, 1972).

[39] J.R.W. Stott, *Christian Mission in the Modern World* (Downers Grove: InterVarsity, 1975) 23.

The Semitic Background of the Gospel of John

Jack P. Lewis

Scholars have found the home of the Fourth Gospel in Palestinian Judaism, in Philonic Judaism, in Hellenistic Judaism, in the Hermetic literature, and in oriental Gnosticism. Under the impact of Nag Hammadi discoveries which increased knowledge of Gnosticism and of Qumran discoveries which revealed the diversity of first century Judaism, opinion again centers on a possible Palestinian background.

The purpose of this paper is to consider only one side of the complexity — that of the Semitic background — of the Johannine story set (as is true of the material of all the gospels) in Palestine. Jesus does not move out of the Holy Land, nor does he have direct contact with individual Gentiles. While Greeks come to him (12:20ff.), and people suppose that he might go to the Dispersion among the Greeks (7:35), he is recognized as a Jew by the Samaritan woman (4:8); and his work is among Jews.

The Readers

There is no dispute that the writer who wrote the Fourth Gospel wrote for a Greek audience on whose part he can assume a knowledge of the Old Testament. John 1:19-23 has references to priests, Levites, the Messiah, Elijah the prophet, and Isaiah — all from the Old Testament.

The writer gives explanations of customs which have been thought intended for the non-Jew, including allusion to the festivals to be discussed later. The life of the people is reflected in the marriage customs (2:1-11), in the friend of the bridegroom (3:29; cf. *M. Sanh.* 3:5),[1] in the six stone jars of water for purifying (2:6), in matters of ceremonial purification (3:25; 11:55; 18:28; 19:31), in events about the burial of Lazarus (11:17-44), and in the concern to avoid defilement which would disqualify one from eating the Passover (18:28,38). There are Jewish burial customs (19:40); however, the right of execution had been taken from them (19:31).

---

[1] Israel Abrahams, *Studies in Pharisaism and the Gospels*. 2nd series (Cambridge: University Press, 1924), p. 213.

John never refers to the Gentiles (*ta ethne*).² *Ethnos* to him means the Jewish nation (11:48-52; 18:35). His interest is in the way Jesus came to Israel.

Despite what should be deduced from the writer's use of the epithet "the Jews," there is a recognition of the Jews' special claim to be the people of God. Nathaniel, as a believer, is a true Israelite (1:47). The writer has Jesus coming to his own home and his own people (1:11). He has Jesus identify himself with the people of the Old Testament and to say, "We worship what we know, for salvation is from the Jews" (4:22). Those who have rejected the Messiah have alienated themselves from their birthright and stand outside the true Israel; those who believe in him and continue in his word are truly his disciples (8:31). Other sheep not of this fold will be brought, and there will be one flock (10:14-16). Jesus would die not for the nation only but to gather into one the children of God who are scattered abroad (11:51,52). Jesus spoke of his having taught the Jews (13:33; 18:20), and of his being handed over to them (18:36).

The writer used "the Jews" (sixty-nine times), often in a geographical sense of Judeans, those who live in Judaea (7:1; 9:7,8; 11:8; and perhaps others),³ which usage is paralleled in Josephus, *Ant.* 17:254ff.; *Life* 346; but there is a different connotation in 18:20 and 19:20,21. "The Jews" designates unbelievers who reject the gospel of Christ (sometimes the authorities and not the total community of Jews) in opposition to Jesus. They seem to reflect the attitude of Jerusalem (1:19), and they ask for a sign (2:18). The Jews oppose cures on the sabbath (5:10ff.). They oppose Jesus' calling God his father, making himself equal with God (5:18). They object to Jesus' teaching on the bread of life (6:41,52), silence the multitude in Jerusalem (7:11-13), insist that they are Abraham's children (8:31ff.), and would have stoned Jesus (8:59; 10:31) had he not avoided them. They are feared by believing Jews (7:13), by the parents of the healed blind man (9:22), by Joseph of Arimathea who remains a secret disciple (19:38), and by the disciples on resurrection day (20:19). In other passages they marvel (7:15), wonder about Jesus' statements (7:35; 8:22); have a divided opinion (10:19), ask for a clear declaration of Jesus' claim (10:24ff.), and would have stoned him (10:31). Many believe (2:23; 7:31; 8:30,31; 11:42,45; 12:10f., 42). The unbelieving group is identified with the world (*kosmos*); 15:18-25).

The Old Testament

Though quotations form only a small part of the use of the Old Testament in the Johannine writings, the eighteen formal quotations in the gospel have

---

²J.A.T. Robinson, "The Destination and Purpose of St. John's Gospel," *New Testament Studies* 6 (January 1960) 118.

³Malcolm Lows, "Who Were the IOUDAIOI?" *Novum Testamentum* 18 (April 1967) 101-30; Massey H. Shepherd, Jr., "The Jews in the Gospel of John, Another Level of Meaning," *Anglican Theological Review*, Sup. Ser. 3 (1974) 95-112.

a variety of introductions. The cry of the triumphal entry which comes from Psalm 118:26 has no introduction (John 12:13). A "fulfill" citation in John 18:9 used for a saying of Jesus comes from an unidentified source.

While C.C. Torrey claimed that all the quotations were from Hebrew and were all made from memory with customary freedom and arrangement,[4] according to Bernard,[5] the O.T. citations show a knowledge of Hebrew (1:23; 6:45; 12:15,40; 13:18) as well as of the Septuagint (2:17; 12:38; 17:17; 19:24); however some citations are indecisive on this issue (6:31; 7:42; 8:17; 10:34; 12:13,34; 15:25; 19:28,36).

Things done, like the cleansing of the temple (2:17), the hatred of the people (15:25), the loss of Judas (17:12), the division of the garments and the casting of lots for the robe (19:23f.), the expression of thirst (19:28), the limbs left unbroken (19:36), and the pierced side (19:37) are said to fulfill O.T. passages. These all form a basis of faith (19:35).

In addition to the specific quotations, the Fourth Gospel is replete with echoes of the O.T. The prologue opens with identical words to the Greek Genesis: "In the beginning" (*en arche*), and begins to speak of light and darkness (1:5) which were separated in the first chapter of Genesis. The vocabulary *arche* ("beginning"), *phos* ("light"), *zoe* ("life"), *skotos* ("darkness"), *sperma* ("seed"), and *kosmos* ("world") is found alike in Genesis 1:1-2:1 and the gospel. The link between Genesis and the Johannine material may be Psalm 33:6,9 which speaks of creation of the heavens by the word of God's mouth, and of his commanding and things coming to be. God is still working after the six days of creation (5:17).

The Scriptures are in preparation of the Messiah (5:39), and the three O.T. figures Abraham, Jacob and Moses are mentioned in connection with him. Abraham looked to Christ's day (8:56), Moses wrote of him (5:46), and a greater than Jacob opened a well (4:12ff.). The Lamb (*amnos*) of God who takes away the sin of the world (1:29,36) likely echoes Isaiah 53:7-12 (cf. I Pet. 2:21-25). The Messiah is the one of whom Moses and the prophets wrote (1:45).

Old Testament images represent the relation of Christ and his people. The Good Shepherd figure (10:1ff.) recalls several O.T. passages (Ps. 23:1ff.; Isa. 40:11; Jer. 23:1-4; Ezek. 34:1ff.; 37:24) as also does the vine and the branches (15:1ff.; cf. Ps. 80:8-13; Isa. 5:1-7; Jer. 2:21; Ezek. 15:1ff.; 19:10,14; Hos. 10:1). While the use of the O.T. in the Johannine corpus reflects Jewish exegetical tradition to the time of the writing, it has its own modifications of that tradition.

---

[4]C.C. Torrey, *The Four Gospels. A New Translation* (N.Y. and London: Harper and Brothers, 4th edition, 1933), p. 275.

[5]J.H. Bernard, *A Critical and Exegetical Commentary on the Gospel According to St. John*. The International Critical Commentary. 2 vols. (New York: Scribner's Sons, 1929), 1:lxxix; see also Leon Morris, *Studies in the Fourth Gospel* (Grand Rapids, Michigan: Eerdmans, 1969), p. 231; Edwin D. Freed, *Old Testament Quotations in the Gospel of John* (Leiden: Brill, 1965), p. 126.

The Spirit resting upon Jesus is an echo of Isaiah 11:2 where the Septuagint uses *anapausetai* ("will rest"), the verb John uses. The angels ascending and descending echo the Jacob's ladder episode (Gen. 28:12; John 1:51). The Passover is alluded to three times (John 2:13,23; 6:4; 11:55), and some scholars argue that the writer presents Jesus as the Passover lamb. Jesus claims superiority to the temple (2:19). The writer makes use of the serpent (3:14) and the manna in the desert (6:31) episode and Jacob's giving the well in Samaria (4:12). The law only judges a man after having him a hearing (7:51); the testimony of two witnesses is true (8:17; cf. Deut. 19:15). Circumcision from the patriarchs is given by Moses (7:22). The woman taken in adultery is to be stoned (8:1ff. [text problem]; cf. Lev. 20:10; Deut. 22:22). There is a two-fold resurrection — to life and to judgment (5:29; cf. Dan. 12:2). The symbols of lamb and light of the world go back to the O.T., but were there applied to Israel. The bringing of other sheep (the Gentiles) rests upon Isaiah 56:8.

Palestinian Geography

The Gospel of John reveals a considerable knowledge of Palestinian geography. References to Galilee are in 2:1-12; 4:3-54; 6:1-71; 7:1-9. In Galilee there is Bethsaida the city of Andrew, Peter (1:44) and Philip (12:21). Nazareth, the home of Jesus, is an insignificant place (1:46); Cana in Galilee (2:1,11; 4:46; 21:2) is not in any other earlier known writing; but from Cana Jesus goes "down" (2:12; 4:47,49,51) to Capernaum (6:17,24,59). Whichever of the two candidate sites one chooses for Cana, one drops from above sea level to more than six hundred feet below in the descent.

The Sea of Galilee is also called the Sea of Tiberias (6:1; 21:1), and on its shores is Tiberias (6:23). Storms come on the sea (6:18ff.), and three or four miles [twenty-five or thirty stadia] as a distance of rowing is given (6:19). From the sea, Jesus goes up into the hills (6:3).

Jesus goes "up" (*anabainein*) from Galilee to Jerusalem for the Passover (2:13,23); and in going from Jerusalem to Galilee passes through Samaria (4:4); and near there is Sychar, a town of Samaria, which is near the field that Jacob gave Joseph (4:5). Jacob's well which is deep (the deepest in Palestine) is there (4:6,11), and from the well fields ready for harvest (4:35) would be visible at the proper season. The mountain (Mt. Gerizim) is near (4:20).[6] Earlier John had baptized at Eanon near Salim where there was much water (3:23), a place now identified as being only across the mountain from Shechem.[7]

Near Jerusalem is the Kidron valley (*cheimarrous*; 18:1) and its garden. Also near is the Mount of Olives (8:1 [text problem]). The Praetorium into

---

[6]R.J. Bull, "An Archaeological Context for Understanding John 4:20," *Biblical Archaeologist* 38 (May 1975) 54-59.

[7]Claude R. Conder, "On the Identification of Aenon," *Palestine Exploration Quarterly* n.v. (July 1874) 191-92.

which Jesus is led (18:28) with its pavement (*lithostroton*) which in Hebrew is *gabbatha* is in the city (19:13); but whether on the corner of the temple area or near Herod's palace is not determined.⁸

Priests and Levites who question John are from Jeusalem (1:19); John baptizes at Bethany beyond the Jordan (1:28; 10:40) which is to be distinguished from the other Bethany, the village of Mary (11:1; 12:1) two miles (fifteen stadia) from Jerusalem (11:18). A town near the desert is called Ephraim (11:54). The place of a skull (Golgotha), near the city (19:17,20), is not definitely located. There was a garden (*kepos*) and in the garden a new tomb (19:41) whose owner Joseph is from Arimathea (19:38).⁹

Reflections of Jewish Life and Belief

The Semitic background of the Fourth Gospel is to be seen in the allusions to observances of the Jewish festivals: Passover, Tabernacles (7:2,10), Dedication (10:22,23), and an unnamed feast (5:1). Jesus is in Jerusalem for each of these though observance of Dedication did not require presence there. Jews go early to Jerusalem at Passover to purify themselves (11:55). Allusion is made to the day of Preparation (19:31,42; cf. Josephus, *Ant.* 16.6.2 [163]) and to the observation of the sabbath (5:9-18; 9:16); to the last day which is the great day of the feast of Tabernacles (7:37), and to Greeks who come to the Passover (12:20).

The Fourth Gospel reflects popular Jewish views in Galilee (1:4,46,49; 6:14,28,30f.), in Samaria (4:25,29,42), and in Judea (5:39,45f.; 7:26f.,40-43; 8:30f.; 10:24; 12:34).¹⁰ Scribes (8:3), Pharisees (1:24; 3:1; 7:32,48; 11:47,57) and chief priests (7:32; 12:10; 18:35; 19:6,15) who have their officers (*huperetai*; 7:32,45; 18:3,12,18,22; 19:6) furnish opposition to Jesus. They plot the death of Lazarus (12:10). Though the writer does not mention the Sadducees, he knows of those who hold official posts in Jerusalem (11:49f.). Notice is taken of Annas, father-in-law of Caiaphas (18:13) and of the high priesthood of Caiaphas (11:49-51; 18:13,14,24), of the council (*sunedrion*; 11:47), and of fear of the Romans (11:48). A man has a hearing before he is condemned (7:51). The Jews bring Jesus before Pilate (18:29,33;

---

⁸W.F. Albright, *The Archaeology of Palestine* (Harmonsworth, Middlesex: Penguin Books, 1949), p. 245; "Recent Discoveries in Palestine and the Gospel of St. John," in W.D. Davies and D. Daube, eds., *The Background of the New Testament and Its Eschatology* (Cambridge: U. Press, 1964), pp. 158, 159.

⁹R.D. Potter, "Topography and Archaeology of the Fourth Gospel," in *The Gospels Reconsidered* (Oxford: Basil Blackwell, 1960), pp. 90-98; see also my essay, "Topography and Archaeology of the Gospel of John," pp. 225-35 in *"That Ye May Believe"* Lubbock Christian College Bible Lectures (Lubbock, Texas: Lubbock Christian College Bookstore, 1976).

¹⁰E. Basil Redlich, *An Introduction to the Fourth Gospel* (London/New York: Longmans, Green and Co., 1939), p. 48.

19:8,12,19,38). The priests and the Pharisees act together (7:32,45; 11:47,57; 18:3). At times the writer speaks only of "the authorities" (*hoi archontes*; 7:26,48; 12:42). The chief priests are always in the lead (cf. 11:47; 12:10; 18:35; 19:6,15,21).

The Pharisees inquire of John's baptizing (1:24; 4:1), and question the man born blind (9:13-18). They scornfully reject the opinion of the multitude (7:47), question the authority of Jesus (8:13), condemn his miracles done on the sabbath (9:13ff.), excommunicate Jesus' followers (9:22; 12:42), and admit frustration after the triumphal entry (12:19). The writer is well acquainted with the practices, beliefs, and schools of thought within later Judaism.

One has said, "Although the nationalistic Messianism is not shared by John, he stands on the ground of Jewish messianic belief."[11] To the Jews the Messiah is to be a political king (6:15; 11:48; 12:13). Messianic expectations are reflected in the use of the term *Messias* (not found in the other gospels) which is twice explained to mean *Christos* (1:41; 4:25). *Messias* is a title only to be understood in the Jewish sphere. It is not used in Greek religious thought (cf. Justin, *Apol.* 1.49.5). and is not used by Philo and Josephus. The gathering into one the children of God that are scattered abroad (11:52) is a Messianic work.[12] John is aware of Messiah's meaning as a synonym to "king of Israel."[13] Of the expected one, Moses in the law and the prophets wrote (1:45). The Scriptures bear witness (5:39). He was not expected out of Galilee, but from Bethlehem (1:46; 7:41-43,52; cf. *Targum* Micah 5:1). The expectation of the Christ (1:20), of Elijah (1:21), and of the prophet (1:21,25; 4:19; 6:14; 7:40-52; 9:17), but not a prophet from Galilee (7:52), are reflected. Also the expectation of a hidden Messiah is echoed (7:27), but in common expectation, rather than dying, the Christ remains forever (12:34).[14] Jesus is king in quite another sense (18:33-37). Jesus performed signs, even the Christ could not be expected to perform more (7:31).

Contemporary with the temple was the synagogue in which Jesus could teach (6:59; 18:20); but there is a tension with the synagogue. Though Jesus spoke openly to the world, in the synagogues, and in the temple (18:20), the one who confesses the Christ is to be put out of the synagogue (*aposunagōgos genesthai*; 9:22). The authorities though believing in Jesus would not confess it lest they be put out of the synagogue (12:42), and Jesus warns that his

---

[11]W.C. van Unnik, "The Purpose of St. John's Gospel," in *The Gospels Reconsidered* (Oxford: B. Blackwell, 1960), p. 180.

[12]P. Volz, *Die Eschatologie der judischen Gemeinde im neutestamentlischen Zeitalter* (Tübingen: J.C.B. Mohr, 1934), pp. 345f.

[13]N.A. Dahl, "The Johannine Church and History" in William Klassen and Graydon F. Snyder, eds., *Current Issues in New Testament Interpretation* (New York: Harper & Row, 1962), p, 129; Walter Grundmann, "The Understanding of Christ in the Johannine Writings," in *Theological Dictionary of the New Testament*, ed. Gerhard Friedrich, trans. and ed. G.W. Bromiley (Grand Rapids, Mich.: Eerdmans, 1974), 9:566-73.

[14]N.A. Dahl, "The Johannine Church," p. 130.

followers would be put out of the synagogue and killed as a service to God (16:2; cf. Justin Martyr, *Trypho* 95:4; 133:6; *Martyrdom of Polycarp* 13:1).[15]

The tensions between the Jews and Samaritans in which "Jews have no dealings with Samaritans" (4:9) and in which Jesus can be called derogatorily a Samaritan who has a demon (8:48) are reflected. The controversy over whether Jerusalem or Mount Gerizim is the place of worship is brought up (4:20).

There was a clash between Jesus and the Jews over his healing on the sabbath (5:9-18); 9:1ff.,14); it was not lawful to carry a pallet on it (5:10), and there were other sabbath regulations; however, there were matters like circumcision on the eighth day which were recognized to take precedence over the sabbath rest (7:22,23). Bodies were not left hanging on a cross over the sabbath (19:31,42).

The Rabbinic Background

Another part of the Semitic background of the Johannine literature is seen in those elements it holds in common with later rabbinic literature. The dating of rabbinic literature is a problem in evaluating this element. Existing rabbinic literature is considerably later than the Johannine literature; however, it is a commonly accepted assumption that some of the views expressed in rabbinic sources are older than the present form of the sources. With this assumption, some of the views may be contemporary with the date of the writing of the Johannine material.

The rabbis saw the law as pre-existent as John describes the *logos* to be pre-existent (1:1). C.H. Dodd, whose work this section summarizes,[16] pointed to affinities between the Fourth Gospel's use of "law" (*nomos*) and rabbinic use of *torah*. He paralleled John 7:51, "Does our law judge a man without first giving him a hearing?" to *Exodus R.* 21:3: "Flesh and blood, if it hear the words of a man, judges him; if it does not hear, it cannot establish his judgment." Also 8:17, "In your law it is written that the testimony of two men is true," based on Num. 35:30, Deut. 7:6; 19:15, is paralleled in *Siphre* on Numbers 35:30, paragraph 161. "It is written in the law" (10:34; 15:25) is a common rabbinic formula (*M. Abodah Zarah* 3:4; *Lev. R.* 4:6; *Qoh. R.* 1:8; 11:1). However, what the rabbis ascribed to the law, John declared to be fulfilled in Jesus.

That the law was given by Moses (1:17; 7:19,23) is the common rabbinic view. *Siphre* on Deut. 31:14, #305 states: "Blessed be God who gave the Torah to Israel through Moses our teacher." Dodd notices that the attitude expressed in 7:49, "But this crowd who do not know the law, are accursed,"

---

[15]Wolfgang Schrage, "*Aposunagōgos*," in *Theological Dictionary of the New Testament*, ed. Gerhard Friedrich, trans. and ed. G.W. Bromiley (Grand Rapids, Mich.: Eerdmans, 1974), 7:848-52.

[16]C.H. Dodd, *The Interpretation of the Fourth Gospel* (Cambridge: University Press, 1953), pp. 74-96.

parallels rabbinic attitudes toward the *'amme ha 'arets*, those who do not scrupulously follow the requirements of the law.[17] Hillel said, "A *bor* [a brutish man] does not fear sin and no *'am ha 'arets* [ignorant man] is pious" (*M. Pirke Aboth* 2:6).

The casuistry involved in the sabbath argument of John 7:22-24 parallels the rabbinic "light and heavy" (*qal wachomer*) type of argument. The law permits circumcision on the sabbath because the act must be done on the eighth day (*P. Ned.* 38b; *Tos. Shab.* 15:16). From that premise in a light and heavy argument, Jesus reasoned that the entire man could also be healed on the sabbath. Eliezer ben Azariah (ca. A.D. 100) put it, "If circumcision which affects one of our 248 members, repels the Sabbath, how much more must the whole body repel the Sabbath?" (*b. Yoma* 85a-b).

Despite the parallels with later rabbinic thought, examples of which could be multiplied, Dodd points out that the differences are also great.[18] The author of the Gospel of John writes as one outside the Jewish system, using the terms "your law" and "their law" (8:17; 10:34; 15:25). He contrasts the law which came through Moses with grace and truth which came through Jesus Christ (1:17). The rabbinic view is that grace and truth are attributes of God: "Grace: that means God's acts of love, truth: that means the Torah" (*Midrash Ps.* on Ps. 25:10). In many rabbinic passages study is the way to eternal life (*M. Pirke Aboth* 7:6; *Mech. Exod.* 13:3; *Pesiqta* 102b); but for John the study of the law is inadequate (5:39). Rather than the law's being life, Christ's words are life (6:63).

Twice Jesus is called Messiah (1:41; 4:25) which is then translated "Christ." Solid evidence for the use of this term for a future appearing figure in pre-Christian Judaism is elusive apart from Daniel 9:25, 26. "Anointed" is used in the O.T. for the reigning king, and there is the promise of a prince of the house of David. The future monarch of the house of David is called *christos kurios* in Ps. Sol. 17:36 which is assumed to be a translation of *meshiach 'adhonai*. The term then appears in the Apocalypse of Baruch 29:3-30:1 about A.D. 100 and occurs in one recension of the *Zadokite Document* 9:10. The term is used in the Targums. According to I. Abrahams, the term became common in rabbinic usage after the destruction of the temple and was well established after the Bar Cochba War (A.D. 135).[19]

Some people were inclined to accept Jesus as the Messiah on the basis that he performed signs (7:31; cf. 6:30f.) and greater ones could not be expected of the Messiah. Rabbinic sources stress signs of the Davidic Messiah's coming rather than his miracle working power.[20] The signs stressed in John, though

---

[17]H.L. Strack and Paul Billerbeck, *Kommentar zum Neuen Testament aus Talmud und Midrasch*, 6 vols. (München: C.H. Beck'sche Verlagsbuchhandlung, 1924), 2:494-5.

[18]C.H. Dodd, *The Interpretation of the Fourth Gospel*, pp. 74-96.

[19]Israel Abrahams, *Studies in Pharisaism and the Gospels*, 1st series (Cambridge: University Press, 1917), p. 137.

[20]Joseph Klausner, *The Messianic Idea in Israel*, W. F. Stinespring, trans. (London: George Allen and Unwin, 1956), p. 506.

convincing to believers, would have little convincing power to those of such expectations. However, in a typology, the prophet-Messiah like Moses was expected to do things like Moses did, dealing with manna, riding a donkey (*Qoheleth Rabba* 1:8,4), and furnishing water. The writer of John has the crowd expect a miracle, but when they see a miracle, they fail to recognize the sign.

The Messiah is a descendant of David born at Bethlehem (7:42). The descent from David is a standard part of the messianic belief (Ps. Sol. 17:23-36; 18:6-8). John rejects the idea that he is a man born of men (cf. Justin, *Trypho* 8:3; 49:1); he is "from above," "from God," "from heaven" (3:31; 6:38; 8:23,42). The rabbinic expectation of the return of David is not alluded to in the N.T. Micah 5:2 is not frequently cited in the literature. Allusion to a messianic birth in Bethlehem comes in the fourth century. One has to reckon with the possibility that though the expectation was a part of contemporary first century expectation, O.T. claims favored by Christians were abandoned later in rabbinic schools.

Qumran[21]

It is widely recognized that rather than there being a direct dependence between Qumran and the Johannine corpus, the Qumran materials find their importance in showing that there was a Palestinian atmosphere in which the vocabulary and religious ideals of the corpus would have been understood.[22] Ideas which formerly were known only in second century Gnosticism can now be dated to the first century.

No other literature furnishes the close terminological and ideological parallels to the Johannine literature which the Qumran literature does. While both have an O.T. background, they diverge from it. Creation is traced to God (John 1:2; 1QS 3:15; 11:11; 1QH 1:20; 10:9); however, in John, God works through his Word (1:1), while in Qumran it is through his knowledge (1QS 3:15; 1QH 1:20). In Qumran the two spirits were created (1QS 3:25); the Gospel of John does not raise the question.

The scrolls and the Johannine writings have a dualism under one God the creator in which good and evil are opposite each other. In Isaiah 45:7 the Lord is said to "form light and create darkness," but the struggle depicted in the Johannine literature and in Qumran is not so precisely delineated in the O.T. In Qumran all men are aligned either with light or darkness; and in the Johannine writings light and truth struggle with darkness and evil. The dualism is ethical and eschatological rather than being metaphysical as is that of the second century Gnostics.

---

[21]This material is indebted to the study of Raymond E. Brown, "The Qumran Scrolls and the Johannine Gospel and Epistles," in *New Testament Essays* (Garden City, N.Y.: Doubleday & Co., 1968), pp. 138-73.

[22]See J.A.T. Robinson, "A New Look on the Fourth Gospel," in *The Gospels Reconsidered* (Oxford: Basil Blackwell, 1960), p. 159.

In the Gospel of John, with the advent of Jesus, light has come into the world (John 1:4,9; 12:46), and he is the light of the world (9:5). He is quite different from Qumran's created angel of light, and the terminology used for the leader of the forces of darkness in Qumran differs from that of John. While John speaks of darkness and mentions the devil or Satan who is the ruler of this world (John 12:31; 14:30; 16:11), John does not characterize him as an angel of the forces of darkness as Qumran does.

Whereas the Johannine literature reflects a struggle which has some parallels in the Qumran picture, its details are different. In Qumran the struggle between good and evil, light and darkness (though light is ultimately to be victorious) is to continue until the end. The victory is in the eschatological future. In John the victory has already been determined with the coming of Jesus into the world (16:28). Light is victorious over darkness. Darkness did not overcome the light (1:5). "He who walks in darkness does not know where he goes" (12:35); cf. 1QS 3:2). The prince of this world is cast out (12:31), and Christ has overcome the world (16:33).

In Qumran the sons of light are the members of the community who live by its rule: "All who dedicate themselves to do God's ordinances shall be brought into the covenant of friendship to be united in God's counsel" (1QS 1:7-8). Refusal to do God's will makes one a son of darkness. The member of the community was expected to manifest truth, humility, patience, compassion, understanding, wisdom, zeal, and purity (1QS 4:2). Misbehavior was seriously punished. Contrasting with this acceptance of the community's interpretation of the Law is the fact that in the Gospel of John one in the light believes in Jesus (12:36,46) and follows him (8:12). The figure of Christ and his revelation is a significant difference between the two groups.

In Qumran one must hate evil and love the good (1QS 1:3-4; CD 2:15). The members must hate the sons of darkness (1QS 1:10), curse the sons of Belial (1QS 2:4-5), and separate themselves from perverse men (1QS 5:11; 9:17-18). Yet they were not to return evil for evil (1QS 10:18); they were to respond humbly before the haughty (1QS 11:1). One must love the sons of light (1QS 1:10) and not speak to a brother in anger (1QS 5:25). The theme of brotherly love is prominent in the Gospel of John (John 13:34,35; 15:12); but to hate is foreign.

Other contrasts are that John has nothing of Belial as the personification of evil (1QS 1:18,24; 1QM 1:1ff.). He uses the Jewish term "Satan" only at 13:27, but three times uses the Greek word *diabolos* (6:70; 8:44; 13:2). John has nothing of an eschatological war (1QM), of a New Covenant concept which is characteristic of Qumran (CD 6:19f.), of hatred of outsiders (1QS 1:4,10), of degrees of rank among members (1QS 2:20-23; 6:4-23), of repentance (CD 2:5; 8:16), community punishments (1QS 7:1ff.), and numerous other doctrines.[23]

Many features in the Fourth Gospel have no parallel in Qumran. The Messiah as incarnate God (1:14), abiding in the Son of God (15:1-8), "Son of

---

[23]This material is dependent upon Howard M. Teeple, "Qumran and the Origin of the Fourth Gospel," *Novum Testamentum* 4 (October 1960) 8-9.

man" as a Messianic title (1:51; etc; thirteen times), new birth (3:3), flesh and spirit as opposite (3:6), and eating the flesh of the Son of man (6:53,54) are all foreign to Qumran. The *Ego eimi* ("I am") predictions, the coming from above, and the being born from above concepts have no point of connection in Qumran.[24] God as God of love, not merely of righteousness, the ministry of healing of the Messiah, his coming to save all sinners, not merely the elect, and his atoning death are foreign to Qumran.[25]

The Gospel of John would never have been written in the Qumran community. While the scrolls show that vocabulary and ideas which scholars previously thought were to be dated in the second century are now known to be present in the first, their meaning to Qumran and John are not identical. Furthermore, the scrolls have helped to break down the clear division of thought previously made between Palestinian and Hellenistic Judaism. Previously known Palestinian materials had been predominantly Pharisaic. The Qumran scrolls enable scholars to see sectarian Judaism from its own presentation.

Essenes (if the Qumran people were Essenes) were in every city of Palestine (Josephus *War* 2.8.4 [124]); however, the Qumran movement did not lead people to Christ. The Johannine materials, though sharing some terminology, did not arise out of Qumran. However, the materials seem to establish the possibility of a Palestine background for the Johannine materials. W.F. Albright, while leaving open the possibility of later editing, argued that the parallels make acceptable the argument that the gospel contained memories of the Apostle John from within the first century rather than being late as some had argued.[26]

Language

The Semitic element in the language of the Fourth Gospel is difficult to demonstrate to those who read neither Semitic nor Greek. Aramaisms (cf. 9:18), but not Hebraisms, have been identified.[27] Semitisms are constructions which are present in both Hebrew and Aramaic (cf. 1:27) but are not native to Greek. Septuagint influence is not thought to be an adequate explanation for their presence. Scholars like Burney[28] and Torrey[29] argued inconclusively for an Aramaic original which had been translated into Greek, but E.C. Colwell argued for use of a non-literary koine Greek, insisting that there is

---

[24] See Teeple, "Qumran and the Origin . . . ," p. 10, for other items.

[25] W.F. Albright, "Recent Discoveries in Palestine . . . " p. 170.

[26] W.F. Albright, "Recent Discoveries in Palestine . . . ," pp. 170-71; R.E. Brown, "The Qumran Scrolls," p. 170.

[27] Schuyler Brown, "From Burney to Black: The Fourth Gospel and the Aramaic Question," *Catholic Biblical Quarterly* 26 (July 1964) 323-39.

[28] C.F. Burney, *The Aramaic Origin of the Fourth Gospel* (Oxford: Clarendon Press, 1922), 176pp.

[29] C.C. Torrey, *Our Translated Gospels* (New York and London: Harper & Brothers, 1936), 172pp.

nothing to justify the claim that the author of the Fourth Gospel thought in Aramaic but wrote in Greek.[30] Others like Howard[31] and Black[32] have said that the author did think in Aramaic but wrote in Greek.[33] Bultmann thought his hypothetical signs source of the Gospel was by a Greek speaking Semite.[34] Dodd speaks of irresistible evidence for an underlying Semitic idiom.[35] Turner points out that the language is more Semitic than that of the other Gospels.[36]

Cases of alleged mistranslation which could be rendered back into Aramaic for slight correction and retranslation into Greek to correct the difficulty (the stock in trade of the argument of Burney and Torrey) were reduced by Black to two (8:34; 11:33,38).[37] Barrett rejected even these, arguing that the existing Greek is not such as to need conjecture.[38]

The Semitic coloring in vocabulary is seen first in the words which are given in Semitic form and translated: Rabbi (1:38; etc), Rabbouni (20:16), Messias (1:41; 4:25), Cephas (1:42), Siloam (9:7), Thomas (11:16; 20:24; 21:2), Bethzatha or Bethesda (5:2), Gabbatha (19:13), and Golgotha (19:17). Other words which are not translated include "amen" ("truly"; 3:3; etc.), "hosanna" (12:13), and "manna" (6:31,49).

Other English words and phrases from strongly Semitic colored Greek are "behold" (1:47) and "answered and said" which occurs 31 times.[39] Others are "grace and truth" (1:14,17), "believe on the name" (1:12; 2:23; 3:18), "the name" referring to God and his nature (12:28; 17:6,11,12,26), "does what is true" (3:21), "rejoice greatly" (3:29), "has given all things into his hand" (3:35), "seed" for descendants (7:42; 8:33,37), "sons of light" (12:36), "son of perdition" for the lost one (17:12), "the devil had already put into the heart" (13:2), and "all flesh" for *kol basar* (17:2). "Come and see" (1:39,46; 11:34) is common in rabbinic materials inviting to that which is unusual,[40] often

---

[30]E.C. Colwell, *The Greek of the Fourth Gospel* (Chicago: University Press, 1931), pp. 130f.

[31]J.H. Moulton, gen. ed., *A Grammar of New Testament Greek*, 4 vols. (Edinburgh: T. & T. Clark, 1919), vol. 2. *Accidence and Word Formation* by W.F. Howard, p. 484.

[32]M. Black, *An Aramaic Approach to the Gospels and Acts* (3rd ed., Oxford: Clarendon Press, 1967), pp. 272-74.

[33]Edwyn Hoskyns and Noel Davey, *The Riddle of the New Testament* (London: Faber and Faber: 1931), p. 284.

[34]R. Bultmann, *The Gospel of John, A Commentary*, G.R. Beasley-Murray, trans. (Oxford: Basil Blackwell, 1971), pp. 98-99, n. 6.

[35]Dodd, *The Interpretation*, p. 75.

[36]J.H. Moulton, gen. ed., *A Grammar of New Testament Greek*, 4 vols. (Edinburgh: T. & T. Clark, 1976), vol. 4: *Style*, by N. Turner, p. 64.

[37]M. Black, *An Aramaic Approach*, pp. 171, 240-43.

[38]C.K. Barrett, *The Gospel According to St. John* (London: S.P.C.K., 1960), pp. 10, 283-84.

[39]N. Turner, *Style*, pp. 68, 69.

[40]N. Turner, *Style*, p. 64.

claimed as a parallel, is rejected by Smith.[41] "You have well said" is paralleled in *Mechilta* 19:24.[42]

Qumran texts often illustrate Johannine usage. The double "truly" (*amen*) which occurs twenty-five times (3:3; etc) is found in 1QS 1:20; 2:10,18. "Deeds were evil" (3:19; 7:7) parallels "works of darkness" (1QS 2:7; 1QM 15:9). "Do the truth" is paralleled in 1QS 1:5; 5:3; 8:2 but is also in Tobit 4:6; 13:6. "The wrath of God rests upon him" is paralleled in 1QS 4:12, but is common in Judaism. "Spring of water" is paralleled in the *Damascus Covenant* 3:16; 8:22. "Witness to the truth" (5:33; 18:37) is paralleled in 1QS 8:6. Other examples include "walk in darkness" (8:12; 12:35), "the ruler of this world" (12:31; 14:30; 16:11, and "sons of light" (12:36).

In syntax, Semitic influence can be seen in the use of *casus pendens* where *pan* ("all") refers to the personal pronoun (6:39; 15:2; 17:2). There are twenty-four cases of the dangling clause.[43] The partitive *ek* with the omission of *tis* (1:24; 3:25; 7:40; 16:17) occurs which is usual in Semitic and frequent in the Septuagint. *Pas* is put before a conditional participle resulting in the translation of "whoever" (or "every one") . . . " (3:8,15,16,20; 4:13; 6:40,45; 8:34; 11:26; 12:46; 15:2b; 16:2; 19:12). It is also seen in the imperative with *kai* used for the future (1:39; 2:19; etc), and the imperative is used with a second imperative (1:46; 7:52; 11:34).

The Greek is characterized by the use of parataxis in which short sentences are connected by *kai* ("and," "but," and "then"), rather than using particles and subordinating clauses in examples too numerous to list (cf. 1:10,11; 3:10,16-21; 5:24; etc.) in narrative and in reports of discourse (5:39,43; 17:8,10,11). John 9:6ff. may be cited for its five occurrences of *kai*. *Kai* is also used adversatively (cf. 1:5; 17:11; etc) in twenty-two cases.

After making allowance for the occurrence of some of the phenomena in Greek not known to be Semitic and for the influence of gospel tradition upon the writer of the Fourth Gospel, C.K. Barrett summarizes:

> Perhaps it is safest to say that in language as well as in thought John treads, perhaps not unconsciously, in the boundary between the Hellenic and the Semitic; he avoids the worst kind of Semitism, but retains precisely that slow and impressive feature of Aramaic which was calculated to produce the effect of solemn, religious Greek, and may perhaps have influenced already the liturgical language of the church.[44]

R. Schnackenburg, from whom this survey is condensed, concludes that "John was written in Greek from the start even though the language displays

---

[41]Strack and Billerbeck, *Kommentar*, 2:371; Morton Smith (*Tannaitic Parallels to the Gospels* [Philadelphia, Penna: Society of Biblical Literature, 1951], pp. 25, 26, 41, nn. 67, 68) denies the parallel but sees a partial parallel in John 7:52.

[42]M. Smith, *Tannaitic Parallels*, p. 27.

[43]N. Turner, *Style*, p. 71.

[44]C.K. Barrett, *The Gospel According to St. John*, p. 11.

many Semitisms or Semitic colouring."[45] R. Brown is more cautious but also feels that the evidence is inadequate to demonstrate that the gospel according to John ever existed in Aramaic.[46]

Space limitations prohibit an exhaustive consideration of all Semitic aspects of the Fourth Gospel. We have looked at only one strand of its complexities. After one has discounted the material the Fourth Gospel has in common with the Synoptic Gospels the data we have collected substantiates the opinion that "the Fourth Gospel . . . is one of the most Jewish of the early Christian writings. . . . At the same time it attests some of the diversity of Judaism in the first century.[47] It remains disputed whether this atmosphere was to be found outside of Palestine as well as in Palestine. Scholars who reject the gospel's Palestinian background will continue their struggle to explain how such an atmosphere was transplanted out of Palestine.

---

[45]R. Schnackenburg, *The Gospel According to St. John*, Kevin Smyth, trans., 2 vols. (London: Burns & Oates, 1968), 1:110.

[46]R. Brown, *The Gospel According to John*. The Anchor Bible, 2 vols. (Garden City, N.Y.: Doubleday, 1966), 1:cxxx.

[47]W.A. Meeks, " 'Am I a Jew?' Johanninne Christianity and Judaism," p. 185 in J. Neusner, ed., *Christianity, Judaism, and Other Greco-Roman Cults*, 4 pts. (Leiden: E.J. Brill, 1975), 1:185.

Metaphors and an Obligational Norm for Ministry in the Fourth Gospel

Stuart L. Love

Ministers and church leaders are concerned with *practical* theology. It is their concern to ask, "How will a study of ministry in the Gospel of John relate to the church's ministry today?" "Do we find examples of congregational life in the Fourth Gospel like we find in Paul's correspondence to the Thessalonians or Corinthians?[1] And, if so, do those situations sufficiently parallel contemporary church challenges?"[2] At this juncture, I have found the work of Don S. Browning helpful. Browning believes three generalizations can be made about practical theology: 1) it "tries to answer the question of what we should do in the face of problems and challenges to faithful action," 2) "it consists of several different levels," and 3) "it is correlational and critical."[3]

---

[1] The relationship of the Fourth Gospel to the Johannine Epistles concerning church structure and organization will be addressed momentarily as well as the setting of John's gospel and its implications for christology. Suffice to begin with a statement of D. Moody Smith, "If, as seems likely, the Johannine community felt 'hemmed in' by a hostile world, that narrowness is reflected in its doctrine and ethos." "Theology and Ministry in John," in *A Biblical Basis for Ministry* edited by Earl E. Shelp & Ronald Sunderland (Philadelphia: Westminster Press, 1981), p. 214.
[2] From a sociological perspective the major changes are from an "agrarian" (ancient) society to an "advanced industrial" society. See Gerhard and Jean Lenski, *Human Societies: an Introduction to Macrosociology*, 4th ed. (New York, et al.: McGraw-Hill Book Co., 1982) for a macrosociological description and ethnographical analysis.
[3] Don S. Browning, "Integrating the Approaches: A Practical Theology," in Carl S. Dudhey, ed., *Building Effective Ministry* (New York: Harper & Row, 1983), pp. 222-223. Browning states in a footnote that he is following the tradition of practical theology associated with the names of Daniel Day Williams, Seward Hiltner, and David Tracy. For a fuller development of Browning's position see Don S. Browning, "Pastoral Theology in a Pluralistic Age," *Pastoral Psychology* 29:1 (Fall 1980) 24-35, and *Religious Ethics and Pastoral Care* (Philadelphia: Fortress Press, 1983). Browning cites as examples of the literature of this tradition, Daniel Day Williams, "Truth in a Theological Perspective," *Journal of Religion* 28:4 (October 1948), and *The Minister and the Care of Souls* (New York: Harpers, 1961); Seward Hiltner, *Preface to Pastoral Theology* (New York: Abingdon Press, 1958); David Tracy, *The Blessed Rage for Order* (New York: Seabury Press, 1975), and *The Analogical Imagination* (New York: Crossroad, 1981).

All three of Browning's generalizations are germane to our study, but the second is especially so. Within it Browning sets forth five "analytically distinct levels to practical theological thinking."[4] First is the metaphorical level which parallels systematic theology and is concerned with the great metaphors which symbolize our faith experience. God as creator is an example. Second is the obligational level which parallels formal theological ethics and is concerned with moral development. The golden rule is an example. Third is the need-tendency level, the psychological plane concerned with personal emotional motivational development. The concern for justice and love in a marriage relationship is an example. Fourth is the contextual-predictive level, the sociological dimension wherein "we try to interpret the situation that confronts us in our ethical deliberation."[5] An inner city church's struggle for survival as it attempts to find resources to care for the homeless in its community is an example. Finally there is the rule-role communication level, the point in which "specific rules and roles for organizing our practical action" takes place, both for individuals and groups.[6] Paul's command to the Thessalonians, "if any one will not work, let him not eat" (2 Thess. 3:10) is an example. It is essential for practical theologians to work at all of these levels, although the last three are the traditional areas for doing practical theology.

Although the Fourth Gospel may not address actual congregational settings, it does set forth at least three "ministry metaphors" and an "obligational norm" which relate the Biblical message to contemporary church ministry.[7] In this study I will work with the metaphorical and obligational levels (the first two) using the Fourth Gospel as my guide. Admittedly, my effort will be incomplete, but hopefully it will be an illustration of an essential step since practical theology as Browning puts it "cannot afford to ignore the higher levels, the metaphorical and the obligational."[8]

Preliminary Considerations

First, however, three preliminary but concise considerations require our attention: 1) a comparison of John with the Synoptics concerning the topic of ministry; 2) a consideration of the reality of "church/ministry" in John; and, 3) a brief development of three related theological themes: "incarnation," "the world," and "sending."

---

[4]Don S. Browning, "Integrating the Approaches:" *op cit.*, p. 223. The elements of the list are a compilation I have created from Browning's data, *ibid.*, pp. 222-223.
[5]Don S. Browning, *Religious Ethics and Pastoral Care* (Philadelphia: Fortress Press, 1983), p. 70.
[6]*Ibid.*, p. 70.
[7]This is a hermeneutical challenge which cannot be ignored, but can not be adequately addressed in such a limited study.
[8]Don S. Browning, "Integrating the Approaches:" *op cit.*, p. 224. Browning's use of "higher" and "lower" levels is not intended to mean that the lower levels are less important — only that they are dependent on "certain judgments at the higher levels for their proper positioning." *Ibid.*

Comparing John with the Synoptics

Although ministry in all four of the gospels is predicated on the ministry of Jesus, it is expressed and emphasized differently by each writer.[9] However, in the Synoptics there are usually three ministry activities attributed to Jesus — preaching, serving and healing. In John the vocabulary and thought patterns for these activities are significantly modified. For example, the terms "gospel" and "preaching" are nearly absent from John's vocabulary. Instead, emphasis is given to "testimony" and "witness." Further, in the Synoptics (as for most of the New Testament) ministry focuses upon "service."[10] The Fourth Gospel speaks of "slaves," "servants," and "service" with some regularity, but to my knowledge in only three instances, 12:26; 13:17 and 15:15, does the language seem to relate to ministry. Similar observations can be made of the third activity, healing. Jesus' ministry in the Synoptics is characterized by frequent healings and/or exorcisms, vital demonstrations of the power of God's Kingdom over Satan.[11] In John, the vocabulary for "healing" and the "kingdom" is used infrequently.[12] Only four miracles are healings,[13] a small number in comparison to the Synoptic record. Even more noticeable is the absence of exorcisms in John, a prevalent activity in the Synoptics (Mark 3:15). True, in John, Jesus is accused of having a demon, but never is there an exorcism. In fact, the miracles of Jesus are not described as miracles but as his "works" (5:36; 9:3; 10:32-33; 14:10), and/or "signs" (2:11,23; 3:2; 4:54 et al) which have the force of testimony and are given for the purpose of producing faith. Miracles in the Fourth Gospel, Smith states, "have the express function of raising the question of who Jesus is and suggesting an answer."[14]

---

[9] The question of why John is so different from the Synoptics along with a more in-depth treatment of the similarities and differences between them relating to the topic of ministry, is provided by D. Moody Smith, "Theology and Ministry in John," pp. 186-200.

[10] The theological importance of *diakonia* for ministry is described well by C.E.B. Cranfield, "It is a theological necessity having its ground in the Gospel itself, in the grace of God in Jesus Christ." "Diakonia in the New Testament," in *Service in Christ, Essays Presented to Karl Barth on his 80th Birthday*, edited by James I. McCord and T.H.L. Parker (Grand Rapids: Eerdmans, 1966 the Epworth Press), pp. 39-40.

[11] The gospels variously treat the purpose of miracles. For example, Mark indicates that miracles and faith do not always go together (e.g., 3:19b-35; 4:35-6:6). Concerning Mark, Charles H. Talbert states, "to confess Jesus as Christ on the basis of his power is only partial vision and must be supplemented by the vision of his cross (e.g., 8:14-21,22-26,27-30, 10:46-52)." *Reading Luke: A Literary and Theological Commentary on the Third Gospel* (New York: Crossroad, 1986), p. 59. Faith, however, seems important to Luke's presentation of miracles; see Paul J. Achtemeier, "The Lukan Perspective on the Miracles of Jesus: A Preliminary Sketch," in *Perspectives on Luke-Acts*, ed. Charles H. Talbert (Danville, Va.: ABPR, 1978), p. 161. Talbert says of John: "The fourth evangelist has the most inclusive view of miracle in the NT:" *Reading Luke*, p. 59.

[12] 3:3; 4:47; 5:10,13; 12:40; 18:36.

[13] They are: the military officer's son (4:46-54); the lame man on the sabbath (5:1-18); the man blind from his birth (9:1-41); and the raising of Lazarus (11:1-57).

[14] *Ibid.*, p. 368.

Even though certain ministry vocabulary and thought patterns in the Synoptics are missing and/or modified in John, a rich message of ministry remains. Testimony leads people to choose life or judgement.[15] Service is stressed through the love commandment (John 13:34,35; 15:12-13,17) and the footwashing scene (13:1-11,12-20).[16] The works of Jesus are integral to his ministry. In saying this, though, we must be careful. The Fourth Gospel does not express matters differently without reason. The language, structure, and activity of the gospel are fundamental to its purpose.

Ministry and Church in John

But what about the reality of church and ministry in John? Raymond Brown points out that up to 1965 most of the discussion concerning this topic was negative.[17] For example, it was argued there is no explicit reference to church order and governance or to the Lord's Supper or baptism or the "people of God" in the gospel, and, like Mark and Luke, John does not use the term "church." On the other hand, reflecting a consensus of scholarship today, there is implicit evidence for the church as a community within the gospel. The symbolic discourses on the Shepherd and Vine include sheep and branches, images not just of individuals, but of the disciples, a community of believers. The frequent controversial discourses probably reflect struggles within and without the community encompassing the pre-gospel period as well as the time of the gospel.[18] The discussion on worship in John 4 probably

---

[15]This point will be developed shortly.
[16]D. Moody Smith, "Theology and Ministry in John," pp. 217-228.
[17]Raymond Brown, "Johannine Ecclesiology — The Community's Origins," *Interpretation*, XXXI 4 (October 1977) 379. See also Brown's discussion in the introduction to his commentary, *The Gospel According to John*, I-XII (Garden City, N.Y.: Doubleday & Co., Inc., 1966), pp. cv-cxi, and bibliography cxxvii, and his *The Community of the Beloved Disciple* (New York, et al.: Paulist Press, 1979), pp. 13-24. A more complete bibliography is provided by Ernst Haenchen, *John*, translated by Robert W. Funk, Funk and Ulric Busse, eds., Hermeneia (Philadelphia: Fortress Press, 1984), section 37.
[18]J. Louis Martyn's *History and Theology in the Fourth Gospel*, second revised edition (Nashville: Abingdon Press, 1979), first published 1968, was the beginning of several studies that maintain the gospel operates on two levels, the author's present as well as Jesus' past. We must not forget, however, the importance of the pre-Easter Jesus. Talbert, in discussing the theological importance of apostleship in Luke, makes a statement with a broader significance. "Theologically, this view of apostleship is significant as it places the church's proclamation under the control of the career of the pre-Easter Jesus as known through his witness." *Reading Luke*, p. 62. For a helpful overview of other efforts in the reconstruction of the milieu out of which the gospel and epistles arose see Raymond E. Brown's *The Community of the Beloved Disciple*, pp. 171-182. I assume that the gospel works with both the faith and life of the Johannine circle as well as the pre-Easter Jesus. But I also agree with Smith that the gospel has a polemical setting which helps account for its apparent distinctive emphasis upon Christian conviction and "the vigor, and even vehemence, of the Fourth Gospel's Christological affirmation." "Theology and Ministry in John," pp. 214-215.

points to the church's worship in spirit and in truth (4:23-24). The mission and witness of the disciples seem to prefigure the church.[19] Teaching on love, prayer, obedience, the Spirit, bearing fruit and persecution in the world suggests a community of disciples with a fellowship and ministry. The prayer of Jesus in John 17 includes the future — "those who believe in me through their word," (John 17:20). Our study cannot settle the contemporary debate concerning Johannine ecclesiology, but it is a defensible assumption to work with the reality of the church in the Fourth Gospel, especially when the evidence of the Johannine epistles is considered.[20] If we may speak of the church as a community we must speak of its ministry as well. Edward Schillebeeckx expresses the matter well in his much broader study. There is "no community without ministry," and conversely there is "no ministry without community."[21]

Themes Which Inform

Finally, there are at least three interrelated themes which inform and narrow our topic: incarnation, the world and the role of sending. All three could be viewed as metaphors of ministry, but we will reserve that designation for three more specific matters.

Incarnation and ministry. No writing in the NT has a higher christology than John. Not only does the gospel parallel in its own way Paul's conviction that God has acted decisively in Jesus (cf. Rom. 1:1-4,16-17; 3:21-22), it affirms also the pre-existence and universal importance of Christ. Smith states, "The cosmic significance of Christ, . . . is now expressed in a Gospel, . . . " and a central early Christian "tenet is now taken to mean that Jesus is, at least functionally, equivalent to God."[22]

John's high christology contains as well the fullest expression of Jesus' humanity — the incarnation. Jesus is declared to be the "only Son" who

---

[19]C.K. Barrett, *The Gospel According to St. John* (London: S.P.C.K., 1955), pp. 78-82. I am dependent on Barrett for most of what follows.

[20]A variety of opinions for and against church order in the gospel and epistles exists. Opposed is Eduard Schweizer, *Church Order in the New Testament* (SBT 32; London: SCM, 1961). Schweizer's argument centers around the absence of the notion of "the people of God" in the Johannine theology. A more balanced view is that of S. Pancaro, "People of God in St. John's Gospel," NTS 16 (1967-68) 114-129. Smith asserts, "It cannot be shown that either the Gospel of John or the Johannine epistles evince a highly developed church organization," "Theology and Ministry in John," p. 218. The most recent analysis to my knowledge is Edward Schillebeeckx, *The Church With a Human Face* (New York: Crossroad, 1987), pp. 94-99 who sees a Spirit led community in the gospel with the possible exception of 21:15-19 which is a structure based on the authority of love.

[21]*The Church With a Human Face*, p. 128.

[22]"Theology and Ministry in John," p. 216.

"became flesh" (1:14).[23] I will cite several examples which emphasize both the human and transcendent dimension of Jesus' ministry. Jesus participates in a wedding feast (2:1-11), at which time he reminds his mother, "What have you to do with me? My hour has not yet come." (2:4). Jesus, weary, sits down at a well in Samaria and reveals to a woman her past (4:1-42). Agitated in spirit, Jesus weeps at the tomb of Lazarus and in the same moment reveals himself to be the resurrection and the life (11:33,35,25). During the last supper Jesus lays aside his garments and washes the disciples' feet (13:3-5). John introduces this scene by stating "when Jesus knew that his hour had come to depart out of this world to the Father, having loved his own who were in the world, he loved them to the end" (suggesting the footwashing is symbolic of his death). At the hour of his glorification, his death, he thirsts (18:28). Resurrected, he shows the disciples bodily evidences of his death and then commissions them (20:20-21). One week later, he tells Thomas to touch and to handle the bodily signs of his suffering — believing (20:27), which leads Thomas to confess, "my Lord and my God" (20:28).

Further, the incarnation is underscored by statements which identify and depict the solidarity of Jesus and the disciples. If people persecute Jesus they will persecute the disciples (15:20). If the world hates the disciples it is because the world first hated Jesus (15:18). If anyone receives the disciples that person receives Jesus, and the one who sent him (13:20). As the Father has sent Jesus into the world in like fashion Jesus sends the disciples (20:21). Jesus prays not for the disciples to be taken out of the world, but that the Father will protect them from the evil one (17:15). Sometimes the fullness of John's christology is most clearly expressed by Jesus' opponents, "It is not for a good work that we stone you but for blasphemy; because you, being a man, make yourself God" (10:33). Smith states, "It is not the intention of the Fourth Evangelist to present the revelation of God in Jesus in such a way as to negate his humanity or to make his experience foreign, and therefore irrelevant to his followers."[24]

A corollary of the incarnation is the gospel's view of "flesh." Flesh is not evil, nor does it stand in opposition to God. Flesh is simply "the sphere of the

---

[23]The incarnation is set forth as a historical event. In it is found a paradox. Rudolf Schnackenburg states, "It expresses the unmistakable paradox that the Logos who dwelt with God, clothed in the full majesty of the divinity and possessing the fullness of the divine life, entered the sphere of the earthly and human, the material and perishable, by becoming flesh." *The Gospel According to St John: Volume One, Introduction and Commentary on Chapters 1-4*, tr. by Kevin Smyth (London and New York: Burns & Oates, Herder and Herder, 1968), p. 268. Four examples stand out. A "high" christology is found in the prologue (1:1-2), is uttered in prayer by Jesus (17:20), is indicated in Jesus' conversation with Philip (14:9-11), and is confessed by Thomas after the resurrection (20:28).

[24]"Theology and Ministry in John," p. 217.

human and the worldly as opposed to the divine, . . . "[25] Through Jesus' flesh, John affirms, "we have beheld his glory, glory as of the only Son from the Father" (1:14). Flesh cannot avail (6:63) because it is transitory and helpless, but through it the glory of God is revealed in Jesus and through it the community of believers by the Spirit continues Jesus' mission and ministry to the world. H. Richard Niebuhr describes the gospel's view of flesh:

> . . . whatever is is good . . . . the physical, material, and temporal are never regarded as participating in evil in any peculiar way because they are not spiritual and eternal. On the contrary, natural birth, eating, drinking, wind, water, and bread and wine are for this evangelist not only symbols to be employed in dealing with the realities of the life of the spirit but are pregnant with spiritual meaning. Spiritual and natural events 'are interlocking and analogous.'[26]

Bultmann perhaps best depicts John's meaning of flesh when he says, "This is the paradox which runs through the whole gospel: the *doxa* (glory) is not to be seen *alongside* the *sarx* (flesh), nor *through* the *sarx* as through a window; it is to be seen in the *sarx* and nowhere else."[27]

A theology of incarnation is crucial to the church's self-understanding and sense of ministry.[28] T.F. Torrance aptly conveys the significance when he states, "Thus through the Incarnation is revealed to us that God in His own Being is not closed to us, for He has come to share with us the deepest movement of His divine heart, and so to participate in our human nature that the heart of God beats within it."[29] The church through the incarnation, Karl Barth believes, is the community that exists for God, but in so doing it must understand that God exists for the world which means that in existing for God the church must exist for the world.[30] In John the church and its ministry are shaped by the imperative of the incarnation. This leads us to a second theme.

---

[25] Rudolf Bultmann, *The Gospel of John: A Commentary*, tr. by G.R. Beasley-Murray et al. (Westminster Press, 1971), p. 62. Bultmann distinguishes the meaning of several related words including "flesh," "spirit," "world," and "darkness." Flesh stresses the "transitoriness, helplessness and vanity" of the worldly sphere. "Spirit" emphasizes the divine, especially the divine power. "Darkness" is "the worldly sphere in its enmity towards God, . . . " "World" can be used both in the sense of "flesh" and "darkness."

[26] H. Richard Niebuhr, *Christ and Culture* (New York: Harper & Brothers, 1951), p. 197.

[27] Rudolf Bultmann, *The Gospel of John: A Commentary*, p. 63.

[28] Ray S. Anderson, editor, *Theological Foundations for Ministry* (Edinburgh: T. & T. Clark and Grand Rapids: William B. Eerdmans Publishing Company, 1979), p. 493.

[29] James I. McCord and T.H.L. Parker, editors, *Service in Christ: Essays Presented to Karl Barth on his 80th Birthday* (Grand Rapids: William B. Eerdmans Publishing Company, The Epworth Press, 1966), pp. 4-5.

[30] Karl Barth, *Church Dogmatics*, IV (Edinburgh: T. & T. Clark, 1962), pp. 762-63.

The world. If the means of ministry is the Spirit working through the flesh, the object of ministry is the world.[31] But, what constitutes the world in John? Niebuhr believes the world is one of the Fourth Gospel's apparent paradoxes.[32] First, it refers to the totality of creation.[33] Within the notion of creation it focuses especially upon the world of men, of human affairs, of humankind capable of knowing and comprehending.[34] Both creation and humanity are transitory. They belong to the world that is below in contrast to the world that is above (8:23; 18:36). In this sense "the world" is comparable to "flesh."

But, the world also, and often in the same context, refers to humankind rejecting Christ, living in darkness, doing evil, being ignorant of God, and exulting over Jesus' death.[35] In this sense flesh and the world are not synonymous. This world, Bultmann declares, "stands over against God and confronts him with hostility; . . . " This world has made itself "independent of God." Its synonym is darkness, the "darkness of lies and sin."[36] God sent his son to both the world of creation and alienation (3:16). But "this world," the world of darkness and under the power of its ruler, hated Jesus and hates his disciples. It rejected Christ and refused to believe. This world is judged and not saved (3:18; 5:24; 9:39; 12:47-48). Jesus' disciples, the community of faith, are in an alienated and hostile world but are not of it (17:11,15). Accordingly, they are opposed and suffer tribulation (16:33), but are encouraged since Jesus through his death overcomes the world (12:31; 14:30; 16:11).

To accept this apparent paradox is important for the church and its ministry. It must "love" the world, "die" for the world, be involved with the world, all the while knowing it is still flesh. It must know that it came out of the world, but it is not of the world. The church cannot accept the world's

---

[31]Care must given at this point. Jesus is sent into the world, but the object of his work is to do his Father's will (4:34; 5:30; 17:4 et al.). At his death he exclaims, "It is finished" (19:30). His work was done. He had glorified his Father by loving the world. Ray Anderson states, "All ministry is God's ministry. Jesus did not come to introduce his own ministry. His ministry was to do the will of the Father and to live by every Word that proceeds out of the mouth of God." "A Theology for Ministry," *Theological Foundations for Ministry,* p. 7. In turn, the call of discipleship is to serve Jesus (12:26). The disciple who does this will be honored by the Father. Helmut Thielicke, in a carefully developed argument, maintains care must be given that theology does not begin with the "Cartesian self" with its subjective tendencies but with testimony and work of the Holy Spirit. *The Evangelical Faith,* Vol. I, (Grand Rapids: William B. Eerdmans Publishing Company, 1974). See especially pages 129-160, 193-205.

[32]*Christ and Culture,* p. 198.

[33]1:9; 8:12; 9:5; 11:9; 17:5,24; 3:19; 12:46 et al. It is God's good creation. Niebuhr states, "in his convictions about creation through the Word and about the incarnation of the Word, John expresses his faith in God's wholly affirmative relation to the whole world, material and spirit. Creation means what redemption does, that 'God so loved the world that he gave his only Son,' " *Christ and Culture,* p. 197.

[34]Barrett, *The Gospel According to St. John,* p. 135.

[35]7:7; 8:23; 14:17; 15:18ff.; 17:25 et al.

[36]*The Gospel of John: A Commentary,* pp. 54-55. Bultmann in footnote 3, p. 55, refers the reader to John 8:21-29,30-40,41-47; 9:39-41; 15:21-25; 16:8-11.

values, live by its strength, measure its success by the world's standards, or share its dreams. It must never forget the only way to transform the world is through the Word made flesh. Schnackenburg states, " . . . in the Johannine theology of incarnation and mission, the greatness of God's act is manifest in the very bridging of the chasm between God and the 'world'."[37]

Sending. Finally, the themes of the incarnation and the world as foundational realities for the church's ministry are closely related to the church's commission and authority expressed primarily in the gospel by a theology of "sending."[38]

God's mission to the world is carried out through the "sending" of John the Baptist, the Son, the Spirit, and the disciples who represent four aspects of a single mission.[39] The ultimate "sending," though, is of the Son (3:17) from which the other three gain legitimacy and significance.[40] In other words, each aspect of the one mission has a christological focus. Although the sending of the disciples is central to Jesus, it is connected to the sending of John and the Spirit as well.

For example, John the Baptist is sent by God to witness to the light (1:6-7). His mission has import only because he is sent by God. Its purpose is that all should believe in the "Lamb of God."[41] Even though John does not know Jesus, he "came baptizing with water, that he might be revealed to Israel" (1:31). His testimony is that Jesus is the Lamb of God (1:29,36); that he is the one who is able to baptize with the Spirit (1:33; 3:34); and that he is the Son of God (1:34). His witness also includes his own confession (1:20; 3:28) and complete abnegation before Jesus.[42] In this John's joy is fulfilled (3:29). The truth of John's witness, even though delimited by his role, makes him a paradigm of discipleship.[43]

---

[37]Rudolf Schnackenburg, *The Gospel According to St John: Volume One, Introduction and Commentary on Chapters 1-4* (London and New York: Burns & Oates, Herder and Herder, 1968), p. 399. Earlier, Schnackenburg emphasizes the meaning of the incarnation as an event in history, *ibid.*, pp. 266-67.

[38]The Greek verbs *pempein* and *apostolein* are used interchangeably. Barrett states, "The two verbs seem to be used synonymously in this gospel." *The Gospel According to St. John*, p. 473. For example, following Barrett's study of Christ's being sent by the Father cf. 3:17,34; 5:36,38; 6:29,57; 7:29; 8:42; 10:36; 11:42; 17:3,8,18,21,23,25 (*apostellein*); 4:34; 5:23f.,30,37; 6:38f.,44; 7:16,18,28,33; 8:16,18,26,29; 9:4; 12:44f.,49; 13:20; 14:24; 15:21; 16:5 (*pempein*). In the three Paraclete passages (14:26; 15:26; 16:7) *pempein* only is used. In the case of the disciples 4:38; 17:18 *apostellein* is used, but in 13:(16),20 *pempein* is found. Both are used in 20:21. *The Gospel According to St. John*, p. 473.

[39]David Lertis Matson, *Theology of Sending in the Fourth Gospel*, unpublished M.A. thesis, Pepperdine University, 1984.

[40]For John the Baptist see 1:6-7; 3:28; for the Spirit see note 2 above for a list of appropriate references.

[41]This is demonstrated when two of his disciples hear John's witness and follow Jesus (1:35-37).

[42]Jesus comes after John but ranks before him (1:27,31). His witness is: "He must increase, I must decrease" (3:30), and "No one can receive anything except what is given him from heaven," (3:27).

[43]In the Synoptics John is referred to as being least in the kingdom (Mt. 11:11; Lk. 7:28).

The Spirit's mission is parallel to the Son's (15:26). The Spirit's primary function is to teach — not his own thoughts — but only the teachings of Jesus (14:26). Together, the Spirit and the disciples bear witness to Christ (15:26), but only after the Son's glorification (7:39; 16:7; 20:22). The Spirit is the church's source of life and the world's salvation.[44] Without the Paraclete there is no church or ministry.

The sending of the disciples is inextricably united to the sending of the Son and modeled after his mission (20:21; 4:38; 13:16,20; 17:18). When some of the key elements of Christ's sending are listed, the church's self-understanding and motivation for ministry in relationship to Christ are implicitly portrayed.

1. The Son is sent to do the Father's will and not his own (4:24; 6:38).
2. In so doing the Son does only what pleases the Father (8:29).
3. He does not seek his own initiative or glory (5:30; 8:42; 12:49; 7:18).
4. Rather, he honors the Father (5:23).
5. He honors the Father by acknowledging that his teaching, words and works are his Father's and not his own (7:16; 8:26; 14:24; 9:4).

In other words, the Son's life, mission, authority and self-identity are bound up in his unity with the Father (6:57; 17:21), and that unity includes the disciples "that the world may know and believe that thou didst send me" (11:42; 5:24; 12:44-45). Jesus, the Son, is the model apostle.[45]

Now, we believe the statements pertaining to the sending of the disciples become clearer.

---

[44]Barrett, *The Gospel According to St. John*, p. 405. In 20:22 parallels to the first creation (Gen. 2:7) are evident. For John the breath of Christ resulting in the reception of the Spirit is the beginning of the new creation, the church, Barrett, *ibid.*, 474-75.

[45]Jesus is called "apostle" only once in the NT (Heb. 3:1). However, the usage of the verbs *apostelein* and *pempein* in the gospel is consonant with the affirmation of the book of Hebrews. Karl Rengstorf, "*apostolos*," *TDNT*, ed. Gerhard Kittel, trans. Geoffrey W. Bromiley (Grand Rapids: Wm. B. Eerdmans Publishing Co., 1964, I), 443. See note 2 above for references. It is evident the phrase "he who sent me" (or its equivalent) on the lips of Jesus becomes a statement of " 'missional self-understanding.' " See David Lertis Matson, *Theology of Sending in the Fourth Gospel*, pp 72-78. Sent into the world by God, Albert Winn writes, "lies at the very core of Jesus' self-understanding." *A Sense of Mission* (Philadelphia: The Westminster Press, 1981), p. 22. Barrett states, 'The fundamental thought of John is that the Father sent the Son to be the Savior of the world; it is because he is sent that the Son has authority, and because he is the Father's envoy that in him and in his mission men encounter the Father himself." in "The Theological Vocabulary of the Fourth Gospel and the Gospel of Truth," *Essays on John* (Philadelphia: The Westminster Press, 1982), p. 51. And in his commentary he writes, "The ministry of Jesus has no significance apart from the will of the Father; it is not an independent achievement of humanity but the fruit of submission." *The Gospel According to St. John*, p. 201.

4:38 — I sent you to reap that for which you did not labor; others have labored, and you have entered into their labor.

13:16 — Truly, truly, I say to you, a servant is not greater than his master; nor is he who is sent greater than he who sent him.

13:20 — Truly, truly, I say to you, he who receives any one whom I send receives me; and he who receives me receives him who sent me.

17:18 — As thou didst send me into the world, so I have sent them into the world.

20:21 — Peace be with you. As the Father has sent me, even so I send you.

In conclusion, what can we say specifically concerning the church's commission? Its mission is not its own, but is defined in reference to God. Its self-understanding — its identity — is inseparably linked to its message so that its election and message coincide. Its ministry is not the result of its own resources or facilitation. Rather, its service is a faithful response to God who through his Son sends his witnesses into the world to lead others to follow Jesus. In this commitment there is an absolute sense of necessity. The church, like John, confesses its abnegation — "I must decrease, he must increase" — and therein its joy is fulfilled.

Three Metaphors for Ministry

Our three metaphors, "following," "bearing fruit," and "serving," are found in one passage, 12:23-26, which provides " . . . a splendid commentary on the meaning that the hour of Jesus' death and resurrection will have for all men."[46] The first metaphor, "following," stands for the commitment of discipleship. The second, "bearing fruit," is part of a parable comparing the death of a grain of wheat as the means of bearing much fruit to the death of Jesus as the means by which "all men" are "drawn" to Christ (12:32). The third, "serving," characterizes the loving behavior of those who belong to Jesus. The unifying theme is life through death. Bultmann refers to verses 23-26 as "The Law of Access."[47] The way to glorification for Jesus leads through death. This law, "to which Jesus is subject," is extended to the disciples.[48] The three metaphors are interrelated and are set within the framework that Jesus' hour has come.[49]

---

[46]Brown, *The Gospel According to John*, I-XII, p. 475. Alone, the passage serves as a conclusion for chapters 11-12 (Brown, I, p. 469). When combined with the epilogue (John 12:36b-50) it is a part of the conclusion of Jesus' public ministry (John 1:19-12:50) — a kind of climax to what Brown calls the "book of signs," (Brown, I, xi). The passage also serves as a transition to the second division of the gospel (John 13-21).

[47]Bultmann, *The Gospel of John: A Commentary*, p. 424.

[48]*Ibid.*, p. 425.

[49]This moment is precipitated by the coming of the Greeks who symbolize the universality of his work.

First Metaphor — Following Jesus

To follow Jesus is to accept a fundamental reality of discipleship — "He who loves his life loses it, and he who hates his life in this world will keep it for eternal life" (12:25).

Instances of following (or rejecting or denying discipleship) are found several times in the gospel. There is the call of the first disciples of Jesus (1:35ff.).[50] When this instance is carefully examined other crucial words for discipleship appear — "abide (dwell)," "come," and "see."[51] Jesus asks the two men sent to him by John, "What do you seek?"[52] The men wish to "abide" with Jesus (1:38) to which Jesus responds, "Come and see" (1:39). Bultmann points out that " . . . the essential meaning of the narrative is hidden behind these events."[53] Discipleship is at stake. John the Baptist's proclamation had led two disciples to follow Jesus. Andrew then finds Simon and brings him to Jesus the Messiah.[54] So, Brown concludes, the disciples must begin to act like apostles and bring others to Jesus.[55]

In John 6 the term "follow" (used in the sense of discipleship) does not occur, but the theme pervades the chapter. First, we are told a multitude "followed him" (6:2). Later, when the people seek Jesus he tells them they seek him "not because you saw signs, but because you ate your fill of the loaves" (6:26). The Bread of Life discourse is then given and ends with many of his disciples drawing back (6:66) which prompts Jesus to ask the twelve, "Do you also wish to go away?" Peter then confesses for all (6:68-69). In this instance discipleship is predicated upon Jesus' claims and teaching.

In the Light of the World discourse (8:12-10:21) the man born blind (9:1-41) is healed and becomes Jesus' disciple despite significant persecution revealing that the person who follows Jesus "will not walk in darkness, but will have the light of life" (8:12).

In the passage on the shepherd who gives his life (10:1-42), the sheep follow Christ for two reasons: 1) he goes before them and they know his voice (10:4); and 2) he lays his life down for the sheep (10:11ff.).[56] The theme of death and discipleship parallels 12:23-26.

---

[50]"Follow" appears in vss. 37, 38, 40, and 43.

[51]Brown points out that "Throughout John the theme of "coming" to Jesus will be used to describe faith (iii 21, v 40, vi 35,37,45, vii 37, etc.). Similarly, "seeing" Jesus with perception is another Johannine description of faith." *The Gospel According to John*, I, p. 79.

[52]It should be noted that Jesus takes the initiative by turning and speaking to the men which parallels John 10:16 "It is not you who chose me. No, I chose you."

[53]Bultmann, *The Gospel of John: a Commentary*, p. 100.

[54]Throughout the passage Jesus' identity is expressed through christological titles — "Messiah" (vs. 41), "Moses in the law and also the prophets wrote" (vs. 45), "Rabbi, you are the Son of God! You are the king of Israel!" (vs. 49).

[55]Brown, *The Gospel According to John*, I, p. 79.

[56]The theme of leadership as well as following can be observed in the passage. Jesus' leadership, a model for his followers, is contrasted with "strangers" and "thieves." The theme of "feeding" and leading through love is the topic of 21:15ff. as well.

The incident of Peter's premature discipleship (John 13:36ff) follows the footwashing scene (13:8) and demonstrates that Peter remains "too proud to countenance the humility of Jesus."[57] Peter's response, "Lord, why cannot I follow you now? I will lay down my life for you" (13:37) is sincere, but unenlightened (good intentions are inadequate) as he struggles over what his own will is. Jesus tells him "the cock will not crow, till you have denied me three times" (13:38).[58] The reinstatement of Peter, the reversal of his threefold denial, is found in the post-resurrection appearance of Jesus in Galilee (21:15-22). The question is asked three times "Do you love me?" It is reminiscent of Peter's triple denial (18:17,25-27) and ends with Christ's challenge, "Follow me" (20:19).

Among contemporary theologians discipleship has been shown to be a major expression of church and ministry. For example, Avery Dulles has developed a major model of the church as a community of disciples.[59] He builds a Biblical basis for the model first out of the book of Acts, but then turns to the gospels. He states "when the evangelists speak of the common life of the disciples with Jesus, they are quite conscious of the ecclesial significance of their statements."[60] Focusing on the latter chapters of John, Dulles speaks first of the role of the Paraclete, but then turns to the post-Easter experience and dwells on the necessity of Peter's obeying "the precept 'Follow me' (21:19)." He states, "Discipleship for John achieves its fullest meaning in the post-Easter situation for only then is the Holy Spirit given in fullness."[61] I believe Dulles demonstrates that discipleship is a major means by which the church's response to the work of Christ is made known. The call to discipleship in examples like Peter suggests a corresponding parallel to the community of faith. The church must die to itself to follow Christ. It can only follow, abide, come, and see as it gives its life to Christ for the sake of the world.

Second Metaphor — Bearing Much Fruit

If the heart of discipleship is a call to hate one's life in this world (12:25) and to follow Jesus unto death, a striking parallel is the metaphor of bearing fruit. Jesus states, "Truly, truly, I say to you, unless a grain of wheat falls into

---

[57]Bultmann, *The Gospel According to St. John*, p. 375.

[58]Rudolph Schnackenburg, *The Gospel According to St. John*, 3, pp. 55-56. Once more the logion in 12:26 is echoed. Denial is the opposite of confession. Peter's denial is found in 18:15-18.

[59]Avery Dulles, *A Church to Believe In Discipleship and the Dynamics of Freedom* (New York: Crossroad, 1987), pp. 1-40. In an earlier book *Models of the Church* (Garden City, N.Y.: Image, 1974) Dulles developed five models of the church — Institution, Mystical Communion, Sacrament, Herald, and Servant. His latest effort on discipleship is designed to overcome some of the barriers between some of his earlier models, especially the institutional and mystical communion examples.

[60]*Ibid.*, p. 7.

[61]*Ibid.*, p. 8.

the earth and dies, it remains alone; but if it dies, it bears much fruit" (12:24). The verse, Schnackenburg states, is " . . . an impressive little parable" by which "Jesus illustrates the fruitfulness of his death, a fruitfulness which will lead to his glorification."[62]

But what does it mean to bear fruit in the gospel? Fruit bearing is emphasized in three contexts: 1) in our present text, 2) in the conversion of the Samaritans (4:31-42), and 3) in the allegory of the vine (15:1-17)[63]

The immediate context. The coming of the Greeks (12:20) symbolically anticipates the future after Jesus' crucifixion when the church would include both Jews and Gentiles (cf. 10:16; 11:52).[64] Their request to see Jesus (12:21) depicts the theme of discipleship and is reminiscent of the disciples' call of 1:35-51. But, the time of the Gentiles first requires the glorification of the Son of man (12:23), illustrated by Jesus' statement comparing his death to the sowing of a seed of grain. Hoskyns believes this parable should not be applied "primarily to the lives of the disciples of Jesus, as though their fruitful obedience to the will of God was to burst forth independently on its own. They are the fruit of the isolated (xvi. 32) obedience and death of Jesus; and their fruitfulness springs from His death, and is joined organically to it."[65]

The harvest of the Samaritans. Jesus tells his disciples "He who reaps receives wages, and gathers fruit for eternal life," (4:36). Here again, gathering "fruit" stands for making converts to the Christian faith, most immediately the Samaritans.[66] As in 12:24 Schnackenburg compares the passage to the work of Jesus which precipitates a rich missionary harvest.[67] Interestingly, it is the woman's testimony, not the disciples', which leads to the conversion of the Samaritans (4:39). Witness as evangelism is important for John.

However, the relationship of the two, witness and evangelism and/or preaching, must be carefully weighed.[68] The gospel emphasizes that the

---

[62] *The Gospel According to St. John*, 2, p. 383.

[63] Imagery for sowing and seeds is found in the Synoptic Gospels (Mark 4:3-9,26-29,31-32; Matt. 13:24-30). It is used by Paul in 1 Cor. 15:36-38 which seems to have similarities to John 12:24. Brown acknowledges that there are no good parallels to John's parable in the OT but suggests the possibilities of Isa 55:10-11 and Dan 4:12 in the Greek, *The Gospel According to John*, I, p. 472.

[64] In recent years Johannine scholars have largely supported a non-evangelistic purpose for the gospel. D.A. Carson challenges that view as he reconsiders the possibility of viewing the gospel's purpose to be found in 20:3. Carson supports the position of W.C. van Unnick, J.A.T. Robinson and K. Bornhäuser that the "the Fourth Gospel is designed to serve as an evangelistic tool aimed at converting Hellenistic Jews to Jesus Messiah." D.A. Carson, "The Purpose of the Fourth Gospel: John 20:31 Reconsidered," 639-651 (quotation cited from p. 646).

[65] *The Fourth Gospel*, p. 424.

[66] Barrett, *The Gospel According to St. John*, p. 202.

[67] *The Gospel According to St. John*, 1, 450.

[68] Our goal is to present a balanced perspective. Witness in the sense of proclamation focuses on raising the question of either "Who is Messiah?" or "Who is Jesus?" which when received by an individual leads to confession and discipleship. Rejection of course is a live option. In the discourses involving Jewish audiences, especially those with the religious leaders (the Jews), the question Carson demonstrates is, "Who is Messiah?" "The Purpose of the Fourth Gospel," pp. 644-646.

works of Jesus done in his Father's name bear witness to him (10:25).⁶⁹ Jesus challenges both "the Jews" (10:37-38; 5:36) and his disciples (14:11) to believe his works. If they do, they will know the Son's unity with the Father (10:37; cf. 14:11).⁷⁰ The mission of Jesus is "to *do* the will of him" who sent him, and to accomplish his *work*" (4:34).⁷¹ The "now" of his hour (12:23; 13:1; 17:1) is the work of God for the salvation of the world. Word and deed are one.

The discourses of Jesus are often the outgrowth of his deeds.⁷² Two examples are given.⁷³ First, the "sign" of the feeding of the five thousand (6:1-14) is followed by the discourse on the bread of life (6:25-59) and the response of Jesus' disciples (6:60-71). The unity of sign and discourse, deed and word, reaches a climax when "many of his disciples draw back" (6:66), except for the Twelve (6:69). A second example is the healing of the man with congenital blindness (9:1-40), a demonstration that Jesus has come for judgement as well as for salvation (9:39-41). The theme and discourse, Jesus the light of the world (8:12), precede the sign. The dynamics of both discourse and deed lead to acceptance and rejection — acceptance on the part of the blind man (9:38), rejection on the part of Jesus' opponents.⁷⁴

Finally, as previously noted, the "signs" (the works) of Jesus function to produce faith, but not "simply a belief in miracles."⁷⁵ Jesus' signs should never be confused with the "food that perishes" since they symbolize the food which "endures to eternal life," (6:27). Word and deed are one.⁷⁶ The witness of the church that produces faith requires both preaching and practice, a connection and unity between its words and its deeds. Dulles states, "the goal of preaching is not mere profession of faith in the message, but rather a communion of life and love."⁷⁷

---

⁶⁹In other words, words alone are an inadequate witness.

⁷⁰In reference to the disciples Jesus promises them that they will do even greater works (14:12).

⁷¹That is, the lifting up of Jesus in death (3:14; 8:28; 12:32,34).

⁷²His deeds often are referred to as "signs."

⁷³Space limitation necessitates the examination of only two examples.

⁷⁴The gospel does not seem to allow for neutrality in human encounters with the witness of Jesus. It necessitates decision for or against. A positive response is faith which leads to confession, following and eternal life. A negative response is rejection and/or denial which leads to judgment (12:44-50).

⁷⁵D. Moody Smith, "The Presentation of Jesus in the Fourth Gospel," *Interpretation*, p. 368. We are reminded of an earlier observation by Smith that the signs have "the express function of raising the question of who Jesus is and suggesting an answer." *Ibid.*, p. 369.

⁷⁶Overall, the Fourth Gospel supports what has been emphasized by G.E. Wright, *God Who Acts: Biblical Theology as Recital* (Chicago, H. Regency, 1952) and Gerhard von Rad, *Old Testament Theology* (New York: Harper & Row, 1962-67, 2 vols.), in their studies of the OT. Words cannot be emphasized over deeds. The two go together. Again, space limitations necessitate that we break off this development. It should be remembered, however, that believing is more than a cognitive activity. It is knowing God in a relationship. Knowing God includes love, obedience and mutual indwelling. Faith, too, is the work of God (6:29).

⁷⁷*Models of the Church*, pp. 91-92.

The allegory of the vine. Perhaps the most familiar passage of bearing fruit is the allegory of the vine (John 15:1-17). Fruitfulness, service to God, is related to answered prayer, and is produced by obedience in love. Bearing fruit "is simply living the life of a Christian disciple (see vv. 5, 8); perhaps especially the practice of mutual love (v. 12)."[78] For Bultmann, the nature of fruit-bearing "is every demonstration of vitality of faith, to which, according to vv. 9-17, reciprocal love above all belongs."[79] Obedient love is the essential element in the growth of faith. It is expressed through the image of mutual abiding. Abiding and bearing fruit constitute a reciprocal relationship. A believer cannot abide in the vine without bearing fruit nor can one bear fruit without abiding in Christ. Thus, we must not equate bearing fruit with human merit or achievement. The church is a created being. It owes its existence to the Word of God. It is not its own master, nor can it make its own beginning or end. Only because of the vine is the church enabled to keep the new commandment (13:34-35), and by its keeping a witness is given that "all men will know that you are my disciples" (13:35).[80]

Third Metaphor — Serving Christ

As noted earlier, although the gospel speaks of "slaves," "servants," and "service" with some regularity in only three instances, 12:26; 13:17 and 15:15, does the language seem to relate to ministry. Two of the passages (13:17; 15:15) belong to the theme of the new commandment of love. The other (12:26) is a part of the passage containing our three metaphors (12:23-26).

The lesson from the allegory of the vine serves to introduce our last metaphor — "for apart from me you can do nothing" (15:5). Christian service originates with Christ and is rendered to him — "If any one serves me, he must follow me;" (12:26a). Service is given to *Christ* because it belongs to Christ. This includes service rendered to others since "washing the feet" of others actually means washing Jesus' feet.[81] The church ministers to its own and the world by facing Christ. When this is accomplished its service has God's power, life and authority — it is of the Spirit and not the flesh. Chris-

---

[78]C.K. Barrett, *The Gospel According to St. John*, p. 395.

[79]*The Gospel of John*, pp. 532-33.

[80]The branches represent individual believers, but the community of faith is implied. Note, that even though obedient love is specifically expressed in "loving one another" (*doing* service for the *church,*) the end result is a *witness* to the *world*.

[81]We are emphasizing the solidarity of Christ and his followers which originates and ends with Christ. The two are embedded, organically one. The identity and work are Christ's as Christ's identity and work are bound up in the Father. This parallels the Matthean notion, " 'as you did it to one of the least of these my brethren, you did it to me.' " (Matt. 25:40,44).

tian service cannot have a human origin. Self-originating service and/or human-centered service denies the gospel's theology of sending and faith.[82]

So far we have emphasized the first half of Jesus' statement, "if any one serves me, he must follow me; . ." The second half is equally significant. To serve Christ means to *follow him*. Serving Christ is predicated on dedicated discipleship.[83] The model for service and following is the footwashing scene (13:4-11,12-20). In the first section (13:4-11) Peter struggles with Jesus, refusing at first to permit him to wash his feet. Bultmann maintains that Peter reflects the natural man who simply does not want this kind of service.

> The service in question is not just any personal act of kindness — for why should this not be acceptable to the natural man? — but it is service performed by the incarnate Son of God. And even if man can reject it out of pride, Peter's words do not just express this kind of pride, but rather the basic way men think, the refusal to see the act of salvation in what is lowly, or God in the form of a slave.[84]

The struggle of discipleship in reference to service is more than a question of humility or submission. The difference is the acceptance in faith of both realities in the face of the incarnation.

If the point of issue in the first section (13:4-11) is the unwillingness of Peter to permit Jesus to wash his feet, the second section (13:12-20) stresses the disciples' need to similarly serve others in the community of faith.[85] This is "impossible" without first accepting the loving service of Christ.[86] God's love in Christ is the prerequisite for Christian service. *When* the church knows and accepts the incarnation, *then* it is called to serve its own by loving them.

Consequently, in light of John 15:15, the believer is more than a mere servant — he is a *philos* (loved one) of Jesus.[87] Brown states, "Thus . . . the

---

[82]We are not denying the reality of Christian humanism. We are only affirming that Christian humanism begins and ends with God. Only then is it authentically human.

[83]The reader is encouraged to re-examine the section on "following."

[84]*The Gospel of John*, p. 468.

[85]It is too trite to say the passage means that Jesus' followers cannot serve without loving and they cannot love without serving. Or, that the only person who can love is the person who first is loved. These may be true statements but they are moralisms in light of the theology of the incarnation. The incarnate love of God defines the nature of Christian service.

[86]John 13:1 opens the section with the statement that "Jesus knew that his hour had come to depart out of this world to the Father, having loved his own who were in the world, he loved them to the end." The scene is then enclosed by the new commandment in 13:34-35. The first precedes the second.

[87]Biblical servanthood begins with the prophets who speak of themselves as the servants of God (Amos 3:7). It is stressed by Jesus when he instructs the disciples to say, "We are unprofitable servants" (Luke 17:10). Jesus, without hesitation accepts the address as "Lord" which implies that his disciples are servants (John 13:13; see also 13:16 and 15:20). Paul views himself to be the "servant of Jesus Christ" (Rom. 1:1) and yet he stresses that Christians are sons and not slaves (Gal. 4:7).

Christian remains a *doulos* (slave) from the viewpoint of service that he should render, but from the viewpoint of intimacy with God he is more than a *doulos*."[88] The friendship of Jesus defines the environment of service and bathes it with divine dignity.

Finally, Jesus also affirms, "if any one serves me, the Father will honor him" (12:26). Nowhere else does John use *timan* (honor) with God as subject.[89] Probably, the language parallels Mark 10:30,43 and depicts the reward of following. But it conveys more than a promise to the servant to follow Christ into death. It is a promise that reaches beyond the cross to the completion of Jesus' glorification (12:23). The middle member of verse 26 "and where I am, there shall my servant be also;" should not be overlooked. It probably refers to the permanent fellowship the disciples will share with Jesus after his death and resurrection (John 14:2-3; see also 13:33,36). The church's call to service receives God's honor. Christian service is rendered by a martyr church, but not a church with a martyr's complex. The call to self-denial is not without reward. The Father honors those who serve him.

The Ethical Norm for Ministry — the New Commandment

We have examined three themes and three metaphors. The themes, the incarnation, the world and the divine sending, serve as necessary foundational assumptions for ministry in John. The three metaphors, following Christ, bearing fruit and serving Jesus, function as analogies for faith development.

But, as noted, Browning sets forth *two* "higher levels" for practical theology — metaphors and ethical norms. The latter, to which we now turn, and in the gospel there is but one, shape and guide moral development.

The ethical norm for the Fourth Gospel is the new commandment of love (13:34-35).

> A new commandment I give to you, that you love one another; even as I have loved you, that you also love one another. By this all men will know that you are my disciples, if you have love for one another (13:34-35).

Why is the new commandment an ethical norm? First, its very nature is marked by a sense of duty. Bultmann points out that the disciples "are directed towards an existence that has the character of an 'ought'."[90] It is *ethical* in nature.[91] The command is given to guide and regulate the interper-

---

[88]*The Gospel According to John*, II, p. 683.
[89]Barrett, *The Gospel According to St. John*, p. 353.
[90]*The Gospel of John*, p. 525.
[91]"Love," *Harper's Bible Dictionary*, Paul J. Achtemeier, general editor (San Francisco, et al.: Harper & Row, Publishers, with the Society of Biblical Literature, 1987), p. 581.

sonal behavior of the disciples. Second, it is *the* commandment that encompasses all other commandments and governs their meaning.[92] Third, although the command is relegated to a specific group, the community of believers, within that group it is universal in scope. Mutual love is bound upon all — every disciple is obligated by it. Fourth, it is not an optional command, nor is it operative under certain conditions. It guides the church at all times.

Why is it a "new" commandment? First, let us state some negatives. It is not to be confused with a universal love for the fatherhood of God and the brotherhood of men, or the love of enemies or even the love of neighbors.[93] Neither is it new because it is a spontaneous and unmotivated love directed to human beings who are sinners and unworthy of love.[94] Why, then, is it new? Barrett, I believe, is correct when he sees the newness as God's love in and for the new age made possible by Jesus' life and death.[95] It is new because it is defined by the cross. This view fits the context and parallels the message of our three metaphors. Standing behind it and informing it is the revelatory character of the mutual love which regulates the relationship of the Father and Son (10:18; 12:49f; (14:31); 15:10). Jesus' statement in John 15:10 to the disciples conveys this thought, "If you keep my commandments, you will abide in my love, just as I have kept my Father's commandments and abide in his love." Accordingly, the new commandment creates and sustains the fellowship of the Christian community — the church. It affirms that the moral norm which governs the church is the cross.

Further, Brown is correct in seeing it as "the basic stipulation of the 'new covenant' of Luke xxii 20."[96] "This covenant was to be interiorized and to be marked by the people's intimate contact with God and knowledge of Him — a knowledge that is the equivalent of love and is a covenantal virtue."[97]

What effect does the new commandment have within the Christian community? Brown points out that the new commandment keeps alive the spirit of Jesus among the disciples as they continue to live their life in the world.[98] Barrett states the notion similarly, "The disciples cannot accompany Christ in his death; they are to be left to live in this world . . . For the direction of their

---

[92]See the gospel's emphasis on "commands" in 14:15,21; 15:10 and the reiteration in 15:12 "This is my commandment, that you love one another as I have loved you."

[93]We are not saying Christians are unconcerned for all of these noble expressions of love. They are. But none of them touches upon the newness of the command.

[94]Here, I disagree with Brown who follows Anders Nygren's classic argument in *Agape and Eros*. I am not denying that God loves like that and Christians are called to model their lives accordingly. But such love may be experienced outside the Christian community. *The Gospel of John*, II, p. 614

[95]*The Gospel According to St. John*, p. 377.

[96]*The Gospel According to John*, II, p. 614. This is the Christian understanding of the fulfillment of the vision of Jeremiah 31:31-34.

[97]*Ibid*. Intimacy, knowledge and mutual indwelling are major themes of chapters 13-17.

[98]*Ibid*. p. 612.

life in this new situation (a messianic community living between the advents of the Messiah) Jesus leaves one new commandment."[99]

Finally, what effect does the new commandment have among outsiders? It serves as a witness.[100] Its practice will lead outsiders to recognize the distinctiveness of Christian love. This is a part of Jesus' prayer, "I in them and thou in me, that they may become perfectly one, so that the world may know that thou hast sent me and hast loved them even as thou hast loved me" (John 17:23). The practice of the new commandment is a proof of Christian discipleship and an authentication of the revelation of the Father in the Son.

Conclusion

We have demonstrated that faith and moral development are a central concern of John. It is at these two levels (theology and formal theological ethics) that essential reflection is made concerning the other three (the need-tendency, contextual-predictive, and rule-role communication levels).

All of the levels, however, are essential in doing practical theology. Our study supports Browning's contention that practical theology "cannot afford to ignore the higher levels, the metaphorical and the obligational."[101] Biblical theology and ethics provide an enduring basis for specific contemporary ministry applications.

We have shown as well that the witness of the ancient church, even when apparently lacking specific examples of congregational life, does speak to ministers and churches today. The message of the Fourth Gospel including the incarnation, the world, sending, following, bearing fruit, and serving relates to contemporary ministry challenges. In other words the ministry message of one gospel can enlighten and assist the efforts of both ministers and members to anchor their personal ministries and the churches they serve in a theology of ministry. Theology can be practical.

Our effort is unfinished and ongoing. Not all of the possible metaphors for ministry in the gospel have been explored. One striking omission is the metaphor of "feeding" or "tending" and "shepherding" in John 21:15ff. and John 10. Also, the three metaphors and single ethical norm could be probed with greater depth both textually and theologically. And, especially unfinished and of necessity, is the completed task of practical theology. What we have learned requires translation into the specific experiences of people and churches at the social, psychological and rule and role levels. This, the Fourth

---

[99] *The Gospel According to St. John*, p. 377.

[100] Barrett believes the two functions of ministry in the gospel are witness and love, exemplified by Peter and the Beloved Disciple. He equates love with the shepherding task of Peter and witness with the role of the Beloved Disciple. He states, "If the wandering preachers did not point to Jesus Christ come in the flesh, and did not love, they were not what John understood by ministers." *Church, Ministry, and Sacraments in the New Testament* (Grand Rapids, Michigan: William B. Eerdmans Publishing Company, 1985), pp. 48-49, quotation from p. 49.

[101] See footnote 2.

Gospel cannot provide. Only people in actual churches of actual communities working out actual life situations in their hour can complete the task of practical theology. This is the gospel applied.

Finally, our study has taught us that the church and its ministry must never stray from Christ and the cross. Only as the community of faith remains close to its Lord can it do God's will, learn the delights of pleasing him, experience the freedom of dedicated discipleship and the reward that honoring the Father brings when the church freely acknowledges its witness and works not to be its own but the fruit of the Vine. The gospel stresses the importance of the church's witness to Christ in its proclamation and deeds and in its love for one another. Witness and love are the bottom line, but only when those who do them point others to Jesus Christ and allow their fruitfulness to spring from Christ's death and to be joined organically to it. The words of Jesus speak to the church today, "Peace be with you. As the Father has sent me, even so I send you."

John 3:14-15: The Raised Serpent in the Wilderness: The Johannine Use of an Old Testament Account[1]

Rick R. Marrs

And as Moses lifted up the serpent in the wilderness, so must the Son of Man be lifted up, that whoever believes in him may have eternal life. (John 3:14-15).

This statement, set within the pericope of Jesus's dialogue with Nicodemus, is replete with intrigue and unanswered questions. John 3:14-15 clearly alludes to an Old Testament event (Numbers 21:4-9). However, the issues surrounding this Old Testament passage and its New Testament citation are both manifold and complex. From the Old Testament perspective, there are multiple concerns. Issues raised concern the form and purpose of this short pericope in Numbers 21, the transmission and redaction of the account, and the larger issue of the place and function of serpents in the Old Testament (and in the ancient Near East). Significantly, explicit citations and/or implicit allusions to this passage are relatively numerous both in later Jewish (Old Testament to Intertestamental) and Christian (New Testament to Patristic) writings.[2] In the Gospel of John, this reference has direct bearing on numerous important and debated matters: Johannine Christology (especially the use of Son of man in John); the Ascent/Descent motif in John; Moses typology in John.

This article intends the following: 1) set and interpret (exegete) Num 21:4-9 in its immediate context (Numbers) and in its larger context (Old Testament and ancient Near East); 2) set and interpret John 3:14-15 in its immediate context (John 3) and in its larger context (Gospel of John); 3) draw appropriate conclusions regarding the theological significance of these two passages.

---

[1] It is a pleasure to be able to dedicate this article to Dr. Frank Pack. Dr. Pack, through his teaching and preaching, has served over the years as a constant mentor and role model for younger scholars. He is a noteworthy reminder of the importance of utilizing scholarship in the service of the church. It is hoped that in some small way this article will exhibit the appreciation of the writer.

[2] A full discussion of the use of Num 21:4-9 in later Judaism is beyond the scope of this paper. For a full discussion, see: H. Maneschg, "Gott, Erzieher, Retter und Heiland seines Volkes," *BZ* 28 (1984) 214-29; A. del Agua Perez, "A proposito de la obra de Maneschg sobre la tradicion derasica de la serpiente de bronce (Nm 21)," *EstBib* 42 (1984) 203-16.

Numbers 21:4-9

From Mount Hor they set out by the way to the Red Sea, to go around the land of Edom; and the people became impatient on the way. And the people spoke against God and against Moses, "Why have you brought us up out of Egypt to die in the wilderness? For there is no food and no water, and we loathe this worthless food." Then the Lord sent fiery serpents (*hnhsym hsrpym*) among the people, and they bit the people, so that many people of Israel died. And the people came to Moses, and said, "We have sinned, for we have spoken against the Lord and against you; pray to the Lord, that he take away the serpents (*hnhs*) from us." So Moses prayed for the people. And the Lord said to Moses, "Make a fiery serpent (*srp*), and set it on a pole; and every one who is bitten, when he sees it shall live." So Moses made a bronze serpent (*nhs hnhst*), and set it on a pole; and if a serpent (*hnhs*) bit any man, he would look at the bronze serpent (*nhs hnhst*) and live.

Num 21:4-9 is situated within a larger block of materials dealing with Israel's successes and setbacks as she journeyed through the desert toward Canaan. Twin themes are the successes enjoyed through Yahweh's sustaining guidance, and the setbacks experienced through the doubt and shortsightedness of the people. Their lack of faith is most clearly manifested in their habitual murmuring.[3] Within the immediate context, there is a repeated interplay between movement (progress) of the Israelites through the sure guidance of Yahweh's hand, and death and stalemate through the repeated grumbling of the people. In Num 20, Miriam dies (20:1) and the people complain about imminent death in a desert without water (20:2-9). Moses' shortness of temper in providing water for the people (20:10-13) results in death coming near both to him and to Aaron. When the Israelites are denied passage through Edom (20:14-21), they journey to Mount Hor (where Aaron dies and his leadership is transferred to his son Eleazar [20:22-29]). Num 21 opens recounting the complete defeat and destruction of Arad (21:1-3).[4] Num 21:4-9, picking up on 20:22-29, recounts another instance in which death entered the Israelite camp because of murmuring and shortsightedness. Several of the elements in these verses pick up or parallel earlier accounts. The people, as they set out to circumvent the land of Edom (see 20:14-21), once again grumble concerning the lack of water and the miserable dietary conditions. In response, Yah-

---

[3] For a fuller discussion of these themes in the book of Numbers, see P. Buis, "Les conflits entre Moïse et Israël dans Exode et Nombres," *VT* 28 (1978) 257-70; G. Coats, "The Wilderness Itinerary," *CBQ* 34 (1972) 135-52; idem., *Rebellion in the Wilderness* (Nashville: Abingdon, 1968); S. de Vries, "The Origin of the Murmuring Tradition," *JBL* 87 (1968) 51-58; T. Fretheim, "Life in the Wilderness," *Dialog* 17 (1978) 266-72; W. Harrelson, "Guidance in the Wilderness," *In* 13 (1959) 24-36.

[4] The placement and appropriateness of Num 21:1-3 is variously interpreted. See the commentaries for discussion of the passage and proposed relocations of the material.

weh afflicts the camp with poisonous snakes. Strikingly, the people's contention with Moses gives way to confession and request for intercession. In response to Moses' prayer, the Lord instructs Moses to set a bronze snake on a pole so that those bitten may look at the bronze snake and be healed. Although quite brief, this pericope is filled with theological import and varies significantly from earlier accounts. Response to the people's murmuring is swift and decisive; further, emphasis is placed on the people's confession and the role of Moses as intercessor. Most noticeably, the poisonous snakes are not removed; rather, Yahweh provides deliverance through the gazing at an elevated bronze serpent. After this passage, we have another wilderness itinerary (21:10-20), followed by an account of the defeats of Sihon of Heshbon and Og of Bashan (21:21-35). Whereas the Israelites acceded to the refusal of the Edomites to allow passage, here the Israelites do not circumvent the land but defeat these kings and take control of their territories.

Interestingly, in Num 21:4-9 the people's discontent with the frugal life of the desert does not lead (as previously) to an act of divine help, but to punishment.[5] The punishing serpents sent by Yahweh have been understood in several ways. Although they are variously designated in the Hebrew (see above), most discussed is the nature of their "fiery" (*srp*) quality. Two interpretations have been most common: 1) *srp* refers to their appearance (they have a shiny, incandescent appearance); 2) *srp* refers to their stinging bite (its venomous quality produces a burning sensation). Although certainty is perhaps impossible, it seems not unlikely that both nuances may be intended. If these poisonous snakes are cobras (a most menacing and poisonous desert snake), both appearance and bite could aptly be described as fiery.[6]

Providing deliverance from the venomous snake bites is a bronze (or perhaps copper)[7] serpent elevated on a pole (*nes*).[8] Although some scholars have wanted to see here a case of sympathetic magic (or an act closely akin to

---

[5] M. Noth, *Numbers* (OTL; Philadelphia: Westminster, 1968) 157. J. Mays (*The Books of Leviticus and Numbers* [LBC 4; Atlanta: John Knox, 1963] 114) notes that Israel was *supposed* to recite: "the Lord brought us out . . . " (Deuteronomy 6:20-25; 26:5-9); here the confession of faith has been turned into lamenting doubt ("why have you brought us out? . . . ").

[6] For a fuller discussion, see the various commentaries. Conversely, G. Coats (*Rebellion*, 117), following a suggestion by Holzinger, considers these creatures mythical. Thus, *srp* is a borrowed name with no connection to the Hebrew root *srp*. Similarly, N. Snaith ("Numbers," *PCB* [Berkshire, Eng.: Von Nostrand Reinhold, 1982] 264) considers these serpent demons jinn of the desert appearing in snake form. Given the geographical locale of this incident, I see no reason to doubt the reality of a life threatening snakebite epidemic.

[7] A snake of bronze (an alloy of copper and tin) or of copper (*nhst* can refer to pure metal, see Deut 8:9) seems most appropriate here. This would strikingly resemble the copper color of the cobra. Further, archaeological excavations have unearthed copper snakes at several sites in the Negeb (see below).

[8] Interestingly, this term is translated by *semeion* ("sign") in the LXX.

such),[9] the later rabbinic commentators were careful to let the reader know that it was the Lord, not the snake, who restored the bitten one to health.[10] Significantly, Moses functions here solely as intermediary. He intercedes on behalf of the people; he elevates the bronze serpent on the pole.[11]

To understand this passage its form and purpose must be determined.[12] Significantly, although some scholars have considered Num 21:4-9 an aetiology for 2 Kgs 18:4 (Hezekiah's removal of Nehushtan from the Jerusalem

---

[9] For a lucid presentation of this approach, see K. Joines, "The Bronze Serpent in the Israelite Cult," *JBL* 87 (1968) 245-56; R. Boraas, "Of Serpents and Gods," *Dialog* 17 (1978) 275-77.

[10] The Aramaic Targums provide elaboration and clarification concerning the precise nature of the restoration of the one bitten:

> ... and it shall be that when a serpent hath bitten any one, if he behold it, then he shall live, if his heart be directed to the Name of the Word of the Lord. And Mosheh made a serpent of brass, and set it upon a place aloft; and it was, when a serpent had bitten a man, and the serpent of brass was gazed at, and his heart was intent upon the Name of the Word of the Lord, he lived. (Tg. Onq.)

> And Mosheh made a serpent of brass, and set it upon a high place; and it was that when any one had been bitten by a serpent, and his face was uplifted in prayer unto his Father who is in heaven, and he looked upon the brasen serpent, he lived. (Tg. Jon)

Cf. also the rabbinic statement in Mish. Ros. Has. iii.8:

> but could the serpent slay or the serpent keep alive! — it is rather, to teach thee that such time as the Israelites directed their thoughts on high and kept their hearts in subjection to their Father in heaven, they were healed; otherwise they pined away.

(Targumic and rabbinic citations are from J. Etheridge, *The Targums of Onkelos and Jonathan ben Uzziel on the Pentateuch* [NY: KTAV, 1968] 411)

[11] Some scholars have suggested that the bronze snake was none other than a metal serpent entwined about Moses's rod (so W. Eichrodt, *Old Testament Theology* [II,; Philadelphia: Westminster, 1967] 112). However, for Eichrodt, in Num 21 the importance of the pole as the leader's rod has been omitted; prominence has been given rather to the pole and serpent as an apotropaic sacred object.

[12] Determining the form and purpose of this unit is integrally related to elucidating its literary history. In this matter there is little agreement. Although vocabulary variations exist within the verses (e.g., Elohim/Yahweh; *nhs/nhs srp*), few scholars are inclined to see 21:4-9 as a compilation of multiple sources (however, see J. de Vaulx, *Les Nombres* [SB; Paris, 1972] 236-37). Since the narrative progresses smoothly, 21:4-9 is usually considered a single, unified pericope. However, assignation to a particular source is disputed. Numerous scholars derive these verses from E (e.g., Gray; Gressmann; Noth); others find here the J writer (e.g. Rudolph; Fritz; Coats); finally, several simply see a JE combination. Not surprisingly, those who argue for J authorship point to the affinities between 21:4-9 and Numbers 11:10-33a; 11:1-3 and the Act-Consequence schema of J. Those positing E authorship point to the affinities of 21:4-9 and 20:14-21 and the ethical sensitivities present in the text). Fortunately, our interest in the passage is largely unaffected by its presumed literary history. For a clear summary of the different approaches to this text, see R. Boraas, "Of Serpents and Gods," 275-77.

cult),[13] M. Noth, a most forceful and eloquent proponent of aetiological analysis throughout the Pentateuch, denies that Num 21:4-9 is an aetiology.[14] As a short narrative unit, 21:4-9 clearly is linked to the murmuring tradition. These verses seem to have two main purposes: 1) to state unequivocally that the outbreak of death from poisonous snakes in the Israelite camp was the direct result of Israel's murmuring against the Lord and against Moses; 2) to recount another manifestation of Yahweh's gracious intervention on behalf of his faithless followers. Two further aspects are worthy of note. Within the context of the murmuring tradition, this passage represents the final and most extensive response to the continual murmuring tradition. Punishment is not reserved for a few key instigators; death penetrates the whole camp. Further, whereas elsewhere Yahweh often responds to the cry of his people by removing the assumed danger (e.g., by providing food and water), here he allows the poisonous snakes to continue. Instead, he provides a way of deliverance and restoration within the context of danger and death.[15]

Finally, some attention should be given to the significance and multivalent nature of serpents in the ancient Near East and in the Old Testament. The ancients (like most moderns) were fascinated by serpents. We have ample evidence, both literary and artifactual, showing the ambivalent feelings of the ancients toward snakes. From the literary world, besides the obvious nar-

---

[13]The relation of Num 21:4-9 and 2 Kgs 18:4 is beyond the scope of this article. Clearly a relationship is evident; less clear is the nature of that relationship. Although many scholars consider Num 21:4-9 an aetiological narrative providing legitimacy and theological rationale for the presence of the bronze serpent in the Jerusalem temple in the days of Hezekiah, this conclusion is neither self-evident nor necessary. Further, the thesis that the bronze serpent was originally a Canaanite cult symbol transferred into the Jerusalem cult by David, which eventually became an idolatrous cult symbol, is lacking in substantial proof. For detailed discussions of these matters, see H. Rowley, "Zadok and Nehushtan," *JBL* 58 (1939) 113-41; G. Coats, *Rebellion*, 118-127; G. Gray, *Numbers* (ICC; Scribners, 1903) 275; P. Budd, *Numbers* (WBC; Waco: Word, 1984) 233f.; V. Fritz, *Israel in der Wuste* (Marburg: N.G. Elwert, 1970) 94f.; J. Fichtner, "*ophis*," *TDNT* 5 (1967) 576 n. 3; J. Gray, *Numbers* (OTL; Philadelphia: Westminster, 1964) 670f.; K. Joines, *Serpent Symbolism in the Old Testament* (N.J.: Haddonfield, 1974) 61-63. J. Tabick ("The Snake in the Grass: The Problems of Interpreting a Symbol in the Hebrew Bible and Rabbinic Writings," *Religion* 16 [1986] 158) notes interestingly that most modern scholars have concerned themselves with attempting to elucidate the identity of the bronze serpent, while the ancient rabbis were concerned with determining why God chose serpents for the original attack.

[14]Although Noth ("Num. 21 als Glied der 'Hexateuch'-Erzahlung," *ZAW* 58 [1940/41] 178-80) denies that 21:4-9 is formally an aetiology, he does consider that the the reason for this story being told is the later existence of the bronze serpent in the Israelite cult. The purpose of Num 21:4-9 was not to legitimize the snake as a Mosaic relic, but to remind the people that if the bronze serpent did heal, it did so only at God's behest. Similarly, G. Coats (*Rebellion*, 118) denies that 21:4-9 in form represents an aetiology, but thinks it clear that an aetiological purpose undergirds the tradition.

[15]The prominence given to the people's repentance is noteworthy. In the murmuring traditions, Yahweh's aid more typically comes in response to *complaint* by the people.

rative texts in which snakes play a central or subordinate role, come snake omen texts[16] and incantation texts against snakebites.[17] This same fascination and fear is evidenced also in ancient Jewish literature.[18] Significantly, snakes were often perceived ambivalently as aid or opponent, as bringing death or life, and were not infrequently related to fertility and marital rites.[19] This fascination with serpents is also evidenced in the artifactual remains from the ancient Near East. Bronze serpents have been discovered at Megiddo,[20] Gezer,[21] Hazor,[22] and Shechem. Apart from Palestine, a bronze serpent figurine has been found in a Hittite shrine in North Syria,[23] and a pair of bronze serpents appear situated beside each of the four entrances of the Temple of Esagila.[24] Perhaps most important is the discovery of a copper snake at Timna. At Timna (c. 15 miles north of Eilat), at the foot of one of the pillars of Solomon was discovered a small copper snake. Here the excavator B. Rothenberg unearthed an Egyptian temple of Hathor (used in the thirteenth century B.C.). It is thought that this site was taken over by the Midianites

---

[16]See, e.g., R. Whiting, "Six Snake Omens in New Babylonian Script," *JCS* 36 (1984) 206-10.

[17]The most famous snakebite incantation text comes from Ugarit (RS 24.244). For a discussion of this text and fuller bibliographic information, see: J. Nougayrol (ed.), *Ugaritica V* (Paris, 1968) 564-74; A. Rainey, "Ugaritic Texts in Ugaritica V," *JAOS* 94 (1974) 194 [bibliography]; T. Gaster, "Sharper than a Serpent's Tooth: A Canaanite Charm against Snakebite," *JANES* 7 (1975) 33-51; idem., "The Ugaritic Charm against Snakebite: An Additional Note," *JANES* 12 (1980) 43-44; M. Dietrich, et al., "Bemerkungen zur Schlangenbeschwörung," *UF* 7 (1975) 121-25; C. Bowman and R. Coote, "A Narrative Incantation for Snake Bite," *UF* 12 (1980) 135-39; J. de Moor, "Some Remarks on U 5 V, No. 7 and 8 (KTU 1.100 and 1.107)," *UF* 9 (1977) 366-67; I. Kottsieper, "KTU 1.100 — Versuch einer Deutung," *UF* 16 (1984) 97-110.

[18]See especially J. Tabick, "Snake in the Grass," 155-67; B. Bokser, "Wonderworking and the Rabbinic Tradition: The Case of Hanina ben Dosa," *JSJ* 16 (1985) 42-92. Tabick finds the reoccurrence of three major themes: the snake as a servant of God; the snake as a symbol of rebellion against God; the snake as a creature independent of God.

[19]For a discussion of the role of serpents in some marriage dramas or in fertility/sexual rituals, see D. Young, "With Snakes and Dates: A Sacred Marriage Drama at Ugarit," *UF* 9 (1977) 291-314; R. Coote, "The Serpent and Sacred Marriage in Northwest Semitic Tradition," *HTR* 65 (1972) 594-5 [dissertation abstract]; K. Joines, *Serpent Symbolism*, 64-66.

[20]Two have been discovered here: one from Stratum X (c. 1650-1550 B.C.); one from Stratum VIIIB (c. 1250-1150 B.C.).

[21]A bronze snake with an upraised head was found at the high place.

[22]Two serpents were discovered here in the Holy of Holies of Temple Area H (Stratum I [LB II]).

[23]Here a bronze statue (c. 1460-1190 B.C.) of a god holding a serpent in one hand and a staff in the other appears.

[24]These were placed by King Neriglissar (c. 559-56 BC). From a much earlier period, Naram-suen of Esnunna places a pair of metal serpents on the Temple gates at the completion of construction. This event may be recorded both in a year formula and in a royal inscription (see D. Frayne, "Naram-Suen and the Mushussu Serpents," *JAOS* 102 [1982] 511-13).

when abandoned by the Egyptians, who covered it with curtains to construct a tent shrine. The little snake was found inside the tent.[25]

These larger contexts are helpful, for they allow us to view again Num 21:4-9 from a somewhat different context. Although the ancient Israelites knew that the desert was a hostile environment, filled with dangers and potential harm (note especially Isa 14:29; 30:6), they were in need of constant reminder that her safety lay solely in Yahweh's gracious and faithful protective guidance. Especially appropriate is Deut 8:14b-16:

> . . . and you forget the Lord your God, who brought you out of the land of Egypt, out of the house of bondage, who led you through the great and terrible wilderness, with its fiery serpents (*nhs srp*) and scorpions and thirsty ground where there was no water, who brought you water out of the flinty rock, who fed you in the wilderness with manna which your fathers did not know, that he might humble you and test you, to do you good in the end.

This brief passage is a reminder of the essence of the covenant relationship between God and his people. The poisonous snakes are not removed; rather, a means of deliverance is provided. The threat of death remains lest the people again suppose they can treat God disdainfully with no consequences. However, a way of life, available only through faith, is provided.[26] As Fretheim states so well:

> Yet even in the wilderness God is responsive to the needs of these his complaining people. He provides what the context could not. The protests are answered, the cries are heard, quite undeservedly. There is a gift of healing where the pain experienced is the sharpest. Deliverance comes, not in being removed from the wilderness, but in the very presence of the enemy. The movement from death to life occurs within the very experience of godforsakenness. The death-dealing forces of chaos are nailed to the pole. God transforms death into a source of life. A sanctuary is provided in the wilderness.[27]

---

[25] According to B. Rothenberg (*Timna. Valley of the Biblical Copper Mines* [London: Thames and Hudson, 1972]) Midianite sherds are present, as are holes for tent poles. Rothenberg considers this evidence striking elucidation of the materials in Num 21:4-9. G. Wenham (*Numbers* [TOTC; Intervarsity, 1981] 156f.), like Rothenberg, utilizes this evidence to draw close links between Moses and the Midianite clans (e.g., Moses may have gotten the idea for the tabernacle and the copper snake from his Midianite relatives). Wenham then attempts to understand the underlying significance of the elevated serpent in Num 21:8-9. He considers the clue to lie in the general principles underlying sacrificial and purificatory rites in the Old Testament. Just as in the sacrificial system animals die so that sinful men may live, and polluting blood sanctifies men and articles, so here those inflamed and dying through the bite of living snakes are restored to health through a dead snake. For him, the red symbolizes first the inflammation, then the atonement and purification. For a rather different analysis, see K. Joines, *Serpent Symbolism*, 91-93.

[26] Mays, *Numbers*, 115.

[27] "Life in the Wilderness," 270.

John 3:14-15

When we turn to the citation of Num 21:4-9 in John 3:14-15, we are at once aware that John (and his audience) inherited not only the text of Num 21:4-9, but also (and perhaps more importantly) later interpretations and speculations that went with it. Thus, to understand fully and appreciate the use of this reference by Jesus (and John), we must have an awareness of various first century understandings of Num 21.[28] This information must then be related to John's highly freighted and nuanced vocabulary and theology.

Verses 14-15 are an integral part of the tightly structured and crafted pericope of 3:1-21.[29] Cohesiveness and coherence are created through repetition of key terms and phrases. Partial *inclusio* appears in vv 2, 10-11:

---

[28]In Wis 16:5-7 we find a midrash on Num 21:4-9: "Even when the terrible fury of beasts came upon them, and they were perishing through the bites of tortuous serpents, your anger did not abide to the end; only for a while were they thrown into disarray as a warning, possessing as they did a symbol of your salvation to remind them of the commandment of your law. For whoever turned towards it was saved not by the sight beheld, but through you, the savior of all (Translation of D. Winston, *The Wisdom of Solomon* [AB 43; N.J.: Doubleday, 1979]).

The citation of Num 21:4-9 in Wis occurs as a third example (antithesis) contrasting Yahweh's treatment of the Israelites with that of the Egyptians (see Wis 11-19). In the Targums, the significance of looking on the serpent is addressed: "It means turning one's heart toward the name of the memra of God" (Tg. Ps.-J.). (Note that Ps.-J. mentions the name of the memra, just as John 3:18 mentions the name of God's only son.) For further discussion of the Targumic readings of these verses, see above, n. 10. Not insignificantly, T.W. Manson ("The Argument from Prophecy," *JTS* 46 [1945] 129-133) considers John 3:14 evidence of an ongoing debate between Palestinian Christianity and Judaism. John 3:14 represents Palestinian Christian proofs; m. Ros. Has. iii.8 represents Palestinian Jewish rebuttals (for m. Ros. Has. iii.8, see n. 10).

[29]The literary structure, development, and origin of John 3 has been hotly debated. A literary analysis and discussion of possible source(s) behind the materials and the unity/disunity of this chapter is beyond the scope of this paper. For a thorough discussion of these topics, see R. Bultmann, *The Gospel of John* (Philadelphia: Westminster, 1971). (Bultmann's views on the larger context are well known: the primary element in this section is discourse; this chapter reflects the editorial work of the Evangelist; this material was derived from the "revelation-discourses.") Specifically, Bultmann thinks vv 14f. may have been composed by the Evangelist himself, since his source was uninterested in establishing a positive connection with the OT. He thinks it probable that vv 14f. replaced a sentence in the source, which spoke of the necessity of the Son of man's exaltation. For more balanced discussions, see E. Haenchen, *John 1* (Hermeneia; Philadelphia: Fortress, 1984); R. Brown, *The Gospel According to John I-XII* (AB 29; NY: Doubleday, 1966); C. Dodd, *The Interpretation of the Fourth Gospel* (Cambridge: University Press, 1963); R. Schnackenburg, *The Gospel according to St. John* (I; NY: Herder and Herder, 1968) 361-2. Schnackenburg considers vv 13-21 part of a kerygmatic exposition originally independent of the gospel narrative. Further, these verses were not the beginning of this "kerygmatic discourse," but were preceded by vv 31-36 (which contrast "who comes from above" with "who is from the earth" and speak of his heavenly "testimony"). Vv 13-21 suitably follow these verses. All this unmistakable Johannine style and content must come

Nicodemus: we know (*oidamen*)that you are a teacher (*didaskalos*) come from God . . .
Jesus: Are you a teacher (*ho didaskalos*) of Israel and yet you do not understand (*ou ginoskeis*) this? . . . We speak of what we know (*ho oidamen laloumen*).[30]

Twice Nicodemus responds to statements by Jesus with "how can this be?" (*pos dunatai* [vv 4, 9]). The first responds to Jesus's statement that " . . . unless one is born anew (*ean me tis anothen*), he cannot see the kingdom of God." The second query follows Jesus' enigmatic statements concerning the wind, introduced by "You must be born anew" (*dei humas gennethenai anothen*). Finally, vv 14-15 may echo implicitly v 8. In v 8, Jesus concludes his illustration of the wind: "so (*houtos*) it is with everyone who is born of the Spirit." In some way Spirit birth is analogous to or can be elucidated by the activity of the wind. In vv 14-15, Jesus concludes his citation of Num 21:4-9: "so must (*houtos dei*) the Son of Man be lifted up." Significantly, in vv 14-15, the complete grammatical framework of *kathos . . . houtos* appears. In some way, the lifting up of Jesus is analogous to or can be elucidated by the incident of Moses and the serpent (*kathos Mouses hypsosen ton ophin . . . houtos dei hypsothenai . . .*). The construction *kathos . . . houtos* occurs elsewhere in the NT to provide comparisons or analogies. Perhaps the most striking parallels are:

Luke 11:30: For as (*kathos*) Jonah became a sign to the men of Nineveh, so (*houtos*) will the Son of man be to this generation.
Luke 17:26: As (*kathos*) it was in the days of Noah, so (*houtos*) will it be in the days of the Son of man.[31]

---

from the evangelist himself. He considers it probable that a dialogue with Nicodemus occasioned the composition of this "kerygmatic discourse." Schnackenburg explains the present arrangement thusly: vv 13ff. were linked to v 12 on account of the *epourania* of v 12; vv 31-36 were attached to the words of the Baptist because "he who is from earth" was interpreted as the humble speaker of v 30). Conversely, F. Moloney ("The Johannine Son of Man," *BTB* 6 [1976] 180) sees these verses as part of a larger pericope (2:23-3:36) dealing with the problem of various types of faith. Chapter 3 consists of two "reasonably credible narratives" (vv 1-10, 22-30) divided by two mini-discourses (vv 11-21, 31-36) in parallel.

[30]Another *inclusio* may be intended with the reference to Nicodemus coming to Jesus at night (v 2). In vv 19-21, Jesus states that the Light has entered into the world, and those who would be followers must opt for the Light and come out of the darkness into that Light. For further structural links, see J. Neyrey, "John III — A Debate over Johannine Epistemology and Christology," *NT* 23 (1981) 115-127.

[31]Cf. the similar structure in v 24: "For as (*hosper*) the lightning flashes and lights up the sky from one side to the other, so (*houtos*) will the Son of man be in his day." *Kathos* is a standard part of introductory formulae for OT quotations in the NT. For a fuller discussion of NT citations of OT passages, see J. Fitzmyer, "The Use of Explicit Old Testament Quotations in Qumran Literature and the New Testament," *NTS* 7 (1961) 297-333 (reprinted in: *Essays on the Semitic Background of the New Testament* [Missoula, MT: Scholars, 1971] 3-58).

In both instances comparisons are drawn from OT accounts; in both instances it is Jesus as Son of man that is compared.[32]

This comparison raises several significant issues for interpretation and understanding. A primary issue involves the significance of the term *hypsoo* in v 14. Its importance encompasses a number of concerns. Central are the determination of its nuance(s) and background, and the recognition that it is Jesus as Son of man who is lifted up. Another key issue concerns the precise point of comparison between the citation of Num 21:4-9 and John 3:14-15, and its importance for both the immediate and the larger context.[33]

The nuance and significance of the term *hypsoo* has been debated extensively.[34] Clearly in John (and elsewhere) it can have and has a meaning referencing death on the cross (see John 8:28; 12:32-34). However, numerous scholars are convinced that the primary meaning of *hypsoo* is that of exaltation (and thus the ascension is the primary focus [see e.g., Acts 2:33; 5:31]). At issue is which of these meanings is intended in John 3:14 (or whether both).[35] If Jesus were speaking Aramaic, it is quite plausible that he would have used the Aramaic verb *zqp*, a term that has the dual nuances of crucifixion and exaltation.[36] Thus, a dual nuance for *hypsoo* in this passage is quite

---

[32]Of some interest is the change of subject in 3:14. At issue is the specific point of the comparison. The Son of man is not the counter to Moses, but apparently to the serpent that was lifted on the pole. (For a similar grammatical change using *kathos . . . houtos*, see 2 Cor 1:5.)

[33]Important ancillary issues within this context are the motif of ascent and descent and the apparent Moses typology in the Gospel of John (and its possible influence in this passage).

[34]For a full discussion of *hypsoo* in Judaism and early Christianity, see G. Bertram, "*hypsoo*," *TDNT* 8 (1972) 602-20. For further discussion, see below, n. 40.

[35]The issue is quite complex, since it involves not only the nuance of the particular verb, but also is closely related to the immediately preceding statement in v 13 ("No one has ascended [perf: *anabebeken*] into heaven but he who descended from heaven, the Son of man"). The use of the perfect tense in this case is quite striking. Opinions and proposed solutions are varied. Some scholars consider this use a clear indication of the post-Easter Evangelist reflecting back on Jesus's past ascension; other scholars argue that the past tense is utilized to deny that up to that point in time anyone had gone up to heaven to inquire and gain knowledge of heavenly things (see v 12). (For further elaboration of this interpretation, see below, n. 43.) R. Brown (*John*, 132) thinks this latter interpretation was perhaps the original meaning of the verse, but that with the passage of time the clause came to refer to the ascension. In a decidedly different direction, J.L. Martyn (*History and Theology in the Fourth Gospel* [NY: Harper and Row, 1968] 137) links this verse to the Paraclete. For Martyn, the Paraclete makes effective the presence of Jesus as the awesome Son of man. The Son of man ascends to heaven on a cross, but in some sense returns to earth in the person of the Paraclete and can therefore enter into conversation with "Nicodemus" as he who "has ascended" to heaven. The Paraclete makes Jesus present on earth as the Son of man who binds together heaven and earth (1:51).

[36]Conversely, M. McNamara (*The New Testament and the Palestinian Targum to the Pentateuch* [AB 27; Rome: Pontifical Biblical Institute, 1966] 145-49) sees behind *hypsoo* the Aramaic term *slg*. For McNamara, the dual nuance involves exaltation/*death* rather than exaltation/crucifixion. (Interestingly, the Hebrew term *ns* also can convey this twofold sense of death and exaltation (see Gen 40:13,19).

plausible. However, its significance is variously interpreted. John may understand the crucifixion — resurrection — ascension as one continuous action. That is, Jesus inaugurates his return to the Father in his crucifixion which culminates in the ascension. This is the "upward swing of the great pendulum of the Incarnation corresponding to the descent of the Word which became flesh."[37] Expanding upon this issue, the exposition of B. Lindars is most suggestive. He argues that the term *hypsoo* is a most inappropriate term for crucifixion. (It simply means "lift up," which is not the same as "set on a pole" or "fix to a cross.")[38] The linkage with the crucifixion resulted from an implicit association with Isa 52:13. There the Servant of the Lord is "exalted and lifted up."

The introduction of Isa 52:13 into the discussion brings us to a central issue: the larger backdrop against which these lines should be read. Numerous scholars have noted that the three *hypsoo* sayings in John's Gospel (3:14f.; 8:28; 12:32-34) correspond to the Passion predictions in the Synoptic Gospels (e.g., Mark 8:31; 9:31; 10:32f.).[39] Such a recognition is crucial, since it further elucidates the point of John's choice of this particular OT analogy and his use of terminology. Not insignificantly, just as the suffering servant of

---

[37]So R. Brown, *John*, 146. For Brown, this understanding elucidates John 8:28: "When you lift up the Son of man, you will realize that I AM."

[38]B. Lindars (*The Gospel of John* [NCB; Greenwood, SC: Attic, 1972) is neither the first nor the only scholar to note this. His exposition is cited rather as representative. G. Nicholson (*Death as Departure. The Johannine Descent-Ascent Schema* [SBL Diss. Ser. 63; Chico, CA: Scholars, 1983] 75, 103) articulates clearly the notion that *hypsoo* referred primarily to exaltation rather than execution. He downplays the centrality of the crucifixion in this passage, arguing that of central importance is the exaltation of the Son of man to heaven; this lifting up of the Son to the Father takes place through the medium of the crucifixion. P. Duke (*Irony in the Fourth Gospel* [Atlanta: John Knox, 1985] 113-4) finds powerful irony in John's use of *hypsoo* in this context (" . . . the scandalous irony of history is ironized"). As G. MacRae ("Theology and Irony in the Fourth Gospel," in *The Word in the World: Essays in Honor of F.L. Moriarty* [ed. R. Clifford; G. MacRae; Cambridge: Weston, 1973]) states:
> His interpretation of the death of Jesus as exaltation and return to the Father, the 'lifting up of the Son,' is his unique and crowning irony.

Conversely, F. Moloney (*The Johannine Son of Man* [Rome: LAS, 1976] 62) finds here *only* a reference to the cross. His argument centers primarily on the analogy with the snake. Since the snake in Num 21 did not ascend to heaven, no suggestion of the ascension of Jesus should be imported into the Johannine text. Such reasoning fails to take seriously the elaboration and expansion of OT themes and motifs, and reads OT analogies far more tightly than the ancient evidence would suggest.

[39]Parallel terms occur (e.g., *dei*; *huios tou anthropou*). Significantly, some scholars have attempted to show that John's use of *hypsoo* and *doxazo* is the thematic equivalent of the Synoptic use of *anistemi, paradidomi*, et al. For a full discussion, see F. Borsch, *The Son of Man in Myth and History* (Philadelphia: Westminster, 1967) 283-91. He concludes:
> It is clear from these examples that strong overtones of vindication and even of *exaltation* and glory are not missing in the use of the verbs *qum* and *anistemi* and that in these senses they can be related to the verbs *hypsoo* and *doxazo* found in John (p. 287).

Isa 53 serves as a backdrop for the Synoptic Passion predictions, so John 3:14 strikingly echoes Isa 52:13 (LXX):

'Idou sunesei ho pais mou kai hypsothesetai kai doxasthesetai sphodra.[40]

Viewing John 3:14 from such a perspective suggests that John intends the reader not only to look to Num 21:4-9 as a backdrop, but also to be reminded of the life and death of the Servant of the Lord in Isaiah.[41]

Thus, it is not surprising that it is Jesus as Son of man who is exalted. Such a motif accords well with the aforementioned backdrops.[42] From this con-

---

[40]The MT uses the verbs *rwm* and *ns*. Cf. similar uses of *ns* in Isa 5:26; 13:2; 11:12; 18:3; 62:10. *Hypsoo* in the LXX manifests a variety of uses (see Bertram, "hypsoo," 602-20). It can refer to the exaltation of God, who alone as the exalted one is able to exalt and elevate men. In the OT, Israel's deliverance is almost equivalent to exaltation. To be exalted means to be drawn nearer to God (this is especially true of the Servant of the Lord). Most striking is the linkage of exaltation and abasement. Abasement is often the presupposition of the exaltation of the righteous. "To turn abasement into exaltation and lowliness into loftiness is the affair of God alone and it will be a sign of the time of salvation" (*ibid.*, 607).

[41]P. Borgen (*Philo, John and Paul. New Perspectives on Judaism and Early Christianity* [BJS 131; Atlanta: Scholars, 1987] 110-112) understands the use of *hypsoo* as pivotal. He argues that both Isa 52:13 and Dan 7:13 are the context from which John 3:14 must be read. For him, both these OT passages depict installation in a royal office. Thus, the context is *enthronement*. The thematic ties he sees are extensive.

> It is thus probable that John 3:13 combines elements from Dan 7:13 and from Exod 19:20,23; 24:1-2,9,13; 34:2-4 in a way which corresponds to the fusion of elements from Dan 7:13 and Ps 110:1 in Acts 7:56. In a corresponding way John 3:14 weaves together elements from Dan 7:13f; Is 52:13 and Num 21:9 . . . to the paraphrase of John 3:13-14 previously given (no person, not even Moses on Mt Sinai, has ascended into heaven) the following can be added: only he who descended from heaven to execute his office, the divine being, the Son of Man, has ascended to heaven for the installing in office prior to his descent. The subsequent return of the Son of Man to his prior place of glory (John 6:46; 17:5,24) must take place as an exaltation through the death on the cross, to mediate life to those who believe. (112).

[42]A detailed discussion of the Son of man theology in the Gospel of John is beyond the scope of this paper. The literature on this topic is vast. For a good overview of the issues and a sampling of various approaches and interpretations, see: F. Moloney, "Johannine Son of Man," 180ff.; idem., *Johannine Son of Man*, 56f.; R. Kysar, *John, the Maverick Gospel* (Atlanta: John Knox, 1976) 35-40; M. Black, "The 'Son of Man' Passion Sayings in the Gospel Tradition," *ZNW* 60 (1969) 5-7; S. Schulz, *Untersuchungen zur Menschensohn-Christologie im Johannesevangelium* (Gottingen; 1957); F. Borsch, *Son of Man*, 272-73; E. Sidebottom, "The Ascent and Descent of the Son of Man in the Gospel of St. John," *ATR* 115-22; W. Meeks, *The Prophet-King. Moses Traditions and the Johannine Christology* (SNT 14; Leiden: Brill, 1967); idem., "The Man from Heaven in Johannine Sectarianism," *JBL* 91 (1972) 57; S. Smalley, "The Johannine Son of Man Sayings," *NTS* 15 (1968/9) 298-9; P. Borgen, *Philo, John and Paul*, 110; J. Coppens, "Le fils de l'homme dans l'Evangile Johannique," *ETL* 52 (1976) 28-81. In some ways, John 5:27 may be the most "traditional" Son of man saying in the whole NT. However, in the other eleven references to the Son of man in the Gospel of John, some surprises appear. The Son of man is linked to OT figures (e.g., Jacob [1:51] and Moses [3:14]); he is depicted as a descending/

text, four passages seem especially germane to a proper understanding of John 3:14-15:

> Truly, truly, I say to you, you will see heaven opened, and the angels of God ascending and descending upon the Son of man. (1:51)

> For as the Father has life in himself, so he has granted the Son also to have life in himself, and has given him authority to execute judgment, because he is the Son of Man. (5:26-27)

> So Jesus said, 'When you have lifted up the Son of Man, then you will know that I am he, and that I do nothing on my own authority but speak thus as the Father taught me.' (8:28)

> '... and I, when I am lifted up from the earth, will draw men to myself.' He said this to show by what death he was to die. The crowd answered him, 'We have heard from the law that the Christ remains for ever. How can you say that the Son of man must be lifted up? Who is this Son of man?' (12:32-34)

Two things seem worthy of note in these verses. First, there is movement connected with the Son of man. This movement is depicted variously as "ascending/descending"[43] and otherwise as being "lifted up." Second, this

---

ascending Redeemer (3:13; 6:62); he uses the language of sacramental mystery (6:27,53); key verbs associated with the Son of man are *hypsoo* and *doxazo* (3:14; 8:28; 12:23,34; 13:31); finally, he is the object of the blind man's confession (9:35ff). (For a fuller discussion, see J. Martyn, *History and Theology*, 131ff.). Especially debated are the provenance of the Son of man passages and their significance within the larger context of Johannine theology. Although several scholars still consider the Gnostic Redeemer myth a plausible backdrop for much of the Son of man thinking, this position has been decidedly undermined in recent years. For a significant rebuttal to this interpretation, see R. Schnackenburg, *John*, Excursus VI: "The Gnostic Myth of the Redeemer and the Johannine Christology." Also P. Borgen (*Philo, John and Paul*, 103-20) provides evidence demonstrating that much of the supposed Gnostic motifs (especially the ascent/descent motif) were known throughout the Mediterranean basin, especially within the Jewish tradition.

[43]The motif of ascending/descending in the Gospel of John is beyond the scope of this paper. Three aspects of this motif merit brief comment: 1) the background and origin of this motif; 2) the use of the perfect tense of *anabaino* (v 13); 3) the sequential order (ascent/descent vs. descent/ascent). Although some scholars have suggested Gnostic origins (e.g., Bultmann) or a Johannine apologetic against Mandaean or Hermetic literature (so H. Odeberg, *The Fourth Gospel* [Amsterdam: B.R. Gruner, 1929]), most scholars now assume that this passage more likely reflects an apologetic against a current stream of Jewish piety which claimed that ancient greats (such as Elijah, Isaiah, and especially Moses) had been allowed to ascend into heaven to receive their knowledge of God. Such ideology can be seen in several places in later Jewish literature (see e.g., the Targums on Deut 30:11-14 and Ps 68:19; the Mart. Isa. 2:9; 3:7-10; 1 Enoch 71; 4 Bar. 2:1-8; T. Abr., Recension A:10-15; Recension B:8-12). This motif may be further elucidated with reference to Prov 30:4: "Who has ascended into heaven and come down?" (An answer of "no one" seems implicit [cf. also Wis 9:16-18; Bar. 3:29.) Especially helpful is the tannaitic Midr. Mek. on Exod 19:20:

movement in some way expresses the purpose of Jesus as Son of man. Not insignificantly, Jesus as Son of man demands that onlookers acknowledge his authority from the Father (8:28). Further, the lifted up Son of man "draws men to himself" (12:32).

In these four passages, the Son of man theology in the Gospel of John is presented forcefully. Viewed from one angle, Jesus as Son of man is exalted before the eyes of the world. However, this exaltation occurs ironically in the

> *l lh msh w lyhw lm lh*
> *wl yrd hkbwd lmth*
> *ouk anebe Mouses kai Elias ano*
> *kai ou katebe he doxa kato*
> "Neither Moses nor Elijah ascended above nor did the Glory descend below."

If the backdrop for the ascent/descent motif in John is the Jewish speculation of the ascent of certain privileged ancients into heaven for revelations, then John's use increases in significance.

The use of the perfect continues to be understood variously (see above, n. 35). As mentioned earlier, numerous scholars consider it simply a reflection of the stance of the final editor and addressed community. I.e., at the time of the writing, Jesus as Son of man has ascended and is enjoying exalted status in heaven. However, such a comment remains enigmatic placed on the lips of Jesus. In striking contrast, P. Borgen (*Philo, John and Paul*, 103ff.) argues that v 13 refers to the pre-existent installation of Jesus into office. Once the installation is accomplished ("ascent"), the agent (i.e., Son of man) is discharged to execute his function ("descent"). Borgen concludes:

> These words about God's ascent in the Old Testament and in Jewish exegesis show that the "spatial" movement of ascent expresses a change in role and office and not a change in degree of divinity nor a change of a being's nature from an existence that is not divine into that of divinity.

He paraphrases 3:13:

> . . . No person, not even Moses on Mt. Sinai, has ascended into heaven, except the heavenly being who descended to execute his office; by his ascent into heaven he was installed and empowered for his descent.

(For a rebuttal to Borgen, see Nicholson, *Death as Departure*, 96-7).

Perhaps most significant is the order of the terminology. Strikingly, within the Jewish literature the sequence is consistently ascent/descent. I.e., a human agent is allowed access to the heavenly realm (ascent) and then commissioned to return with revelatory material to earth (descent). In the Gospel of John, the ascent/descent motif only occurs in discourse (not narrative) and typically is introduced into the middle of something (i.e., as an explanation of another issue). However, most striking is that the Johannine sequence is always descent/ascent. I.e., Jesus as Son of man *originates* in the heavenly realm and then descends to enter the human arena. W. Meeks ("Man from Heaven," 50) has shown in a compelling fashion that a key point of this motif is to demonstrate that the story of Jesus is played out on earth, even though he belongs elsewhere. I.e., Jesus as the descending/ascending Son of man is the stranger par excellence on earth. In contrast to the ancient greats who supposedly ascended into heaven, the Son of man originated in heaven and brought God's revelation in his descent. Not insignificantly, in 1:51 Nathanael is promised a vision of "greater things;" in 3:12 Nicodemus (a teacher of Israel) is told he will not see (believe) heavenly things! Wherever the motif of ascent/descent occurs, there is a primary emphasis on the inability of men of "this world" to understand and accept Jesus (note especially the discourse on bread from heaven in John 6 [see *ibid.*, 58]).

event of the crucifixion. Further, in the cross, Jesus as heavenly revealer reveals the quintessence of his heavenly revelation — his own identity! Jesus as exalted Son of man is revealed most clearly when he is lifted up on a cross! Viewed from another angle, when Jesus is viewed as the exalted Son of man lifted up on the cross, judgment takes place (vv 16-21). However, for those who view this exaltation properly (i.e., through the eyes of faith), the place of judgment becomes a place where life is granted rather than condemnation (v 15). The reversal is complete: the judged and condemned receive eternal life through faith! As F. Moloney states:

> The elevated Son of Man will always be the place where man can find God's revelation to men and judge himself by accepting or refusing it. . . . It is sufficient to recognize what this title meant in the Johannine Church: Jesus as the place where men will judge themselves.[44]

Notice of the above aspects allows us to consider now the point of comparison intended between Num 21:4-9 and John 3:14-15. Most striking perhaps are the potential elements for comparison left unexploited by the Gospel of John. In the LXX, the stake upon which the bronze serpent is placed is translated with *semeion* (John's term for the miracles of Jesus). Further, no analogy is drawn between the necessity for the OT people to "look upon" the serpent (and consequently the necessity to "look upon" Jesus for salvation).[45] Clearly the point of comparison is not between Moses and Jesus, since Moses is the lifter of the serpent, while Jesus is the one lifted.[46] The immediate point of comparison seems simply the lifting up that occurs in both scenes.[47]

---

[44]"Johannine Son of Man," 185f.

[45]Seeing is often a metaphor (both in the OT and the NT) for (coming to) faith. These possible points of interpretation of utilization were not left unattended by the early church Fathers. For a full discussion of the use of Numbers 21 and John 3 among the early church Fathers, see C. Lee, "Moses' Serpent as a Patristic 'Type,' " *Dialog* 17 (1978) 251-60; J. Bowman, *The Fourth Gospel and the Jews* (PTM 8; Pittsburgh: Pickwick, 1975) 358, n. 136; L. Goppelt, *Typos. The Typological Interpretation of the OT in the New* (Grand Rapids: Eerdmans, 1982) 18, n. 55.

[46]For an extensive discussion of the importance of Moses in the Gospel of John, see: R. Kysar, *The Fourth Evangelist and his Gospel* (Minneapolis: Augsburg, 1975) 141-44; T. Glasson, *Moses in the Fourth Gospel* (SBT 40; Naperville, IL.: Allenson, 1963) 33-39; J. Martyn, *History and Theology*, 93-109; W. Meeks, "Moses as God and King," in *Religions in Antiquity* (ed. J. Neusner; Leiden: Brill, 1968) 354-68.

[47]Not all scholars conclude that John only intended the lifting up for comparison. F. Moloney ("Johannine Son of Man," 60) understands three points of comparison: the lifting up; the gazing upon; the gaining of faith. Alternatively, R. Schnackenburg (*John*, 395-96) comments:

> John exploits three points which he sees as intrinsically connected: the 'exaltation,' its salvific power and the divine plan behind all (*dei*). The other features should not be allegorically interpreted. The point of the comparison is neither the stake nor the serpent, but 'exaltation.' Even the fact that the mortally wounded 'look upon' the stake is not mentioned, and hence can hardly be exploited in favour of a theory of the meaning of

Thus, again it appears that John 3:14-15 is dependent not only upon Num 21:4-9, but also is drawing upon Isa 52:13.

Although clearly the precise point of comparison is the lifting up that occurs in both passages, it may be suggested that John also knew well the language of Num 21 and stated his passage accordingly:

    Num 21:8 (LXX):   *pas ho dedegmenos idon auton zesetai*
    John 3:15:   *pas ho pisteuon eche zoen aionion.*

If the similarity is intentional, then the motif of life occurring in the place of expected death may be implicitly at the heart of John 3:13-15. Whereas gazing upon the uplifted bronze serpent restored one to health, the uplifted Son of man grants eternal life. The Johannine paradoxes of death/life and judgment/salvation are brought together in these few verses. Just as the desert serpent brought both death and life to the Israelites, so the cross of the Son of man transmitted both death and life. What begins as a discourse of confusion for Nicodemus becomes an entrance into the depth of the meaning and significance of Jesus as the Son of man. Jesus, the Son of man whose origin is heaven, comes as judge (5:27). However, precisely at the point of judgment, salvation (eternal life) is meted out to those who respond in faith to the exalted Son of man. Paradoxically though, the realization of Jesus's exaltation occurs and is demonstrated unequivocally in the crucifixion. Ironically, life comes through the death of the Son of man. The consistency and faithfulness of the Father is seen both in the deliverance from death in the wilderness and the redemption from death in the life-giving death of the Son. As Mays correctly states:

> In both cases the punishment for sin is the instrument for its healing. Men who look in faith behold in the Cross simultaneously the reality of their sin and the means of their redemption from it.[48]

    'faith.' (At most, one could compare the 'looking upon' the pierced body of Jesus in 19:37.) Rabbis and Jewish mystics speculated on this 'looking.' John does not do so . . . .
[48]*Numbers*, 115.

Counseling From the Gospel of John

Carl Mitchell

It is clear that any attempt to deduce principles of counseling from the Gospel of John will be to a great extent subjective. The basic document of the Judeo-Christian religion, the Bible, was not written specifically as a guide or text on counseling. However, it is equally clear that it does offer a great deal of insight and guidance that can be useful in the counseling process.

The Bible is a book about people and their problems . . . problems of the family, of the workplace, of adjustment, of human loss and misery, of purpose and meaning, of motivation . . . in fact there is hardly a contemporary situation which is not in some way reflected in Biblical life. Those who have believed in Jehovah have been convinced that Divine solutions to the human predicament were better than purely human solutions.

Since the prophets of the Old Testament had so much to say about how people were to live, it would seem to follow logically that the ultimate prophet so frequently depicted by them (Deut. 18:18) would have something to say of a counseling nature. The records of the life of Jesus do indeed picture him as a helper and guide to people in trouble with their lives.

The Gospel of John has been a favorite of believers through the ages precisely because it offers such comfort and help to those who read it. Therefore, in the following pages, after first giving a "style of the art" resume of psychological counseling and something of the development of Christian psychological counseling, concepts will be drawn from those portions of the Gospel of John which seem best to apply to the counseling situation. Emphasis will be placed upon the figure of Jesus as a counselor, and upon the methodology that he used.

Backgrounds of Psychological Counseling

cĒtsah and *boulē*, both of which may be translated ADVICE, are the most frequent words for counsel in the Hebrew and Greek Scriptures. While it is probable that most people today think of counseling in terms of giving advice, the contemporary technical definitions tend to include much more. English and English lament the limited view of counseling as advice giving, stating:

Counseling is a two-way affair involving both counselor and counselee. Unfortunately, both noun and verb COUNSEL retain an older meaning of advice-giving, which is now conceived as only part of the counseling process.[1]

It would be possible to fill many pages with various shades of meaning given in the terms counsel, counseling, or counselor. It appears that most of them can be included under two headings: those which center upon the counselor or the counsel given, and those which center upon the quality of the interaction of the participants. Williamson and Foley illustrate the former. Counseling is:

> ... a face to face situation in which, by reason of training, skill or confidence vested in him by the other, one person helps the second person to face, perceive, clarify, solve and resolve adjustment problems.[2]

Wren's definition of counseling is one which stresses the quality of the relationship of the participants.

> Counseling is a personal and dynamic relationship between two people who approach a mutually defined problem with mutual consideration for each other to the end that the younger or less mature, or more troubled of the two is aided to a self-determined resolution of his problems.[3]

While counseling as a specific discipline is relatively new, the resources used are as old as mankind. Almost since the beginning of human history the constructive influences of human beings upon each other have been known and appreciated. Hiltner suggests that the first recognized counselor was Jethro the father-in-law of Moses, who became Moses' advisor.[4] Those with a more negative view of counseling might see the beginning of counseling as a Biblical subject in the influence of Satan upon Eve, or of Eve upon Adam. Whatever the opinion may be, all must admit that counseling and counselors have been around for a long time, and the outcome of counseling may be either good or bad.

The twentieth century will certainly be remembered as that point in time when both the number of counselors available to the public, and the number of theoretical approaches to counseling, made a quantum leap. Today, there are literally hundreds of approaches to counseling, whose varied and some-

---

[1] Horace B. English and Ava C. English, *A Comprehensive Dictionary of Psychological and Psychoanalytical Terms* (New York: David McKay Co., Inc., 1985), p. 127.
[2] Edmond G. Williamson and John G. Foley, *Counseling and Discipline* (New York: McGraw-Hill, 1950), p. 192.
[3] Charles G. Wren, *Student Personnel Work in College* (New York: Ronald Press Co., 1951), p. 59.
[4] Seward Hiltner, *The Counselor in Counseling* (New York: Abingdon-Cokesbury Press, 1952), p. 8.

times contradictory theoretical approaches leave the public confused, to say the least. One writer, echoing frequently expressed misgivings, states,

> . . . there has been a bewildering proliferation of theoretical orientations to psyhotherapy. Each new system of therapy has faulted its predecessors on one ground or another and has claimed superiority to them. These schools, often lacking a base of research evidence, have presented an array of oppositional definitions, objectives, and therapeutic methods.[5]

In view of the above, it must be admitted that the development of psychology as a discipline has been the result of both subjective and objective factors. On the subjective side, there has been injected a mixture of folk-wisdom, intuitive insights, and often untested theoretical constructs. Usually these constructs were an outgrowth of personal philosophy or belief as to the nature of life, the role of human kind, and what constitutes successful living . . . all intermingled with opinions as to how individual personalities and qualities develop. A good example is the individual who has served more than any other to bring psychology to its present state, Sigmund Freud. Notice the following assessment of his work:

> . . . psychotherapy has never reached the stage of a truly causal science. From the beginning, classical psychotherapy stressed its own truth. Emerging out of a biological background, psychotherapy acknowledged causality as well as it could. At base, however. Freud's focus was on the degree of consonance between a patient's "reality principle" and his or her neurotic denial of it. Had the patient failed to become master of his existential options and limitations? Freud wanted to make his patients accountable for the mature planning that leads to reasonable enjoyment of life's potential — and to do it essentially from the patient's own vantage point.[6]

On the scientific side, in as far as possible (given the uniqueness of every individual) extensive effort has been made to approach psychology scientifically . . . to make it in fact a science. English and English define science as any body of organized knowledge which has been gathered through the use of systematic methods of investigation.[7] The terms "systematic methods of investigation" are usually applied to the traditional triad of description, prediction, and control. It is safe to say that almost every claim of psychologists has been subjected to the scientific scrutiny of others in the psychological community, no matter how sacred the memory or how broadly acclaimed a particular theorist may be. In fact, among American psychologists, there appears to be a trend away from "great leaders" and particular schools and a

---

[5]Darrel Smith, "Trends in Counseling and Psychotherapy," *American Psychologist* 37:7 (July 1982) 802ff.

[6]Ivan Boszormenyi-Nagy and Barbara Krasner, *Between Give and Take: A Critical Guide to Contextual Therapy* (New York: Brunner/Mazel Inc., 1986), p. 6.

[7]Horace English and Ava English, op. cit., pp. 479-480.

movement toward a "creative synthesis" or a "systematic eclecticism."[8] The just mentioned source further indicates that the longer a therapist has been working as a professional, the more likely that he or she is in transition toward an eclectic approach.

This mix of subjective and scientific elements sometimes makes people a little uncomfortable. For the general public, it is probable that the terms "science" or scientific" usually describe something more exact than that which the discipline of psychology affords. Also, the working of the scientific process itself has sometimes raised doubt as to how much actual help may be forthcoming from professionals in the field of psychotherapy. In the past several years, there have been numerous studies designed to test the claims of various forms of therapy. Some of the general conclusions on the basis of these studies are reviewed in a contemporary popular textbook in psychology.

> There have been many studies showing that approximately 66 percent of clients show improvement with psychotherapy. However, of this 66 percent, only a small percentage show impressive results, most show only some type of positive results. Moreover, approximately 33 percent of clients treated with psychotherapy show no improvement or, in a very small number of cases, actually get worse. There are also studies of people who have problems but do not seek psychotherapy. Of these, approximately 33 percent report improvement without therapy.[9]

As might be expected, given the rather tentative state of much of the discipline of psychology, this area of study has not been without its critics. Within recent years, numerous titles have attracted attention to some of the excesses and problems of modern psychology in its practical application (*The Psychological Society* by Martin Gross, *The Myth of Psychotherapy* by Thomas Szasz, and *Psychological Seduction* by William Kirk Kilpatrick, to name a few). One author, with tongue in cheek, was moved to comment that counseling is " . . . an unidentified technique applied to unspecific problems with unpredictable outcomes. For this technique we recommend rigorous training."[10]

Care must be exercised not to throw out the baby with the bath water! As research has shown, 66 percent of those seeking psychological help do benefit by it. The ongoing challenge to professionals in psychology centers on the discovery of ways to benefit the 33 percent who at present seem to show no improvement in therapy.

In the above paragraphs, an effort has been made to depict the present state of psychotherapy. What is seen is a sometimes uncomfortable mix of subjective and scientific approaches to human problems. Much of psychology

---

[8] Darrel Smith, ibid.
[9] Rod Plotnik and Sandra Mollenauer, *Introduction to Psychology* (New York: Random House, 1986), pp. 531-532.
[10] Earl Ubell, "Has Psycho-Probing Helped Anyone?" in *Morality and Mental Health*, ed. O.H. Mowrer (Chicago: Rand-McNalley and Co., 1967), p. 19.

appears to be in transition as many of the theoretical structures of the past are put to the test and found wanting. Consequently, some of them are modified and put back into the arena for further testing, while others may be discarded entirely. In the meantime, occasionally, here and there, progress is being made, and individuals are thereby better served.

Additionally, the subjecting of the theoretical substructures and claims of psychology to scientific investigation seems to be creating a greater spirit of humility and openness on the part of those who ply their trade in the field of psychology. A few years ago, some were making outlandish claims about the potential of psychology for an almost religious salvation of mankind.[11] For example, a former president of the American Psychological Association claimed that only a "rigorous, tough-minded" psychology could save mankind and guarantee the survival of the human race."[12] Another former president of this organization urged a very evangelistic "giving away" of psychology, which he claimed to be potentially "one of the most revolutionary intellectual enterprises ever conceived by the mind of man."[13] More recent appraisals recognize that real help in psychotherapy appears to come more from the personal qualities of the therapists than from a supposed "life-giving" body of psychological knowledge or insight. Comparisons of effectiveness of various approaches to dealing with human behavioral and emotional problems have shown approximately equal beneficial results. The conclusion has been that non-specific factors have been the key to improvement. In other words, while therapists have held varied and sometimes contradictory approaches to psychotherapy, they have been very similar in their personal qualities such as approachability, warmth, ability to listen, optimism about human potential, love for people, and empathy.[14]

The Development of Christian-Psychological Counseling

In an earlier period, there was frequently a spirit of diffidence and sometimes of competition between psychology and religion. This was largely due to the influence of Freud who considered religion a centering on an unreal father figure created by mankind as a result of the sense of impotency exacted by the overpowering negative forces of life.[15] Also in the development of his theories of the id, ego, and superego, which resulted in the unreasonable

---

[11]Paul Vitz, *Psychology as Religion* (Grand Rapids: Eerdmans, 1977).

[12]Kenneth Clark, "The Pathos of Power: A Psychological Perspective," *American Psychologist* 26 (1971) 1047ff.

[13]George Miller, "Psychology as a Means of Promoting Human Welfare," *American Psychologist* 24 (1969) 1063ff.

[14]Rod Plotnik and Sandra Mollenauer, op. cit., pp. 532-535.

[15]Sigmund Freud, "Obsessive Actions and Religious Practices," (1907), "Totem and Taboo," (1913), "The Future of an Illusion," (1927), in *The Standard Edition of the Complete Psychological Works of Sigmund Freud*, 9, 13, 21, ed. and trans. James Strachey (London: Hogarth, 1959).

inhibiting of the id . . . the root cause of much emotional trauma. As a result, the efforts at disinhibiting the id (centering on weakening the power of the superego) seemed to the church to be little short of the work of the Devil.[16]

In the ensuing years, the climate has warmed, and today many ministers are trained in psychology, and see counseling as an important component of their spiritual ministry. The word "psychology," comes from two Greek terms: *psychē*, which means "soul," and *logos*, which means "word." Literally then, "a study of the soul."[17] Germane to this definition are the comments of Szasz.

> The soul is the essence of the human personality; it distinguishes persons from animals or things and "causes" them to be moral agents. . . . Actually, psychotherapy is a modern scientific-sounding name for what used to be called the "cure of souls." The true history of psychiatry thus begins not with the nineteenth-century psychiatrists, but with the Greek philosophers and the Jewish rabbis of antiquity and it continues with the Catholic priests and Protestant pastors, over a period of nearly two millennia, before the medical soul-doctors appear on the stage of history.[18]

Given the "soul" nature of psychology, it is no marvel that those preparing for marriage, the elderly, the young, those experiencing difficulties with their marriage, the depressed, those with drug and alcohol problems . . . in increasing numbers find their way to "soul specialists" (ministers) in their quest for aid. One older study showed that about 42 percent of all individuals seeking help in the United States turn first to the church for that help. This same study reported that 65 percent of those who were counseled by ministers felt they had improved as a result (this as compared to 45 percent reporting improvement who went instead to mental health professionals.)[19]

While hardly a groundswell, ministers and psychologists/psychiatrists have begun to work together more closely. Clinebell, in a volume he edited on community mental health, includes a section on the role of ministers as active participants in mental health clinics.[20] Across the nation, a variety of programs are being instituted by which ministers can be trained for the important supportive contributions they can make to sound emotions. One of the earliest of these was the "Lilly Kokomo Project" held at the University of

---

[16]O.H. Mowrer, *The Crisis in Psychiatry and Religion* (New York: Van Nostrand, 1961), pp. 114-116.

[17]John Drakeford, *Psychology in Search of a Soul* (Nashville: Broadman Press, 1964), p. 2.

[18]Thomas Szasz, *The Myth of Psychotherapy* (New York: Anchor Press/Doubleday, 1978), p. 26.

[19]E.M. Pattison, "The Role of Clergymen in Community Mental Health Programs," [International Psychiatry Clinics] 5:4 (1969) 245-256.

[20]Howard Clinebell, *Community Mental Health: The Role of Church and Temple* (Nashville: Abingdon Press, 1970), pp. 160-192.

Chicago in 1950.[21] Since that time, such offerings have proliferated greatly. In addition, this relative "newcomer" to psychology called "Pastoral Psychology" has already begun to make its own important contributions to the broader field, including some very fine journals.[22]

Meanwhile, on the side of the secular practitioner in psychology, there appears to be an increasing awareness of the importance of the spiritual side of mankind. In part, this awareness of the need of psychologists and ministers to work together may be related to the complaint of clients themselves who bemoan the fact that while their religion forms a very important part of their lives, their analysts often completely ignore the subject.[23] Also, in the living experience of offering psychotherapy to clients, the ongoing interrelationship of the physical and the spiritual cannot escape notice. This important truth was penned centuries ago by king David in one of his confessional statements.

> There is no soundness in my flesh because of thy indignation, there is no health in my bones because of my sin. For my iniquities have gone over my head, they weigh like a burden too heavy for me. My wounds grow foul and fester because of my foolishness, I am utterly bowed down and prostrate; all the day I go about mourning, for my loins are filled with burning, and there is no soundness in my flesh. I am utterly spent and crushed; I groan because of the tumult of my heart (Psalm 38:3-8 RSV).

One must be impressed with the number of theorists who are presently stressing ideas similar to king David's. Mowrer, a past president of the American Psychological Association, related all emotional problems to sin and accused the church of having betrayed mankind in turning the treatment of the mentally disturbed over to those outside of the church.[24] Jung, formerly an associate of Freud, worked to bring religion back into legitimate relationship to psychology and psychiatry[25] Allport, perhaps the greatest American psychologist, also wrote and lectured widely in an attempt to bring about a rapprochement between religion and psychology in order that both spiritual and mental health practitioners might benefit from each others' areas of accomplishment and expertise.[26] Glassar, the developer of "Reality Therapy," underscores the distructive nature of irresponsible behavior, and holds

---

[21]Granger Westberg, "The Role of the Clergyman in Mental Health," *Pastoral Psychology* 11:104 (1950) 18-22.

[22]E.g., *Journal of Psychology and Theology, Pastoral Psychology, Religious Education, The Journal of Religion and Health,* and *Review of Religious Research.*

[23]Philip Woollcott, Jr., "The Psychiatric Patient's Religion," *Journal of Religion and Health* 1:4 (1962) 337-349.

[24]O.H. Mowrer, op. cit.

[25]Carl G. Jung, *Psychology and Religion* (New Haven: Yale University Press, 1938); see also Carl G. Jung, "Psychotherapists or the Clergy," *Pastoral Psychology* 7:67 (1956) 27-43.

[26]Gordon Allport, *The Individual and His Religion* (New York: MacMillan, 1950).

that if man refuses to live responsibly in terms of what he believes to be right, he will not be able to cope satisfactorily with life.[27] Frankl has developed Logotherapy (which Carl Rogers calls one of the outstanding contributions to psychological thought in the last fifty years) on the premise that mental health is inexorably intertwined with purposes and ideals that are of sufficient value to merit the cost and the pain of living. In his experience, this leads many to search for the super-meaning that can be found in God.[28] Blazer, a psychiatrist and leading gerontologist, reports a study showing that 40 percent of American psychiatrists believe in God and attend church either regularly or occasionally, while 53 percent send their children to religious schools.[29] Pullias, widely respected as an eminent professor of psychology and education, and as a practicing psychologist for almost 50 years, gave the following recommendation in an open letter to his former students:

> The important things in life are the things of the spirit. Whatever one may achieve in material possessions, in worldly prestige, in physical power is as nothing compared with those qualities of heart and mind which partake of the nature of God. All other things come and go with the uncertain turns of fortune. But true greatness of spirit cannot be moved. Material things are good when they are kept in their place — that is, subordinate to the spiritual.[30]

Jesus as Counselor

In the foregoing paragraphs, an effort has been made to establish two principles: the first is that due to the varied nature of human kind, a strong element of psychology has been, and will no doubt continue to be, subjective and intuitive; the second is that the soul nature of psychology, and the spiritual nature of persons, legitimizes a spiritual approach to the treating of human problems. Now some indications will be offered from the Gospel of John centering on Jesus as a counselor and upon the methodology that he used.

In one of the important Messianic passages of Isaiah, one of the titles given the one who was to come was the term "counselor." "For to us a child is born, to us a son is given, and the government will be upon his shoulder, and his name shall be called Wonderful Counselor, Mighty God, Everlasting Father, Prince of Peace," (Isa. 9:5 [Heb.]; Isa. 9:6 [Eng.]) The Hebrew word *yāʿats*, which is translated "counselor," connotes "one who gives counsel."

In the body of the Gospel of John, Christ is never referred to specifically as "counselor," although this term is applied repeatedly by Christ to the Holy

---

[27]William Glassar, *Reality Therapy* (New York: Harper and Row, Pub., 1965).
[28]Viktor Frankl, *Man's Search for Meaning* (New York: Simon and Schuster, Inc., 1984).
[29]Dan Blazer, *Healing the Emotions* (Nashville: Broadman Press, 1979), p. 9.
[30]E.V. Pullias, *A Search for Understanding* (Dubuque, Iowa: Wm. C. Brown Pub., 1965), pp. 55-56.

Spirit (14:16,26; 15:26; 16:7). However, in John 14:16 it is implicit that Jesus also considered himself to be a counselor. Notice his statement: "And I will pray the Father, and He will give you another Counselor, to be with you forever, even the Spirit of truth . . . " Jesus, in the larger context, is discussing his impending departure with his disciples, and is attempting to prepare them for his absence. In stating that "another Counselor" will be given, it is clear that he considered himself to be their present counselor.

> *Parakletos* . . . is primarily a verbal adjective, and suggests the capability or adaptability for giving aid. It was used in a court of justice to denote a legal assistant, counsel for the defense, an advocate; then, generally, one who pleads another's cause, an intercessor, advocate, as in 1 John 2:1, of the Lord Jesus. In the widest sense, it signifies a succourer, comforter. Christ was this to His disciples, by the implication of His word "another" (*allos*, another of the same sort, not *heteros*, different) Comforter," when speaking of the Holy Spirit . . .[31]

Kittle and Friedrich go somewhat more extensively into the history and background of the term *parakletos*, but their conclusion is essentially in agreement with Vine's.

> The use of the term *parakletos* in the New Testament, though restricted to the Johannine writings, does not make any consistent impression. . . . In 1 John 2:1, where Jesus Christ is called the *parakletos* of sinning Christians before the Father, the meaning is obviously "advocate," and the image of a trial before God's court determines the meaning. . . . The Spirit, however, is not the defender of the disciples before God but their counsel in relation to the world. . . . What is said about the sending, activity and nature of this *paraclete* (16:7,13-15; 15:26; 14:16ff., 26) belongs to a very different sphere, and here (cf. Jesus in 14:16) *parakletos* seems to have the broad and general sense of "helper."[32]

He was identified as a counselor.

Jesus was seen as a source of help by those who had need. There was something discernable in him that struck people with the thought, "Here is a person who can give the assistance that I seek." When the disciples of John were brought into contact with Jesus, they immediately used the term "rabbi," which means "teacher" (1:38). His demeanor and teaching were so electrifying that very soon huge multitudes were following him wherever he went (6:1-2), so much so that at times he would separate himself from them (6: 15-21), only to have the crowd search him out again (6:22-25). Eventually, Jesus'

---

[31]W.E. Vine, *An Expository Dictionary of New Testament Words* (London: Oliphants, Ltd., 1957), p. 208.

[32]Gerhard Kittel and Gerhard Friedrich, eds., *Theological Dictionary of the New Testament*, 5 (Grand Rapids: Eerdmans Pub. Co., 1968), pp. 803-804.

fame and popularity became so great that he began to pose a political problem to the religious and political leadership in Jerusalem. "The Pharisees then said to one another, 'You see you can do nothing; look, the world has gone after Him'." (12:19). It is interesting that a sort of final summation of the qualities of Jesus as a "people helper" is given by John toward the close of the Prologue when he declares, "And from His fulness have we all received grace upon grace. For the law was given through Moses, grace and truth came through Jesus Christ," (1:16-17). Counseling is as much a gift as it is a skill, and people seem able to individuate those who have this gift.

He was available.

Jesus made himself available to the people who needed and desired his help. He did this by being in their midst. John depicts Jesus encountering people in the public streets (1:35-39), at a wedding feast (2:1-10), at a well by the side of the road (4:3-26), by the seaside (6:1-14), in the temple area (8:1-11), in a private home (12:1-3) . . . in short, wherever there were people, there we find Jesus in their midst, always open to being approached by those needing help.

He identified with the people.

Jesus had the ability to identify with people in all their areas of living. He grew up in a family where sometimes he had to encounter contrasts with those who were his own kindred (7:1-5). Eventually, perhaps the bulk of his own physical family, and certainly the majority of his fellow countrymen, rejected him and his claims (1:11). He had to deal with considerable vaciliation on the part of his closest friends and followers (18:25-27), with one of them eventually betraying him (18:2-13). He knew what it meant to be tired and thirsty (4:6-7). In fact, the writer of the book of Hebrews makes the claim that no human problem or trial eluded Jesus, because that was a vital part of his identification with humankind in order that he might become the succorer of those who are in trouble (Hebrews 2:14-18). A summation of the degree to which Jesus understood the human condition is presented by John in these words, " . . . He knew all men and needed no one to bear witness of man, for He Himself knew what was in man," (2:25).

He was word oriented.

The Gospel of John begins with the much discussed Prologue, where John centers upon the Eternal-Word nature of the Messiah (1:1-18). It is not the purpose of this writer to delve into the various possible meanings that have been attributed to Jesus being characterized as the Word. What is important for this writing is the fact that the Bible presents God as the source of language (Genesis 1 and 2), and as one who communicates by the spoken word to humankind (as the Bible itself evidences). While thoughts, deeds, and feelings constitute the heart of humanity, the spoken word is invariably the medium by which such are interpreted for the benefit of the understanding of others. Even the most thorough-going Rogerian finds it necessary to rely upon words in the process of psychotherapy. Little wonder, then, that the Counselor of the ages would personally be referred to as the Word, and that he would use the word as the means by which his counsel would be made known to all persons (17:7-8,20-21). Counselors who are effective are always good communicators. In fact, it may be said that counseling is communication.

He used an eclectic approach.

In present day language, Jesus appears to have used an eclectic approach in dealing with people and their problems. It is clear that he varied his manner of intervention in terms of his interpretation of the need. However, it is interesting to see how often he used a confrontational approach, especially with those who were attempting to avoid facing up to their own reality (4:16-18; 6:26-27); or those who were not being honest with themselves or with Jesus and needed to be shocked into facing up to the seriousness of their circumstances (8:44); or those who just needed a very direct-loving reminder of the course to follow (5:14); or finally, those who were in danger of making a serious error and needed to be warned in very clear terms (13:38).

He was not judgmental.

As an aftermath of having taught counseling at the graduate level for 15 years, this writer has observed that one of the most difficult aspects of counseling, perhaps especially for ministers, is that of learning to withhold judgment. A most human tendency is the feeling that in every situation one must decide if he or she is for or against something, or if something is good or bad, or if he or she likes or dislikes the thing in question. The predisposition to be judgmental has been documented in a well-known study undertaken at the University of Illinois, where Osgood and others demonstrated that the majority of the meaning content of words is evaluative (an instrument called the Semantic Differential resulted from this research).[33] Early in his ministry, Jesus made it very clear that he did not come into the world to judge humanity, but to show all how to live successfully (3:17). A notable example of his intent to heal rather than to judge or condemn is found in the case of the woman caught in the act of adultery and brought to Jesus for judgment. After having dampened the ardor of her accusers for making a scapegoat out of her by reminding them of their own personal sin (some suggest that he may have been implying that they had all been guilty of this same sin) he then encourages her to sin no more and tells her that he does not accuse her (8:1-11). Jesus always made it clear where he stood on moral and ethical issues, and he never left people with the feeling that he somehow approved of their wrong actions. However, he came across as someone who wanted to understand, who was

---

[33]Charles E. Osgood, George J. Suci, and Percy H. Tannenbaum, *The Measurement of Meaning* (Urbana: University of Illinois Press, 1957).

very sympathetic with human weakness, and who held out forgiveness, acceptance, and help, rather than condemnation.

He was optimistic about people.

A key characteristic of Jesus as a counselor was his ability to see clearly the potential of the persons with whom he came in contact. It was his practice to urge them on to their potential rather than evaluate them and be turned off by their present circumstance. He very obviously had a basic optimism about people. Nothing could illustrate this better than his selection of his disciples. Imagine one who intended to initiate a world movement that was to last until the end of time, deciding to do this with the likes of those whom he chose to be his apostles . . . a tax collector, a politic activist, barely literate fishermen . . . if Jesus had had a public relations person working with him, he would probably have resigned over such choices. John tells about the call of Simon, the impetuous fisherman. As he was presented to Jesus by his brother Andrew, Jesus looked at him and told him that he was going to change his name from Simon to Cephas or Petros (Aramaic and Greek words for rock) (1:40-42). What a marvelous prospect and challenge for this rough unstable man to be informed that in Jesus' view he had the quality to become something as strong and consistent as a rock. Interesting too, is the fact that the very writer of the Gospel of John, widely heralded as the "apostle of love," was at the time of his call so anger-prone and combatant that Jesus calls him a "son of thunder" (Mark 3:17). Jesus knew that this intense energy which early on could have been so destructive (Luke 9:54) could later be rechanneled into equal intensity for the noble and for the lovely. One of the most important qualities of the successful counselor is the ability to project this kind of optimism and hopefulness in order that the client, too, can catch the vision of the possible in his or her life.

He believed in the freeing power of truth.

Jesus believed in and was irrevocably committed to the power of truth. It was the truth that would set one free (8:32). He himself was the source of truth (14:6). His purpose in coming into the world was to make truth available to God's creation (1:17). He dramatically set forth the difference between the life based on untruth which would shun the light and seek to live in darkness, and the life based on truth which would seek the light because his or her deeds do not need to be hidden (3:20-21). Those who have worked very extensively with emotionally distressed persons will have noted the degree to which deeds of darkness often lurk in the background of such problems. Jesus also demonstrated how one can walk toward one's destination and goals without stumbling when truth and openness and light characterize his or her conduct (11:9). He implies that his own mission was to offer the light by which his disciples would be able to walk successfully (12:35). Jesus indicated that his own consistent walking in the light of truth made it possible for him to go ahead unafraid of the threats that surrounded him personally

(11:8-10). In counseling, it is especially the case that only those who seek honestly to find the truth of their situation (regardless of what this may mean or demand) have the opportunity of becoming free.

He avoided being manipulated.

Jesus did not allow himself to either be manipulated by or forced to play the games of the people with whom he associated. On one occasion, a large group of persons that in his view were not sincerely interested in his message, but rather were looking for the easy handout, had this brought to their attention in no uncertain terms: "Truly, truly, I say to you, you seek me, not because you saw signs, but because you ate your fill of the loaves. Do not labor for the food which perishes, but for the food which endures to eternal life; which the Son of Man shall give to you . . . " (6:26-27). When the politically minded began thinking how advantageous it would be to have as their king one who had such marvelous powers, they decided to try to force Jesus to become king. He promptly withdrew himself from them and literally headed for the hills (6:15). Every counselor has felt the pressure at times to say what people want to hear, or to do what they want done when in his or her heart it was obvious that this would not be best and would be a sacrifice of principle. Jesus' example is a marvelous demonstration of how important it is that counselors maintain integrity at all times.

He was always consistent.

There was a perfect consistency between Jesus' standards, words, and actions. His challenge to those who questioned his claims was that until they could find some inconsistency in his life, they should accept the truth of his statements (8:46). His stinging rebuke of his distractors was that they had more interest in peer acceptance than in living up to the standards of Abraham or of the Law of Moses (5:44-47; 8:39). John includes an unhappy note on some of the main Jewish leaders who, while being convinced of the truth of Jesus' claims, valued acceptance by the Pharisees more than personal integrity, and therefore refused to act upon their faith (12:42-43). By way of contrast, Jesus, in the presence of the priestly court, claimed that all he had taught and done had been out in the open with nothing being done secretly (18:20). The failure to be consistent with one's beliefs or standards . . . to live up to what the individual perceives as "right," is a major issue in mental health. It is not only legitimate but essential as well that counselors insist that clients' deeds be examined in the light of the clients' own belief systems.

He prized purpose.

The famous logotherapist, Viktor Frankl, is fond of quoting Neitzsche's statement, "He who has a why to live can bear with almost any how."[34] He

---

[34] Viktor Frankl, op. cit., p. 9.

also draws attention to research done in France which indicated that 89 percent of those polled stated that people need something to live for. Additionally, 61 percent admitted that there was either something or someone that was so important to their lives that they would even be willing to die for that person or thing if necessity demanded it. He quotes a similar study undertaken by researchers from Johns Hopkins University involving some 48 colleges. They found that 78 percent of the students participating said that the number one goal of their life was to find purpose and meaning.[35] This writer's conclusion after 21 years experience as a therapist is that what is lacking in many lives is precisely a cause that is important enough to them that it will at least match the personal investment demanded by life. What is for the moment unsupportable can become supportable when one's cause is upgraded. Jesus knew that his own personal death was a part of his progress toward the successful completion of his mission (3:14-15; 8:28; 12:32-33). He was careful to specify that he would not be constrained to die by the hand of others, but that it was his choice and that he would do so voluntarily because his cause demanded it (10:17-18,27-28). He made it very clear to his disciples that following him would (for at least some of them) eventually lead to their death as well (15:20; 16:1-3). From his viewpoint, the most critical problem was not the fact that one must suffer for a cause, but rather that many would find no cause greater than physical life itself (12:24-25). Those who would successfully embrace whatever trials or suffering lay in the way to their goals as followers of Christ were assured that the subsequent reward would be great (12:26). There is, in fact, much joy to reward those who stand by their purposes through whatever trials until their goals are achieved. The writer of the book of Hebrews shows how Christ was drawn toward the cross by the anticipated joy that lay beyond it, and from Jesus' example encourages his followers to be similarly steadfast.

> . . . let us lay aside every weight, and the sin which clings so closely, and let us run with perseverance the race that is set before us; looking to Jesus the pioneer and perfecter of our faith, who for the joy that was set before him endured the cross, despising the shame, and is seated at the right hand of God. Consider him who endured from sinners such hostility against himself, so that you may not grow weary or fainthearted, (Hebrews 12:1-3).

He loved people.

Jesus had a genuine love for and concern for people. In fact, it may be said that the total investment of his life hinged on two great laws: to love God with all of one's heart, soul, and mind; and to love one's neighbor as one's self (Matthew 22:37-39). He was the good shepherd who lived for the benefit of his sheep . . . and who would eventually die for them (10:1-15). Those who are experienced in the art of counseling say that it best proceeds as a sort of

---

[35]Ibid., p. 105.

love affair between counselor and client (a serving rather than exploiting love). It is in the climate of such care and concern that individuals are frequently emboldened to dig out long denied or hidden realities about themselves or others. Emotionally detached cold psychological specialists may make a living but they will not be able to lead to life.

He was committed to the power of love.

Jesus was thoroughly convinced that love is the most awesome and invincible power available . . . that there was no weapon known to Satan or man that could withstand it. His own record demonstrates that. As Durant wrote, "Caesar and Christ had met in the arena, and Christ had won."[36] Jesus based the continuity of his mission on this particular virtue. He commanded his disciples to love each other as he had loved them (15:12,17) . . . not a superficial casual, costless love, but a deep burning commitment love that would give one the power to die for a friend (15:13). In a personal way, Jesus designates love as the key to whether or not his will would be respected by his followers. Those who did not put Jesus' will into practice, even to the point of preempting their own will, could not claim to be his disciples (14:15,21-24; see also I John 2:3-6). The sweet aftermath of such loving obedience would be that both Jesus and the Father would make that person their dwelling place (14:23). The badge of distinction of his followers would be that they loved each other. In Jesus' view, this would authenticate their claim that they were his followers (13:34-35). The finished work of Jesus was intended to be a demonstration to all persons that God loves them and that his greatest desire and joy (and that of Jesus as well) was that Jesus' followers eventually be with him to participate in his glorification (17:22-26). Perhaps a conclusion of all the above for counseling is that love will pay the price. Christ is of course talking about *agapē*, the freely offered, non-exploitative love which comes from the free choice of the individual, and can therefore be commanded. This writer has seen repeated instances where such a choice and commitment to love has held persons steady in the most trying of circumstances, and made it possible for them to conquer in battles with persons and with conditions.

He felt with others.

Jesus was a man of empathy. He was touched by the plight of an embarrassed host and was moved to turn water into wine (2:1-11). He was angered by those who exploited people for their own gain and misrepresented God the Father in the process (2:13-17). He wept at the death of a friend as he beheld the misery and the grief of the family (11:33-35). He was touched by the anxiety of a father whose son was grievously ill and healed the son (4:46-54). As elsewhere observed, such personal qualities as empathy and understanding

---

[36]Will Durant, *Caesar and Christ* [The Story of Civilization: Part III] (New York: Simon and Schuster, 1944), p. 652.

are the distinctives of successful therapists even more than the particular theoretical framework used by the therapist. A study that was made of the counseling ability of hairdressers, bartenders, family lawyers, and work supervisors showed very positive results, no doubt due to just such personal qualities.[37]

He reinterpreted the stimulus.

The thrust of at least some of Jesus' instructions to his disciples fits the psychological concept of "reinterpreting the stimulus." (See for example his discussion of how one should respond to violence or to an enemy in Matthew 5:38-48). The basic idea involves going beyond the immediate stimulus (word, act, mood, attitude) to try to understand the motivation or cause that lies behind it. This, then, affords one the opportunity of responding in either a more satisfying or a more appropriate way. Until this is done, the interaction between people is often like that of two sparks bouncing off of each other. The original stimulus thus has an almost dictatorial power to set the response. By reinterpreting the stimulus, it is possible to respond to others in terms of either their needs or what is best, as opposed to what they may seem to deserve. A good example would be Jesus' treatment of Peter after he had repeatedly denied being Jesus' follower (21:15-17). Even though Peter had failed him miserably, Jesus reinstated him as an apostle and commissioned him to "feed his sheep." In a broader sense, Jesus exercised this principle in dealing with the people generally. Even though they had rejected him and demanded his death, he was willing to die for them because they had acted in ignorance (Acts 3:14-17), and even while on the cross he prayed for their forgiveness (Luke 23:34). It was Jesus' hope that after his death and resurrection many of those who had momentarily rejected him would come to believe in him through the teaching of the apostles (17:20-21). The very writing of John was calculated to fulfill that hope (20:30-31). It is frequently true that in interpersonal conflict power shifts from the one presenting a destructive and disruptive stimulus to the one who has the insight and the will to go beyond the immediate stimulus thereby giving a different and more constructive reply. One can make a difference!

He was a spontaneous counselor.

There are of course many ways to categorize counselors. Some counselors (one would hope it is the bulk of them) have a genuine concern for the well being of their clients. To the best of their ability they attempt to relate to their needs. There are others (one would trust that they are few in number) who enter into a counseling relationship primarily for their own benefit. This may be referred to as the "spontaneous" versus the "impulsive" approach to counseling. The spontaneous counselor does not try to solve his or her own

---

[37]Emory L. Cowen, "Help Is Where You Find It," *American Psychologist* 37:4 (April 1982) 385ff.

problems at the expense of the counselee . . . nor does he or she project either personal problems or personal solutions onto the client. The spontaneous counselor has sufficient insight into self to be able to keep his or her feelings, needs, solutions and experiences separate from those of the person being served. Special care will be taken to do this when the counselor begins to register similarities between self and the client. If he or she should arrive at a point where it was very difficult to maintain such a separation, he or she would refer the client to another therapist. The impulsive counselor makes the mistake of mixing his or her own personal baggage with that of the client, so that it becomes unclear as to who is being helped. As a result, indications, solutions, or attitudes of the counselor may be imposed on the one seeking help. Jesus was definitely a spontaneous counselor. In reference to his own mission, he was able to make a distinction between his own glory and that of God who had sent him (7:18). In reference to others, he was the "good shepherd" who would lay down his life for the benefit of his sheep (10:11) . . . this as distinguished from the "hireling" whose only interest in the sheep was for whatever personal gain might be forthcoming. The "impulsive" shepherd would very readily abandon the sheep in the face of danger (10:12-13). Occasionally, this writer has been called to the assistance of persons who were used, sometimes even sexually, or otherwise manipulated by the very person they had gone to in trust for help.

He was disciplined.

Jesus modeled personal discipline as a concommitment of life. Any who have been involved in counseling know the trials and heartaches (brought on self and others) by individuals who lack personal discipline. To leap and then look, to decide and choose primarily on the basis of feeling, to initiate without carrying to conclusion, to fail to have a well-thought-out plan and purpose for life, to fail to have some thoughtful means of prioritizing . . . are all disastrous and hopelessly complicating for life. It is frequently true that a lack of discipline (impulsivity) is the key to depression, hostility, nervousness, and assorted other personal problems. Jesus had a blueprint for his life. He had chosen to fulfill God's plan for the redemption of the world, a plan which involved words, deeds, and eventually Jesus himself being offered as a sacrifice for sin; and he held to it unswervingly (8:14,26-29). Furthermore, he carried God's purpose through to its completion. His words on the cross, "It is finished," almost certainly carry a greater meaning than just indicating the moment of his death (19:30). Jesus was a hard worker who was diligent in the fulfillment of his obligations (4:35). Before his death, he claimed that he had done all the work assigned to him (17:4). Because he had a clear purpose and plan, he was able to prioritize in a meaningful way (4:31-34). What he knew to be first really did come first in his life. Jesus was a man of discipline and was able to teach his main clients (the apostles) to be so as well, as their later lives showed.

He was well developed socially.

Jesus was human in the best sense of that word. He was friendly, social, and appears to have had a good sense of humor (His humor is not as visible in the Gospel of John as it is in the Synoptics . . . see for example Matthew 19:24; 23:24; Luke 13:32). Humor has long been noted as a sign of health. On the other hand, the loss of humor accompanies the development of various forms of mental illness. Frankl, in his description of the fight for survival in the concentration camps under Hitler, refers to the value of humor as a symbol of somehow being able to rise above the momentary circumstance, of not being defeated by it.[38] Being an attractive, sociable, optimistic, and humorous person is very important to the counseling process. Jesus was all of these.

He modeled a servant spirit.

People who seek counseling are often confused as to the purpose of life. The media have helped many to erroneously believe that the fundamental goal of life is to be happy, or to be successful, or to be assertive, and on and on. From the Biblical perspective, the question of purpose is easily answered. Jesus penpoints servanthood as the highest position available to a human being. One of the last acts of Jesus before his death was the washing of his disciples feet (13:3-17). Notice his words in verse 15, "For I have given you an example, that you also should do as I have done to you." John does not include scenes described in the Synoptics where the disciples are vying with each other for position in the coming kingdom (Matthew 20:20-28; Mark 10:35-45; Luke 22:24-27). Jesus responds to their selfish ambition by affirming that the greatest in the kingdom will be the one who most perfectly becomes the servant of others. Trouble in homes and throughout society characteristically grows out of a selfish desire to be served. Even those who spend their time serving others have sometimes been so brainwashed by contemporary ways of thinking that they end up feeling reduced and bitter because they are servants. Once a person begins to realize the divine status of serving and starts to experience the joy and satisfaction of serving, a lot of tension subsides and life becomes sweeter. Paul recalls the precise words of Christ. "It is more blessed (happy) to give than to receive," (Acts 20:35). When tried, it works!

He emphasized the blessings of productivity.

Every person in the world would like to experience inner peace and joy, although many are extremely disillusioned as to the prospect. Jesus, as a counselor, in fact promises peace and joy to those who follow him and his indications. By identifying with Jesus, it is promised that peace will result, even though life will always present its challenges and difficult times. Jesus

---

[38]Viktor Frankl, op. cit., p. 54.

can promise peace because he has met and overcome the world (16:33). He encouraged his followers to not be intimidated by the world. His peace, which is freely given, differs from worldly peace in that it has the power to calm the heart even while external turmoil may continue (14:27). Realistically, he promises adequate help in time of need (16:7,13). Joy is promised to those who ask and receive in his name (16:24). In part, this joy is related to being productive in one's own life (15:1-11). At the conclusion of the passage just indicated where Jesus stresses the urgency of a fruitful existence, he says, "These things I have spoken to you, that my joy may be in you, and that your joy may be full." One does not have to live very long in this world to realize that there is not much fun in just being a consumer. As the years pass, there is very little satisfaction in looking back at an essentially parasitic life . . . but there is a great deal of satisfaction in looking back at work well done, at the meaningful development and use of potential, and at persons who have been served (these all seem basic to the concept of self-actualization). Jesus also encourages the joy of anticipating his future reward. Isaiah had prophecied that the "suffering servant" would divide the "spoils" of his victory with others (Isaiah 53:12). Toward the end of his ministry, Jesus promised that troubled hearts can be eased by contemplating his return and the sharing of his heavenly home with those who believe in him (14:1-6).

He was a man of emotion.

Jesus was an emotional man (11:34,38), but he was not controlled by his emotions. It can be learned from the life of Jesus that the more consistency there is between one's deeds and principles, the more spontaneous it is possible to be in the displaying of emotion. Jesus' displays of emotion were always perfectly suited to the occasion. His love for his disciples was expressed in everything he did which involved them (13:1). While he was not foolhardy, his courage is clearly evident (18:3-8). His anger flamed hot against those who by their evil actions misrepresented the Father and discouraged the believers (2:13-17). On the other hand, he knew how to dominate emotions which, if acted upon, would have carried him away from his purpose (12:27). A very significant part of being a person consists in the emotional makeup of humankind. It is important to express emotion in as much as it is consistent with personal faith and purpose. However, some potential emotional response is not appropriate because it may be incorrectly motivated, or because it may be damaging to another person. While one does not have direct control over one's feelings, it is possible to choose whether or not a particular emotion should be expressed, and in what way. Eventually, the only real control possible over emotions is achieved by monitoring one's thoughts and actions. It is possible to think and act one's way into different and more appropriate ways of feeling (see Genesis 4:6-7).

He taught individual responsibility.

Several years ago, this writer took a graduate class in ministerial counseling to visit a mental hospital. There, we had the opportunity to sit in on a small patient-led group. At a certain point, almost as one person, the group turned on one of their fellows who had been in the hospital the longest, and told him he should leave the hospital and begin taking care of himself. When he tried to excuse himself, the group stayed on his case. Finally, he said, "You are saying to me that unless I become responsible for myself, I cannot be a person." Psychology has been through a long dark night in which it (in at least some of its elements) flirted with the idea that people are not to be held responsible for themselves and their actions. Thankfully, the few who still hold to this concept appear to be a vanishing breed. While it is clear that many persons (and especially one's own family) exert tremendous influence upon him or her, in the final analysis, if there is to be any progress, an individual must accept responsibility for self and for what one can do. Jesus warned that all must finally appear before God to answer for their lives (5:28-29). Even in what is a favorite scene for most, the case of the woman taken in adultery, Jesus stresses both forgiveness and responsibility: "Neither do I condemn you; go your way; from now on, sin no more," (8:11). The bottom line appears to be that until one accepts responsibility for oneself, that person is destined to either be a perennial babe, or a perennial victim of life's circumstances. Jesus, however, did not follow the erroneous practice of his contemporaries who foolishly attributed blame to persons for conditions for which they were not responsible (9:1-3,34).

He believed in individual freedom of choice.

The Judeo-Christian religion is a teaching religion. In both the Old and the New Testaments, God appealed to the minds of those who were willing to hear him. Jesus draws attention to this truth when he quotes from the prophet Isaiah, "And they shall all be taught of God," (6:45). Elsewhere, it is stated that God's will is that none perish, but that all be saved (2 Peter 3:9). It is obvious that so far as salvation is concerned, God will not have his way. While it is his desire that all be saved, few will be (Matthew 7:13-14). The reason . . . God created humankind with the freedom of choice, a freedom which he will not preempt! Jesus regretfully acknowledged this when he said, ". . . you are unwilling to come to me, that you might have life," (5:40). Yet, he encourages that right choice by saying, "If any man is willing to do his will, he shall know of the teaching . . . ," (7:17). Even though it may be so deeply hidden as to be almost lost, counselors must believe that some degree of choice remains for their clients. An important part of the route to mental health involves the thoughtful exercise of that choice. This usually will demand the often time-consuming process of teaching and leading toward personal discovery of wiser and more successful ways of responding to one's situation. Experience will show that this is the way to growth and to autonomy. Counselors who make decisions for clients lack respect for the God-given right of choice and promote dependency rather than autonomy. While Christ very emphatically spoke the truth and laid out alternatives, he never violated individual right of choice.

He followed up on his contacts.

Jesus, as occasion demanded, followed up on those whom he had helped. After his encounter with the Samaritan woman, he remained for two days to work further with her and with the people of her city (4:40). He sought out the lame man whom he had healed shortly before at the Pool of Bethesda, and gave him further indications as to what he should do (5:14-15). The man who had been born blind, who was healed by Jesus, soon found himself in contrast with the local religious authorities as a result of his having been healed. His own parents refused to come to his aid out of fear of these same authorities. John states that Jesus, "having found him," came to his assistance (9:13-39). It is frequently the case that genuine care is shown by taking the time to make a phone call, or write a letter, or even to make a personal visit just to see how a client is doing.

He gave greater importance to the spiritual.

The distinctive of Christian counseling is the holistic approach that is used. Not only is the spiritual part of persons recognized and given attention (along with the social, physical and intellectual) but the spiritual is considered the most important. When Nicodemus came to Jesus at night, Jesus went immediately to the spiritual, insisting that unless there is an encounter between the Spirit of God and the human spirit (He called it a rebirth of water and of the Spirit) then one cannot enter the kingdom of heaven (3:1-10). When conversing with the Samaritan woman at the well of Jacob, he bypassed her interest in the purely physical water, counseling instead that she give attention to the spiritual water which he was prepared to offer her (4:13-14). To the physically hungry people who were following him for the "loaves and the fish," Jesus countered that there was a spiritual food that they would do well to seek above the physical (6:27). There appears to be an increasing number of therapists who believe that a great deal of human problems are primarily spiritual in nature and to some degree must have a spiritual solution (Mowrer, Jung, Frankl, Allport, Oates, Clinebell, Tournier, Blazer, Faulkner, Dobson, Peck, et al.). The world is filled with spiritually hungry persons, and Christian counselors believe there is a spiritual food for the soul that is curative and satisfying. Wise use of confession, restitution, repentance, prayer, Scripture reading, forgiveness, and worship (both corporate and private) are viable aids to emotional health and furnish a firm foundation for a better future.

Conclusion

Many years ago, one of my students wrote the following words:

> There is a sense in which the aims of . . . counseling are the same as those of the Church itself — bringing people to Christ and to the Christian fellowship, aiding them to acknowledge and repent

of sin and to accept God's freely offered salvation, helping them to live with themselves and their fellowmen in brotherhood and love, enabling them to act with faith and confidence instead of the previous doubt and anxiety, bringing peace where discord reigned before . . . .[39]

Even as the religiously oriented counselor should not separate the spiritual from the physical, social, and the intellectual; it is equally inadvisable for others to separate the physical, social and intellectual sides of humankind from the spiritual. While a counseling session is not a church service or an occasion for preaching, it is certainly a proper place in which to explore the spiritual and ethical values of those clients who acknowledge their importance. As one psychiatrist has stated:

> It is a classical distinction between the preacher and the therapist that the former preaches, and the latter does not . . . the former professes himself to be an advocate of a formal morality, whereas the latter, theoretically at least, considers matters pertaining to morals and ethics as irrelevant to his detached and scientific pursuit of psychological understanding. In the actual practice of psychotherapy I have long found this classical distinction to be both irrelevant and inapplicable to the chief business at hand, namely, the assistance demanded by the patient and required of the therapist . . . Perhaps we have underestimated the importance of morality to the individual . . . Unlike the preacher, we do not advocate any particular code of ethics, nor, by and large, are we to prescribe any particular course of action. But, we must, I think, insist with our patients that they consider the right and wrong of their actions carefully in the light of their own standards; that they expose their standards to the buffeting of diverse opinion; and that they try hard to identify and dispel excuses and rationalization and to arrive at the essential truth of their position . . . Integrity is, I submit, the goal of all therapy. In its attainment, moral issues, for from being treacherous bogs to be avoided, are the proper arena for our therapeutic battles — battles which will require of the therapists on occasion a far more active intervention than is provided for in the psychoanalytic model.[40]

The Christian counselor takes what Allport called a "step beyond" the above position, seeing in Jesus and his teachings essential truths for successful living. Such truths (counsel) are particularly evident in the Gospel of John. As Allport has written:

> We may rightly ask, "After tranquilizers, what? After energizers, what? After electroconvulsive therapy, what? After psychoanal-

---

[39]Robert C. Ard, "Pastoral Counseling," (*Unpublished Paper*, Pepperdine University, Spring, 1968).

[40]Wolfgang Lederer, "Some Moral Dilemmas Encountered in Psychotherapy," *Psychiatry* 34:1 (February 1971) 75-85.

ysis, what?" Here, religion enters its claim. When the psychiatrist says, "We must integrate this life," religion replies, "I am the potential integration you need."[41]

---

[41] Gordon Allport, "Behavioral Science, Religion and Mental Health," *Journal of Religion and Health* 2:3 (1963) 187-197.

The Theology of the Signs in the Gospel of John

Thomas H. Olbricht

Much attention in recent years has been directed to the significance and function of signs in the Gospel of John. The focus on signs has resulted from studies in the redaction, structure and theology of the gospel.[1] I wish to concentrate on the theological role of the signs, with reference to structure or redaction insofar as these impinge on the theology.

The Central Role of the Signs

In John 20:30-31, the signs are clearly assigned a fundamental role in respect to the purpose of the gospel.

> Now Jesus did many other signs in the presence of the disciples, which are not written in this book; but these are written that you may believe that Jesus is the Christ, the Son of God, and that believing you may have life in his name.

These verses are universally recognized as the purpose of the gospel in its present form.[2]

Identifying the purpose has become complicated because of revised understandings of the structure of the gospel. Rudolf Bultmann argued that three sources lie embedded in the gospel: a signs source, a discourse source, and a passion narrative.[3] J. Louis Martyn, building on Bultmann, contended that

---

[1] Smalley in a recent article identifies the contemporary preoccupation in Johannine studies with tradition, structure, the nature of the community, and the theology, but not all of these are so directly related to the theology of signs. Stephen S. Smalley, "Keeping up with Recent Studies, XII. St John's Gospel," *Expository Times* 97 (1986) 102-108.

[2] Rudolf Bultmann, *The Gospel of John A Commentary*, trans. G.R. Beasley-Murray (Philadelphia: The Westminster Press, 1971), pp. 698f.; Robert Kysar, *John* (Minneapolis: Augsburg Publishing Company, 1987), pp. 309ff.; Rudolf Schnackenburg, *The Gospel According to St. John* (New York: Crossroad, 1982) I, pp. 154-156; Massey H. Shepherd, Jr., "The Gospel According to John," *The Interpreter's One-Volume Commentary on the Bible*, ed. Charles M. Laymon (Nashville: Abingdon Press, 1971), p. 7.

[3] Bultmann, *John*, pp. 16-18, 111-129. The first German edition of the commentary was dated 1941. For a discussion of contemporary source analysis see: Robert

the signs source was basic, to which was added and interlaced the discourse material.[4] Robert Fortna argued that the signs source was a proto-gospel and influenced the canonical gospel throughout.[5] That the gospel was constructed from sources and has undergone redaction is now commonly accepted by critical scholars.[6] John 20:30-31, accordingly is the purpose of the signs source, but may not reflect the purpose of the whole gospel.

In my perspective the gospel is a literary unity, and John 20:30-31 does indeed set forth the purpose of the gospel, which in turn highlights the theology of the signs.[7] Certain features noted by scholars are therefore not so much interlaced sources, but the result of the manner in which the gospel reached its canonical form,[8] a position similar to that of Raymond Brown, Rudolf Schnackenburg, and C.K. Barrett.[9]

The Central Theology in John

According to John 20:30-31, the signs which Jesus performed were many.[10] It is my judgment, despite a popular view that the specific signs number seven, the author, in fact, did not intend a catalog comprised of any specific

---

Kysar, *The Fourth Evangelist and His Gospel* (Minneapolis: Augsburg Publishing House, 1975), pp. 10-81.

[4]J. Louis Martyn, *History and Theology in the Fourth Gospel* (New York: Harper and Row, 1969); J. Louis Martyn, "Source Criticism and Religionsgeschichte in the Fourth Gospel," *Perspective* 11 (1970) 247-273.

[5]Robert T. Fortna, *The Gospel of Signs*, SNTSMS 11 (Cambridge, Cambridge University Press, 1970); Robert T. Fortna, "Source and Redaction in the Fourth Gospel's Portrayal," *Journal of Biblical Literature* 89 (1970) 151-166.

[6]Bruce Vawter, "Some Recent Developments in Johannine Theology," *Biblical Theology Bulletin* 1 (1970) 33-40. Stephen S. Smalley, "Keeping up with Recent Studies XX. St. John's Gospel," *Expository Times* 97 (1986) 104f.; So Kysar, *John*, pp. 11-15.

[7]While I am not impressed by all the details I concur with Smalley's methodology in establishing the unity of the gospel. Stephen S. Smalley, "The Sign in John XXI," *New Testament Studies* 20 (1974) 275-288.

[8]I think Smalley, "Recent Studies," p. 104. is essentially correct, " . . . we can allocate . . . three major steps in its composition: stage 1, the apostle John in Palestine transmits his version of the Jesus tradition to his immediate circle of disciples; stage 2, the Johannine group, with the apostle, moves to Ephesus, and the fourth evangelist begins a first draft of the Gospel, at which point the *distinctiveness* of the Johannine account of the Christian gospel begins to emerge; and stage 3, after the death of John, the beloved disciple, the Fourth Gospel is redacted, authenticated and published by the Johannine church."

[9]Raymond E. Brown, *The Gospel According to John* (Garden City: Doubleday, Vol. 1, 1966; Vol. II, 1970) xxiv-xl; lxxxvii-civ.; Schnackenburg, *John*, I, pp. 44-104; C.K. Barrett, *The Gospel According to St. John* (Philadelphia: The Westminster Press, 1978). In regard to "a source containing a sequence of miracle stories . . . " Barrett wrote: "I see no evidence that proves, or indeed could prove, that it was so, or even that the hypothesis has such weight of probability as to make it a valuable exegetical tool." p. 19.

[10]Other mention of many signs are: 2:23; 3:2; 4:45; 6:2; 7:4; 7:31; 9:16; 11:47; 12:37. The first two signs are specifically numbered and from this fact some scholars conclude that the next five are thereby adumbrated. But a specific sign is also cited

number.[11] What is significant about the first two signs is that they occurred in Cana of Galilee.[12] The RSV translates 2:11 "This, the first of his signs, Jesus did at Cana in Galilee . . . " Though he is not arguing my point, Barrett translates it, "Jesus did this as the first of his signs [in Cana of Galilee]."[13] While scholars freely substitute among the specific signs, they seldom challenge the number as seven. The reason is that seven serves as a wedge for championing a non-consensus entry.[14] A better ground, I contend, is frank recognition that the seven framework is a scholarly construct.[15]

---

with the catching of the 153 fish (John 21:11). Kysar lists eight signs by including the 153 fish. Robert Kysar, *John the Maverick Gospel* (Atlanta: John Knox Press, 1976), p. 68; Also, Donald Guthrie, "The Importance of Signs in the Fourth Gospel," *Vox Evangelica* 5 (1967) 77.

[11]The traditional catalog of seven is: 1) the water changed into wine (2:11); 2) the healing of the nobleman's son (4:54); 3) healing the man at Bethesda; 4) feeding the 5000; 5) walking on water; 6) healing the blind man; and 7) raising of Lazarus. See, for example, Merrill C. Tenney, "Topics from the Gospel of John, Part II: The Meaning of the Signs," *Bibliotheca Sacra* 132 (1975) 147-154. These are the ones narrated in some detail; Brown, *John*, p. cxxxix. While in Jerusalem between sign one (2:11) and sign two (4:54) Jesus performed many signs (2:23) showing that the emphasis is upon signs one and two occurring in Cana. Those who disavow 2:23 as signs either attribute the comment to the redactor rather than the sign source, or disregard the significance, so Brown, p. 528. The best explanation is, however, that neither early or late versions of the gospel envision a seven sign limitation.

[12]The question arises as to why Cana of Galilee is singled out. Shepherd, "John," p. 712, proposes that Cana ties the wedding events with the Nathanael story immediately preceding (1:43-51), since Nathanael was from Cana (21:2). He also notes that Cana is part of a cycle of stories, a point made by several others including Brown, *John*, pp. cxl-cxliv, and Francis J. Moloney, "From Cana to Cana (John 2:1-4:54) and also the fourth evangelist's concept of correct (the two Cana signs) and incorrect faith," *Studia Biblica* II 80 (1978) 185-213. It is these two signs as part of a cycle that I find the most convincing. Grassi asserts that the Galileans receive the first benefits of God's salvific acts, citing Acts 2:7. Joseph A. Grassi, "The Wedding at Cana (John II 1-11): A Pentecostal Meditation?" *Novum Testamentum* 14 (1972) 133; De Jonge suggests that the two signs contrast with those in Jerusalem which did not lead to true faith. M. De Jonge, "Signs and Works in the Fourth Gospel," Supplement *Novum Testamentum* 48 (1978) 107-125; Brown in addition cites the scholars who see the singling out of Cana and the numbering as evidence of the sign source, pp. 194f.; Collins says it is simply that. R.F. Collins, "Cana (Jn. 2:1-12) — The First of His Signs or the Key to His Signs?" *Irish Theological Quarterly* 47 (1980) 83.

[13]Barrett, *John*, p. 193. On 4:54 he wrote, "The whole verse refers back, through vv. 3, 43, to the miracle at the marriage feast at Cana," p. 248.

[14]Varying views exist as to which events qualify in the seven. Smalley, "The Sign in John XXI," *New Testament Studies* 20 (1974) 275-288, argues that the catch of 153 fish is the seventh sign, and thus chapter 21 is not an appendix; Marc Girad, "La Composition structurelle des sept 'signes' dans le quartieme evangil," *Studies in Religion* 9 (1980) 315-324, followed by Joseph A. Grassi, "Eating Jesus' Flesh and Drinking his Blood: The Centrality and Meaning of John 6:51-58," *Biblical Theology Bulletin* 17 (1987) 24-30, argue for the blood and water upon Jesus' death as a sign.

[15]The seven catalog is not presupposed by Sandra M. Schneiders, "The Face Veil: A Johannine Sign (John 20:1-10)," *Biblical Theology Bulletin* 13 (1983) 94-97; Gerald L. Borchert, "The Fourth Gospel and Its Theological Impact," *Review and Expositor* 78 (1981) 254, who claims the cleansing of the temple as a sign, *contra*

Many incidents in addition to the detailed miracle stories at minimum possess the same stages of faith as signs and perhaps therefore qualify as signs, for example, Jesus' encounter with Nathanael, his remarks to Nicodemus regarding being born from above (John 3:1-13), Jesus' statements to the woman at the well (John 4:10-19),[16] and most importantly the death and resurrection of Jesus (John 20:10-29) which immediately preceded the signs statement.[17] I will argue this conclusion again in discussing Nathanael and the woman at the well. The signs were legion, suggesting accumulative proof, but John was not interested in numbers for numbers' sake. Faith building, for him, involved recounting certain powerful signs from among the myriads which occurred. I conclude that neither the structure nor the theology of John is dependent on the elsewhere significant number "seven."[18]

The purpose for the signs was either to bring people to belief, to confirm beliefs already held, or both.[19] I am inclined to think John had in mind first of all deepening the faith of believers, but he was also concerned with bringing others to faith, aroused by those who single mindedly believed in Jesus. The signs lead to a faith which specifically affirms Jesus as "the Christ, the Son of God."[20] In the language of the gospel this means concretely that Jesus was sent from God (John 5:36) and therefore possessed the very nature of God (1:1-3).[21] This faith results in life for the believer. In the context of the gospel,

---

Smalley, "The Sign in John XXI," p. 277, fn. 5; Guthrie, "Importance," and Peter Riga, "Signs of Glory, The Use of 'Semeion' in St. John's Gospel," *Interpretation* 17 (1963) 402-424.

[16]Riga discussed the encounters with Nicodemus and the woman at the well from this perspective. Peter Riga, "Signs of Glory," pp. 408-410.

[17]Since I do not have time to discuss the resurrection, I point to 2:18-22 where the sign given the Jews is the resurrection. See Fortna, "Source and Redaction," p. 166. Guthrie, "Importance," argues for the resurrection as a sign on the grounds that Thomas sought physical signs, the other disciple believed because of the empty tomb (20:29), and that no sign is more important in the gospel than the resurrection; also Paul Ciholas, "The Socratic and Johannine *semeion* as Divine Manifestation," *Perspectives in Religious Studies* 9 (1982) 260; De Jonge affirms the crucifixion and resurrection as important for explaining the significance of the signs, p. 117; Brown, however, controverts the resurrection as a sign, (p. 1059).

[18]For example, the seven churches of Asia (Revelation 2-3) and the seven seals (Revelation 5:1-8:5).

[19]C.K. Barrett, *The Gospel According to John*, 1978) argues on grounds of both the Greek tense and internal evidence that Riesenfeld is right that " . . . the gospel belongs within the church and is not a missionary tract," p. 575; Also Brown (pp. 1055-1061) and Schnackenburg (III, 337-339); But W.D. Dennison, "Miracles as Signs: Their Significance for Apologetics," *Biblical Theology Bulletin* 6 (1976) 190-202, admits that nothing can be settled by the tense of the verbs, but argues that John had an evangelistic or apologetic intent, pp. 190-194.

[20]20:31. Note the confession of Nathanael which has early import in the gospel. "Rabbi, you are the Son of God! You are the King [messiah?] of Israel!" (1:49).

[21]Bultmann focuses on Jesus as the "revealer" even though one section heading (45) is "The Sending of the Son," Rudolf Bultmann, *Theology of the New Testament* (New York: Charles Scribner's Sons, 1951, 1955) II, pp. 33-69. I think Hans Conzelmann, *An Outline of the Theology of the New Testament* (New York: Harper & Row, 1969), pp. 341-347 is more correct in emphasizing the son as sent.

"life" no doubt connotes "eternal life" (John 3:15-16; 4:13-14) which begins here and now, though death occurs even for the believer.[22]

These then are the central theological seams running through the gospel. The question remains as to the manner in which John perceives the signs as bringing about deepened faith. Do the signs automatically and without misappropriation or failure lead to faith?

The Signs as the Route to Faith

John and the Synoptics

In the Gospel of John the signs are pointers. It is appropriate first of all to ascertain that to which they point. By contrasting John with the synoptics the object of faith becomes clear. In John the miracles are focused upon who Jesus is, that is the preexistent one sent from God. This purpose is unmistakable in John 12:37: "Though he had done so many signs before them, yet they did not believe in him." For John, what is at stake is the recognition and confession of Jesus as divine son.

In the synoptics the miracles of Jesus are primarily acts of power through which the reign of God is established in a world of opposition and evil. They also serve as indicators that the prophecies in regard to the Messianic age are being fulfilled.[23] The word most typically used is *dynamis*, commonly translated either "mighty work" or "miracle" but most frequently "power" or "powers."[24] In contrast with the synoptics, John reports no miracles which serve to counteract the power of Satan including even exorcisms, though hostility exists between Satan and Jesus (13:27; 14:30; 16:33).[25]

In John, the divinely empowered actions of Jesus are normally called "works" or "signs."[26] "Works" as a description of Jesus' activities, equates what Jesus did with the prior work of God. "My Father is working still, and I am working," (5:17). "Works" has a larger field of meaning than either sign or miracle, but it includes both. Jesus' work encompasses his words as well as his action. "The words that I say to you I do not speak on my own authority; but the Father who dwells in me does his works," (14:10). The manner in

---

[22]C.H. Dodd, *The Interpretation of the Fourth Gospel* (Cambridge: Cambridge University Press, 1968), pp. 144-150; Raymond Brown, *John*, pp. cxvii-cxxi. Brown, correctly I believe, argues for a launched eternal life rather than eternal life fully realized (eschatology) in John.

[23]Brown, *John*, p. 525-526.

[24]Karl Heinrich Rengstorf, "Semeion" *Theological Dictionary of the New Testament*, Gerhard Kittel and Gerhard Friedrich, eds., trans. Geoffrey W. Bromiley, (Grand Rapids: Wm. B. Eerdmans Publishing Company, 1971) VI, p. 230. It is instructive that while *dynamis* occurs 38 times in the synoptics it does not appear in John.

[25]Kysar, "John the Maverick Gospel," p. 10; Brown, p. 525.

[26]The synoptics employ *ergon* 9 times as compared with John's 27 times. *Semeion* is found in the synoptics 28 times, or an average of 9, and in John 17 times.

which the works of Jesus are paralleled with those of God make it clear that his works identify him as sent from God. "The works which the Father has granted me to accomplish, these very works which I am doing, bear me witness that the Father has sent me," (5:36).

In John, signs are divinely empowered acts or words which demand a decision for or against who Jesus is, that is, the preexistent one sent from God. In the synoptics, in contrast, the heavenly signs are either eschatological clues heralding the inbreaking of the kingdom, or a proof demanded by unbelievers. In Acts, signs and wonders are the miracles of Jesus and the apostles.[27] Signs do not occur in John to adumbrate the coming kingdom (that is eschatological) perhaps because for John the incarnation of Jesus means that the kingdom is now present. "Signs" occur in John as a demand (2:18; 6:30), but more characteristically signify the decisive works or miracles of Jesus. They are a stage on the way to belief, and ultimately to sonship (1:12) and life for those who epitomize true faith. They point beyond themselves. As Brown stated, "If Jesus gives life to Lazarus, the remarks of Jesus (xi 24-26) show that the restoration of physical life is important only as a sign of the gift of eternal life."[28] But the signs obviously do not always attain their intended end.

Signs of Faith

We are now ready to address the question of how it is that signs bring about faith in Jesus as the Christ, the Son of God (20:31).[29] It is helpful to identify five stages on the road to faith. The sign at the wedding in Cana may function as a paradigm.

As the text now stands, Andrew affirmed that Jesus is Messiah, though earlier he had called him Rabbi. Other disciples attached themselves to Jesus; one unnamed (1:35-41), as well as Peter, Philip and Nathanael. It is these disciples and perhaps others who were invited to the wedding in Cana. Since the disciples are the ones singled out, we need to focus on them. 1) The first stage of faith is the inclination or predisposition to believe that Jesus possesses unusual powers.[30] These followers are already predisposed to expect the extraordinary from Jesus. A second factor now enters, the confidence or faith of Mary who preceded both Jesus and the disciples to the wedding (2:1-5). Mary is committed to the power of Jesus' word, "Do whatever he tells you," (2:5).[31] 2) The faith of another (or others) is a catalyst for a chain reaction of faith in the presence of a sign.

---

[27]Rengstorf, pp. 234-240; Brown, p. 527.

[28]Brown, p. 529.

[29]Most helpful for this pursuit is Robert Kysar's chapter 3, "Seeing is Believing — Johannine Concepts of Faith" in *John the Maverick Gospel*, pp. 65-83.

[30]Kysar discusses this point from the perspective of which comes first, faith or knowledge, and concludes that faith only occurs where extra-sensual perception already exists.

[31]Cf. Moloney, "From Cana to Cana," p. 191, who points to the parallel circumstance in the second sign. He argues that the official was likewise committed,

The sign now occurs. Six stone jars for Jewish rites of purification were filled to the brim. Jesus asked the servant to draw some out and take it to the steward. The steward after tasting it declared the water now wine superior to that served earlier. 3) The sign commences with a common, ordinary physical entity. But something occurs to that entity as the result of Jesus' word, which points beyond the physical, demanding explanation. The sign therefore elicits wonder, a puzzle, and to some looking on a misapprehension. The steward could not fathom the quality of the wine.[32] The revision in the physical entity itself points to a caring, helping God. A crisis was averted at the wedding by the abundant supply of wine.[33] The sign is not a marvel for its own sake. In the words of Barrett, it is " . . . a symbolic anticipation or showing forth of a greater reality of which the *semeion* is nevertheless itself a part."[34]

An explanation for a sign is more often than not endemic to the context, rather than an overt verbal explication. In this case the water turned to wine not only demands powers from beyond, but also prefigures a radical change in the grounds of purification for all humankind.[35] The sign therefore points beyond itself with twofold or even multifold meanings.[36]

4) With people for whom signs create belief one discovers a curiosity, an openness to the prospect that there is more to the specific word or action than meets the eye. Behind and beyond this physical event are powers reaching in from God himself. The steward had cause for wonderment, but he knew little about the chain of events. The servants knew from where the liquid in the jars came, but they knew little about Jesus. The disciples, however, were primed with expectancy. They were open. "His disciples believed in him," (2:11). Their faith had now reached a higher plateau. This was not yet the apex, but they were launched.[37] Even after the resurrection, signs from ear-

---

"The man believed the word" (4:50), which served as a catalyst for the belief of his household (4:53).

[32]Dennison, "Miracles as Sign," p. 196 finds three essential elements in the sign: (1) the parable (*semeion*), (2) miscomprehension, and (3) explanation.

[33]Collins, "Cana," pp. 79ff. He declares that through the signs Jesus "ministers to man in his need."

[34]Barrett, *John*, p. 76.

[35]Collins, "The First of His Signs," p. 89. "He is contrasting the old era of God's gifts to his people, the era of the Jewish dispensation, with the new era of Jesus' messianic gifts to the people, effected in the hour of his glorification." Cf. Ernst Haenchen, *John* (Philadelphia: Fortress Press, 1984) I, p. 179.

[36]Kysar, *John*, p. 46, "teaming with meaning." The scholars who declare a sign source and redaction find the overlay of the change of the dispensations in the contribution of the final author. Since however, this author includes all these details they all somehow contribute to his theology of signs.

[37]Additional signs also heighten their faith, which is not yet mature, 6:4-9; 11:14. Jesus told the disciples that what he was about to do in regard to Lazarus was for enhancing their faith, 11:15 "so that you may believe." Notice the Greek construction is the same as 20:31, supporting the position that the signs are to heighten faith in those who already possess a measure. Of the six traditional signs the lame man and the man born blind apparently know nothing of Jesus before their healing. We aren't told whether the former came to faith, and the later came to faith only after a second

lier moments etched indelibly on the memory, additionally deepened faith (2:18-21).

But what is the faith of the disciples when they believed in him? It was, of course, commitment to Jesus as a person.[38] The sign was not the reality. It pointed to the reality — Jesus sent from God — and demanded faith. 5) In the context already established in John, the events at the wedding established with additional clarity that Jesus was the "Word become flesh," the "only Son from the Father," (1:14). His glory was manifested (2:11), that is, his divinity, the same as when God tented among his people in the past, pinpointed by the presence of his glory (Exodus 40:34-38).

It is now appropriate to isolate the five stages of faith and ascertain, first of all, whether these characterize the traditional catalog. The five stages are: (1) a predisposition to believe that Jesus possesses extraordinary powers, (2) a person or group of strong faith providing a catalyst, (3) the sign, involving both event and contextual interpretation, (4) an openness to perceive the transcendent dimension to which the sign points, and (5) a profound conviction that Jesus is Son of God, was sent to reveal God, and to die for the sins of humankind. Examining the other six traditional signs with the five stages in mind, these difficulties accrue: no predisposition on the part of the man born blind is suggested in the text; no catalyst is identified in the healing of the lame man and the feeding of the five thousand, though the disciples presumed to be present likely serve this function; in the case of Jesus walking on the water stages 1 and 2 are obscure, and 4 and 5 missing;[39] and finally, it is not clear in the case of the lame man that he came to faith. Despite these few difficulties, however, the succeeding six traditional signs confirm, in an amazing manner, the stages of faith in our paradigm — the water changed to wine at Cana.

I now turn to the surprising presence of these stages in the encounters of Jesus with Nathanael, Nicodemus, and the Samaritan woman at the well, but developing at length only the latter. On John's grounds, extraordinary statements during the encounters qualify at minimum as faith inciters, but we are justified, I think, in perceiving them as signs even though scholars with empirical predilections locate the signs in action rather than in words.[40]

---

encounter with Jesus. Signs, therefore, may be the occasion to one to knows little to come to faith, but not upon the action alone. This seems to support the view that signs deepen the faith of those who already have begun a trust relationship with Jesus.

[38] Kysar, *The Maverick*, makes John's view of faith clear, pp. 77-79.

[39] The ambiguity of the stages in this case may lend support to the professed inadequacy of this event as compared with the other signs.

[40] The significance of this observation is not blunted by agreeing with Kysar that hearing is sensory, *The Maverick Gospel*, p. 75. Empiricists from Aristotle on have assigned priority to seeing and touching over hearing. It is possible to argue that the fundamental sense in the Biblical faith among the five, is hearing, e.g., Deuteronomy 6:4, and John 5:24 " . . . he who hears my word and believes him who sent me has eternal life." In this light it is instructive that "hear" occurs in John 50 times even though "see" in its various forms is more frequent, and "see" is the only word of the two used in connection with *semeion*. Bultmann calls Jesus' comments to Nathanael "miraculous power," and discusses the resulting faith, *John*, pp. 104ff.

Kysar paves the way by noting that the path to faith involves hearing as well as seeing,[41] but he fails to follow through, identifying as signs only actions which may be seen.

I would like now to notice briefly how the encounters with Nathanael and Nicodemus involve the characteristics of a sign. The sign in each case is an extraordinary — necessitating power from beyond — statement. In the Nathanael story Jesus' statement, "Before Philip called you, when you were under the fig tree, I saw you," (1:48) has these features, as also does Jesus' declaration to Nicodemus, "You must be born anew," (3:7). In regard to the other steps: (1) the predisposition of each is obvious (1:47; 3:2); (2) others of faith are present in the case of Nathanael (1:45), and perhaps the disciples with Nicodemus though the text does not so state; (3) the sign, i.e., the statement creates wonderment; (4) the openness to Jesus as God is clear with Nathanael (1:49), and perhaps later with Nicodemus (19:39), and (5) both begin the road to faith that Jesus is Son of God, Messiah (1:49). So whether signs, and I think in John's sense they qualify, these astounding statements replicate the same path to faith.[42]

The account of the woman at the well exhibits the same characteristics. She is not predisposed to sense anything unusual about Jesus, but her puzzlement grows until she rushes home in astonishment. She is first struck by the fact that he, a Jew, speaks with her (4:9). Then she is puzzled by his comments on living water (4:10-15). But what really triggered the numinous was Jesus' remarks about her husbands (4:28-29). Because of what he described in regard to her private life, she sensed divine presence. The Samaritan woman's excitement was catalytic. The people were predisposed to hear Jesus out (4:39). Jesus spent two days with the Samaritans, who believed because they heard for themselves (4:42). Notice that belief resulted from what the woman and and her fellow inhabitants heard! According to Kysar, "Belief in the word (logos) of Christ is for John more mature and authentic than faith in his works."[43] The word creating faith had a divine aura; it was not an ordinary word. The word sired the same progeny as the sign, and just perhaps qualified as a sign. At their optimum efficacy signs point to Jesus as sent from God, and lead ultimately to faith in Jesus as disclosing the true reality both here and beyond.

When the Signs Fail

The signs do not automatically produce faith. They by no means exhibit *ex opera operato*. The offspring of Bultmann's source theory locate a tension in the text regarding signs and faith. The assertion is that the signs source regarded the signs as maximizing faith, whereas the later redactor (for conve-

---

[41] Kysar, *The Maverick Gospel*, pp. 73-77. "So faith-hearing, if you will, is the act of discerning the presence of the Ultimate in the voice of this man, Jesus," p. 75.
[42] Riga, "Signs of Glory," pp. 408-411.
[43] Kysar, *John*, p. 70.

nience designated John) mitigated, if not repudiated those who believed because of the signs.[44] It is appropriate to ask whether Bultmann has not inadvertently distracted scholars from the tension in humankind to a so-called tension in the text. The gospel makes it clear that faith travels a rocky road. An intense moment of faith may be followed by a groping in the dark. Faith lifts the believer out of the chasm only to stand by as he sinks back into the abyss for rescuing anew (6:6,18,66,68-69; 14:5; 18:17). No single ground of faith settles the plight of man once for all, whether action or word. The vicissitudes of faith are more than a pedestrian tension in the text. They are the ultimate reality of humanness. For John it takes the full action of God and the Counselor (15:26-16:11) in sign and word to overcome the human failure to recognize (1:10) the savior of the world (4:42). Tensions do exist in the text and we are indebted to those who call them to our attention. Can it be that the tensions are theological rather than literary?

We will scrutinize 6:25-34 as a paradigm for the failure of signs, with reference to other texts.[45] This pericope follows the feeding of the five thousand and refers back to it. The feeding was explicitly identified as a sign (6:14). To those who crossed the sea, Jesus declared " . . . you seek me, not because you saw signs, but because you ate your fill of the loaves," (1:26). Those so accused are called the people (*ochlos*). Most typically in John those who fail to believe are the Jews,[46] but also the world (7:7; 16:9), and Judas (6:64). Unbelief therefore does not commence from closure to transcendent reality or to divine activity in human history. Unbelievers in John confess the God of Israel and his mighty deeds, past and present. Belief fails, the signs collapse, rather because these descendants of Abraham do not perceive divine Sonship in Jesus. Jesus exhorts the crowd to labor for a different food supplied by the son of man (6:27).[47] The word "labor" caused them to ask what they must do so as to do the works of God. By his answer Jesus made it clear that to see the sign is to recognize transcendence in his ministry. "This is the work of God, that you believe in him whom he has sent," (6:29).

Despite the fact that they had experienced the multiplication of the loaves and fishes they did not perceive the power of God. They were so closed off, they unwittingly proposed as an example of a sign Moses' manna, oblivious to

---

[44] Kysar, *John the Maverick Gospel*, p. 70.

[45] See Joseph A. Grassi, "Eating Jesus' Flesh and Drinking his Blood: The Centrality and Meaning of John 6:51-58," *Biblical Theology Bulletin* 17 (1987) 24-30; Frederick A. Rusch, "The Signs and the Discourse — The Rich Theology of John 6," *Currents in Theology and Mission* 5 (1978) 386-390; and Hans Weder, "Die Menschwerdung Gottes Uberlegungen zur Auslegungsproblematik des Johannesevangeliums am Beispiel von Joh 6," *Zeitscrift für Theologie Und Kirche* 82 (1985) 325-360.

[46] As if "Jew" is synonymous with unbelief 5:10,38; 7:48; 8:44-45; 9:18; 10:22-26. Jews also believed 11:45, but many did not confess for fear they would be put out of the synagogue 12:42-43.

[47] In the words of Riga, "Signs of Glory," p. 114. "They did not go beyond the material to see the hand of God in the event and the justification of Christ as the envoy of the Father."

the food Jesus miraculously supplied. Jesus pointed out that it was God who supplied the bread; furthermore, he provides the true bread which is Jesus himself (6:35). Belief, a human manifestation of the work of God (6:29), results in believers who are given the Son by God (6:37). Those who believe in the Son will have eternal life and will be raised up in the last day (6:40).[48] Contrariwise, those who fail to believe are condemned now and forever (3:18). Clearly, therefore, when the signs become an end in themselves and do not point to the reality, that is, the power of God in Jesus, they fail. Signs produce genuine faith when they bring those observing them to a single-hearted conviction that "Jesus is the Christ, the Son of God," (20:31).

Conclusions

John makes it clear that people believe when circumstances or a community of faith empowered by the Holy Spirit attest to Jesus' Sonship. It is then that signs may direct the believer to the transcendent reality, that is, God himself. Signs contribute to the stages of faith, but they are never an end in themselves. A community of faith which relishes miracles above the God who gives them is on the wrong track. The signs they see dazzle and blind them to the God who loves and extends eternal life (17:20-26). Faith is not a once-for-all intense possession. Faith grows and flourishes through a willingness to see and hear the continuous activity of God, in his church (the sheepfold 10:27-29; the vine and branches 15:1-11), and in the nexus of the life, light, truth, love and glory authenticated by the Son.

---

[48]Schnackenburg's comments on this chapter are extensive and helpful, *The Gospel According to John* II, pp. 10-78.

Contemporary Apocalyptic Scholarship and the Revelation

James E. Priest

Introduction

It is neither necessary nor possible to give a full survey of apocalyptic literature in this article which has as its primary interest the New Testament Apocalypse. However, for sake of clarity, it is important that several terms be explained which are central to the study. This is essential for two major reasons: First, the literature on the subject often reflects an ambiguity of thought and a tendency to generalize which makes definition of terms elusive.[1] Second, critical studies in apocalyptic literature since WWII, and the availability of additional materials such as the Dead Sea Scrolls, have resulted in scholarship which offers new insights and new or adjusted definitions of pivotal terms.

Additionally, the following sections of this paper discuss characteristics of apocalyptic literature. The New Testament Apocalypse is briefly described in light of these characteristics and placed in the broad context of biblical and non-biblical apocalypses, both Jewish and Christian. Specific biblical backgrounds for the New Testament Apocalypse are given. Then, historical and literary features of the Apocalypse are presented. Pertinent New Testament apocalyptic passages precedent to the Apocalypse are examined. The purpose of all this is to prepare the reader to appreciate why apocalyptic language was chosen to express its contents and to expect what is actually found in the Revelation, especially regarding the *parousia* of Jesus.

Definitions

In this paper, with its special emphasis on the New Testament Apocalypse, the following terms are used according to the definitions given below.

An *apocalypse* is a genre of revelatory literature with a narrative framework, in which a revelation is mediated by an otherworldly

---

[1]Klaus Koch, "What Is Apocalyptic? An Attempt at a Preliminary Definition" in: *Visionaries and Their Apocalypses* [Issues in Religion and Theology, No. 2, ed. Paul D. Hanson] (Philadelphia: Fortress, 1983). See pp. 16-20 where the author discusses what he calls "The Cloudiness of Current Definitions."

being to a human recipient, disclosing a transcendental reality which is both temporal, insofar as it envisages eschatological salvation, and spatial insofar as it involves another, supernatural world.[2]

Apocalypticism is a system of thought produced by visionary movements; [which] builds upon a specific eschatological perspective in generating a symbolic universe opposed to that of the dominant society.[3]

Apocalyptic[4] is used in this paper as an *adjective*[5] to describe, e.g., the literary features of a particular apocalypse, or the system of thought and eschatological perspective of a specific type of apocalypticism.[6] The inconsistent use of the term "apocalyptic"[7] in the relevant literature as both a noun and an adjective has not helped to create the sharpness of perspective needed to deal properly with the complex issues involved.[8]

---

[2]John J. Collins, *The Apocalyptic Imagination* (New York: Crossroad, 1984), p. 4, (emphasis added).

[3]Paul D. Hanson, "Apocalypticism" in: *Interpreter's Dictionary of the Bible*, Supp. Vol. (Nashville: Abingdon, 1962), p. 28, (emphasis added). See Christopher Rowland, *The Open Heaven: A Study of Apocalyptic in Judaism and Early Christianity* (New York: Crossroad, 1982), for a mitigating view of the role of eschatology in apocalyptic writings.

[4]Paul D. Hanson, *The Dawn of Apocalyptic* (Philadelphia: Fortress, 1975), pp. 11-12. Cited by Barry Ray Sang, *The New Testament Hermeneutical Milieu: The Inheritance and the Heir* (Madison, N.J.: Drew University, 1983), p. 170. "Apocalyptic is a form of eschatology (and hence a religious perspective) which focuses upon the usually mysterious disclosure to the elect of the cosmic vision of Yahweh's sovereignty." Hence, the nominative use of the word 'apocalyptic,' *contra* this paper.

[5]T.F. Glasson, "What Is Apocalyptic?" *New Testament Studies* 27:1 (Oct. 1980). After presenting a very lucid case, this author states, "I would advocate the abandonment of the word Apocalyptic. I know what an apocalypse is, and I see there is a place for the adjective 'apocalyptic' to denote matters relating to this type of literature. But, . . . Apocalyptic has no agreed and recognizable meaning," p. 105.

[6]Paul D. Hanson, "Old Testament Apocalyptic Reexamined [First published in: *Interpretation* 25 (1971) 454-79]; now in: *Visionaries and Their Apocalypses* [Issues in Religion and Theology, No. 2, ed. Paul D. Hanson] (Philadelphia: Fortress, 1983). "Apocalypticism is in vogue. . . . there is ample evidence that apocalyptic has come out of a long eclipse into the full light of a wide audience," p. 37.

[7]Koch, ibid., On page 16 the writer states, "The adjective apocalyptic is not directly derived from the general theological term *apokalypsis*, in the sense of revelation, at all; it comes from a second and narrower use of the word. . . . as the title of literary compositions which resemble the Book of Revelation." He goes on to say that, "The collective term apocalyptic, which came into use at the beginning of the nineteenth century (Johann M. Schmidt, *Die jüdische Apokalyptic: Die Geschichte ihrer Erforschung von den Anfängen bis zu den Textfunden von Qumran*. Neukirchen-Vluyn: Neukirchener, 1969), can therefore still be retained today," p. 29.

[8]Paul D. Hanson, "Apocalyptic Literature" in: *The Hebrew Bible and Its Modern Interpreters* [eds. Douglas A. Knight and Gene M. Tucker] (Philadelphia: Fortress; Chico, Ca.: Scholars Press, 1985). Hanson uses "apocalyptic" as both adjective and noun, i.e., as a description of a literary genre and as the genre itself. However, he concedes that "Apocalyptic is a complex and many-faceted phenomenon, and matters are not simplified by the restless development that characterizes its passage through time," p. 483.

Eschatology is also a term which has been cloaked in various garb. For example, with Schweitzer, eschatology became "thoroughgoing."[9] Dodd emphasized "realized" eschatology.[10] Bultmann advocated an "existential" eschatology.[11] Bowman saw a distinction between "prophetic" eschatology and "apocalyptic" eschatology.[12] Robinson developed an "inaugurated" eschatology.[13] Ladd opted for a "realistic" eschatology which is confined to the eschatology contained in the Hebrew/Jewish traditions.[14] This diversity is mentioned simply to point out that it is essential to delineate terms used in discussing a specialized subject. In this paper the term "eschatology" remains close to its linguistic roots (Gr. *eschatos* = end, last things). It has to do with *telos*, the ultimate end, purpose, or consummation of history and the world, (Rev. 22:13). It is vividly portrayed in the New Testament Apocalypse.[15]

The Milieu of the Apocalypse

When examining the New Testament Apocalypse it is helpful to place it, as much as possible, in its literary, historical, cultural, and theological milieu. From a literary point of view, the genre has a rich heritage. A significant contribution has been made in the last decade shedding considerable light on the nature of apocalypses. It is now known that apocalypses fall into two major groups, those which contain otherworldly journeys and those which do not.[16] This kind of classification makes possible an insight enabling better analysis of the various apocalypses; and, importantly for this paper, points out some of the unique features of the New Testament Apocalypse vis-à-vis Jewish and Greco-Roman apocalypses.

The topic of this paper does not call for a discussion of the many individual apocalypses which would be an inherent part of a larger survey of the litera-

---

[9]E.g., Albert Schweitzer, *The Quest of the Historical Jesus* [Trans. W. Montgomery] (New York: Macmillan, 1910).

[10]E.g., C.H. Dodd, *The Parables of the Kingdom* (New York: Scribner's, 1961). Also Oscar Cullmann, *Salvation in History* [Trans. Sidney G. Sowers] (New York: Harper & Row, 1967).

[11]E.g., R. Bultmann, *History and Eschatology* (New York: Harper & Row, 1957).

[12]E.g., John Wick Bowman, *Prophetic Realism and the Gospel* (Philadelphia. Westminster, 1955).

[13]E. g., John Thomas Robinson, *In the End, God.* . . . (London: Clarke, 1950).

[14]E.g., George Eldon Ladd, "The Place of Apocalyptic in Biblical Religion," *The Evangelical Quarterly* XXX (1958) 75.

[15]Rowland, ibid., "The fact that the apocalypses offer such important evidence of the dominance of eschatological beliefs within Jewish and early Christian religions is demanding a reappraisal of this element within contemporary Christianity," p. 447.

[16]John J. Collins, "Introduction: Towards the Morphology of a Genre," *Semeia* 14 *Apocalypse: The Morphology of a Genre* [ed. John J. Collins] SBL (Missoula, Mt.: University of Mt. Press, 1979), pp. 14-15.

ture. However, in order to "place the New Testament Apocalypse," something should be said about its appearance among other apocalypses.

Although the book of Daniel is seen as the only full apocalypse in the Old Testament, it has been repeatedly pointed out that Ezekiel 38-39, Isaiah 24-27, 40-45, 56-66, Zechariah 9-11, Joel 2, and Amos 5:16-20 are apocalyptic sections within these prophetic books. Although it is wise to acknowledge there is dispute among scholars whether certain writings should be included among Jewish and Christian apocalypses, it is probably safe to say that the following non-biblical Jewish apocalypses do in fact "bracket" the New Testament Apocalypse in time and thus give some kind of basis for comparative analysis of the genre during the period they cover. These books are: Apocalypse of Abraham, I Enoch, Psalms of Solomon, Assumption of Moses, Apocalypse of Moses, Sibylline Oracles, Apocalypse of Esdras/4 Ezra 3-14, Book of Elijah, II Enoch, Apocalypse of Baruch, Testament of Abraham, Testament of the Twelve Patriarchs, Ascension of Isaiah, and many of the Dead Sea Scrolls, e.g., the War Scroll.

As mentioned above, along with one full apocalypse in the Old Testament, Daniel, there are several apocalyptic sections. The same may be said of the New Testament. The Revelation is the one full apocalypse, but there are several apocalyptic sections found in other New Testament books. Some of them are Mark 13, Matthew 24-25, Luke 21:5-36, I Thessalonians 4-5, II Thessalonians 2:1-12, and I Corinthians 15.[17] Additionally, there are numerous non-biblical Christian apocalypses which stress common apocalyptic themes such as heaven, hell, manifest destiny by God's bursting into history, etc. Some of these apocalypses are: The Sophia of Jesus Christ, The Apocalypse of Paul, The Apocryphon of John, The Apocalypse of Peter, and The Apocalypse of Mary.[18]

Characteristics of Apocalyptic Literature[19]

Compiling a list of characteristics is difficult since no full set fits each document and because general descriptions of apocalyptic literature found in current discussions often fail to draw distinctions between literary features and content. A descriptive approach blending the literary features with the

---

[17]Paul D. Hanson, "Biblical Apocalypticism: The Theological Dimension" *Horizons in Biblical Theology* 7 (Dec. 1985), "The New Testament stands . . . as the most important and authoritative guide to the Christian's interpretation of all apocalyptic writings," p. 8.

[18]Cf. Adela Yarbro Collins, "The Early Christian Apocalypses," *Semeia* 14 *The Morphology of a Genre* [ed. John J. Collins] SBL (Missoula, Mt.: University of Mt. Press, 1979), pp. 61-71 for a survey of twenty-four such texts, including the New Testament Apocalypse.

[19]See Ithamar Gruenwald, "Jewish Apocalyptic Literature," in: *Aufstieg und Niedergang der römischen Welt* [Herausgegeben Wolfgang Haase] (Berlin-New York: Walter de Gruyter, 1979), *Principat*. II.19.1, pp. 89-118 for helpful insights, esp. on apocalyptic and prophecy, pseudepigraphy, history, and eschatology.

attitudinal positions of the writers provides a framework to note some major literary techniques and beliefs of the apocalyptists.

Pseudonymity is a common trait of an apocalypse. Various conjectures account for this. For example, the "demise of prophecy" made the writer believe that his work would not receive a hearing unless it purported to originate from a great hero of the past. This view is strengthened by the fact that the works are not anonymous; they are almost invariably pseudonymous.[20]

Many apocalypses exhibit the *ex eventu* ("predictions" of past events) approach to prophecy. Pseudonymity, along with history "predicted" as prophecy (correctly, of course!), would further assure acceptance of the apocalypse.

Use of symbolic language is thoroughly typical of apocalyptic literature.[21] This feature was no doubt more than a conventional literary technique, although there is often a detectable conventionalizing of symbols, e.g., the use of *gematria*.[22] Symbolism would allow the writer to convey truths to intended readers who understood the symbols used without that knowledge becoming widespread; or, symbolism could be used to describe reality where literal language would fail.

The pessimism noted in much of this literature has to do with the various writers' views of the world in light of the general fallen state of mankind. Things would not get better. God was their hope. Most of them saw themselves as living near the end of time, an event which God would bring about. They would *then* be vindicated and God would be glorified. Their pessimism for this world did not dampen their enthusiasm for the next. God would have the last word. Their salvation would be supra-historical.

Dualism is characteristic of most apocalyptic writings. It becomes very apparent in the contrasting tendencies so often present such as evil vs. good, God vs. Satan, world vs. kingdom of God, this age vs. the age to come, etc. These features show a persistent dualism, but it is not dualism in the absolute sense. Their ultimate view was basically monotheistic.

Ethically, these writings are designed to offer comfort and consolation to the elect, rather than berating or rebuking them. There is, of course, a parenetic element present. Generally speaking, however, apocalyptic literature tends to confirm the stance of the faithful instead of reforming the wicked. This emphasis is likely due to the author's pessimistic view of the world and the belief in the nearness of the End-time.

---

[20]Cf. Bruce Metzger, "Literary Forgeries and Canonical Pseudepigrapha," *Journal of Biblical Literature* 91 (1972) 3-24 for a discussion of deception, etc., as motives for pseudonyms.

[21]Leon Morris, *Apocalyptic* (Grand Rapids: Eerdmans, 1972), pp. 34-37.

[22]E.g., D.S. Russell, *Between the Testaments* (Philadelphia: Fortress, 1960), pp. 98-101. The extensive use of *gematria* is illustrated when Russell says, "The popularity of the number seven is obvious in the Book of Revelation, where it occurs fifty four times," p. 101.

A chief trait of practically all apocalyptic writing is the deep-seated conviction that all history is predetermined by God.[23] This is usually articulated in the literature with episodic or dispensational type of language.[24] In a paradoxical sort of way, this view of history was a comfort to the apocalyptists. It gave meaning to the horrors of the world. God would not act until the Endtime. It added stamina to their faith. God *would*, in his own appointed "time," redeem those predestined to glory. This view also explains the general lack of "evangelistic" emphasis in the literature as implied above.

The concept of revelation is at the heart of an apocalypse. What the apocalyptist wrote about was purportedly what had been revealed to him, i.e., to the great person of the past as indicated by the pseudonym. Thus, the heavenly mysteries, angelic hosts, scenes of hell, judgment, etc., were elements which could not have been known, from the writer's point of view, except by revelation. Therefore, revelation, for the apocalyptist, did not emphasize God's working in history so much as the apocalyptic eschatological soteriology of his people.

Apocalypticism

The definition of apocalypticism needs to be recalled at this point because the following enumeration of major beliefs emphasizes, for the most part, the content of the literature in contrast to the literary features of the genre. Admittedly, the fine line between the package and its contents is sometimes difficult to draw. However, for the sake of emphasis, the following beliefs are cited:

1. The radical transformation of this world lies in the immediate future (Dan. 12:11-12; Rev. 22:20; II Bar. 85:10; IV Ezra 4:50).

2. Cosmic catastrophe (war, fire, earthquake, famine, pestilence) precedes the end (Dan. 7:11; II Bar. 70:8).

3. The epochs of history leading up to the end are predetermined (Rev. 20:6ff.; Dan. 9; II Bar. 27; 4 Ezra 7:28; I Enoch 85, 93; Apoc. of Abr. 29).

---

[23]James H. Charlesworth, *The Old Testament Pseudepigrapha: Apocalyptic Literature and Testaments*, Vol. 1 [ed. James H. Charlesworth] (Garden City, New York: Doubleday, 1983). Here the writer says that within the nexus of pseudepigraphical literature generally, there are at least four significant theological concerns which are often emphasized in apocalyptic fashion: "[1] preoccupations with the meaning of sin, the origins of evil, and the problem of theodicy, [2] stresses upon God's transcendence, [3] concerns with the coming of the Messiah, [4] and beliefs in resurrection that are often accompanied with descriptions of Paradise," p. xxix.

[24]Martin Hengel, *Judaism and Hellenism*, 2 Vols. [Trans. John Bowden] (Philadelphia: Fortress, 1974), Vol. 1, p. 181.

4. A hierarchy of angels and demons mediate the events in the two worlds (this world and the one to come) and victory is assured to the divine realm (Dan. 10:20ff.; I Enoch 89:59ff.; Rev. 16:14; Apoc. of Abr. 10:17).

5. A righteous remnant will enjoy the fruits of salvation in a heavenly Jerusalem (Rev. 4-5; Dan. 12; II Bar. 50ff.; 4 Ezra 7:32; I Enoch 22:51; Rev. 21; II Bar. 6:8ff.; 4 Ezra 8:52-55; I Enoch 48ff.; Apoc. of Abr. 29:17).

6. The act inaugurating the kingdom of God and marking the end of the present age is his (or the Son of Man's) ascension to the heavenly throne (Rev. 20:11; Dan. 7:19; II Bar. 73:1; 4 Ezra 7:33; Apoc. of Abr. 18).

7. The actual establishment of the New Kingdom is effected through the royal mediator, such as the Messiah or the Son of Man, or simply an angel (Dan. 7:13ff.; Assump. of Mos. 10:2; Dan. 12:1).

8. The bliss to be enjoyed by the righteous can only be described as glory (Rev. 21:1ff.; II Bar. 30:1; 32:4; Dan. 12:3; I Enoch 50:1; 51:4).[25]

It is obvious that most of the above apocalyptic beliefs, with slight modifications, are found in the New Testament Apocalypse. What produces such a confluence of religious beliefs? Why are they presented in apocalyptic form? The answers to these and many related questions are vigorously debated in the scholarly literature. This short article can only address such matters by referring to some major developments in the history of investigation into apocalyptic literature.[26]

As the 19th century closed, the German scholar Hermann Gunkel was struggling with the question of coherence in the apocalyptic materials. He called attention to the apocalyptist's use of myth as well as traditional materials to suit his own purposes; thus, the symbolism and the message were of one piece, as the language of poetry is to truth.[27]

---

[25]Klaus Koch, "What Is Apocalyptic? An Attempt at a Preliminary Definition" in: *Visionaries and Their Apocalypses* [Issues in Religion and Theology, No. 2, ed. Paul D. Hanson] (Philadelphia: Fortress, 1983). First appeared in *The Rediscovery of Apocalyptic* [Trans. M. Kohl] (London: SCM Press, 1972]. Summarized and condensed from pp. 24-29. See esp. profuse text references, both biblical and non-biblical.

[26]Lawrence Boadt, *Reading the Old Testament: An Introduction* (New York: Paulist Press, 1984). See pp. 511ff. for pointed comments on specific apocalyptic books, a developmental chart of apocalyptic literature, some major elements common to this genre, and "some of the lasting values basic to all apocalyptic thinking that Christians and Jews must never forget."

[27]E.g., Hermann Gunkel, *Schöpfung und Chaos in Urzeit and Endzeit* (Göttingen: Vandenhoeck & Ruprecht, 1895).

As the 20th century opened, the interest in apocalyptic literature was aroused by the work of Johannes Weiss,[28] Albert Schweitzer,[29] F.C. Burkitt,[30] and R.H. Charles.[31] Questions of eschatology were sparked by the two former scholars while emphases on texts and translations marked the efforts of the latter two.

From the 1940's into the 1960's perhaps the most widespread and influential works on apocalyptic writings were those of the British scholars H.H. Rowley[32] and D. S. Russell.[33] One of the major features in their inquiries was their attempts to relate closely Old Testament prophecy and apocalypse, and to show Old Testament prophecy as the primary inspiration for apocalyptic writings.[34]

Although not the first to advance the theory, Gerhard von Rad took the position that the apocalypse had its roots in Wisdom literature and thought, not prophecy and prophetic traditions.[35] Although his position has not received general acceptance, neither has it been dismissed altogether.[36]

Since the late 1950's there has been a burgeoning of books and articles on apocalyptic literature. Some major theologians, as well as Bible scholars, have found apocalypticism to be crucial.[37] Advancements have been made on many fronts. For example, renewed directions of emphasis in the research

---

[28]E.g., Johannes Weiss, *Jesus' Proclamation of the Kingdom of God* [Trans. and eds. Richard H. Hiers and David L. Holland] (Philadelphia: Fortress, 1971).

[29]E.g., Albert Schweitzer, *The Quest of the Historical Jesus* [Trans. W. Montgomery] (New York: Macmillan, 1910).

[30]E.g., F.C. Burkitt, *Jewish and Christian Apocalypses* (London: Oxford Universversity Press, 1914).

[31]E.g., R.H. Charles, *Apocrypha and Pseudepigrapha of the Old Testament*, 2 Vols. (Oxford: Clarendon Press, 1913).

[32]E.g., H.H. Rowley, *The Relevance of Apocalyptic* (London: Lutterword, 1947).

[33]D.S. Russell, *The Method and Message of Jewish Apocalyptic* (Philadelphia: Westminster; London: SCM, 1964).

[34]Shaye J.D. Cohen, *From the Maccabees to the Mishnah*, [Library of Early Christianity, ed. Wayne A. Meeks] (Philadelphia: Westminster, 1987). Cf. pp. 195-201 where the author describes the relationship of prophecy and apocalypse as that of *transformation*.

[35]Gerhard von Rad, *Old Testament Theology*, Two Vols., [Trans. D.M.G. Stalker] (New York: Harper and Row, 1965), II. p. 306.

[36]*Contra* the definition of apocalypticism given earlier in this paper, if one sees apocalyptic literature with its origins in Wisdom writings, as does von Rad, then another definition is forthcoming. Jonathan Z. Smith, "Wisdom and Apocalyptic," [First published in *Religious Syncretism in Antiquity*, ed. B.A. Person, (1975), pp. 131-56]; now in: *Visionaries and Their Apocalypses* [Issues in Religion and Theology, No. 2, ed. Paul D. Hanson]. Smith states, "Apocalypticism is Wisdom lacking a royal court and patron and therefore it surfaces during the period of Late Antiquity not as a response to religious persecution but as an expression of the trauma of the cessation of native kingship," p. 115.

[37]E.g., cf. below Ernest Käsemann; also Wolfhart Pannenberg, "Redemptive Event and History" in: *Basic Questions in Theology*, Vol. I, ed. George H. Kehm (Philadelphia: Fortress, 1970), pp. 20ff.

have been in the areas of (1) definitions, (2) sources, (3) structure of the apocalypse, (4) time of origin, (5) function of eschatology, (6) *Sitz im Leben*, and (7) theology.

Biblical Backgrounds for the New Testament Apocalypse

Of course, prophecy is a persistent theme running through much of the Old Testament, as well as the New Testament. It is significant that eschatology is a part of both Old Testament and New Testament prophecy. It is also important to note that apocalyptic features appear in both Old Testament and New Testament prophetic contexts. Thus, it is possible to speak of Old Testament prophetic eschatology and apocalyptic eschatology and New Testament prophetic eschatology and apocalyptic eschatology.[38]

But there is a difference in perspective between prophetic eschatology and apocalyptic eschatology.[39] Prophetic eschatology had to do with historical events leading up to the End. Those predicted events were, in the mind of the prophet, the eventual working out of God's oversight of the world and its history. God was at the helm of reality. All events were in his hands. History was the working out of his will in his own time, and prophetic eschatology emphasized those phenomena pointing toward time's consummation. All of this was according to the *telos* of God.[40]

On the other hand, apocalyptic eschatology appears to be mainly expressions of apocalyptists who had "turned loose of history," so to speak. Despairing of transformation or reformation of this world in this age, they expected God's sovereignty to be displayed at the glorious End, not in the history of the world.

With this dichotomy in mind, it is easy to empathize with the ecstasy and agony of the Old Testament prophets. In their use of prophetic eschatology,

---

[38] See George Eldon Ladd, "The Origin of Apocalyptic in Biblical Religion," *The Evangelical Quarterly* XXX (1958) 146, where he makes the observation "that while both Jewish apocalyptic and New Testament apocalyptic developed principles fundamental in the Old Testament prophetic eschatology, Jewish apocalyptic developed in certain non-prophetic directions which sets it apart from its biblical counterpart, which we may describe by the term prophetic-apocalyptic to distinguish it from the non-prophetic apocalyptic of late Judaism."

[39] John J. Collins, *The Apocalyptic Imagination: An Introduction to the Jewish Matrix of Christianity* (New York: Crossroad, 1984). "In all [apocalypses] there are also a final judgment and a destruction of the wicked. The eschatology of the apocalypses differs from that of the earlier prophetic books by clearly envisaging retribution beyond death," p. 5.

[40] George Eldon Ladd, "Why Not Prophetic-Apocalyptic?" *Journal of Biblical Literature* 76 (1957), "The underlying theology of apocalyptic eschatology is a view of the world in which the kingdom of God can be realized only by an inbreaking of the divine world into human history," p. 197.

they were sensitive to God's mighty acts in *history* which were leading up to the eventual overthrow of all opposing powers and the glorious restoration of Israel and the perpetuation of God's Davidic kingdom. On the other hand, when they utilized the speech of apocalyptic eschatology they often broke through the historical boundaries. In other-worldly language, they described God's inbreaking as the End-of-time phenomenon which would usher in the new age in which God's rule would be fully exercised in his kingdom and his people would be vindicated and exalted.

Historically speaking, eschatology tended to arise in Old Testament prophetic activity when the "the world tumbled in" and the prophets were living and serving during a period of great upheaval, displacement, agony, and distress for them and their people.[41] Their prophetic utterances reflect a conviction that, although the present time was terrible and traumatic, God would not forget his people. There would be a rescue operation, a restoration of the kingdom. All this was seen as the consummation of God's purposes for his people which would eventually be realized in *history*.

It is not surprising, then, that the historical context of the fall of Judah and the Babylonian captivity in the late 7th century and the early 6th century produced an emphasis on prophetic eschatology.

What happened? The Jews were eventually allowed to return to Judea, beginning about 536 B.C.E. Life under Persian rule was better than it had been under the Babylonians. However, the kingdom was *not restored.* The Jews were still under subjection to foreign rule. This was followed by Greek domination of the East. After Alexander's death (323 B.C.E.), the conflicts between the Seleucids of Syria-Mesopotamia and the Ptolemies of Egypt reduced Judea to a "political football" kicked repeatedly in the larger struggles of the Eastern Mediterranean world. All of this is too well-known to belabor.[42]

In the post-exilic period many of the Jews saw the conditions described above as flying in the face of the prophetic eschatology which had been a comfort and a source of strength for them in those earlier times.[43] Even the prophetic voice was silent.[44]

Why the *DELAY,* the agonizing *DELAY?* Out of the maelstrom of these post-exilic centuries the Jewish apocalypses flourished, both biblical and non-

---

[41]John J. Collins, "The Apocalypse — Revelation and Inspiration," *The Bible Today* 6 (Nov. 1981) 363.

[42]George W.E. Nickelsburg, *Jewish Literature Between the Bible and the Mishnah* (Philadelphia: Fortress, 1981). Cf. pp. 9-18 for a brief but helpful historical overview.

[43]Richard J. Bauckham, "The Rise of Apocalyptic," *Themelios* 3 (Jan. 1978). "Those who now denigrate apocalyptic rarely face the mounting problem of theodicy which the apocalyptists faced in the extended period of contradiction between the promises of God and the continued subjection and suffering of his people," p. 20.

[44]I Macc. 1:41; 4:46. Also, see Gruenwald, ibid., pp. 102-107.

biblical.⁴⁵ Apocalyptic eschatology came to the fore. Faith in history, as such, was shaken. The previous visions of glory, restoration, and kingdom were frequently pushed into meta-history, where the "new heaven and new earth" would be the stage upon which God would reign in full sovereignty and fellowship with his people.⁴⁶ How else could the *DELAY*, the baffling, traumatizing, agonizing *DELAY*, be positively explained? How else could faith harmonize the God of history and eternity?

Approaching the Book of Revelation

This paper is obviously not a commentary on the Revelation. It is not intended to be. It is, rather, an attempt to present the New Testament Revelation as an apocalypse and explain why it was written as an *apocalypse*.⁴⁷ By the very nature of the case, scholarship concerned with apocalyptic literature in the past has dealt with Jewish apocalypses and related literature far more than the New Testament Apocalypse and non-biblical Christian apocalypses.⁴⁸ Therefore, it is not surprising to find that the Apocalypse of the New

---

⁴⁵Emil Schürer, *The History of the Jewish People in the Age of Jesus Christ* (175 B.C. - A.D. 135), 4 Vols. [New English version revised and edited by Matthew Black, Martin Goodman, Fergus Millar, Geza Vermes, Pamela Vermes] (Edinburgh: T. & T. Clark, Ltd., 1986). In Vol. III, Pt. I, Geza Fermes says of the prophetic-apocalyptic pseudepigraphic Jewish literature of this period, "A new type of composition, and *the best-loved and most influential in this period*, is the prophetic-apocalyptic pseudepigrapha," (emphasis added), p. 241.

⁴⁶John J. Collins, "Apocalyptic Literature," *Early Judaism and Its Modern Interpreters* [eds. Robert A. Kraft and George W.E. Nickelsburg] (Philadelphia: Fortress; Atlanta: Scholars Press, 1986). Although the "Son of Man" phrase was not a title in intertestamental Judaism, "the idea of a heavenly Savior figure was current and provides the natural context for the NT expectation of the Son of Man who will come on the clouds with his angels," p. 352.

⁴⁷James H. Charlesworth, "The Jewish Roots of Christology: The Discovery of the Hypostatic Voice," *Scottish Journal of Theology* 39 (May 1986). "We do not come to [the Apocalypse of John] at the end of the canon. There was no New Testament canon in John's day. We should read the Apocalypse and try to understand its penetrating brilliance in light of the continuum of apocalypses," p. 40.

⁴⁸Joshua Bloch, *On the Apocalyptic of Judaism* (Philadelphia: The Dropsie College for Hebrew and Cognate Learning, 1952). In speaking of the late Jewish apocalypses, the author states, "Growing excitement and rising despair on the present order furnished the urge to look for the realization of the promise of miraculous deliverance for the righteous and a new era of power and splendor for a regenerate Israel. Naturally in such a day the belief in the advent of a messiah heralding 'the end of days' was widespread. The apocalyptic writings in which this belief is proclaimed were very popular, and began to make inroads into Judaism, its votaries drew upon them for support in their claims for the messianic character of Jesus of Nazareth," p. 45.

⁴⁹George Eldon Ladd, "The Revelation and Jewish Apocalyptic," *The Evangelical Quarterly* XXIX (1957) 94-95.

Testament has several features which are not characteristic of most Jewish apocalypses. First, the book is identified as a prophecy (*prophēteia*), as well as a revelation (*apokalypsis*), (Rev. 1:3; 22:7,10,18-19). Second, it is neither anonymous nor pseudonymous.[49] Third, Revelation, in contrast to any other known apocalypses, is set within epistolary perimeters (Rev. 1:4-8; 22:10-21).[50] Fourth, the Revelation does not engage in the practice of *ex eventu* prophecy,[51] a common feature of apocalyptic literature in general.[52] Fifth, and most important, difference between the Revelation and Jewish apocalypses is the emphasis on Jesus, especially his death and glorious exaltation.

It has been said that the "Apocalypse of John is more structurally complex than any other Jewish or Christian apocalypse, and has yet to be satisfactorily analyzed."[53] Since a finalized, undisputed structure of Revelation has yet to be established,[54] the following uncomplicated outline is presented here as an aid in grappling with this perplexing feature.[55]

I. Prologue	1:1-8
Preface	1:1-3
Prescript and sayings	1:4-8
The seven messages	1:9-3:22
The seven seals	4:1-8:5
The seven trumpets	8:2-11:19

---

[50]David E. Aune, *The New Testament in Its Literary Environment* [Library of Early Christianity, ed. Wayne A. Meeks] (Philadelphia: Westminster, 1987), p. 240-241.

[51]Some scholars see in Rev. 17:9-12 an example of *ex eventu* prophecy. E.g., cf. Bernard McGinn, "Early Apocalypticism: The Ongoing Debate," in: *Apocalypse in English Renaissance Thought and Literature* [eds. C.A. Patrides and Joseph Wittreich] (Ithaca, New York: Cornell University Press, 1984), p. 211.

[52]John J. Collins, "Pseudonymity, Historical Reviews and the Genre of the Revelation of John," *The Catholic Biblical Quarterly* XXXIX:3 (July 1977). "The most basic function of *ex eventu* prophecies was rendered superfluous by the historical context of Revelation," p. 333.

[53]Aune, ibid.

[54]David Hellholm, "The Problem of Apocalyptic Genre and the Apocalypse of John," *Semeia 36 Early Christian Apocalypticism: Genre and Social Setting* [ed. Adela Yarbro Collins] SBL (Decatur, Ga.: Scholars Press, 1986). Here a five-fold perspective of Revelation is given based on complex levels of communication, which, according to the author, serve as *meta-levels* for other levels. This all leads to the most embedded text of the book, 21:5-8, which is probed to eight levels (!), pp. 43-46.

[55]Aune, "The Apocalypse of John and the Problem of Genre," *Semeia 36 Early Christian Apocalypticism: Genre and Social Setting* [ed. Adela Yarbro Collins] SBL (Decatur, Ga.: Scholars Press, 1986). The reader is reminded to be alert to *content* and *function*, as well as *form*, in studying the Apocalypse, since apocalypses are generically described in the literature in these terms, p. 65.

II. Seven unnumbered visions	12:1-15:4
The seven bowls	15:1-16:20
Babylon appendix	17:1-19:10
Seven unnumbered visions	19:11-21:8
Jerusalem appendix	21:9-22:5
Epilogue	22:6-21
Sayings	22:6-20
Benediction	22:21 [56]

The Revelation may be best studied in light of its historical context, other apocalyptic literature of its time, its unity as an apocalypse, and the severity marked by Christian martyrdom and false teachers.[57] This requires as accurate knowledge as possible of the date the book was written.[58] The two dates which have received more serious consideration than any others are 68-69 C.E.[59] and 95-96 C.E.[60]

There is no difficulty in geographically locating the Apocalypse in Asia Minor. It is apparent in the letters addressed to the seven churches that the seer of Patmos is looking to that locale. However, there is considerable dispute of long standing about the authorship of the Apocalypse. The earliest extant witnesses affirmed apostolic Johannine authorship for the Apocalypse. Among them were Justin Martyr [d. 165], Clement of Alexandria [d.c. 220], Hippolytus [d.c. 236], and Origen [d.c. 254]. It was not until the time of Dionysius [d.c. 265] that the apostolic authorship of Revelation was called in question.[61] Athanasius [d. 373] won the East back to belief in apostolic authorship after which the church, both East and West, generally held to the

---

[56] Adela Yarbro Collins, "Persecution and Vengeance in the Book of Revelation," *Apocalypticism in the Mediterranean World and the Ancient Near East* [ed. David Hellholm]. Proceedings of the International Colloquium on Apocalypticism, Upsalla, August 12-17, 1979, Tübingen: J.C.B. Mohr (Paul Siebeck), 1983, p. 731.

[57] James H. Charlesworth, *The New Testament Apocrypha and Pseudepigrapha: A Guide to Publications with Excursuses and Apocalypses* (Metuchen, N.J.: Scarecrow Press, Inc., 1987), pp. 19-27.

[58] Cf. Adela Yarbro Collins, "Dating the Apocalypse of John," *Biblical Research* XXVI (1981) 33-45. Although suggesting a Domitianic date, this article clearly presents the major problems and alternatives. The literature on this point is extensive.

[59] Albert A. Bell, "The Date of John's Apocalypse: The Evidence of Some Roman Historians Reconsidered," *New Testament Studies* 25:1 (Oct. 1978) 93-102. Here is an extended argument for the early date with the author's statement, "The inescapable conclusion is that the Apocalypse was written between June 68 and 15 January 69 . . . . or a few weeks later. . . ," p. 100.

[60] Alan Johnson, "Hebrews-Revelation," [*The Expositor's Bible Commentary*, Vol. 12, eds. Frank E. Gaebelein and J.D. Douglas] (Grand Rapids: Eerdmans, 1981). "Though the slender historical evidence on the whole favors a later date (81-96), in light of the present studies, the question as to when Revelation was written must be left open," p. 406.

[61] Leon Morris, *The Revelation of St. John* [ed. R.V.G. Tasker; Tyndale House] (Grand Rapids: Eerdmans Publishing Company, 1969). See pp. 25-34 for sources and citations on the subject. His cautious comments point to John the apostle; however, he concedes "the subject is certainly one of great difficulty," p. 26.

Johannine apostolic authorship of the Apocalypse until the time of the Reformation, at which time Luther and others were vocal in anti-apostolic views concerning the authorship of the Revelation.[62] The question remains unresolved.

Unfortunately for the question, the author only identifies himself as "John," (1:1,4,9; 22:8). He implies he is a prophet, (22:9), and his book is called a prophecy (1:3; 22:7,10,18-19). Fortunately, unresolved questions about authorship, in themselves, do not in any way negate the Apocalypse's authority, integrity, or importance within the New Testament canon. Although there was a time when many scholars tended to see the Revelation as a composite work, like many other apocalypses, there is now a growing conviction that the Apocalypse stands as a unity from beginning to end, including the epistolary framework, and that it is the composition of a single author.[63]

New Testament Apocalyptic Antecedents to the Revelation

The reasons why apocalyptic literature flourished among the Jews from about 200 B.C.E. to around 100 C.E.[64] have already been discussed above.[65] Now, what does one see when the New Testament is opened? The first records to appear after the ascension of Jesus and the beginning of the church were some of the early Pauline epistles addressed to various congregations. In these one finds a strong conviction concerning the imminent return of Christ. For example, in I Thessalonians 4:13-18, Paul states "For this we declare to you by the word of the Lord, that *we who are alive, who are left until the*

---

[62]"My spirit cannot accommodate itself to this book. There is one sufficient reason for the small esteem in which I hold it — that Christ is neither taught in it nor recognized," (Martin Luther, 1522). Quoted by G. B. Caird in: *The Revelation of St. John the Divine* (New York: Harper & Row, 1966), p. 1.

[63]See G. Mussies, *The Morphology of Koine Greek as Used in the Apocalypse of St. John* (Leiden: E.J. Brill, 1971), p. 351 for one author and unity position; cf. Charlesworth, ibid., pp. 24-25 where literary integrity of the Apocalypse is affirmed.

[64]Anthony J. Saldarini, "Apocalypses and 'Apocalyptic' in Rabbinic Literature and Mysticism," *Semeia* 14 *Apocalypse: The Morphology of a Genre* [ed. John J. Collins] SBL (Missoula, Mt.: University of Mt. Press, 1979), "200 B.C.E. - 100 C.E.," p. 189. There are variations in the dates within contemporary literature.

[65]Michael Brennan Dick, *Introduction to the Hebrew Bible: An Inductive Reading of the Old Testament* (Englewood Cliffs, N. J.: Prentice Hall, 1988). Dick points to another factor which produced apocalyptic literature, viz., "inner-community strife," p. 135. The complexities of this sectarianism are discernible in broad outline, but space does not allow their development.

coming of the Lord, shall not precede those who have fallen asleep," (emphasis added, v. 15).[66] This letter (5:1-11) and II Thessalonians show the "day of the Lord" was a day of salvation for the righteous and judgment for the wicked (2:1-8), but, of course, it had not come yet (2:2).

In a dramatic apocalyptic eschatological passage addressed to the Corinthian church, Paul ties together in an intimate way (1) the resurrection, (2) Christ's coming, (3) the "end," (4) the kingdom, and (5) the ultimate and complete victory of Christ over all opposition, including death (I Cor. 15:24-26).[67] Although this is yet future, the language of Paul clearly leads one to conclude that he saw the end approaching. "I mean, brethren, the appointed time has grown very short. . . . For the form of this world is passing away," (I Cor. 7:29a, 31a). He insists the kingdom of God cannot be inherited by "flesh and blood, . . . but we shall all be changed, in a moment, in the twinkling of an eye, at the last trumpet," (I Cor. 15:50-52).[68]

Biblical scholars are aware of the "now" but "not yet" tension present in scripture. There is a present reality to salvation (I Cor. 15:1-2). Justification and glorification for those predestined and foreknown by God are accomplished (Rom. 8:29-30). This "realized eschatology," mentioned earlier, needs no elaboration here. However, it is clear that the "not yet" is separated from the "now" by the inevitable judgment on that Day (Rom. 14:10b; I Cor. 3:13; II Cor. 5:10). Between the two poles of "now" but "not yet" the early Christians often lived with anxieties and afflictions, as well as hope and confidence. The longing was to "be away from the body and at home with the Lord," (II Cor. 5:8b). The Christians faced the future with courage. "He who has prepared us for this very thing is God, who has given us the Spirit as a guarantee," (II Cor. 4:16-5:10, v. 5 quoted). Paul posited this transcendental possibility of consummate, eschatological salvation in one Person, Jesus Christ, when he said, "Therefore, if any one is in Christ, he is a new creation,

---

[66]J. Massyngberde Ford, *Revelation* [Anchor Bible; eds. William Foxwell Albright and David Noel Freedman] (Garden City, New York: Doubleday & Company, Inc., 1975). "The oldest apocalyptic text in the N.T. appears to be I Thess. 4: 16-18. It describes the coming, Gr. *parousia*, of Jesus succeeded by resurrection...," p. 4.

[67]John J. Collins, "Apocalyptic Literature," *Harper's Bible Dictionary* [gen. ed. Paul J. Achtemeier] (San Francisco: Harper & Row, 1985). "Apocalyptic ideas played a *crucial* role in the formation of early Christian beliefs in the resurrection and Second Coming of Christ," (emphasis added), p. 36.

[68]Paul J. Achtemeier, "An Apocalyptic Shift in Early Christian Tradition: Reflections on Some Canonical Evidence," *The Catholic Biblical Quarterly* 45:2 (April 1983) 234-237.

the old has passed away, behold, the new has come," (II Cor. 5:17).[69]

After Paul's early letters, one comes chronologically to those Synoptic documents of "good news," the gospels. The reader is soon reminded of how the Old Testament book of Malachi closed with his apocalyptic announcement, "Behold, I will send you Elijah the prophet before the great and terrible day of the Lord comes," (4:6a).

The gospel of Mark shows Jesus explaining to the people why Elijah would arrive "before the great and terrible day of the Lord comes." "Elijah does come first to restore all things. . . , (Mk. 9:12a). ". . . But I tell you that Elijah has come . . . (9:13a). This pronouncement was interpreted by the disciples of Jesus as a reference to John the Baptist, (Matt. 18:10-13). Elijah (John the Baptist), like Jesus, preached repentance in view of the fact that "the kingdom of God is at hand," (Mk. 1:15; Matt. 3:1; 10:7). Such a proclamation would fan the hopes of the Jews. This was what they had yearned for in the past. But how would this kingdom come about and who would reign over it?

Jesus affirmed he was the answer to such questions. "Truly, I say to you, there are some standing here who will not taste death before they see the kingdom of God come with power," (Mk. 9:1 and parallels Matt. 16:28; Lk. 9:27). The very keys of the kingdom were promised as an apostolic possession to be used during the lifetime of the apostolic band, (Matt. 16:16-19). Matthew records the following teaching of Jesus,

> So every one who acknowledges me before men, I also will acknowledge before my Father who is in heaven; but whoever denies me before men, I also will deny before my Father who is in heaven. (Matt. 10:32-33, with parallels Mk. 8:38; Lk. 12:8-9).

Then, there were those electrifying apocalyptic teachings of Jesus, especially those concerning the destruction of the temple and Jerusalem and the end of the world (Mk. 13 with parallels Matt. 24; Lk. 21).[70] No doubt many Jews who heard these teachings believed this predicted holocaust to be the time of their own redemption in the new epoch which would be inaugu-

---

[69] Walter Schmithals, *Die Apokalyptik: Einführung und Deutung* (Göttingen: Vandenhoeck & Ruprecht, 1973) [Trans. John E. Steely] *The Apocalyptic Movement: Introduction and Interpretation* (Nashville: Abingdon, 1975). Of paramount importance is that "the resurrection of Jesus was originally interpreted as the beginning of the general resurrection of the dead. According to Paul in I Cor. 15:20, Jesus arose as the 'first fruits of those who have died.' Thus Jesus' resurrection signals the onset of the end-events; it introduces the time of judgment and the inbreaking of the new eon," p. 157.

[70] F.F. Bruce, "A Reappraisal of Jewish Apocalyptic Literature," *Review and Expositor* LXXII:3 (Summer 1975). "Jesus was not himself an apocalyptist. . . . but it was the popular expectations generated by apocalyptic visions that provided the setting for much of his message," p. 315.

rated.[71] In this context the following words of Jesus would have special meaning to them. "Come, O blessed of my Father, inherit the kingdom prepared for you from the foundation of the world;" . . . (Matt. 25:34).

After his death, burial, and resurrection,[72] and the confirming appearances to many of his followers, Jesus continued to teach his apostles, "speaking of the kingdom of God," (Acts 1:3b). Their eager question was "Lord, will you at this time restore the kingdom to Israel?" (Acts 1:6b). It is difficult for a 20th century reader to catch the sense of immediacy in their question! They actually expected the kingdom *at that time*, the fulfillment of the hopes and dreams of centuries.

Why the Apocalypse?[73]

This question calls for two answers. The first answer deals with why the writer chose this genre of literature for his message. The second answer is concerned with why the author said what he did.[74]

---

[71]Donald Sneen, *Visions of Hope* (Minneapolis: Augsburg, 1978). Note how Sneen shows the continuity of apocalyptic thought and teaching from Jesus of Mark, through Matthew and Luke, and finally into Revelation, pp. 116-117:

Mark 13:7-9, 24-25	Matt. 24:6-7, 9, 29	Lk. 21:9-12, 25-26	Rev. 6:2-7:1
1. wars	1. wars	1. wars	Seal 1: war
2. international strife	2. international strife	2. international strife	Seal 2: international strife
3. earthquakes	3. famines	3. earthquakes	Seal 3: famine
4. famines	4. earthquakes	4. famines	Seal 4: pestilence, Death, Hades
5. persecutions	5. persecutions	5. pestilence	Seal 5: persecutions
6. eclipses of the sun and moon, falling of the stars, shaking of the powers of heaven	6. eclipses of the sun and moon, falling of the stars, shaking of the powers of heaven	6. persecutions 7. signs in the sun, moon, and stars, men fainting for fear, shaking of the powers of the heavens	Seal 6: earthquakes, signs in sun and moon, stars falling, men calling on rocks to fall on them, shaking of the power of heaven, four destroying winds

[72]E. Frank Tupper, "The Revival of Apocalyptic in Biblical and Theological Studies," *Review and Expositor* LXXII:3 (Summer 1975). "The question of Jesus' eschatological destiny lurks behind all evaluations of the relevance of apocalyptic in Christian theology. Theological inquiry into the definition of man and the reality of God intersect in the question of the historicality of Jesus' resurrection," p. 302.

[73]James J. Megivern, "Wrestling with Revelation," *Biblical Theology Bulletin* 8:4 (Oct 1978). "One does not have to read very much to discover that Revelation has been the most troublesome New Testament book in Christian history," p. 47.

[74]Elisabeth Schüssler Fiorenza, "Apocalyptic and Gnosis in the Book of Revelation and Paul," *Journal of Biblical Literature* 92 (1973). "The New Testament scholars generally agree that the author of Revelation used the apocalyptic genre to depict the religious and political struggles of the churches of Asia Minor [and that] Revelation was written in a time of tribulation and persecution in order to strengthen the faith, endurance, and hope of the Christians. . . ," p. 565.

Even if the above is granted, the two major questions still remain, the answers to which being the chief purpose of this article: "Why use an apocalyptic genre of literature to 'depict religious and political struggles'?" and, "What is the central message that strengthens the 'faith, endurance, and hope of the Christians'?"

Earlier, it was pointed out that two dates for the writing of the Apocalypse have been defended. If Revelation was written in the late 60's C.E.,[75] the blood of the Neronian martyrs had scarcely dried. If the mid-90's C.E.[76] is the correct date, which is the dominant view, severe trials were also present, but there seemed to be no reign of terror against Christians. However, it is obvious that John was preparing his readers for, and encouraging them to endure, intensified persecutions which would soon come upon them, as well as to stand firm in their present trials.[77]

A major point arises here as attention is called to amazing parallels between two earlier historical epochs and the history which is unfolding at the end of the first century, and a way in which biblical writers responded to these times.

The era involving the fall and captivity of Judah was initially addressed by some prophets with a heavy emphasis on a prophetic eschatological message. The restoration of Israel would occur. History would see all of the hopes and dreams of a subjugated people fulfilled. However, that did not happen. The kingdom was not restored. The Jews had no more kings after Babylonian captivity.[78] They remained under foreign domination during Persian, Greek, and Roman times. It was during these times, especially from about 200 B.C.E., that apocalyptic eschatology became a major theme in Jewish writings. What was perceived as a *DELAY* of the fulfillment of the prophetic promises had pushed God's redemptive work beyond the course of ordinary history. Now, his coming and kingdom would inaugurate the new aeon. There would no longer be "mere" history.[79] The transcendental would break into the mundane resulting in a "new heaven and a new earth." The apocalyptic genre of literature provided the language for this perspective of

---

[75]C. van der Wall, "The Last Book of the Bible and the Jewish Apocalypses," Neotestamentica 12 (n.d.). "We cannot accept all the arguments of J.A.T. Robinson in his book *Redating the New Testament* (London, 1976), but we agree with his conclusion that all the books of the New Testament were written before the year 70 A.D.," p. 116.

[76]Frank Stagg, "Interpreting the Book of Revelation," *Review and Expositor* LXXII:3 (Summer 1975). "The New Testament Apocalypse probably comes from the time of the Roman Emperor Domitian (A.D. 81-96)," p. 334.

[77]Elisabeth Schüssler Fiorenza, "Revelation, Book of," *The Interpreter's Dictionary of the Bible*, Supp. Vol. [eds. Keith Crim, Lloyd Richard Bailer, Sr., Victor Paul Furnish, Emory Stevens Bucke] (Nashville: Abingdon, 1962). "Revelation demands unfaltering resistance to the Roman imperial cult, because to give divine honors to the emperor would mean to ratify his claim of dominion over all people," p. 745.

[78]To be sure, there were dissenting views. E.g., some saw in John Hyrcanus (134-104 B.C.E.) all the endowments of prophet, priest and king to qualify him as a "messianic" ruler, (Josephus, *Antiquities*, Bk. XIII, Ch. X, par. 7).

[79]Much in the Dead Sea Scrolls (ca. 150-B.C.E.-68 C.E.) reflects this perspective from the viewpoint of the Qumran Essene apocalyptists. Cf., e.g., the War Scroll.

reality.[80] Prophetic eschatology was no longer sufficient to explain the *DELAY* and encourage the faithful to endure until the final consummation because prophetic eschatology emphasized God's working out *in history* the events up to the End.

This scenario is, in principle, repeated in the New Testament.[81] In a sense, Käsemann was right when he made the statement several years ago that "apocalyptic . . . was the mother of all Christian theology."[82] Christianity came into being in a milieu which had fostered high apocalyptic expectations. Thus, many of the teachings of John the Baptist and Jesus were understood in apocalyptic terms.[83] And, the spectacular birth of the church, described apocalyptically by the prophet Joel ([Heb. 3:1ff.]; [Eng. 2:28ff.] — Cf. Acts 2:17ff.) as God's divine breaking into the world with heavenly and earthly consequences, no doubt seemed a logical answer to the apostles' question put to the resurrected One, "Lord, will you at this time restore the kingdom to Israel?" (Acts 1:6b).

Based upon the apocalypticism of the times, it is not surprising that the ministry of "Elijah" (John the Baptist), some of the apocalyptic teachings of Jesus, and the "fiery" birth of the church following Jesus' ascension, resulted in a group of Christians who were expecting the imminent return of God's Messiah.[84] The early writings of Paul, discussed previously in this article, also fostered these eschatological hopes.[85] The later Pauline corpus mitigates this stance enough to allow the possibility of his own death before Christ's return

---

[80]Charlesworth, ibid., ". . . . we should emphasize that the Apocalypse does not quote any extant apocalypse, nor has it been influenced directly by any of the Jewish apocalypses," p. 24.

[81]Paul Hanson, *Old Testament Apocalyptic* [Interpreting Biblical Texts, eds. Lloyd R. Bailer, Sr., and Victor P. Furnish] (Nashville: Abingdon, 1987). Hanson speaks of "the apocalyptic message as a pattern woven into the fabric of the canon," p. 131.

[82]Ernst Kasemann, "The Beginnings of Christian Theology," [Trans. James W. Leitch] *Journal for Theology and the Church* 6 (1969) 40.

[83]See J. Massyngberde Ford, *Revelation* [Anchor Bible, eds. William Foxwell Albright and David Noel Freedman] (Garden City, New York: Doubleday & Company, Inc., 1975), for the rather startling role assigned to John the Baptist. "Chs. 4-11 contain the revelation given not to John the evangelist after the death, resurrection, and ascension of Jesus, but to John the Baptist, the forerunner of Jesus before his public ministry," p. 50!

[84]John E. Stambaugh and David L. Balch, *The New Testament in Its Social Environment* [Library of Early Christianity, ed. Wayne A. Meeks] (Philadelphia: Westminster, 1986). The writers state that a theme "made most explicit in Revelation but frequently used in Pauline literature and the Gospels, is apocalyptic, the expectation that Jesus will return in ultimate triumph, amid destruction and judgment. In that coming wrath, *which was expected urgently and imminently,* Jesus would save the believers and deliver them," (emphasis added), p. 58.

[85]D.S. Russell, *Apocalyptic: Ancient and Modern* (Philadelphia: Fortress, 1978). See pp. 41-43 for three other germane elements of N.T. teaching that shaped the apocalypticism of the times which cannot be discussed in detail here, viz., Jesus' mastery of demons, the concept of the kingdom as *mysterion*, and the "Son of Man" title associated with Jesus and his *parousia* in glory.

(Phil. 3:10-11, etc.); however, he never teaches anything, including II Thessalonians 2:1-12, that contravenes his early statements concerning the imminent return of Christ.

However, it should be remembered that from forty to sixty years had passed since those anticipatory, exciting times of Jesus' ministry, the flourishing of the first century Christian communities, the early writings of Paul, and the writing of the Apocalypse. What had happened in Christendom between the early and latter decades of the first century? The obvious had occurred. Many Christians had become convinced there had been an undue *DELAY OF THE PAROUSIA.*[86]

Later New Testament statements show that this perceived *DELAY* was recognized and addressed in at least three different ways. First, the "now" of "realized eschatology" tended to mitigate the effects of the *DELAY* since many of the anticipated benefits of the new aeon were already being enjoyed (Cf. esp. Eph. 1-2). Second, to those who were skeptical of the *parousia*, II Peter insists that the *DELAY* is more apparent than real since time means nothing to God. However, the "day of the Lord" *is* coming with all of its apocalyptic consequences, (cf. II Pet. 3:1-15a).

A third way of dealing with the *DELAY OF THE PAROUSIA* is seen is the Apocalypse. The epistolary framework is rooted and grounded *in history*. Seven Asian churches are addressed in specific terms. Their present status is real (probably mid-90's C.E.). They are assured by their brother that he shares their tribulation, the kingdom, and their endurance (1:9). No doubt he is well known to them, since he is a servant (1:1),[87] as well as their brother.

In addition to the seven letters in the epistolary framework, the bulk of the Apocalypse includes the "seven" sections (messages, seals, trumpets, bowls,

---

[86]David L. Barr, "The Apocalypse as a Symbolic Transformation of the World: A Literary Analysis," *Interpretation* XXXVIII:1 (Jan 1984). "How did this strange book prove to be useful when, on the face of it, it failed rather spectacularly to deliver on its promise that Jesus would come 'soon'?" Relying heavily on David Aune, *The Cultic Setting of Realized Eschatology in Early Christianity* (Leiden: E.J. Brill, 1972), he speaks of the "cultic" coming of Jesus in three ways: "in the person of a charismatic prophet, in a visionary christophany, or in a sacramental identification with Christ," and affirms that all three are present in the Apocalypse "in the cultic personal, in the cultic recitation, and in the cultic celebration of the Eucharist," p. 48. All this is very intriguing but less than convincing.

[87]David E. Aune, "The Social Matrix of the Apocalypse of John," *Biblical Research* XXVI (1981). Building on E. Käsemann's argument that the term "servant" in the Old Testament may be honorific (TDNT 11, 268, 276f.) *Commentary on Romans* (Grand Rapids: Eerdmans, 1980), p. 5, Aune goes on to say that in the New Testament "the designation 'servant' had doubtless come to connote one of superior status (Phil. 1:1; Jas. 1:1; Jude 1:1)," p. 17. Thus, John, writing from "above" to the seven churches, seeks to establish a close communion with his readers by rhetorical terms emphasizing he is "one of them."

two sets of unnumbered visions),[88] in which the setting is heavenly with earthly perspectives interspersed throughout.[89] There are also seven beatitudes found throughout the book.[90] The epistolary close may begin at 22:10 and continue to the end.[91] If so, here one sees an "epistolary style" summary which includes commands, promises, blessings, affirmation, invitations, warnings, assurances, and a benediction.

The work of the exegete in specifically interpreting these three sections is the task of expositors who have produced a very large number of commentaries on Revelation through the centuries.[92] The emphasis here is upon one theme which appears in all three sections, i.e., throughout the Apocalypse.[93] It is the assurance to the readers that Christ is coming again and there will be only a brief *DELAY OF THE PAROUSIA*. Notice: "what must SOON take place, (1:1);[94] "the time is near," (1:3b); "Behold, he is coming," (1:7); [the One] "who is to come," (1:8); "hold fast what you have, until I come,"

---

[88]Adela Yarbro Collins, "The Revelation of John: An Apocalyptic Response to a Social Crisis," *Currents in Theology and Mission* 8:1 (Feb 1981). The "seven" sections (cf. Collins' outline above) have "the same underlying pattern and thus the same message. The underlying pattern is threefold and involves: (1) persecution of the faithful, (2) punishment of the persecutors, and (3) victory of God and the Lamb and salvation of the faithful," p. 9.

[89]Bruce M. Metzger, *An Introduction to the Apocrypha* (New York: Oxford University Press, 1957). "The last book of the New Testament contains, in addition to much imagery derived from the Old Testament, a striking parallel to a passage in Tobit. Tobit's 'prayer of rejoicing' contains a remarkable poetic passage which looks forward to the time when

'Jerusalem will be built with sapphires and emeralds
and her walls with precious stones,
and her towers and battlements with pure gold.
The streets of Jerusalem will be paved with beryl and stone of Ophir,'
(13:16-17).

It may well be that these words were in the mind of John when in the Book of Revelation he describes the New Jerusalem as a city of pure gold, with walls of jasper, sapphire, emerald, beryl, and all kinds of precious stones, (21:18-21)," p. 166.

[90]Frank Pack, *Revelation*, Part I (Austin, Tex.: Sweet Publishing Co., 1965). Pack identifies these beatitudes at 1:3; 14:13; 16:15; 19:9; 20:6; 22:7,14, p. 23.

[91]Aune, op. cit.

[92]Paul S. Minear, *New Testament Apocalyptic* [Interpreting Biblical Texts, eds. Lloyd R. Bailey and Victor P. Furnish] (Nashville: Abingdon, 1981). In his chapter, "The Horizons of Apocalyptic Prophecy," the author relates the theme of Christian *vocation* to New Testament apocalyptic expectations, pp. 48-63.

[93]John G. Gager, "The Attainment of Millennial Bliss Through Myth: The Book of Revelation," in: *Visionaries and Their Apocalypses* [Issues in Religion and Theology, No. 2, ed. Paul D. Hanson] (Philadelphia: Fortress, 1983). "The one undeniable fact is that the attention of the community, and thus of its worship, was entirely on the imminent End. 'The end is near' (1:3) and 'Amen, come Lord Jesus' (22:20) frame the work as a whole as much as they express the mood of its hearers," p. 153.

[94]Martin Rist, "Revelation," *The Interpreter's Bible*, Vol. 12 [ed. George Arthur Buttrick] (New York-Nashville: Abingdon, 1957). "It is essential for the author's purpose to stress the immediacy of the coming of the end of this age; . . . the author's own times of course, not ours, being the point of reference," p.367.

(2:25); "I will come like a thief, and you will not know at what hour I will come upon you," (3:3b); "I am coming SOON," (3:11a); [the angel swore] "that there should be no more delay. . . ," (10:6b); [God] "has sent his angel to show his servants what must SOON take place," (22:6b); "And behold, I am coming SOON," (22:7); "Behold, I am coming SOON, (22:12); "Surely I am coming SOON," (22:20a).

To say that "the word 'soon' (*en tachei*; [cf. 1:1; 22:6]) means that the action will be sudden when it comes, not necessarily that it will occur immediately,"[95] is also to say that it may mean SOON and not necessarily "suddenly." This latter meaning seems abundantly clear in this context and is the position taken by many of the major versions,[96] commentaries,[97] and lexicons.[98]

Therefore, it seems warranted to affirm that the apocalyptic literary genre, the historical context, and the content of the Apocalypse demonstrate John's earnest desire to encourage his brethren to keep the faith under all circumstances, even "unto death," (2:10b). His most effective methodology for doing this is his affirmation that the *DELAY OF THE PAROUSIA* would not be long.[99] His use of the apocalyptic genre emphasizes his conviction that the end of history is at hand, the new aeon is rapidly approaching, and the transcendental reality will soon be the realm of the redeemed when the "offspring of David" comes to close the final chapter on human history.[100]

---

[95]John F. Walvoord, "Revelation," *The Bible Knowledge Commentary* [eds. John F. Walvoord and Roy B. Zuck] (Wheaton: [Victor Books] Scripture Press Publishers, Inc., 1983), p. 928.

[96]E.g., Revised Standard Version; New International Version.

[97]G.R. Beasley-Murray, "The Revelation," *The New Bible Commentary* [revisors and eds. D. Guthrie, J.A. Motyer, A.M. Stibbs, and D.J. Wiseman] (Grand Rapids: Eerdmans, 1970, p. 1309.

[98]W. Bauer, *Greek-English Lexicon of the New Testament* [4th ed., rev., trans., and augmented by William F. Arndt and F. Wilbur Gingrich] (Chicago: University of Chicago Press; London: Cambridge University Press, 1957), p. 814.

[99]Barnabas Lindars, "Re-Enter the Apocalyptic Son of Man," *New Testament Studies* 22:1 (Oct 1975). "The delay of the parousia becomes problematical, not simply because of the passage of time, but because of the tension which arises once the death of Christ has been identified as the act in which the evil powers are conquered. To this extent the events of the end time are anticipated, and it is difficult to see why the rest do not follow immediately," p. 64.

[100]Some readers may believe that an absurd, intrinsically self-contradictory position emerges in this article; i.e., how can one insist, after almost 2,000 years have passed, that *en tachei* means "soon" in Revelation when it can, and does, mean "quickly" in other contexts (e.g., Acts 12:7). Higher biblical criticism reminds us that beyond a careful consideration of the lexical meaning of a word(s) that, where optional meanings are possible, one must evaluate the word(s) in light of the purpose of the writer, the cultural, historical, and religious contexts in which the document containing the word(s) is written, the primary audience, the literary genre of the work, the immediate textual context in which the word(s) appears, and such like.

This writer suggests that, within limited scope, this article develops these matters sufficiently, leading to the reasonable conclusion that: (1) the apocalyptic genre was used by John because it was the kind of literature through which he could best

It is significant that virtually the final words of the Apocalypse are John's prayer. If John's use of "amen" stems from the way Jesus used this term, i.e., putting it first to insure the certain fulfillment of his petition,[101] then this short prayer is a virtual guarantee of Jesus' imminent return. "He who testifies to these things says,[102] 'Surely I am coming soon,'[103] 'Amen. Come, Lord Jesus!' " (22:20).

---

accomplish his purpose; (2) his purpose was to encourage, strengthen, and equip his readers to hold firm in the faith in spite of present or anticipated persecutions; (3) his methodology for accomplishing this purpose consisted, for the most part, in presenting a triumphant, reigning Christ returning soon to share his victory with them.

How does this affect the way one looks at predictive prophecy? For further study on this question see J.J.M. Roberts, "A Christian Perspective on Prophetic Prediction," *Interpretation* XXXIII:3 (July 1979) 240-253. Briefly, the author gives four categories of prophetic predictions. The fourth category touches the question at hand as he speaks of "those predictions whose fulfillment, whether already past or yet to be expected, must be regarded as taking place in a way that is less — or more than — literal," (Exp. Ezekiel 37-38/Revelation 20:4-22:5).

It is within the context of this category that Roberts discusses the characteristic fore-shortening of the time element in most prophetic predictions using Jesus' statements of his second coming in Mark 13 and Paul's early ministry as examples. Ultimately, Roberts affirms, "one may try to find the basis for this perplexing problem in the purpose of God himself."

[101] Gerhard Kittle, ed. *Theological Dictionary of the New Testament*, Vol. I [Trans. and ed. Geoffrey W. Bromiley] (Grand Rapids: Eerdmans, 1964). "The point of the Amen before Jesus' own sayings is rather to show that as such they are reliable and true, and that they are so as and because Jesus Himself in His Amen acknowledges them to be His own sayings and thus makes them valid," p. 338.

[102] Matthew Black and H.H. Rowley, eds. *Peakes' Commentary on the Bible* (London: Nelson, 1962). "I am coming soon: this is the motif of the whole book. To our author's mind, everything depends on this speedy return. He can see no other solution for the Church's ills," p. 930b. Cf. also, Robert H. Mounce, *The Book of Revelation* [New International Commentary on the New Testament, ed. F.F. Bruce] (Grand Rapids: Eerdmans, 1977), where he says, "The verse opens with the testimony of Christ that his coming will be without delay, . . . only in Mt. 28:8 does *tachu* mean 'quickly' in the sense of 'at a rapid rate.' . . . Elsewhere it means 'at once' or 'in a short time' (Mk. 5:25; Lk. 15:22; and the five Rev. passages in which it is used of the coming of Christ: 2:16; 3:11; 22:7,12,20)," p. 396.

[103] Mounce, ibid., "The words 'Behold, I come quickly' are those of the risen Lord. . . . *tachu* used as an adverb may mean 'quickly' in the sense of 'at a rapid rate,' although this usage does not fit the context of the five occurrences of *erchomai tachu* in Rev. (2:16; 3:11; 22:7,12,20). It is best to take the utterance at face value and accept the difficulty of a foreshortened perspective on the time of the end rather than to reinterpret it in the sense that Jesus 'comes' in the crises of life and especially at the death of every man. Revelation has enough riddles without our adding more," p. 391. Morris Ashcraft, "Preaching the Apocalyptic Message Today," *Review and Expositor* LXXII:3 (Summer 1975). The adequacy of God's word is stressed. "In the Apocalypse, Christ is known as 'The Word of God' (19:13). He is 'Faithful and True' (19:11). The 'two-edged sword' issues from the mouth of Christ, the Lamb (1:16; 2:12; 19:15)," p. 356. This "Living Word" is the one who encourages his followers by testifying "Surely, I am coming soon."

The Source and Function of Isaiah 6:9-10 in John 12:40

Ronald L. Tyler

We have two major concerns in this article: (1) the question of the source, or origin, of the passage and (2) the issue of the function and use of the passage. It is hoped that this study will contribute to an understanding of John's use of the Old Testament as Christian scripture and to an understanding of these two concerns within contemporary scholarship.

Source

The exact form of the Isaiah 6 passage, as it appears in John 12:40, is elsewhere unattested. This can be seen by comparison and examination of the following textual forms.[1]

Examination of the Text Forms

Make the heart of this people fat, and make
their ears heavy, and shut their eyes;

---

[1] I am placing these in English translation but my remarks will be based upon the original languages. Cf. R.G. Bratcher, *Old Testament Quotations in the New Testament* 2d. rev. ed. (New York: American Bible Society, 1984), for the English translations. For comparison of the textual forms in the original languages, Edwin D. Freed, *Old Testament Quotations in the Gospel of John* (Leiden: E.J. Brill, 1965), remains the most useful source. Of older works, C.H. Toy, *Quotations in the New Testament* (New York: Charles Scribner's Sons, 1884). W. Dittmar, *Vetus Testamentum in Novo: Die Alttestamentlichen Parallelen des Neuen Testaments im Wortlaut der Urtexts und der Septuaginta Zusammengestellt.* (Göttingen: Vandenhoeck & Ruprecht, 1899-1903). D.M. Turpie, *The NT View of the Old* (London: Williams and Norgate, 1872), are the best works for comparing Hebrew and Greek texts. For more recent discussion of the text traditions cf. F. Cross and S. Talmon (eds.), *Qumran and the History of the Biblical Text* (Cambridge: Harvard University Press, 1975).

K. Elliger and W. Rudolph (eds.), *Biblia Hebraica Stuttgartensia* (Stuttgart: Deutsche Bibelgesellschaft, 1966-1977), for the Hebrew text. E. Nestle, *Novum Testamentum Graece*, Rev. by E. Nestle and K. Aland, 26th ed. (Stuttgart: Deutsche Bibelgesellschaft, 1983), for the Greek text. A. Rahlfs, *Septuaginta* (Stuttgart: Deutsche Bibelgesellschaft, 1935), for the Greek of the Septuagint.

Lest they see with their eyes, and hear with
   their ears, and understand with their heart.
And turn again,
And *be healed*. (Isaiah 6:9-10, Masoretic Text)

For this people's heart *is waxed gross*, and
   their ears are dull of hearing, and their
   eyes they have closed;
Lest haply they should see with their eyes,
   and hear with their ears, and understand
   with their heart,
And should turn again,
And *I should heal* them. (Isaiah 6:9-10, Septuagint)

He has blinded their eyes, and he hardened
   their heart,
Lest they should see with their eyes, and perceive with
   their heart,
And should turn,
And *I should heal* them. (John 12:40)

Observations on the Text Forms

The major differences among the readings are underscored. The Hebrew text makes the prophet responsible. Isaiah's word will cause a hardening of heart in the rebellious people which will culminate in their inability to turn and be healed. The Hebrew text is problematical in that impersonal verbs are used, i.e., "might be healed . . . " No active agent is expressed. The main verbs are in the second person singular imperative mood, so that *Isaiah* is commanded to do certain things. The Septuagint rendering supplies a subject, i.e., "I might heal them," and places the responsibility on the people.[2] It uses third person plural forms of the verbs in the indicative mood, so that it is the *people* who are themselves responsible. They have allowed their hearts to become rebellious and hardened. Isaiah found this to be the case when he initially preached his word to them. The Johannine text appears to place the responsibility on *God* who has blinded their eyes and hardened their hearts. John uses the third person singular of the indicative mood, with God being responsible for the action.[3] The shift of tense from the third person to the first is striking in that it may refer to different subjects.[4]

---

[2]The Latin Vulgate does the same.

[3]Cf. Robert G. Bratcher, *Old Testament Quotations in the New Testament* (London: American Bible Society, 1984), p. 24, footnote 6.

[4]John Painter, *John: Witness & Theologian* (London: S.P.C.K., 1975), makes much of this. He makes the point that the Isaiah text has some modifications by John. John *alters* the text so that the one who has blinded the Jews is separate from the one who would heal them. John *adds to* the text "He has blinded . . . " Painter then argues that only one interpretation fits the context, shows why the Jews failed to see

The question of source is further complicated by noting Isaiah 6:9-10 as cited elsewhere in the New Testament: Matthew 13:14-15; Mark 4:10-12 (cf. also Mark 8:18); Luke 8:10; and Acts 28:26ff.[5]

Matthew, Mark, and Luke's use of the passage all occur in the context of Jesus' reason for speaking in parables. Matthew agrees with the Septuagint; making verbs in the third person plural, indicative mood, locating responsibility on the people for allowing their hearts to grow dull and hardened. Mark's emphasis is that parables are given to harden hearts so that they will not turn and be healed. Mark may be alluding to the Isaiah 6 text but, says Black, with affinity to the targum.[6] Luke's focus is similar to Mark's.

The question of the source of the citation is important when one considers the differences in meaning and function which are involved. Is God or Satan the one who hardens? Is the prophet the one who hardens? Is it the word he preached? What does this do to human responsibility?

Explanations of the Text Forms

These textual and theological issues have not passed unnoticed in the history of interpretation.[7] We will attempt to keep this fascinating history in

---

the glory of Jesus' signs and believe, and shows itself consistent with the theology of the Fourth Gospel. Painter affirms that "He," the prince of this world, referring to John 12:31, is the one who has blinded the Jews so that Jesus may not heal them. He justifies this interpretation on the following grounds: (1) the two other New Testament uses of "he has blinded" (2 Cor. 4:4 and I Jn. 2:11), refers to Satan as the one doing the blinding, (2) the dualism is found in the Qumran texts which is significant because Qumran, he feels, offer the best source of material with affinity to the fourth gospel, (3) and the scene in John 8 has the people refusing to believe in Jesus' signs, having mistaken the works of Jesus for the works of the devil.

Such an interpretation can be found as early as Cyril of Jerusalem. Cf. Rudolf Bultmann, *The Gospel of John* (Philadelphia: Westminster Press, 1971).

The view is vulnerable in that it doesn't explain why the textual tradition is so divergent. Furthermore, it isn't necessary in light of the theology of the Old Testament wherein God is often described as hardening hearts.

[5]The passages from the gospels can best be compared in Kurt Aland (ed.), *Synopsis of the Four Gospels* (New York: United Bible Societies, 1985). The passages, along with parallels from non-canonical sources, can be compared in Robert Funk, *New Gospel Parallels*, 2 vols. (Philadelphia: Fortress Press, 1985).

[6]Matthew Black, *An Aramaic Approach to the Gospels and Acts* (Oxford: Clarendon Press., 1954), p. 186.

[7]For a collection of how the fathers viewed the concerns, cf. Thomas Aquinas, *Catena Aurea* which is a *Commentary on the Four Gospels Collected Out of the Works of the Fathers* (Oxford: John Parker, 1845), Vol. IV., Part II, pp. 412-415. W. Sanday and A. Headlam, *Romans* (London: T. & T. Clark, 1895), pp. 269-272. For a further insightful summary of such concerns in the history of interpretation, especially in the twentieth century, cf. E.E. Ellis, "Quotations in the NT," in *The International Standard Bible Encyclopedia*, Volume 4, edited by G.W. Bromiley (Grand Rapids: Wm. B. Eerdmans Publishing Co., 1988), pp. 18-25 with bibliography. Craig Evans, "The Function of Isaiah 6:9-10 in Mark and John," *Novum Testamentum* XXIV:2 (1982) 124-138, contains materials pertinent to the history of the use of the Isaiah passage.

view while recalling that, as a writer in Mediterranean antiquity, John had certain options available to him within which he worked. While his life within the Graeco-Roman world is influential, his context within Judaism and early Christianity largely determined his methodology as a writer.[8]

In first century conceptions, inspiration was a necessary operative in reading and interpreting ancient texts. This expressed itself in various ways such as special speech and insight. While the spoken word was central, serious study of written texts existed in the first century. This is evidenced by the collections of oracle texts, especially the Sibyllines,[9] and by the existence of spurious oracle books written by Jews and Christians to counter pagan oracle collections.[10]

Pagan oracles were often in obscure language which necessitated interpretation. The same was true for much of Greek poetry as well. Some form of inspiration was needed to understand them. The allegorical method came to be used among the Greeks to interpret many of the texts with the end result that a given collection had authority but the original historical meaning was ignored. An ancient text meant whatever an interpreter read into it from the presuppositions which he brought with him.[11]

---

[8]Scholars have recognized that the Gospel of John, as well as Matthew, is a very Hebraic document while, at the same time, noting that Judaism had become very Hellenized in the period prior to the New Testament. Cf. especially G. Delling, "Die Begegnung zwischen Hellenismus und Judentum," in *Aufstieg und Niedergang der Römischen Welt*, edited by H. Wolfgang and H. Temporini, Vol. 20.1, Berlin: Walter de Gruyter, 1987, pp. 3-39, and Martin Hengel, *Judaism and Hellenism*, 2 vols. (Philadelphia: Fortress Press, 1974); with his sequel, *Jews, Greeks, and Barbarians* (Philadelphia: Fortress Press, 1980).

For statements regarding Jewish and Christian exegesis cf. "Contemporary Jewish Exegesis," in E. Earle Ellis, *Paul's Use of the Old Testament* (Edinburgh: Oliver and Boyd, 1957), pp. 39-45 remains one of the best succinct summaries. J.D.G. Dunn, *Unity and Diversity in the New Testament*, (Philadelphia: Westminster Press, 1977). Chapter V deals with the use of the Old Testament in Judaism in the first century and then goes on to show Christian use inherited and growing out of this milieu. Richard Longenecker, *Biblical Exegesis in the Apostolic Period* (Grand Rapids: Wm. B. Eerdmans Publishing Co., 1975). G.R. Beasley-Murray, *John*, Word Biblical Commentary, vol. 36 (Waco: Word Books, Publisher, 1987), pp. lviii-lxvi contains a current summary.

[9]On oracles in general in the religions of the Hellenistic world, cf. Everett Ferguson, *Backgrounds of Early Christianity* (Grand Rapids: Wm. B. Eerdmans Publishing Co., 1987), pp. 166-171. On the Sibyls in particular, cf. pp. 367-368. Cf. especially Emil Schürer, *The History of the Jewish People in the Age of Jesus Christ*, edited by M. Black, G. Vermes, F. Millar, and M. Goodman., Vol. III. 1 (London: T. & T. Clark., Ltd., 1986), pp. 618-654 with bibliographies. Basic to any such study is J.J. Collins, *The Sibylline Oracles of Egyptian Judaism* (Atlanta: Scholars Press, 1972), and "The Development of the Sibylline Tradition," in *Aufstieg und Niedergang...*, *op. cit.*, Volume 20.1, pp. 421-459.

[10]C.K. Barrett, "The Interpretation of the Old Testament in the New," in *The Cambridge History of the Bible: From the Beginnings to Jerome*, edited by P.R. Ackroyd and G.F. Evans, Vol. I (Cambridge: University Press, 1970), p. 378. Schürer, *op. cit.*, pp. 617-618.

[11]*Ibid.*, p. 379.

The Greek background, while important, is less crucial than the Jewish and Christian usages of the Old Testament for understanding John 12:40. Judaism felt itself under the judgment and control of the sacred text and concerned itself with reading and interpreting them. A rich and marked diversity existed within Judaism. Philo and Alexandrian exegesis[12] most nearly resembled much that one might find in pagan usage of texts over against the rabbinic reading of the scriptures. Just how far apart Philo was from the rabbis remains controversial. It appears that for all his eclecticism, excesses, and philological difficiences, he is not so far from Palestinian methods as some scholars have supposed. In reading and interpreting scripture, Judaism in Palestine and in the Hellenistic world was more nearly alike than previous scholars allowed.[13]

Within his Jewish inheritance, and in addition to the original or literal meaning, John had several options open to him regarding his use of scripture: targum,[14] midrash,[15] pesher,[16] typology,[17] and allegory.[18] These methods

---

[12]Philo was an Alexandrian Jew who made allegory a principle method of interpretation. He was aware of literal meanings but, in practice, these were less important than other ideas he found in scripture. On Philo, cf. Ferguson, *op. cit.*, 380-385. On Philo's principles of exegesis cf. F.W. Farrar, *History of Interpretation* (Grand Rapids: Baker Book House, 1961), pp. 149-151. Farrar's lectures were given as the Bampton Lectures in 1885. But cf. especially Jenny Morris, "The Jewish Philosopher Philo," in *The History of the Jewish People in the Age of Jesus Christ*, edited by M. Black, G. Vermes, F. Millar, and M. Goodman., Vol. III.2 (London: T. & T. Clark, 1987), pp. 809-889 with bibliographies. The most important source is *Aufstieg und Niedergang* . . . , Volume 21.1, 1984, pp. 2-553 with several articles on Philo.

[13]Barrett, "The Interpretation of . . . " *op. cit.*, p. 383.

[14]The term is from the Aramaic and means "interpretation" or "translation." The major characteristics of these "paraphrases" of the Hebrew text are (1) they adhere closely to the Biblical text, (2) they were intended for the unlearned, (3) they explained difficult and contradictory passages, (4) they were reverential in speaking of God, (5) they showed great respect for the elders of Israel, (6) they often read later doctrine back into the interpretation and (7) they contained homiletic materials. Cf. M. McNamara, *Targum and Testament* (Grand Rapids: Wm. B. Eerdmans Publishing Co., 1972), pp. 69-78.

There is much interest in the targums today among both Jewish and Christian interpreters. Targums exist for all Old Testament books except Daniel and Ezra-Nehemiah. They appear in several different collections. From the vast literature, cf. especially M.G. Steinhauser, "The Targums and the New Testament," *Toronto Journal of Theology* 2 (1986) 262-278. M. Miller, "Targum, Midrash, and the Use of the Old Testament in the New Testament," *Journal for the Study of Judaism* 2 (1971) 29-82. P. Nickels, *Targum and New Testament: A Bibliography* (Rome: Pontifical Biblical Institute, 1967). E.E. Ellis, "Midrash, Targum and the New Testament Quotations," in *Neotestamentica et Semitica* (Edinburgh: T. & T. Clark, 1969), pp. 61-69. Beyond these, cf. Schürer, *The History of . . .* , *op. cit.*, Vol. 1, pp. 105ff.

[15]The term is from the Hebrew meaning "to inquire" or "to search." Its meaning is an interpretation or explanation of some scripture. Cf. II Chronicles 13:22; 24:27. In practice it involved exegetical, narrative, and literary comments upon scripture. A great deal of diversity and freedom existed in practice with this method. It included comments on scripture, detailed exegesis, cryptic allusions to scripture passages, and retelling of scripture stories. It was " . . . the composition of edifying or doctrinaire enlargement or embroidery upon the text of sacred scripture, in the form

often were combined in actual practice, especially pesher, typology, and alle-

---

of anecdote or of narrative or of the addition of circumstantial detail." Barrett, "The Interpretation of . . . " *op. cit.* p. 413. It has come to include a modern literary way of interpreting the Bible. Cf. Shaye J.D. Cohen, *From the Maccabees to the Mishnah* (Philadelphia: Westminster Press, 1987), pp. 204-209. Cohen's book is an excellent entry level text for seeing how modern scholars have been re-evaluating Judaism in the period 200 B.C.E to 200 C.E. Further bibliography on *Midrashim* may be conveniently found in Schürer, *The History of* . . . , *op. cit.* Vol. I, pp. 90-99. Cf. also, Vol. II, pp. 339-355 for discussion of the nature of Midrash and its actual method and practice, etc. From the prolific Jacob Neusner, reference should be made to *Midrash in Context: Exegesis in Formative Judaism* (Philadelphia: Fortress Press, 1983). Cf. his bibliography on pp. 197-207. G. Porton, "Midrash: Palestinian Jews and the Hebrew Bible in the Graeco-Roman Period," in *Aufstieg und Niedergang* . . . , *op. cit.*, Volume 19.2, pp. 103-138.

This way of using the Bible is similar to what happened among the Greeks in interpreting Homer and among the Romans in interpreting various documents from their tradition. The earliest known extensive use of it in Judaism is in the Dead Sea Scrolls; later it was used by the great rabbis. It is debatable whether they borrowed it from the Qumran group. It is thought by some that the rabbis borrowed it from the Greeks and made it uniquely their own.

[16]The term is from the Hebrew meaning "interpretation" or "commentary." It is a reading of the Old Testament in such a prophetic manner that it speaks directly of events and circumstances in the commentator's own day. What was going on in the prophet's own day is unimportant. What is of issue is to decode the ancient text so as to show it was speaking to the day of the interpreter. K. Stendahl conveniently shows the thirteen principles of interpretation involved in the method in *The School of St. Matthew and Its Use of the Old Testament* (Philadelphia: Fortress Press, 1968), pp. 191-192

This has been central in scholarly discussion since the finding of the Dead Sea Scrolls. The best example of the method at Qumran is the Habakkuk Commentary. The Damascus Document also furnishes us with examples. Helpful from the vast literature is F.F. Bruce, *Biblical Exegesis in the Qumran Texts* (London: Tyndale, 1960), especially pp. 7-11 and 75-88. This method of reading scripture sheds light on the New Testament use of the Old Testament in passages such as concerns us in this study. E.P. Sanders' discussion in *Paul and Palestinian Judaism* (Philadelphia: Fortress Press, 1977), pp. 239-321 is a useful survey of the scrolls in terms of the themes and ideas present. J. de Waard, *A Comparative Study of the OT Text in the Dead Sea Scrolls and in the NT* (Leiden: E.J. Brill, 1965). Romans 10:6ff., with its treatment of Deuteronomy 30:12ff., is a good example of the method used in the New Testament. Cf. also Hebrews 10:5-10; Romans 9:7ff.; I Corinthians 15:54-56; II Corinthians 6:2; Ephesians 4:8-11; Hebrews 2:6-9; 3:7-19.

[17]The term is from the Greek meaning "archetype" or "pattern." In typology, the Old Testament is read with a view to finding events "back there" which foreshadow events, persons, or things in the New Testament. Examples in the New Testament include I Corinthians 10:1-6; Romans 15:14; Hebrews 7, etc. Typology takes seriously the historical dimension of the Old Testament text. It simply sees it as an archetype reading Christian meanings into both persons and events foreshadowing things Jesus said and did. A classic example of Jewish use of the method can be seen in how the rabbis interpreted the Song of Solomon, not to mention the Psalms. G.R. Osborne, "Type; Typology," *International Standard Bible Encyclopedia*, Vol. 4, *op. cit.*, pp. 930-932 offers a brief orientation. Basic to all study of typology is L. Goppelt, *Typos: The Typological Interpretation of the Old Testament in the New*, translated by D. Madvig (Grand Rapids: Wm. B. Eerdmans Publishing Co., 1982) and the 'Foreword' by E. Earle Ellis where pp. 179-194 are especially important. Gop-

gory. Variations existed within all of them.[19] It is nearly impossible to categorize any given sample of ancient exegesis within any one of these groupings.

While all of these approaches can be attested within the New Testament,[20] there is no consensus on the degree to which they are found in the Fourth Gospel. Nor is there agreement as to what light they shed on the question of the origin of the particular citation under consideration. Scholarship has offered several alternatives.

1. It appears that John is not following the Hebrew text. Some disagree, arguing that variant forms of the Hebrew text were in existence in John's day.[21] C.K. Barrett argued in 1946 that it could not be the Hebrew text; he later reversed himself and held that the citation most nearly follows the Hebrew text.[22]

2. It is possible that he is following the Septuagint (hereafter LXX). A stronger argument can be made for his use of the LXX than for the Hebrew text. In support, one notes that the last three words of the citation follow the LXX,[23] variant forms of the LXX may have been available to John,[24] the

---

pelt's article in *Theological Dictionary of the New Testament*, edited G. Kittel and G. Friedrich, Volume VIII (Grand Rapids: Wm. B. Eerdmans Publishing Co., 1972), pp. 246-259 serves to update his book, originally done in German in 1939.

[18]The term is from the Greek meaning "saying something other than what one seems to say." It reads the Old Testament searching for a deeper, hidden spiritual meaning. It sets itself apart from typology in not centering on the original historical meaning of the text. It searches for a meaning beyond and behind the text. Galatians 4:22-31 and I Corinthians 10:1-4 are examples in the New Testament. R.P.C. Hanson's *Allegory and Event* (Richmond: John Knox Press, 1959), while a study of the sources and significance of Origen's interpretation of scripture, contains a long history of the method on pp. 11-129 that remains essential.

[19]Cf. Ellis, *International Standard Bible Encyclopedia*, Vol. 4, *op. cit.*, pp. 19-22 and his *Prophecy and Hermeneutic in Early Christianity* (Grand Rapids: Wm. B. Eerdmans Publishing Co. 1980), pp. 147-172. The issue was likely much more complex than previous scholars postulated. Still, common presuppositions about the Bible and its use existed: (1) the written law contained the revealed will of God, (2) the writings were uniquely from God, (3) the original meanings were important but multiple meanings were inherent in the text, and (4) the use and interpretation of all scripture was for a practical use in the lives of the people of God. Cf. Richard Longenecker, *Biblical Exegesis in the Apostolic Period* (Grand Rapids: Wm. B. Eerdmans Publishing Co.), 1975, pp. 19-20.

[20]As demonstrated by Dunn, *op. cit.*, pp. 87-93.

[21]See S.K. Soderlund, "Text and MSS of the OT," in *International Standard Bible Encyclopedia*, Volume Four, *op. cit.*, pp. 803-805, who characterizes the period from 300 B.C. to 100 A.D. as a "Period of Textual Diversity." A current bibliography is on p. 814.

[22]His earlier viewpoint was expressed in an article entitled, "The Old Testament in the Fourth Gospel," in *The Journal of Theological Studies* 47 (1946) 155-169. Cf. his *The Gospel According to St. John: An Introduction with Commentary and Notes on the Greek Text* (London: S.P.C.K., 1965), pp. 359-360, where he argues that John is closer to the Hebrew than anything else.

[23]". . . and I should heal them."

[24]On this, and all others aspects of LXX research, cf. the most recent analysis of Emanuel Tov, "Jewish Greek Scriptures," *Early Judaism and Its Modern Inter-*

previous citation from Isaiah is from the LXX,[25] and the LXX is the text form most frequently cited in the New Testament.[26]

3. Some posit that the form of the citation existed in the source which John is using. He is then quoting someone else's citation or translation. Representative of such would be Rudolf Bultmann, who sees a "signs-source" throughout John 2-12. Bultmann compares the two Isaiah passages in John 12:38 and 12:40. While the first is the LXX, the second follows no known text. He also notes that each citation has a different introduction. He then argues that John 12:39ff., along with vv. 42ff., go back to the evangelist. Verse 37ff. he then assigns to John's source.[27]

4. It has been suggested that John is following some Targum of Isaiah which was at his disposal. A striking observation is that in the Targum of Isaiah 6:1, "I saw the glory of the Lord" is used rather than "I saw the Lord." (cf. John 12:41).[28]

5. Another suggestion is that John is citing from a "testimony book" of Old Testament texts. J. Rendel Harris has argued that a pre-canonical collection of Old Testament "testimonial" texts were collected when early Christian preachers conflicted with Jewish authorities.[29] Such collections of testimonies did exist but at a much later date.[30]

Observing that citations of the Old Testament in Patristic literature sometimes agreed with each other while having no genetic connection, and not

---

preters, edited by R. Kraft and G. Nickelsburg (Philadelphia: Fortress Press, 1986), pp. 223-237.

[25]John 12:38 cites Isaiah 53:1 as in the LXX.

[26]For the most compelling argument in favor of the LXX forming the background for the citation, cf. E.C. Hoskyns, *The Fourth Gospel* (London: Faber and Faber, 1947), pp. 428-429. He explains the variations from the LXX in light of the author's theological concerns. Charles Goodwin, "How Did John Treat His Sources," *Journal of Biblical Literature* 73 (June 1954) 61-75 remains a major source in favor of the LXX. "Therefore, we have no reason to doubt that the LXX was the source he knew, and we need not consider seriously the possibility of his using some freak version that rendered the Hebrew in this way," (p. 71).

[27]R. Bultmann, *op. cit.*, pp. 452-453 and footnote 2 where Bultmann, correctly, observes that the difference in introductory formulae cannot demonstrate separate sources.

[28]For one of the most lucid arguments in favor of this position, cf. John Wick Bowman, *The Fourth Gospel and the Jews* (Pittsburg: Pickwick Press, 1975), especially pp. 86-89; 196-197; and 266-271. Cf. McNamara, *op. cit.*, "The Targums and the Johannine Literature," pp. 142-159.

[29]Harris' theory enjoyed a period of popularity as the secondary literature shows, but it fell into disfavor or neglect. With the discovery of the Dead Sea Scrolls, it was revived in different forms. Cf. Raymond Brown, The *Birth of the Messiah* (New York: Doubleday, 1977), p. 101, footnote 10. Cf. further his "Apocrypha; Dead Sea Scrolls; Other Jewish Literature," in *The Jerome Biblical Commentary*, edited by R. Brown, J. Fitzmyer and R. Murphy (Englewood Cliffs: Prentice-Hall, Inc.), pp. 550-551, numbers 79-80.

[30]It is in the third century A.D., with Cyprian, that a collection of texts for apologetic texts was collected. Cf. these in *The Ante-Nicene Fathers*, Volume V, edited by A. Roberts and J. Donaldson (Grand Rapids: Wm. B. Eerdmans Publishing Co.), 1965, pp. 507-557. Harris took the name *Testimonia* from this work.

agreeing with any extant Old Testament text, J.R. Harris posited a precanonical collection of Old Testament texts.[31] He said the texts were collected around titles relating to Jesus, such as the "stone sayings," etc. His main reasons were that (1) mixed forms of Old Testament texts existed in more than one writer, (2) different writers improperly identified the Old Testament book being cited, and (3) similar textual variants from all Old Testament texts in Old Testament citations in the New Testament.[32]

6. Another possibility is that John is indebted to a "school" of interpreters who used some form of the pesher method. In some circles of Matthean studies this has come to be an "assured result" of critical studies.[33] Since Matthew and John are increasingly viewed as heavily indebted to the Hebraic-Judaic tradition, it is not surprising that many judgments about Matthew find their way into Johannine studies as well.[34] Stendahl had argued that Matthew's gospel grew out of a "school" led by a converted rabbi.[35] From this "school" came the fulfillment quotations.[36]

---

[31]J.R. Harris, *Testimonies*, 2 vols. (Cambridge: University Press, 1916-1920). This theory found supporters, as a glance at the secondary literature following Harris' work indicates. But doubts were expressed against the notion because the concept of a pre-canonical work of such size was so conjectural. Cf. T.W. Manson, "The Argument From Prophecy," in *Journal of Theological Studies* 46 (1945) 132. Also, the idea of a collection of "proof texts" standing out of their context would be no use in anti-Judaic polemic. Further, C.H. Dodd, arguing against a written testimony book, affirmed that Old Testament citations were orally known in the early church and were pointers or reminders of a broad context from which the passage came. A good example of this is Matthew 1:23 quoting Isaiah 7:14. The context of Isaiah 6:1-9:7 recalls the theological notion of "God is with us" and trust in Him. Cf. his *According to the Scriptures* (London: Nisbet, 1952).

After Manson, Dodd, and others the idea of a testimony collection faded out. But it is striking to observe that among the Dead Sea Scrolls, testimony collections were found showing that written collections existed prior to Christianity. Many note that serious attention to these necessitates reconsideration of Harris' theory.

[32]Harris, *op. cit.*, Vol. I, p. 18. For the best critique of the whole history cf. A.C. Sundberg, Jr., "On Testimonies," *Novum Testamentum* III (1959) 268-281. Krister Stendahl, *The School of St. Matthew* (Philadelphia: Fortress Press, 1968), pp. 207-217 summarizes the work on testimonies. Aware that Harris' theory is in tandem with Matthew's use of the Old Testament, Stendahl judges against Matthew's use of scripture being dependent upon a testimony collection. Negative judgments on Harris' work have functionally rendered it ineffective in solving the problem of text or source of New Testament citations of the Old Testament.

[33]Especially cf. K. Stendahl, *School of St. Matthew . . .* , *op. cit.* Various writings of E. Earle Ellis and R. Gundry also assume this is a *fait accompli*.

[34]Cf. especially the work of Raymond Brown, *The Community of the Beloved Disciple* (New York: Paulist Press, 1979), and his "Other Sheep Not of This Fold": The Johannine Perspective on Christian Diversity in the Late First Century," *Journal of Biblical Literature* 97 (1978) 5-22.

[35]See Matthew 13:52, where Jewish methods of teachings and study were applied to the new faith.

[36]"In these quotations Mt. applies rules for interpretation similar to those used at Qumran and arrives at a substantiation of the claim that the church is right in hailing Jesus of Nazareth as the Christ, and his believers as the true heirs to the prophecies and their promises." Stendahl, *op. cit.*, p. 770.

Some such phenomenon may account for John's use of the Old Testament.[37] However, there is a major difference in what the gospels do in telling a story of Jesus and citing OT citations as fulfilled, and the pesher techniques of Qumran, where the method is a line by line comment on the Old Testament.[38]

7. Next, there is the suggestion that John stood in a mystical, speculative tradition of allegorical and spiritual use of the book of Isaiah.[39] F.W. Young notes that the Targum had trouble with Isaiah's vision resulting in the rendering "I saw the Lord's glory." This opened the door for speculation in Jewish interpretation.[40] John inherited this considerable pre-Christian speculative tradition relating to Isaiah. Young goes on to relate various parts of John with this speculative tradition.[41]

8. There is the possibility that John is not *quoting* any source but only *alluding* to the passage. It is expected that a writer would do this since he was rooted in Jewish methods which were saturated with Old Testament thought and imagery. This can be seen in the Dead Sea Scrolls and the use there of

---

[37] Stendahl's analogy to Qumran aided him in explaining the OT as used in Matthew. The pesher method at Qumran does shed some light on the New Testament's use of the Old, especially in certain instances. Stendahl is correct that such use of the OT did exist among rabbinical schools. But the analog to the Qumran group is the closest. "However, there is a significant difference between Matthew's technique of telling a story about Jesus and accompanying it with OT citations which find fulfillment therein, and the *pesher* technique of Qumran, where the method is a line by line analysis of the OT." R. Brown, *The Birth of . . .* , *op. cit.*, p. 102, footnote 13.

[38] So, correctly, Raymond Brown, *The Birth of . . .* , *op. cit.*, p. 102, footnote 13. Cf. also the critique of Stendahl in W.D. Davies, *The Setting of the Sermon on the Mount* (Cambridge: University Press, 1964) pp. 208ff. Cf. also, J.A. Fitzmyer, "The Use of Explicit Old Testament Quotations in Qumran Literature and in the New Testament," in *Essays on the Semitic Background of the New Testament* (Missoula: Scholar's Press, 1974).

[39] The definitive work on this remains F.W. Young, "A Study of the Relation of Isaiah to the Fourth Gospel," *Zeitschrift für die Neutestamentliche Wissenschaft und die Kunde, der Alteren Kirche*, Heft 3-4 (1955) 215-233.

[40] Young cites Wisdom of Sirach 48:22-25 as an example where additions and deletions are made to the Isaiah 6 text. He argues that the readers would be familiar with what Sirach was doing and would understand him, that speculation of this type was normative, and that this sort of use of the Old Testament continued for the next 200 years. *Ibid.*, pp. 215-221. He next searches the Dead Sea Scrolls for speculative traditions relating to Isaiah. Finally, he refers to the life of Isaiah as found in *Lives of the Prophets*. It contains a legend of Isaiah regarding a miracle story which is called a *sign*. This illustrates further the speculative tradition which Young describes and relates to interpreting the fourth gospel.

[41] *Ibid.*, pp. 221-230. Young's conclusions are that John's Isaiah quotations are more than allusions while not being direct quotations from Isaiah. He is part of a symbolical, even allegorical tradition in using Isaiah. Some use of *testimonia* may be involved but even these are not quoted but read in light of the speculative tradition's methods. John was already part of an "Isaiah tradition." Much of this speculation was already known for up to two centuries before John ever wrote. "There is good reason to believe that the author of the Fourth gospel was one of a group who related themselves to Isaiah in a unique way and drew upon this book for religious inspiration." *Ibid.*, p. 231.

Old Testament imagery and language mingled in with the texts. It certainly fits the general tenor of the Fourth Gospel, which has few direct quotations but is filled with Biblical imagery.

9. Finally, there is the alternative that John is himself responsible for the rendering. R. Gundry, in his work on Matthew, has argued that Christian preachers orally and freely translated the Hebrew text of their choice into Aramaic and Greek as part of their ministry. On occasion, these translations were original; sometimes they reflect in whole or in part existing Aramaic and Greek translations. John, on this view, was his own translator.[42]

The cumulative effect of these nine options is to remind us that John stood in a very complex milieu in which he inherited an interpreted Bible flowing from many different methods.

We do well to remind ourselves of the often cited words of T.W. Manson:

> We are long accustomed to distinguish carefully between the text, which — in more senses than one — is sacred, and the commentary upon it or the expositions of it. We tend to think of the text as objective fact and interpretation as subjective opinion. It may be doubted whether the early Jewish and Christian translators and expositors of Scripture made any such sharp distinction . . . accurate reproduction of the traditional wording of the Divine oracles took second place to publication of what was held to be their essential meaning and immediate application. Odd as it may seem to us, the freedom with which they handled the Biblical text is a direct result of the supreme importance which they attached to it.[43]

We know today that a number of textual traditions existed in John's day in both the Hebrew and Greek traditions. There was no one accepted Hebrew text. There was no single LXX text. There were Aramaic Targums along with many Greek translations of them. There were differing Hebrew wordings. Some of these were closer to the Masoretic text than to the Septuagint. It is unlikely, unless some new evidence surfaces, that we can find a single written source which will settle the use of Isaiah 6:9-10 at John 12:40. While the likelihood of a non-literary origin for the citation seems highly probable, especially John's interpretative rendering of the text, we cannot opt for any of these options as *the* solution.[44]

---

[42]R. Gundry, "The Use of the Old Testament in St. Matthew's Gospel," in *Supplements to N.T.*, Vol. XVIII (Leiden: E.J. Brill, 1975), pp. 172-174.

[43]T.W. Manson, "The Argument From . . .", *op. cit.*, p. 135.

[44]This seems plausible since equally competent Hebraists and Aramaists have judged the issue differently, since we don't know what forms of the MT or the LXX actually existed, since the New Testament itself makes diverse use of the passage, and since the present form of the text of the Fourth Gospel is not a first century form. One can hazard scholarly guesses but they must remain that.

Function

The Isaiah 6:9-10 passage is used in John 12:36b-43 to help explain the reason for the unbelief manifested towards Jesus in previous chapters. The quotation's location within the paragraph serves as an explanation to the reader as to *why* this happened. In so doing, John is addressing a major problem in ancient Christianity: "If Jesus was the son of God and the Christ, why didn't most of the Jewish leaders accept him?"[45] Why did he come to his own and his own did not receive him? (1:14). John 12:36b-43 is the author's explanation of the problem of unbelief.[46] Furthermore, "the purpose of the final summary of the public ministry of Jesus is . . . to point out that the rejection of the Messiah by His own people ought not to surprise those familiar with the Old Testament Scriptures."[47]

Prior to this, John collected a series of clashes or conflict stories between Jesus and various representative types. In each case, unbelief predominates. As the conflict stories progress, the unbelief increases, especially in chapters 5-12. B.F. Westcott long ago observed that the clue to the structure of these chapters is the conflict with unbelief.[48]

John 1:1-18 serves as a prologue which sets forth presuppositions for the story John is about to write.[49] It "lets the cat out of the bag." There the reader learns who Jesus is, how he was received, etc.

John 1:19-4:54 collects together a series of witnesses regarding who Jesus was/is in terms of claims made by Jesus and things others affirmed regarding him.

John 5-12 is the author's collection of the conflict stories. While the growing faith of the disciples and apostles is present, it is the unbelief of the multitudes and the leaders which is central. As this story progresses, the conflict heightens and Jesus' theological reflections become more intense. During all of this the crowds begin to thin out. This process is vivid as early as John 6 with the crisis in Galilee where it looks as though even the apostles might exit.[50] Then, at the end of this, in a few words, John gives his reasons why people did not believe in Jesus, 12:36b-43.[51]

---

[45]Paul gives his discussion of this in Romans 9-11; the author of Hebrews attempts to explain it, etc.

[46]Cf. D. Moody Smith, *Johannine Christianity: Essays on its Setting, Sources, and Theology* (Columbia: University of South Carolina Press, 1984), pp. 90-93.

[47]Hoskyns, *op. cit.*, p. 429.

[48]B.F. Westcott, *Gospel of St. John* (London: John Murray, 1908), p. 80.

[49]From the sea of writings cf. Joachim Jeremias, "The Revealing Word," in *The Central Message of the New Testament* (New York: Charles Scribner's Sons, 1965), pp. 71-90. Morna Hooker, *Studying the New Testament* (Minneapolis: Augsburg Publishing House, 1979), pp. 19-22. Both these treat how the prologue functions in relation to the gospel.

[50]Many of the issues over which conflict occurs can be found in the Synoptic gospels, (such as the Sabbath), but many are unique to this gospel.

[51]Cf. Barclay Newman, "Some Observations Regarding the Argument, Structure, and Literary Characteristics of the Gospel of John," in *The Bible Translator* 26:2 (April 1975).

Verse 36 is a word of command from Jesus giving the imperative for the hearers to believe while they have occasion. Verse 37 then begins with a connective, "but though," forming an antithesis to verse 36. What transpires is the opposite of what is commanded. "Though he had done so many signs before them, yet they did not believe . . . " "He had done" is in the perfect tense underscoring the author's belief that there had been abundant opportunities to understand and believe. Note that Jesus had done "so many signs." It was more than enough for a lover of light and truth. Furthermore, these things were done "before them," not in some hidden place obscured from view.

This is John's way of underscoring the deeds which God has done. Yet, "they did not believe in him." Now the verb tense shifts to the imperfect. Here the imperfect is used with a negative probably suggesting they were not about to believe because the intentionality was nonexistent. The idea is that they don't believe and are not in the mood or habit of believing, i.e., they had no intention of believing him.[52] Again, the focus is that they are responsible and accountable for their own unbelief. John has been carefully describing in chapters 1-12 a process at work in which evidence is presented and rejected. The end product was that "they had no intention" and "they showed no tendency to believe."

In 12:38, Isaiah 53:28 is cited from the LXX, "Lord who has believed our report, and to whom has the arm of the Lord been revealed?" The Isaiah passage indicates an awareness that when people hear truth, they will not believe since they have formed a personal disposition which renders it difficult, if not impossible, to believe.

---

[52]Edwin A. Abbott, *Johannine Grammar* (London: Adam and Charles Black, 1906), pp. 336-339. "With a negative . . . may imply 'I showed no tendency to do.'" "In John . . . the imperfect is frequently used in many shades of meaning not briefly expressible in English." (p. 336). "With a negative, the imperfect may mean 'was not beginning to do,' and this may often mean 'had no intention of doing.'" (p. 338). "In ii:23-4, 'many believed . . . in his name . . . but Jesus himself *did not trust* himself to them,' the meaning is 'did not *even begin to* trust to him,' because He knew their character from the first. It might almost be rendered 'would not trust.'" (p. 338). "The same phrase, applied to nonbelieving Jews in xii. 37 means 'they showed no tendency to believe,' 'did not even make a beginning to believe,' and it is followed by xii.39 'they were not able to believe.'" (p. 338). "Nearly the same meaning is in xxi. 12 'no one *showed a tendency to venture*, or '*so much as began to venture*.'" (p. 338). Cf. also his *Johannine Vocabulary* (London: Adam and Charles Black, 1905), pp. 56-57.

Cf. A.T. Robertson, *A Grammar of the Greek New Testament* (London: Hodder and Stoughton, 1923), p. 885 and the discussion there of "The 'Negative' Imperfect." As examples, he cites Mt. 18:30; Lk. 15:16; 15:38; John 2:24; 7:1; 21:12; Acts 19:30; Mt. 22:3.

Cf. also B.L. Gildersleeve, *Syntax of Classical Greek From Homer to Demosthenes*, Vol. I (New York: American Book Company, 1900), pp. 95ff. and discussion there of the "Negative Imperfect." "The negative imperfect commonly denotes resistance to pressure or disappointment. Simple negation is aoristic."

Cf. further, Maximilian Zerwick, *Biblical Greek* (Rome: Biblical Institute Press, 1963), p. 91, #270.

The "therefore" in verse 39 is a connective relating to what has preceded. What is the result of their refusal? "They could not believe." The judgment of God upon them came after they had rejected the light. The tenor of the paragraph is that God is not the cause of the rejection but rather has done more than enough for an honest heart to accept.

At 12:42, there is a reference to some of the rulers who "believed." The verb here is an aorist stressing fact and point of action. Viewed in the framework of the entire gospel, this is not true belief. John says they "were not in the process of confessing it." Verse 43 tells us why. "They loved the glory of men more than the glory of God."[53] This is a human reason for why they would not openly believe. They feared their peers more than they feared God, which is part of unbelief in this gospel. Man is free and responsible for his own unbelief.

But this is not the entire story. John is saying something else as well. In citing Isaiah 6:9-10 at 12:40 he affirms that the unbelief of the Jews fulfills the prophetic word and that God stands behind this unbelief in a causal sense. 12:39 affirms "the basic thought is not that the unbelief resulted in the fulfillment of the prophecy, but that the prophecy brought about the unbelief."[54]

Given this context, what is the function of Isaiah 6:9-10 at John 12:40? At face value, and without looking at the context, it simply says the rejection occurred to fulfill Isaiah's prophecy and that God is the cause of the rejection.

In a sense, this tension, which is inherent in the Biblical materials, is one of our choosing and creation. Too often in the history of interpretation, a purely psychological explanation is given in which the text is dismissed with a slight of hand: "they would not, therefore, they could not."

Observe that in Isaiah 6, *strong* imagery is used to describe God's action in hardening the heart. Isaiah's message would make the heart of the people *fat*, and their ears *dull*, and their eyes would be *plastered over*, so that they might see and hear but not come to understand.[55] Are such images to be understood as secondary or primary? Were they results brought upon themselves or were they primary causes instituted by God? Von Rad cites with *disapproval* W. Eichrodt,[56] "Deliberate neglect of God's truth and habitual deafness to God's warnings inevitably bring indifference to God's working in their train."

---

[53]C.H. Dodd, *The Interpretation of the Fourth Gospel* (Cambridge: University Press, 1965), p. 380, footnote 2, "The contrast of the true glory and the false echoes v. 44, with all the additional depth given to it by the treatment of the true glory in xii. 23-33. *The mark of the true glory is precisely renunciation of personal security.*" (emphasis mine).

[54]R.E. Brown, *The Gospel According to John I-XII* (New York: Doubleday & Co., Inc., 1966), p. 483.

[55]A healthy corrective to a psychologizing exegesis devoid of an Old Testament orientation is found in G. von Rad, *The Message of the Prophets* (New York: Harper & Row, Publishers, 1967), pp. 122-126, to which much of the present discussion is indebted.

[56]W. Eichrodt, *Theology of the Old Testament*, Vol. II (Philadelphia: Westminster Press, 1967), pp. 380ff.

If one doesn't opt for some such psychologizing exegesis, how does one deal with God hardening the hearts of his chosen people? "How is it that in Isaiah's message Yahweh suddenly withdraws into an obscurity such as Israel had never before experienced?"[57]

John's use of the citation has to be viewed in light of the Old Testament theological context which informs it. In the story of the Pharoah and the exodus, it is said that "Pharoah hardened his heart," "God hardened Pharoah's heart," and "Pharoah's heart was hardened." In Isaiah 6, he was to "make the heart of this people fat and their ears heavy and shut their eyes . . . " In Isaiah 29:9ff., "Stupefy yourselves and be in a stupor, blind yourselves and be blind!" Here responsibility rests with Israel. Then follows, "For the Lord has poured out upon you a spirit of deep sleep, and has closed your eyes, the prophets, and covered your heads, the seers." Here God is the cause.

A common motif in Deuteronomy is that Israel has chosen the way of forsaking the covenant with God because God has blinded them.[58] In the Old Testament the responsibility is sometimes placed on man and sometimes on God. The same thing is true with the use of Isaiah 6:9-10 in the New Testament.

The history of interpretation witnesses to the hesitancy of ascribing God a causal role. The LXX softened the MT. The rabbis were equally bothered by the notion.[59] "The early church fathers often wanted to keep man's freedom opting for God's foreknowledge as a solution.[60] Others have opted for some form of predestination to salvation or damnation. Every imaginable variation on these themes has been proposed. All share in common a concern to avoid making God the cause.

John doesn't have this problem. He is sourced in the thought of the Old Testament. He is thinking of God's hardening in terms of the history of God's salvation and mercy.[61] God hardens that he might redeem. God, in his freedom, remains faithful.[62]

---

[57]von Rad, *op. cit.*, p. 123.

[58]Compare and contrast Deuteronomy 29:24ff. "All the nations shall say, 'why has the Lord done thus to his land? . . . Then men would say, " 'It is because they forsook the covenant of the Lord . . . " and Deuteronomy 29:4: "The Lord has not given you a mind to understand or eyes to see or ears to hear.' " Israel is responsible for hardness of heart yet God has sent hardness to their hearts.

[59]Cf. the study of R. Schnackenburg, *The Gospel According to St. John*, Vol. 2 (New York: Seabury Press, 1980), pp. 265-270.

[60]For an excellent discussion, to which I am indebted, cf. Lester J. Kuyper, "The Hardness of Heart According to Biblical Perspective," *Scottish Journal of Theology* 27 (1974) 459-474. In addition, G. von Rad, *The Message of the Prophets* (New York: Harper & Row, Publishers, 1967), pp. 122-126.

[61]Cf. the excellent remarks of Brown, *John, op.cit.*, pp. 484-486.

[62]Two further considerations sharpen this: (1) the notion of God's hardening hearts is found in the most ancient sources within the Old Testament (Judges 9:23; I Samuel 16:14; 18:10; 19:9; II Samuel 17:14; I Kings 12:15, etc.) and (2) the attribution to a deity of a terrible situation was normative in the ancient near eastern world.

The Old and New Testaments both know that a divine mystery is at work with both God and man involved in the process. At times, a Biblical author will focus on one against the other. Von Rad is correct to criticize a psychologizing exegesis and to source interpretation in the context of Old Testament theology.[63] God hardens but it is not his last word. It was at the beginning of Isaiah's ministry that God hardened hearts yet Isaiah later affirmed, "I will wait for the Lord, who is hiding his face from the house of Jacob, and I will hope in him." God hardens to warn and to have mercy.

Conclusion

Isaiah 6:9-10 has had an interesting history of usage. The majority of Jewish textual traditions, from the LXX thought the rabbis, soften the harshness of the Hebrew text. The same has been done within Christian interpretation from the early fathers to the present day.

Within the New Testament, it is the classic text to explain the rejection of the gospel on the part of the Jews. Writer after writer makes use of the text in this manner.

We cannot, with our present knowledge, know if John had a textual source before him when he wrote. It is probable that he did not but was making his own, creative, use of the Isaiah passage to warn the readers of the devastating power of unbelief in their lives and to remind them of God's hardening of hearts and continuing redemptive work in judgment and mercy.

---

[63]Gerhard von Rad, *The Message of the Prophets* (New York: Harper & Row, Publishers, 1967), pp, 122-126.

Archeology and the Origins of the Fourth Gospel: Gabbatha

John F. Wilson

Introduction

B.F. Westcott claimed that based on internal evidence the author of the Fourth Gospel was a Palestinian Jew who was an eye-witness to the events described in the book.[1] This conclusion was rejected by those who saw in this gospel a "hellenized" theology in contrast to an earlier "hebraic" one. The presence of this "hellenized" theology became the basis for pushing the origins of the Gospel of John far into the second century. The discovery of the Dead Sea Scrolls forced a reevaluation of this rigid hebraic hellenistic dichotomy. The scrolls revealed the existence of a "hellenized" Judaism in first century Palestine. The discovery of early second century papyrus fragments of the Fourth Gospel in Egypt also suggested that the origins of the work should be sought no later than the end of the first century.

While an early date for the origins of the gospel is now generally accepted, the question of whether the author or authors are rooted in first century Palestine is still in dispute. C.K. Barrett, for example, admits that the Fourth Gospel "contains Palestinian, as well as other material" but maintains that "it was drawn up, edited, and published by persons who had no personal contact with John, and perhaps no contact with Palestine; certainly not an apostle."[2]

Raymond Brown, on the other hand, while agreeing that the gospel was written in several stages, still recognizes very early Palestinian roots. Historical, social, and geographical details peculiar to the gospel, especially those which have been illuminated by archeological work, suggest, he says, that the original sources of John date to the period 40-60 A.D. and that, following a forty-year development, the work took its final form about 100 A.D. The gospel, he continues, "reflects a knowledge of Palestine as it was before its destruction in 70 A.D." and "we do not think it unscientific to maintain that John son of Zebedee was probably the source of the historical tradition behind the Fourth Gospel."[3]

---

[1]B.F. Westcott, *The Gospel According to John* (Grand Rapids: Eerdman's, 1908) (reprint, 1954), pp. xx, xxxiv.

[2]C.K. Barrett, *The Gospel According to St. John*, 2nd ed. (Philadelphia. The Westminster Press, 1978) p. 175.

[3]Raymond Brown, *The Gospel According to John*, Vol. I (Garden City, N.Y.: Doubleday and Company, 1966), pp. xliic, c.

Since the Gospel of John refers quite specifically to locations in Jerusalem, mentioning geographical and architectural details, often assigning Aramaic names to them ("Bethesda," 5:2; "Gabbatha," 19:13; "Golgotha," 19:17; etc.) the possibility arises that archeological discoveries which throw light on first century Jerusalem may also provide insights into the question of the origins of the gospel. This essay focuses on one of these locations, the Lithostrotos or Gabbatha (John 19:13), in order to suggest the direction this kind of research into gospel origins might take.

John's account of the trial of Jesus refers to an architectural feature of the Praetorium (Roman Headquarters) in Jerusalem called the Lithostrotos or Gabbatha. This feature is not mentioned in the other gospels; indeed, the term "Gabbatha" is not found elsewhere in contemporary literature. The relevant phrases in the gospel are as follows:

> Then they led Jesus from the house of Caiphas to the praetorium . . . they themselves did not enter the praetorium, so that they might not be defiled . . . So Pilate went out to them . . . Pilate entered the Praetorium again and called Jesus . . . He went out to the Jews again (18:28ff).
>
> He brought Jesus out and *sat down on the judgement seat at a place called The Pavement (Lithostrotos), and in Hebrew, Gabbatha* (19:13).

Our argument will proceed as follows:

I. Archeological and literary evidence converge to identify John's "praetorium" with the palace of Herod the Great.

II. The podium or platform upon which Herod's palace was constructed, or some part of that platform, is John's "Gabbatha."

III. John's use of this term provides evidence of a pre-70 A.D. Judean based source underlying the gospel.

I. The Palace as the Praetorium

For the past several hundred years, Christian pilgrims have located Pilate's headquarters at the site of the Fortress of Antonio, that massive structure erected by Herod at the northwest corner of the Temple Mount. Until this day, this place, now covered by the convent of the Sisters of Zion, becomes the starting point for pilgrims tracing the *Via Dolorossa* (Way of Sorrows) supposedly leading from Jesus' place of condemnation to where he died. The discovery of an extensive pavement made of large well-cut stones led L.H. Vincent to argue that the Lithostrotos or Gabbatha of John's Gospel had been found.[4] Pierre Benoit decisively refuted this theory,[5] however. Archeological

---

[4] L.H. Vincent, "Le Lithostrotos Evangelique," *Revue Biblique* 59 (1952) 513-530.

[5] P. Benoit, "The Archeological Reconstruction of the Antonio Fortress," in *Jerusalem Revealed* [(ed.) Y. Yadin] (Jerusalem: The Israel Exploration Society), pp.

work has proven that the so-called Ecce Homo Arch still standing at this place dates to the reign of the emperor Hadrian and was constructed during the refounding and rebuilding of the city following the Bar Kochba Revolt (135-138 A.D.). Since the pavement may not be dated earlier than this arch, it cannot be the Gabbatha of John. Furthermore, this pavement covers the "Struthion Pool" mentioned by Josephus as having been open to the air in 70 A.D. when it was the site of fighting during the First Revolt (Josephus *War* 5:467), proving that it post-dates the revolt.

Actually, the custom of following the *Via Dolorossa* beginning at the Fortress of Antonio dates only from Medieval times. The Byzantines located Pilate's house at the church of St. Sophia, just west of the Temple Mount, or near the Nea Church, rediscovered by Avigad at the present south wall of the city in the Jewish Quarter. As we shall see, the identification of these locations with the praetorium of Pilate is also incorrect.

Literary evidence supports the conclusion that Pilate's praetorium was the palace built by Herod the Great at the crest of the "Western Hill" across the Tyropoeon Valley, stretching along the present western wall from the Jaffa Gate to the present southern wall of the city. Philo of Alexandria, in his *Delegation to Gaius* (38), plainly speaks of Pilate's residence in "Herod's palace in the Holy City" while visiting Jerusalem during a Jewish feast. He describes the palace as "the residence of the prefects." Josephus says that the governor Florus also "lodged at the Palace" and that there was a *bema* (tribunal or judgement platform) in front of it. Here, the "chief priests, the nobles, and the most eminent citizens then presented themselves before tribunal" (Josephus *War* 2:301). The parallels between Josephus' account and John 19 are striking: "Florus ventured that day to do what none had ever done before, namely, to scourge before his tribunal and nail to the cross men of equestrian rank" (*War* 2:308). (It is, of course, the rank of the victims which makes the incident unusual, not the fact that they were scourged at the *bema* and condemned to crucifixion.)

This incident, though involving a different governor, gives us valuable background for a similar confrontation between Pilate and the Jews. Josephus refers to a *bema* set up by Pilate where, during one of his visits to Jerusalem (the Roman governors normally resided in Caesarea Maritima) he is "surrounded" and "besieged" by an angry mob (*War* 2:175-176). These passages, taken together, indicate that:

1. Pilate resided in the Palace of Herod.
2. This place had, as a part of its complex of facilities, an open area where a *bema* could be located in such a way that a large crowd could surround it.
3. Before this *bema*, he could, as Roman governor, interrogate prisoners, scourge them, and condemn them to crucifixion.

87-89; and "L'Antonia D'Herode le Grand et le Forum Oriental D'Aelia Capitolina," *Harvard Theological Review* 64 (1971) 135-167.

The testimony of the Synoptic Gospels is consistent with these conclusions. During Jesus' trials, Luke says that Pilate "called together the chief priests and the rulers and the people" (Luke 23:13; cf. Josephus *War* 2:301). We may reasonably assume that this gathering took place at the location called by John the Lithostrotos or Gabbatha. Matthew speaks of Pilate's wife who, he says, sent word of her fears concerning the events which were taking place "while he was sitting on the judgement seat" (Greek, *bema*; Matthew 27:19). Mark says that during the trial the soldiers led Jesus away "inside the palace (that is, the praetorium); and they called together the whole battalion" to mock him (Mark 15:16).

This event must have taken place in the northern part of the palace complex, since the military would most likely have been housed close to the three huge defense towers constructed there by Herod (see below). Josephus tells us that during the siege of Jerusalem in 70 A.D. this area was the headquarters of a Roman garrison (*War* 2:438-440). It is reasonable to assume that this had been a military barracks during peacetime as well. Of course, another, likely much larger, Roman garrison was lodged in the Fortress of Antonio. The soldiers at the palace probably functioned as a bodyguard, first for the Jewish kings and eventually for the Roman governors. After the destruction of the palace, as we shall see, the area again became a military barracks.

Josephus has given us a detailed description of the palace of Herod. First, he describes the three lofty towers on the north of the complex: Hippicus, Phasael, and Mariamme. These, he says, stood on a crest above the western hill and were furnished with fine apartments, baths, and reservoirs for water. One of these towers has survived in its lower courses and may be seen today, incorporated into the Turkish Citadel inside the Jaffa Gate. Josephus' description of the residential and ceremonial palace rises to eloquence. Enclosed by its own high wall, it "contained immense banqueting halls and bed-chambers for a hundred guests." Furnishings in the apartments were mostly made of silver and gold, and the walls and ceilings were splendidly decorated. Circular cloisters all around featured open courts and "there were groves of various trees intersected by long walks, which were bordered by deep canals, and ponds everywhere studded with bronze figures, through which the water was discharged, and around the streams were numerous cots for tame pigeons" (*War* 4:156-181).

Herod's palace complex was located in the area presently occupied by the Turkish Citadel (now an archeological park and museum) a police station, and the Armenian Garden and School. Major excavations have been undertaken at the Citadel and in the Armenian Garden, despite the tumultuous political and military upheavals which have occurred there during the last fifty years. The excavators and dates of excavation are:

C.N. Johns (1943-1948)
A.D. Tushingham (1961-1967)
R. Amiran and A. Eitan (1968-1969)
D. Bahat and M. Broshi (1971)
H. Geva (1979-1980)

When Josephus' descriptions of the area are combined with discoveries made during these excavations, a fairly detailed picture of the complex begins to emerge. On the north stood the towers and the military barracks, on the south, auxiliary and utility buildings, and in between, the residential and ceremonial area, itself actually a complex of buildings and gardens.

II. The Podium as "Gabbatha"

Three of the excavations listed above have provided evidence that Herod's "palace" was actually a complex of buildings constructed on top of a huge platform or podium. Tushingham's work in the Armenian Garden showed that this podium was formed by the construction of massive retaining walls. These walls were stabilized by the addition of a network of numerous internal consolidating "walls" designed to contain the immense weight of the earth and stone fill used to build up the platform.[6] Apparently this device was only partially effective. Evidence was found of a severe collapse of at least portions of the retaining walls of the podium on the east and west. The excavator concluded that this damage occurred around the time of the reign of Herod Agrippa I (41-44 A.D.) and quickly repaired.[7] The events of John 18-19 occurred, of course, a decade or so before this accident.

Bahat and Broshi also excavated part of the Armenian Garden in 1970-1971. They, too, found the podium and noted that Herod's builders had used the same technique here as for the Temple (more on this later). They were able to estimate the overall dimensions of the podium: 300 to 350 meters from the north to south and some 60 meters from east to west. The same network of stabilizing "walls" was found, but nothing remained of the buildings of the palace complex which had once stood on the podium. This unfortunate fact, they concluded, is probably the result of events some one thousand years later, when the Crusaders cleared the area in order to construct their own palace.[8]

Fortunately, some remnants of the Herodian buildings were found inside the Turkish Citadel, however, where Amiran and Eitan continued the work began many years earlier by C.N. Johns. At the Herodian level (Level IV) the excavators were confronted "with a radical change in planning as reflected by a considerable artificial rise in the level of the area, a new orientation of the buildings, and certain changes in the city wall." The most striking feature was "a massive platform or podium, three to four meters above the floor level of stratum VI" (the Hellenistic Period). Here they found the

---

[6]A.D. Tushingham, *Excavations in Jerusalem, 1961-1967*, Vol. I (Toronto: Royal Ontario Museum, 1985), p. 32.
[7]Ibid., p. 53.
[8]D. Bahat and M. Broshi, "Excavation in the Armenian Garden," in *Jerusalem Revealed* [(ed.) Y. Yadin] (Jerusalem: The Israel Exploration Society, 1975), pp. 55-56.

same grid of interior "walls" with rubble fill between them as had been discovered by the earlier excavators.[9]

A street of beaten earth and remains of two buildings had survived on top of the podium, along with many fragments of colored plaster, many "terra sigillata" bowls, Herodian lamps and coins — all dating before 70 A.D. Signs of fire indicated that this was the destruction level of the First Revolt, described in detail by Josephus. Above this were floors covering the Herodian ruins, on which were built buildings which "may represent the living quarters of the Tenth Legion which, according to Josephus, was quartered here"[10] (*War* 7:2). The excavators concluded that this was the area between the residential-ceremonial palace(s) and the towers and that it represented the "barracks, servants' quarters and storerooms, or workshops."[11]

The huge podium literally created a new geographical entity and allowed Herod's builders to design a complex on a level surface throughout. John Wilkinson has suggested that this podium so dominated the area that it became the determining factor in the layout of the surrounding streets.[12] At any rate, we must think of a complex of buildings beginning near the present Jaffa Gates with the three towers, extending through a military and service quarter, the residential palace(s) and gardens, and ending with additional auxiliary and service buildings on the south. All of this, except, apparently, the towers, stood on what must have been a most impressive platform with thick walls at least three meters high, crowning the high ridge of the city at its western edge.

This construction technique, as we know, was a favorite one for Herod's architects. The enormous platform by which they extended the Temple Mount is well-known. On the southern end of the Mount, a great series of arches carried the platform out over what had once been a steep slope. Herodian architects also constructed a platform in Hebron, upon which were placed the memorial tombs of the Patriarchs.[13] Jacobson notes the strong architectural links between this structure and the Temple esplanade in Jerusalem. Furthermore, "the two Herodian monuments are related in turn to the *temenos* of Damascus by a common architectural tradition which flourished in Palestine and Syria at the very beginning of the Christian era."[14] The latter structure, built in 15/16 A.D. as a shrine to Jupiter Damascenus, now forms the base for the Great Mosque of Damascus.

Another example of this kind of construction was discovered at Sebaste (ancient Samaria) where Herod's builders created a huge platform 83 meters

---

[9] R. Amiran and A. Eitan, "Excavations in the Courtyard of the Citadel, Jerusalem, 1968-1969," *Israel Exploration Journal* 20 (1970) 13.

[10] R. Amiran and A. Eitan, "Excavations in the Courtyard of the Citadel, Jerusalem, 1968-1969," *Israel Exploration Journal* 20 (1970) 15.

[11] Ibid., p. 17.

[12] John Wilkinson, *The Jerusalem Jesus Knew* (Nashville: Nelson, 1983), p. 56.

[13] D.M. Jacobson, "Plan of Haram el-Khalil, Hebron," *Palestine Exploration Quarterly* 113 (1981) 78.

[14] Ibid., p. 80.

by 72 meters by constructing retaining walls and pouring rubble in on top of earlier structures. On this platform they built a temple to Augustus. Crowfoot, the excavator of the site, notes that "in order to obtain sufficient room for the forecourt, Herod was obliged to build out a great platform to the north. This was supported by massive retaining walls. . . . "[15] Thus, "the general plan of Herod's great temple is plain, and it can be realized what an imposing building it must have appeared, on the summit of the hill, with its great artificial platform and the temple towering above that.[16]

Each of the structures mentioned here was more specifically a *temenos*, that is, a sacred enclosure. While several buildings might stand on them, the central building was a temple. Herod chose to construct his palace complex in this same way, placing his residence at the center of a huge artificial platform which served to level and extend the top of a hill and to dramatize the structures built upon it. We suggest that this particular podium, or some part of it, is what the Gospel of John calls the Lithostrotos or Gabbatha.

Lithostrotos is a straightforward, "generic" term referring to stone pavements in general and, sometimes, to mosaic pavements.[17] That this particular paved area is designated *the* Lithostrotos indicates that it was a public landmark — a gathering place familiar and accessible to the city's inhabitants. But John also knows an Aramaic name for the place: *Gabbatha*. It is not uncommon for bilingual communities to have two names for public locations and first-century Jerusalem must be thought of as essentially bilingual (Aramaic and Greek). The same phenomenon may be observed in modern Israel, where many famous locations carry both Hebrew and Arabic names. More often than not, the names carry meanings in their respective languages which are unrelated. In this case, the Greek designation, *Lithostrotos*, obviously refers to the pavement where public meetings took place and where the *bema* or public tribunal stood. But what is the significance of the other term: *Gabbatha*? The precise form of this word transliterated into Greek characters in John 19:13 does not have an ancient parallel, but the general meaning is clear. The root is *gab*. It may be found in such combinations as *gubta* (a hill), *gabbahta* (a high forehead), *gabbetha* (height), etc. *Gab* signifies "ridge," "hump," or "protrusion," and "connotes in a general way the idea of prominence or height."[18] At John 19:13, the Syriac Version renders Gabbatha *peribolos* ("mound" or "fence"). This accords well with the idea that the Gabbatha was a massive retaining wall which raised the podium above its surroundings.

Josephus makes reference to a place called *Gabath Saoul* (Josephus *War* 5:51; cf. II Samuel 21:6) and explains to his Greek-speaking readers that this

---

[15]J.W. Crowfoot, I. Kenyon, and E.L. Sukenik, *The Buildings at Samaria* (London: Palestine Exploration Fund, 1942), p. 123.

[16]Ibid., p. 126.

[17]P. Benoit, "Pretoire, Lithostroton et Gabbatha," *Revue Biblique* 59 (1952) 545-550.

[18]P. Benoit, "Pretoire, Lithostroton et Gabbatha," *Revue Biblique* 59 (1952) 548.

should be understood *lophos Saoulou*, the *"hill"* of Saul. This explanation throws further light on the connotation carried by the root *gab*.

Let us now return to Josephus' account of the confrontation between the Roman governor Florus and the leaders of the Jews which took place at the *bema* near the palace (*War* 2:301). Thackeray translates the passages as follows:

> Florus lodged at the palace, and on the following day had a tribunal placed in front of the building and took his seat; the chief priests, the nobles, and the most eminent citizens then presented themselves before the tribunal.

A careful analysis of the Greek text reveals significant details not apparent in this translation. For one thing, the Greek text actually refers to the fact that Florus' residence is *en tois basileios*, that is, in the *palaces* (plural), a reference, we think, to the central residential-ceremonial complex which was, as we have seen, made up of several structures.

But it is the next sentence which provides the most direct confirmation of our thesis: *te d'usteraia bema pro auton temenos kathezetai*. This may be translated: "On the next day he seated himself at the *bema* in front of their [that is, the palaces] *temenos*."

The word *temenos* normally refers to the enclosure surrounding a temple. Josephus refers to Herod's temple to Augustus in Sebaste as being "enclosed in a *temenos*, a furlong and a half in length, consecrated to Caesar . . . " (*War* 1:403). In the Septuagint the word is used to refer to the "hill-shrines," "consecrated grounds" or "high places" of Canaanite worship (Ezek. 6:4,6; Hosea 8:14; II Kings 4:6 — Vaticanus only). It is initially curious that Josephus should select this word to describe the setting of Herod's palace, now the Roman praetorium, though the word can mean "a piece of land marked off and assigned as an official domain, especially to kings and chiefs."[19] But his selection of this word is consistent with the fact that the "palace" was actually a complex of buildings, and that these were *elevated*, standing on and within a large podium or platform which functioned as a *temenos*. Josephus' language here squares well with the archeological evidence and we suggest that his *temenos* is nothing other than the Gabbatha of John's Gospel — a huge platform which not only formed the foundation for the buildings of the palace complex but also featured a large open paved area (a *lithostrotos*) accessible to the public, where the ruler could hold public court.

Josephus says that Florus' meeting with the Jewish leaders ended when he ordered his soldiers to sack the Upper Market (*War* 2:305). Avi-Yonah suggests that "when Herod built his palaces on the western edge of the Upper City, he probably appropriated the western half of the agora, which henceforth adjoined the east wall of the palace."[20] Thus, we can picture a large

---

[19]H.G. Liddell and R. Scott, *Greek-English Lexicon*, 9th ed. (Oxford: Clarendon Press, 1940), p. 1774.

[20]Michael Avi-Yonah, "Jerusalem in the Hellenistic and Roman Periods," in *The Herodian Period*, p. 236 [(ed.) Avi-Yonah], Vol. VII of *The World History of the Jewish People* (New Brunswick: Rutgers University Press, 1975).

gathering just inside the palace walls, probably in the eastern part of the middle residential-ceremonial complex, and the soldiers surging out of the gates along the wall (Josephus *War* 2:429) down the stairway which must have carried visitors up to the platform, where they fell on the unfortunate crowds in the marketplace. We may also even speculate that the route of these soldiers as they left the palace had been some four decades before the first leg of the real *Via Dolorossa*.

The archeological evidence also accords well with Josephus' assertion that this part of the palace complex was destroyed during the siege and fall of the city in 70 A.D., and that the area was left in ruins. As already noted, Tushingham found that part of the podium had collapsed and been rebuilt some time during the 40s or 50s A.D. The destruction associated with the Revolt was much more severe, however. Tiles bearing the symbols of the occupying Roman Tenth Legion were found in the debris above the podium. Their presence does not indicate that the army rebuilt there, however. "While indicating that the legionary barracks was probably nearby," these tiles "can suggest only that robbing in the Garden took place during the period of the Tenth Legion's presence in Jerusalem," says Tushingham.[21] Overall, the evidence shows that the area was used as a garbage dump for 500 to 600 years after its destruction in 70 A.D. C.N. Johns did date a building in the immediate vicinity of the towers at the north of the complex to the period after the war and suggested that it was "presumably part of a barrack building" (a drain pipe in the floor bore the Tenth Legion stamp). But even this building was constructed on rubble from the earlier structures on the site.[22]

Amiran and Eitan found a building in the same area *under* John's building which they believe is also a Tenth Legion barracks.[23] They base this conclusion on Josephus' statement that the Tenth Legion used a portion of the western wall of the city "as an encampment for the garrison that was to remain" (*War* 7:2). But the remainder of the site, as Tushingham has shown, was left a pile of debris, a source for stones robbed for use elsewhere, and a dump. Whatever was left of the Gabbatha thus not only ceased to exist as an identifiable architectural feature, but probably was buried under tons of rubble. Geva's findings corroborate this conclusion. The Byzantine wall he discovered "was founded on the earth fill of the Second Temple Period."[24]

III. Dating John's Source

The residential-ceremonial portion of the Herodian palace disappeared in 70 A.D. and along with it the Gabbatha. The towers and some of the western

---

[21]A.D. Tushingham, *Excavations in Jerusalem 1961-1967*, Vol. I (Toronto: Royal Ontario Museum, 1985), p. 61.

[22]C.N. Johns, "The Citadel, Jerusalem," *Quarterly of the Department of Antiquities of Palestine* 14 (1950) 152.

[23]R. Amiran and A. Eitan, "Excavations in the Courtyard of the Citadel, Jerusalem, 1968-1969," *Israel Exploration Journal* 20 (1970) 15.

[24]H. Geva, "Excavations in the Citadel of Jerusalem, 1979-1980," *Israel Exploration Journal* 33 (1983) 67.

wall remained and were transformed into quarters for the occupying Roman garrison. Archeological work has confirmed this general picture. Following the Second Revolt (132-135 A.D.) Hadrian refounded the city and renamed it Aelia Capitolina. A new grid of streets was created based on the classic Roman city plan. Aelia lay essentially north of the site of the palace in what are now the Christian and Moslem quarters of the city and centered in the area later dominated by the Church of the Holy Sepulcher. An eastern gate stood where the Fortress of Antonio had been (the "pavement" under the Convent of the Sisters of Zion was part of this entrance). Extensive remains of a northern gate under the present Damascus gate have also been found.

Avigad's excavations in the Jewish Quarter east of Herod's palace yielded no building remains from the Roman city and only scattered tiles of the Tenth Legion. He concludes: "Our stratigraphic excavations throughout the Jewish Quarter revealed that remains from the Byzantine period always lay directly over the layer of the destruction of Jerusalem (A.D. 70) with no Roman stratum intervening."[25]

The Fourth Gospel's knowledge of the *Gabbatha* thus should be attributed to pre-70 A.D. sources. After that date, the southern part of the city became virtually a desolation, only here and there inhabited, mostly by foreign troops in scattered buildings. When Christian pilgrims began coming to the Holy Land in the fourth century, the site of the Praetorium of Pilate had been forgotten. The earliest pilgrims of this period located it below the Jewish Quarter in the Tyropoeon Valley just east of the temple area.[26] Later the pilgrimage site was moved to the Church of Holy Sion on "Mount Zion" just south of where Herod's palace had actually stood. It is interesting that during this period, quite accidentally, the pilgrims were closer to the correct location than they had been for many centuries previously.

Eventually, as we have seen, the pilgrims' site moved once again — this time to its present location at the site of the Fortress of Antonio north of the temple mount.

Not only is the Fourth Gospel's knowledge of the existence of the platform significant, but also its use of an *Aramaic* name for it. Such an obscure reference, in a language not familiar to John's readers, and so non-essential to the story that it is ignored by the other gospels, suggests the use of a contemporary source with detailed familiarity of the city prior to the First Revolt.

One such reference does not settle all questions concerning the dating of the sources of the Gospel of John. But the investigation in linguistic, literary, and archeological data such as we have conducted, triggered by John's reference to the Gabbatha, an identifiable and datable architectural feature, suggests a fruitful method of bringing archeological discoveries to bear on questions raised by New Testament criticism.

---

[25]Nahman Avigad, *Discovering Jerusalem* (Nashville: Thomas Nelson, 1983), p. 207.

[26]John Wilkinson, *Jerusalem Pilgrims Before the Crusades* (Jerusalem: Ariel Publishing House, 1977), p. 168.

The Old Testament and the Book of Revelation[1]

John T. Willis

It cannot be demonstrated *with certainty* that any passage in the book of Revelation is *quoted directly* from the Old Testament. However, the language and ideas of the book of Revelation are clearly derived from the Old Testament. Of the 404 verses of the book of Revelation, 278 are based directly on Old Testament language and thought.[2] Obviously, it would be impossible to deal with only a fraction of these texts in any meaningful way in a brief essay such as the present one. Accordingly, my intention here is to make a few observations concerning the Hebraisms in the book of Revelation, examine a handful of passages in the book which are based on the Old Testament, and draw some tentative conclusions.

The Language of the Book of Revelation

To anyone who knows the Greek language, it is immediately clear that the author of the book of Revelation had not mastered idiomatic Greek of his day. Rather, his native language was Hebrew. This has led some scholars to argue that the book of Revelation was originally written in Hebrew, and later translated into Greek.[3] Others have contended that its original language was Aramaic, which was later translated into Greek.[4] However, neither of these

---

[1] It is with grateful appreciation that I submit this paper in honor of one of my beloved professors, Dr. Frank Pack, who was the first to introduce me to serious, responsible study of the book of Revelation over three decades ago.

[2] See Henry Barclay Swete, *The Apocalypse of St. John: The Greek Text with Introduction, Notes and Indices* (third edition; London: MacMillan and Co., 1911), p. cxl; Angelo Lancellotti, "L'Antico Testamento nell'Apocalisse," *Rivista Biblica* 14 (1966) 369; Jean-Louis D'Aragon, "The Apocalypse," *The Jerome Biblical Commentary* II (edited by Joseph A. Fitzmyer and Raymond E. Brown; Englewood Cliffs, N.J.: Prentice-Hall, Inc., 1968), p. 468a. See the list in R.H. Charles, *A Critical and Exegetical Commentary on the Revelation of St. John* I (The International Critical Commentary; New York: Charles Scribner's Sons, 1920), pp. lxviii-lxxxii.

[3] So M. Mieses, "Hebräische Fragmente aus dem jüdischen Urtext der Apokalypse des hl. Johannes," *Monatschrift für Geschichte and Wissenschaft des Judentums* 74 (1930), pp. 345-362.

[4] So C.C. Torrey, *The Apocalypse of John* (New Haven, Conn.: Yale University Press, 1958), pp. 47-48.

views has gained widespread acceptance among scholars, because neither accounts for all the data presented in the book itself. Charles is undoubtedly correct when he states: "while he [the author of the book of Revelation] writes in Greek, he thinks in Hebrew."[5] Thus, meanings of words, tenses, cases, and syntactical constructions which do not make sense in the Greek of the book of Revelation, make excellent sense when the Hebrew behind them is understood.

This is a very technical issue, which requires a knowledge of Hebrew and Greek to appreciate fully. Here we may cite three simple examples. (a) In Revelation 3:8, the Greek text says: "Behold, I have given (*dedōka*) before you an open door." This does not make sense or fit the context. But when one realizes that the writer is thinking of the Hebrew qal of *n-t-n*, "give" in the sense of "set," he translates logically, "Behold, I set before you an open door."[6] (b) The Greek text of Revelation 12:7 runs: "And there was war in heaven, Michael and his angels to fight (*tou polemēsai*) with the dragon." Again, this does not make sense. But when one recognizes that the aorist imperative is an attempt to render a Hebrew niphal infinitive into Greek, he immediately detects a normal Hebrew idiom and reads: "And there was war in heaven: Michael and his angels *had to fight* with the dragon."[7] (c) The Greek present *pheugei*, literally, "and death *flies* from them," in Revelation 9:6 does not agree with the context. But since it undoubtedly represents a Hebrew imperfect, it should be translated future, "and death *will fly* from them."[8] The examples could be multiplied.[9]

Specific Passages in the Book of Revelation Based on the Old Testament

The far-reaching dependence of the author of the book of Revelation on the Old Testament becomes clear when one begins to compare passages in the book of Revelation with the Old Testament. The following examples are of necessity selective, but tend to point out the breadth of the author's knowledge of the Old Testament, the ways he uses the Old Testament, and the total dependence of the author on the Old Testament in writing his book.

Revelation 1:6 and 5:10 are based on Exodus 19:6 and Isaiah 61:6. These Old Testament texts declare that Israel was to function as priests between Yahweh and the nations, bringing Yahweh to the nations and the nations to Yahweh. The author of Revelation proclaims the same role for Christians, which agrees with I Peter 2:9-10.

---

[5] Charles, *A Critical and Exegetical Commentary on the Revelation of St. John* I, p. cxliii; see also Lancellotti, "L'Antico Testamento nell'Apocalisse," pp. 373, 383.
[6] See Charles, ibid., pp. cxlviii, 41, 87; Lancellotti, ibid., p. 374.
[7] See Charles, ibid., pp. 321-323.
[8] See Charles, ibid., pp. cxlix, 243-244.
[9] See Charles, ibid., pp. xcliv-clii, Lancellotti, "L'Antico Testamento nell' Apocalisse," pp. 372-383.

To be a Christian is to be both king and priest, but with a sovereignty and priesthood derived from Christ, as his were derived from God. John does not think of Christ as having withdrawn from the scene of his earthly victory, to return only at the Parousia. In and through his faithful followers he continues to exercise both his royal and his priestly functions.[10]

Revelation 20:6 uses this same terminology, but has reference to the relationship of the faithful to Christ at his second coming rather than to the present situation.

Revelation 1:7 combines Daniel 7:13 and Zechariah 12:10. We find this same combination in Matthew 24:30, but in reverse order. Both passages refer to the second coming of Christ, and the mourning of the nations over him as the one whom they have crucified. In the context of Daniel 7, the "one like a son of man" is "the saints of the Most High," as verses 18 and 27 show. The subject of verses 13-14 is a "figure," not a real person, as the comparative "like" indicates.[11] The New Testament quite understandably applies such passages to Jesus Christ, since the term "Son of Man" is used of him frequently in the first century setting.

Revelation 2:14 is based on Numbers 25:1-9 and 31:16. After Balaam had "blessed" the children of Israel on four occasions from the mountains above them, allegedly he returned home (Num. 22-24; notice especially 24:25). However, a comparison of Numbers 25:1-9 with 31:16 (and its context) indicates that he counseled the women of Moab and Midian to entice the men of Israel to come in to them to sacrifice to their gods at Baal-peor, to partake of sacrificial meals, and to commit fornication as an act of worship to Baal. The author of Revelation saw the same kinds of sins being practiced in the church at Pergamum (and probably Ephesus, since the Nicolaitans seem to be identical with those who follow the "teaching of Balaam," cf. Rev. 2:6,15).

Revelation 2:27 is based on Psalm 2:9. Three points need to be stressed here. First, Psalm 2:9 refers to the *king* who has just taken the throne on Zion and is threatened by a rebellion on the part of certain nations that had been subject to Judah under the former king (note verses 6-8, 1-3) whereas Revelation 2:27 refers to Christians at Thyatira who were under severe persecution and whom the author is urging to be faithful to God and Christ. In light of this, it is noteworthy that Psalm 2:9 also forms the basis of Revelation 12:5 and 19:15, both of which refer to Christ as conqueror of Satan (the great dragon) and ruler of the nations. Second, there is an interesting variant between the Hebrew of Psalm 2:9 and the LXX rendering of that verse, which is followed by all three passages in Revelation. The Hebrew text uses the root $r\text{-}^c\text{-}^c$, "to break in pieces, destroy," while the LXX root *poimainō*, "to rule," translates the Hebrew $r\text{-}^c\text{-}h$, "to shepherd, rule." The context and

---

[10] George B. Caird, *A Commentary on the Revelation of St. John the Divine.* Harper's New Testament Commentaries (New York: Harper & Row, Publishers, 1966), p. 77.

[11] See Louis F. Hartman and Alexander A. Di Lella, *The Book of Daniel.* The Anchor Bible 23 (Garden City, New York: Doubleday & Company, Inc., 1978), pp. 218-219.

parallel verbs in the three passages in Revelation make it quite clear that the idea of "destroy" is required.[12] Third, these three passages in Revelation contain the thought that Christ and his faithful followers will ultimately render vengeance on their adversaries, and exalts them for so doing. One is reminded of the imprecatory psalms, in which the authors ask God to render vengeance on their adversaries (see e.g., Pss. 58:6-11; 79:6,10,12; 139:19-22); frequently such are condemned as "sub-Christian." How, then, is one to evaluate passages like Revelation 2:27; 12:5; 19:5? (See further below.)

Revelation 3:5; 13:8; 17:8; 20:12,15; 21:27 are based on Exodus 32:32-33; Psalm 69:28; Daniel 12:1. The idea of God writing a book containing the names of the citizens of his kingdom is well-established in the Old Testament (in addition to the above-mentioned passages, see Psalm 56:8; Malachi 3:16; and possibly Nehemiah 13:14). There, to have one's name written in the book of life meant to share and enjoy the earthly blessings of God's rule among his people. To have one's name blotted out of the book of life meant to be deprived of these divine blessings, which was the same as to die. In the New Testament, this concept is reapplied to the next life, to the eternal kingdom of God in Christ (see Luke 10:20; Phil. 4:3; Heb. 12:23).

The Theophany in Revelation 4 is based on Ezekiel 1 and Isaiah 6:1-4. The similarities in detail are far too many to be listed here. As examples one may cite God sitting on a heavenly throne (Rev. 4:2; Isa. 6:1; Ezek. 1:26), a rainbow round about the throne (Rev. 4:3; Ezek. 1:28), lightning and thunder issuing from the throne (Rev. 4:5; Ezek. 1:4,24,27), four living creatures with appearances like a lion, an ox, a man, and an eagle (Rev. 4:6-7; Ezek. 1:5,10), each creature having six wings (Rev. 4:8; Isa. 6:2), and the cry of these creatures in praise to God, "Holy, holy, holy, is the Lord God Almighty (Rev. 4:8; Isa. 6:3). The vision of Ezekiel 1 is repeated in Ezekiel 10 and (in much briefer form) in Ezekiel 43:1-5. Similar theophanies may be found in Exodus 24:9-11 and I Kings 22:19-23. All such theophanies draw attention to the majesty and glory of God.

The different-colored horses in Revelation 6:1-8 are based on Zechariah 1:7-17 and 6:1-8. The purpose of the horses and their riders in Zechariah is to patrol the earth and return with the report that all is at peace, so that the Jews might be inspired to get back to their work of rebuilding the temple. By way of contrast, the horses and their riders in Revelation bring death and destruction on the earth. Still, the similarities are striking and compelling. Note, for example, the reference to the measuring line stretched out over Jerusalem in Zechariah 1:16 and to the balance in the hand of the rider in Revelation 6:5.

Revelation 6:12-14 is based on Joel 2:10-11,31 and Isaiah 34:4. The description of a cosmic earthquake which will unsettle mankind with the sun being blackened, the moon becoming like blood, the stars falling to the earth,

---

[12]Charles, *A Critical and Exegetical Commentary on the Revelation of St. John* I, pp. 75-76, tries to make a case for understanding *poimainō* as having meant *both* "shepherd-rule" and "destroy." However, this view flounders for lack of substantial evidence, and is unnecessary in light of the explanation offered here.

and so on, is common in the Old Testament and Jewish Apocalyptic of the intertestamental period.[13]

Revelation 7:16-17 is based on Isaiah 49:10. This text in Isaiah describes the return of the Jewish exiles from Babylonian captivity after the decree of Cyrus the Great, King of Persia, in 539 B.C. The author of Revelation applies this language to the eternal bliss of Christians who have been faithful through the great tribulation.

The description of the locusts in Revelation 9:3-11 is based on Joel 2:1-11. In both passages, the locusts come forth after the blowing of a trumpet (Rev. 9:1; Joel 2:1); their appearance is like horses (Rev. 9:7; Joel 2:4); the noise they make is like the noise of chariots (Rev. 9:9; Joel 2:5); people before them are in great fear and anguish (Rev. 9:6; Joel 2:6).

Revelation 9:16 is based on Psalm 68:17 and Daniel 7:10. But there is a striking contrast here. In Psalm 68:17, "twice ten thousand, thousands upon thousands" refers to the chariots of God as he came from Sinai to the holy place, and the similar number in Daniel 7:10 refers to the angels who stand before God as his servants, whereas this number in Revelation 9:16 alludes to the army which comes from hell.

The eating of the scroll in Revelation 10:8-11 is based on Ezekiel 2:8-3:3. The same concept appears in Jeremiah 15:16 in abbreviated form. In both cases, a heavenly voice instructs the prophet to take a scroll from the hand of the heavenly person who is holding it and to eat it; when the prophet does so, it is sweet as honey in his mouth, but becomes bitter in his stomach.

Revelation 11:1-6 is based on Ezekiel 40:3,5; 43:13,18 and Zechariah 4:1-6,11-14. The concept of measuring the temple, the altar, and the court outside the temple (Rev. 11:1-2) has its parallel in Ezekiel. The figure of the two olive trees and the two lampstands (Rev. 11:4) is derived from Zechariah. In Zechariah, there is only one lampstand, which represents the word of the Lord to Zerubbabel that he will complete the building of the temple, not by human might or power, but by God's Spirit; whereas the two lampstands in Revelation represent the churches loyal to Christ under Roman persecution who would be God's witness to the world.[14] Also, the two olive trees in Zechariah are Zerubbabel and Joshua, the political and religious leaders of the Jews who had returned to Jerusalem from captivity, and who were guiding their people in rebuilding the temple and remolding their lives for God (Zech. 4:14); while the two olive trees in Revelation are Elijah and Moses (Rev. 11:5-6). This kind of borrowing and reapplication of Old Testament texts is quite common in the book of Revelation, and indeed throughout the New Testament.

---

[13]Note the references cited in Charles, ibid., pp. 180-181; G.R. Beasley-Murray, *The Book of Revelation.* New Century Bible Commentary (Grand Rapids, Mich.: Wm. B. Eerdmans Publishing Company, 1974; softback edition, 1981), p. 138; J. Massyngberde Ford, *Revelation.* The Anchor Bible 38 (Garden City, New York: Doubleday & Company, Inc., 1975), pp. 111-112.

[14]Compare Zechariah 4:6 and Revelation 11:3,6-7; and see Caird, *A Commentary on the Revelation of St. John the Divine,* pp. 134-135; and Beasley-Murray, *The Book of Revelation,* pp. 176-181.

Revelation 12:7-9 is based on Daniel 10:12-14,20-21; 12:1. The book of Daniel relates a heavenly battle scene between the angelic "prince," Michael, and his angels, and the prince of the kingdom of Persia. Michael defends God's people from their Persian overlords. In a similar way, the passage in Revelation 12 relates a heavenly battle scene between Michael and his angels and "the great dragon, that ancient serpent, who is called the Devil and Satan, the deceiver of the whole world," in which Michael and his angels cast the Devil and his angels down to the earth. One is reminded of the reference to the archangel Michael contending with the devil, disputing over the body of Moses in Jude 9.[15]

Revelation 13:1-7 is based on Daniel 7:3-8,21,25. The passage in Daniel describes four great beasts coming up out of the sea, one like a lion, one like a bear, one like a leopard, and one indescribably horrible. The fourth beast had ten horns, among which was a little horn (Antiochus IV Epiphanes). The little horn prevailed over the saints of the Most High, spoke blasphemous words against the most High, and ruled over his saints "for a time, two times, and half a time" (on this last point, cf. Rev. 12:14). Ultimately, God overthrew this little horn. Similarly, the text in Revelation depicts a beast rising out of the sea, which was like a leopard, whose feet were like a bear's, and whose mouth was like a lion's. He had ten horns with ten diadems upon them. He uttered "haughty and blasphemous words" against God, and conquered God's saints. Ultimately, he was overthrown.[16]

Revelation 14:8 is based on Jeremiah 51:7-8 and Isaiah 21:9. The cry goes out that Babylon has fallen. She had made other nations drink the wine of her impure passion; now she must drink the wine of God's wrath. For this figure, one should also compare Isaiah 13:19; Jeremiah 25:15-29; Isaiah 51:21-23; Psalm 75:8; Habakkuk 2:15-16. "Babylon" actually means Babylon in the Old Testament texts, but has reference to Rome here in Revelation (see the description of the fall of "Babylon" or Rome in Rev. 18).[17]

Revelation 14:14-20 and 19:15 are based on Joel 3:13 and Isaiah 63:1-6. In these texts, there is a figure of God or an angel putting in his sharp sickle, reaping a large harvest of grapes, and casting them into the winepress. Then God treads the winepress until blood flows from it freely. The passage in Joel has reference to the nations who had defeated God's people and scattered them among the nations. The text in Isaiah announces the destruction of Edom. The passages in Revelation concern the destruction of the enemies of

---

[15]See D. Stuart, "Michael," *The International Standard Bible Encyclopedia* 3 revised, gen. ed. Goeffrey W. Bromiley (Grand Rapids, Mich.: William B. Eerdmans Publishing Company, 1986), pp. 347-348.

[16]See William Barclay, "Revelation 13, Great Themes of the N.T.," *The Expository Times* 70 (1958/59) 260-264, 292-296; D'Aragon, "The Apocalypse," pp. 484-485; and S. MacLean Gilmore, "The Revelation of John," *The Interpreter's One-Volume Commentary on the Bible* (edited by Charles M. Laymon; London: William Collins Sons & Co., Ltd., 1972), pp. 960-961.

[17]Cf. C. Anderson Scott, *Revelation*. The Century Bible (Edinburgh: T.C. & E.C. Jack, 1902), p. 246; D'Aragon, "The Apocalypse," p. 485, referring to I Peter 5:13, which uses "Babylon" in referring to Rome.

God's people, the Christians to whom the book of Revelation is addressed. One should note that the description of the destruction of the enemies of Christians is as gory as that of the description of the destruction of the enemies of Israel in the Old Testament. Commenting on verse 20, Ladd writes:

> The metaphor suddenly changes from the treading of grapes to a military slaughter. The flow of *blood* is incredible, literally conceived: *one thousand six hundred stadia* is a distance of about a hundred and eighty-four miles — the entire length of Palestine. The entire land is pictured as being inundated in blood to a depth of about four feet. The thought is clear: a hostility to the reign of God.[18]

Revelation 18 is based on Isaiah 13:1-14:23; 47; Jeremiah 50-51. All of these Old Testament passages describe the fall of Babylon. Here it is impossible to call attention to all the parallels. Two examples may suffice. Revelation 18:7 describes Babylon's boastings when she seemed to be in control of all the peoples under her. The idea and language is strikingly similar to the boastings of Babylon recorded in Isaiah 47:7-8,10. In fact, the thought that such boasting is a major cause of her fall in Revelation 18:8 calls to mind the same concept in Isaiah 47:11. Again, the comparison of Babylon's (Rome's) fall with casting a heavy stone into the sea in Revelation 18:21 has obvious affinities with the symbolic act of binding a stone to a book or scroll containing all the evil (destruction) that was to come upon Babylon and casting it into the midst of the Euphrates in Jeremiah 51:59-64.

Revelation 20:7-10 is based on Ezekiel 38-39. In Ezekiel, Gog is the prince of the land of Magog, but here in Revelation Gog and Magog are nations which Satan deceives to come out against God's people. The identity of Gog and Magog has never been made satisfactorily. These terms are clearly symbolic for Satan's hosts in Revelation. In Ezekiel and Revelation, the attack comes when God's people appear to be enjoying safety and security (see Ezek. 38:8,11,14).

Revelation 21:1 is based on Isaiah 65:17; 66:22, and Revelation 21:4 is based on Isaiah 25:8. The passages in Isaiah all refer to God's blessings on the exiles returning from Babylonian captivity. The previous seventy years in Babylon are obliterated like the heavens and earth of God's initial creation, and their homecoming is like a new beginning with new heavens and a new earth. Their years of mourning are over, so that their tears will be replaced by smiles of joy. The texts in Revelation pertain to faithful Christians living with God eternally. Their home will not be on earth as a physical place, but in a totally new environment. And all the sorrows brought on by their persecutions will give place to eternal joy. The picture of removing every tear from their eyes also appears in Revelation 7:17.

The description of the wall and gates of Jerusalem in Revelation 21:12-14 is based on Ezekiel 48:30-35. Of course, the details and wording are not iden-

---

[18]George Eldon Ladd, *A Commentary on the Revelation of John* (Grand Rapids, Mich.: William B. Eerdmans Publishing Company, 1972, p. 202.

tical. But in both passages there are twelve gates, and on each gate the name of one of the twelve tribes of Israel. Further, there are three gates each on the north, the south, the east and the west.

Revelation 1:8; 21:6: and 22:13 are based on Isaiah 41:4; 44:6; 48:12. All of these texts allude to God (the Father) as "the Alpha and the Omega," that is, "the first and the last," which is a comprehensive term for his sovereignty. But Revelation 22:13 applies this same expression to Jesus Christ, suggesting that he is also divine (God the Son).

Conclusions

In light of the data which have been gathered in the research done for this paper, some of which is reflected in the information given above, several conclusions emerge.

1. The books of Matthew, Hebrews, and Revelation draw from the Old Testament more than any other New Testament books. This suggests that their authors were steeped in Old Testament thought, and that their readers knew the Old Testament well.

2. The author of the book of Revelation uses material from all parts of the Old Testament, but his favorite books are Isaiah, Jeremiah, Ezekiel, Daniel, Exodus, and Psalms. This is because he is concerned with prophetic, eschatological, and apocalyptic language and concepts; he uses figures based on the sea and the plagues (evidently derived from the crossing of the Sea of Reeds and the plagues in Egypt); and he praises God for standing by his persecuted people and overthrowing their enemies.

3. The author of Revelation does not intend to show that Old Testament predictions are fulfilled in events involving Christ and the church. Instead, he used Old Testament language to describe the situation facing his readers. He draws parallels between Old Testament events and ideas and the circumstances in which he and his readers find themselves.

4. There is an underlying assumption of continuity between Old Testament Israel and the New Testament church reflected in the statements and language of the book of Revelation. What happened to God's faithful servants in Old Testament times is happening now to God's faithful servants in New Testament times. And the same God who delivered his people then will deliver them now again.

5. What is said of God in the Old Testament is said of Jesus Christ in the book of Revelation. This is possible because Jesus has shown himself to be divine, especially as him who was raised from the dead by the glory of the Father.

6. Passages in the book of Revelation which call for or describe God's vengeance on the enemies of his faithful people (as 6:9-10; 11:18; 14:9-20; 16:5-7; 18) caution against being too hasty in assigning Old Testament impre-

cations (as Pss. 58:6-11; 79:5-7,12; 139:19-22) a "sub-Christian" status. This whole question needs a careful, sober, scholarly examination.[19]

---

[19]For further study on the use of the Old Testament in the book of Revelation, see Adolf Schlatter, *Das Alte Testament in der Johanneischen Apokalypse. Beiträge zur Förderung Christlicher Theologie*, XVI/6 (Gutersloh: Gutersloher Verlag, 1912); J. Cambier, "Les images de l'A.T. dans l'Apocalypse," *Nouvelle Revue Theologique* 77 (1975) 113-123; G.W. Grogan, "The New Testament Interpretation of the Old Testament," *Tyndale Bulletin* 18 (1967) 54-76, especially pp. 68-72; and D. Moody Smith, Jr., "The Use of the Old Testament in the New," *The Use of the Old Testament in the New and Other Essays. Studies in Honor of William Franklin Stinespring* (edited by James M. Efird; Durhan, N.C.: Duke University Press, 1972), pp. 3-65, especially pp. 61-63. On the problem of asking vengeance on the enemies of God's people in the book of Revelation, see A.T. Hanson, *The Wrath of the Lamb* (London: S.P.C.K., 1957); W. Klassen, "Vengeance in the Apocalypse of John," *The Catholic Biblical Quarterly* 28 (1966) 300-311.

Bibliography of Works Cited

Abrahams, Israel. *Studies in Pharisaism and the Gospels*. Cambridge: University Press, (1st Series) 1917, (2nd Series) 1924.

Achtemeirer, Paul J. "An Apocalyptic Shift in Early Christian Tradition: Reflections on Some Canonical Evidence," *The Catholic Biblical Quarterly* 45:2 (April, 1983).

Albright, W.F. "Recent Discoveries in Palestine and the Gospel of St. John." In: *The Background of the New Testament and Its Eschatology*, (eds. W.D. Davies and D. Daube). Cambridge: University Press, 1964.

_____. *The Archaeology of Palestine*. Harmonsworth, Middlesex: Penguin Books, 1949.

Allport, Gordon. "Behavioral Science, Religion and Mental Health," *Journal of Religion and Health* 2:3 (1963).

_____. *The Individual and His Religion*. New York: MacMillan, 1950.

Amiran, R. and Eitan, A. "Excavation in the Courtyard of the Citadel, Jerusalem, 1968-1969," *Israel Exploration Journal* 20 (1970).

_____. "Excavations in the Jerusalem Citadel." In: *Jerusalem Revealed*, (ed. Y. Yadin). Jerusalem: The Israel Exploration Society, 1975.

_____. "Herod's Palace," *Israel Exploration Journal* 22 (1972).

Andersen, Ward W. *Signs of Jesus's Messiahship: A Biblical-Theological Comparison of the Old Testament Messianic Revelation With the Miracles of John 1-12*. [Ph.D. Dissertation], Bob Jones University, 1985.

Ard, Robert C. "Pastoral Counseling," [Unpublished Paper], Pepperdine University, Spring, 1968.

Ashcraft, Morris. "Preaching the Apocalyptic Message Today," *Review and Expositor* LXXII:3 (Summer, 1957).

Attridge, H.W. "The Philosophical Critique of Religion under the Early Empire," *Aufstieg und Niedergang der römischen Welt*. Principat. II.16.2 (Berlin, 1978)

Aune, David E. "The Apocalypse of John and the Problem of Genre," *Semeia* 36 *Early Christian Apocalypticism: Genre and Social Setting*, (ed. Adela Yarbro Collins). SBL, Decatur, GA.: Scholars Press, 1986.

_____. *The New Testament in Its Literary Environment* [Library of Early Christianity], (ed. Wayne A. Meeks). Philadelphia: Westminster, 1987.

_____. "The Social Matrix of the Apocalypse of John," *Biblical Research* XXVI (1981).

Avigad, Nahman. *Discovering Jerusalem*. Nashville: Thomas Nelson, 1983.

Avi-Yonah, Michael. "Jerusalem in the Hellenistic and Roman Periods." In: *The Herodian Period* (ed. Avi-Yonah), Vol. VII of *The World History of the Jewish People*. New Brunswick: Rutgers University Press, 1975).

Bahat, D., and Broshi, M. "Excavation in the Armenian Garden." In: *Jerusalem Revealed*, (ed. Y. Yadin). Jerusalem: The Israel Exploration Society, 1975).

_____"Jerusalem, Old City, Armenian Garden," *Israel Exploration Journal* 22 (1972).

Bailey, Kenneth. *Poet and Peasant*. Grand Rapids: Eerdmans, 1976.

Barrett, C.K. *The Gospel According to St. John*. London: S.P.C.K., 1960.

_____. *The Gospel According to St. John*, (2nd ed.). Philadelphia: Westminster, 1978.

Barclay, William. "Revelation 13, Great Themes of the N.T.," *The Expository Times* 70 (1958/59).

Barr, David L. "The Apocalypse as a Symbolic Transformation of the World: A Literary Analysis," *Interpretation* XXXVIII:1 (Jan., 1984).

Bartelink, G.J.M. "The démons comme brigands," *Vigiliae Christianae* 21 (1967).

Barth, Karl. *Protestant Thought: From Rousseau to Ritschl*. New York: Simon & Schuster, 1969.

Bauckham, Richard J. "The Rise of Apocalyptic," *Themelios* 3 (Jan., 1978).

Baur, W.. *Griechish-deutsches Wörterbuch zu den Schriften des Neuen Testaments und der übrigen Urchristlichen Literatur;* (4th ed. rev., trans., and augmented by William F. Arndt and F. Wilbur Gingrich), *Greek-English Lexicon of the New Testament*. Chicago: University of Chicago Press; London: Cambridge University Press, 1957.

Baynes, A.C. "St. Anthony and the Demons," *Journal of Egyptian Archaeology* 40 (1954).

Beasley-Murray, G.R. "The Revelation," *The New Bible Commentary;* (revised, eds. D. Guthrie, J.A. Motyer, A.M. Stibbs, and D.J. Wiseman). Grand Rapids: Eerdmans, 1970.

_____. *The Book of Revelation* [New Century Bible Commentary]. Grand Rapids: Eerdmans, 1974.

_____. *John* [Word Biblical Commentary]." Waco: Word, 1987.

Beckwith, R.T. "The Solar Calendar of Joseph and Asenath: a Suggestion," *Journal for the Study of Judaism* 15 (1984).

Bell, Albert A. "The Date of John's Apocalypse: The Evidence of Some Roman Historians Reconsidered," *New Testament Studies* 25:1 (Oct., 1978).

Benoit, P. "L'Antonia D'Herode le Grand et le Forum Oriental D'Aelia Capitolian," *Harvard Theological Review* 64 (1971).

_____. "Pretoire, Lithostroton et Gabbatha," *Revue Biblique* 59 (1952).

_____. "The Archeological Reconstruction of the Antonio Fortress." In: *Jerusalem Revealed*, (ed. Y. Yadin). Jerusalem: The Israel Exploration Society, 1975.

Bernard, J.H. *A Critical and Exegetical Commentary on the Gospel According to St. John*, 2 vols. [The International Critical Commentary]. New York: Scribner's Sons, 1929.

Bertram, G. *"hypsoō," Theological Dictionary of the New Testament* 8 (1972).

Black, Matthew. *An Aramaic Approach to the Gospels and Acts*, (3rd ed.). Oxford: Clarendon Press, 1967.

——————————. "The 'Son of Man' Passion Sayings in the Gospel Tradition," *ZMW* 60 (1969).

Black, Matthew and Rowley, H.H. (eds.). *Peake's Commentary on the Bible*. London: Nelson, 1962.

Blanc, Cécile. "L'angélologie d'Origène," *Studia Patristica* XIV (T.U. 117; Berlin, 1976).

Blauw, Johannes. *The Missionary Nature of the Church*. New York: McGraw-Hill, 1962.

Bettencourt, S. *Doctrina Ascetica Origenis seu quid docuerit de ratione animae humanae cum daemonibus*. Studia Anselmiana 16 (Rome, 1945).

Blazer, Dan. *Healing the Emotions*. Nashville: Broadman Press, 1979.

Bloch, Joshua. *On the Apocalyptic of Judaism*. Philadelphia: The Dropsie College for Hebrew and Cognate Learning, 1952.

Boadt, Lawrence. *Reading the Old Testament: An Introduction*. New York: Paulist Press, 1984.

Boismard, M.E. "L'évolution du thème eschatologique dans les traditions johanniques," *Revue Biblique* 68 (1961).

Bokser, B. "Wonderworking and the Rabbinic tradition: The Case of Hanina ben Dosa," *JSJ* 16 (1985).

Boraas, R. "Of Serpents and Gods," *Dialog* 17 (1978).

Borgen, P. *Bread from Heaven: An Exegetical Study of the Concept of Manna in the Gospel of John and the Writings of Philo* [Supplements to Novum Testamentum 10]. Leiden: Brill, 1965.

——————————. *Philo, John and Paul: New Perspectives on Judaism and Early Christianity* [Brown Judaic Studies 131]. Atlanta: Scholars Press, 1987.

Bornkamm, G. *Jesus of Nazareth*, (trans. I. and F. McLusky and J.M. Robinson). New York: Harper and Row, 1960.

Borsch, F. *The Son of Man in Myth and History*. Philadelphia: Westminster, 1967.

Bosch, David J. "The Structure of Mission: An Exposition of Matthew 28:16-20." In: *Exploring Church Growth* (ed.) W.R. Shenk. Grand Rapids: Eerdmans, 1983.

Bowman, C. and Coote, R. "A Narrative Incantation for Snake Bite," *UF* 12 (1980).

Bowman, John Wick. *Prophetic Realism and the Gospel*. Philadelphia: Westminster, 1955.

——————————. *The Fourth Gospel and the Jews* [PTM 8]. Pittsburgh: Pickwick, 1975.

Brenk, F.E. *In Mist Apparelled: Religious Themes in Plutarch's Moralia and Lives.* Leiden, 1977.

Bretschneider, Karl. *Probabilia de Evangelii et Epistolarum Ioannis Apostoli Indole et Origine Cruditorum Iudiciis Modeste Subjecit.* Leipzig, 1820.

Bright, John. *A History of Israel,* (2nd rev. ed.). Philadelphia: Westminster, 1959.

Brooks, E.W. *Joseph and Asenath* [Translations of Early Documents, Series 2]. London: S.P.C.K., 1918.

Brown, Raymond E. *The Community of the Beloved Disciple.* New York: Paulist Press, 1979.

_____. *The Gospel According to John* [Anchor Bible]. Garden City: Doubleday, (Vol. 1) 1966, (Vol. 2) 1970.

_____. "The Qumran Scrolls and the Johannine Gospel and Epistles." In: *New Testament Essays.* Garden City, N.Y.: Doubleday, 1986.

Brown, Schuyler. "From Burney to Black: The Fourth Gospel and the Aramaic Question," *Catholic Biblical Quarterly* 26 (July, 1964).

Budd, P. *Numbers.* Waco: Word, 1984.

Buis, P. "Les conflits entre Moïse et Israël dans Exode et Nombres," *VT* 28 (1978).

Bull, R.J. "An Archaeological Context for Understanding John 4:20," *Biblical Archaeologist* 38 (May, 1975).

Bultmann, Rudolf. *The Gospel of John: A Commentary,* (trans. G.R. Beasley-Murray). Philadelphia: Westminster, 1971.

_____. *History and Eschatology.* New York: Harper & Row, 1957.

_____. *Theology of the New Testament,* 2 Vols., (trans. K. Grobel). New York: Charles Scribner's Sons, 1955.

Burchard, C. "Ein vorläufiger griechischer Text von Joseph und Aseneth," *Dielheimer Blätter zum Alten Testament* 14 (1979).

_____. "Verbesserungen zum vorläufigen Text von Joseph and Aseneth," *Dielheimer Blätter zum Alten Testament* 16 (1982).

_____. "Zum Text von 'Joseph und Aseneth,' " *Journal for the Study of Judaism* 1 (1970).

_____. "Joseph and Aseneth," *The Old Testament Pseudepigrapha,* 2 Vols. (ed. J.H. Charlesworth). Garden City, N.Y.: Doubleday, 1983-85.)

_____. "The Importance of Joseph and Aseneth for the Study of the New Testament: A General Survey and a Fresh Look at the Lord's Supper," *New Testament Studies* 33 (1987).

_____. *Untersuchungen zu Joseph und Aseneth: Überlieferung-Ortsbestimmung* [Wissenschaftliche Untersuchungen zum Neuen Testament 8]. Tübingen: Mohr, 1965.

Burkitt, F.C. *Jewish and Christian Apocalypses.* London: Oxford University Press, 1914.

Burney, C.F. *The Aramaic Origin of the Fourth Gospel.* Oxford: Clarendon Press, 1922.

Butterworth, G.W. *Origen on First Principles.* London, 1936.
Caird, George B. *A Commentary on the Revelation of St. John the Divine* [Harper's New Testament Commentaries]. New York: Harper & Row, 1966.
_____. *Principalities and Powers: A Study in Pauline Theology.* Oxford: Clarendon Press, 1956.
Calvin, John. *Commentary on the Gospel According to John,* (trans. William Pringle). Grand Rapids: Eerdmans, 1956.
_____. *Institutes of the Christian Religion,* (ed. John T. McNeill; trans. Ford Lewis Battles). Philadelphia: Westminster, 1960.
Cambier, J. "Les images de l'A.T. dans l'Apocalypse," *Nouvelle Revue Theologique* 77 (1955).
Carson, D.A. "The Purpose of the Fourth Gospel: John 20:31 Reconsidered," *Journal of Biblical Literature* 106 (1987).
Chadwick, Henry. "The Evidences of Christianity in the Apologetic of Origen," *Studia Patristica* II (Berlin, 1957).
_____. (trans.), *Alexandrian Christianity* II [Library of Christian Classics] (London, 1954).
Charles, R.H. *A Critical and Exegetical Commentary on the Revelation of St. John.* I [The International Critical Commentary]. New York: Charles Scribner's Sons, 1920.
_____. *The Apocrypha and Pseudepigrapha of the Old Testament in English,* 2 Vols. Oxford: Clarendon, 1913.
Charlesworth, James H. "The Jewish Roots of Christology: The Discovery of the Hypostatic Voice," *Scottish Journal of Theology* 39 (May, 1986).
_____. *The New Testament Apocrypha and Pseudepigrapha: A Guide to Publications with Excursuses and Apocalypses.* Meuchen, N.J.: Scarecrow Press, Inc., 1987.
_____. *The Old Testament Pseudepigrapha: Apocalyptic Literature and Testaments,* Vol. I, (ed. James H. Charlesworth). Garden City, New York: Doubleday, 1983.
Chesnutt, Randall D. "Joseph and Aseneth," *Anchor Bible Dictionary.* Garden City, N.Y.: Doubleday, in press.
_____. "The Social Setting and Purpose of Joseph and Aseneth," *Journal for the Study of the Pseudepigrapha* (in press).
Ciholas, Paul, "The Socratic and Johannine *semeion* as Divine Manifestation," *Perspectives in Religious Studies* 9 (1982).
Clark, Kenneth, "The Pathos of Power: A Psychological Perspective," *American Psychologist* 26 (1971).
Clinebell, Howard. *Community Mental Health: The Role of Church and Temple.* Nashville: Abingdon, 1970.
Coats G. "The Wilderness Itinerary," *Catholic Biblical Quarterly* 34 (1972).
Cohen, Shaye J.D. *From the Maccabees to the Mishnah* [Library of Early Christianity], (ed. Wayne A. Meeks). Philadelphia: Westminster, 1987.
Collins, Adela Yarbro, "Dating the Apocalypse of John," *Biblical Research* XXVI (1981).

_____. "The Early Christian Apocalypses," *Semeia* 14 *The Morphology of a Genre*, (ed. John J. Collins), SBL. Missoula, Mt.: University of Mt. Press, 1979.

_____. "Persecution and Vengeance in the Book of Revelation," *Apocalypticism in the Mediterranean World and the Ancient Near East*, (ed. David Hellholm), [Proceedings of the International Colloquium on Apocalypticism, Upsalla, August 12-17, 1979]. Tübingen: Mohr [Paul Siebeck], 1983.

_____. "The Revelation of John: An Apocalyptic Response to a Social Crisis," *Currents in Theology and Mission* 8:1 (Feb., 1981).

Collins, John J. "Apocalyptic Literature," *Early Judaism and Its Modern Interpreters* (eds. Robert A. Kraft and George W.E. Nickelsburg). Philadelphia: Fortress; Atlanta: Scholars Press, 1986.

_____. "Apocalyptic Literature," *Harper's Bible Dictionary*, (gen. ed. Paul J. Achtemeier). San Francisco: Harper & Row, 1985.

_____. *Between Athens and Jerusalem: Jewish Identity in the Hellenistic Diaspora*. New York: Crossroad, 1983.

_____. "Introduction: Towards the Morphology of a Genre," *Semeia* 14 *Apocalypse: The Morphology of a Genre*, (ed. John J. Collins), SBL. Missoula, Mt.: University of Mt. Press, 1979.

_____. "Pseudonymity, Historical Reviews and the Genre of the Revelation of John," *Catholic Biblical Quarterly* XXXIX:3 (July, 1977).

_____. "The Apocalypse — Revelation and Inspiration," *The Bible Today* 6 (Nov., 1981).

_____. *The Apocalyptic Imagination: An Introduction to the Jewish Matrix of Christianity*. New York: Crossroad, 1984.

Collins, R.F. "Cana (Jn. 2:1-12) — The First of His Signs or the Key to His Signs?" *Irish Theological Quarterly* 47 (1980).

Colwell, E.C. *The Greek of the Fourth Gospel*. Chicago: Chicago University Press, 1931.

Conder, Claude R. "On the Identification of Aenon," *Palestine Exploration Quarterly* n.v. (July, 1874).

Conzelmann, Hans. *An Outline of the Theology of the New Testament*. New York: Harper & Row, 1969.

Coote, R. "The Serpent and Sacred Marriage in Northwest Semitic Tradition," *HTR* 65 (1972).

Coppens, J. "Le fils de l'homme dans l'Evangile Johannique," *ETL* 52 (1976).

Corrie, George Elwes, (ed.). *Sermons and Remains of Hugh Latimer* (For the Parker Society]. Cambridge: Cambridge University Press, 1845.

Cowen, Emory L. "Help Is Where You Find It," *American Psychologist* 37:4 (April, 1982).

Cox, John Edmund, (ed.)."An Answer unto a Crafty and Sophistical Cavillation Devised by Stephen Gardner." In: *Writings and Disputations of Thomas Cranmer Relative to the Lord's Supper* [For the Parker Society]. Cambridge: Cambridge University Press, 1844.

Crouzel, H. *Théologie de l'image de Dieu chez Origène* (Paris, 1955).
Crowfoot, J.W., Kenyon, I., and Sukenik, E.L. *The Buildings at Samaria.* London: Palestine Exploration Fund, 1942.
Cullmann, O. *Christ and Time: The Primitive Christian Conception of Time and History*, (trans. F.V. Filson). Philadelphia: Westminster, 1950.
_____. *Salvation in History*, (Trans. S.G. Sowers). New York: Harper & Row, 1967.
Dahl, N.A. "The Johannine Church and History." In: *Current Issues in New Testament Interpretation*, (eds. William Klassen and Graydon F. Snyder). New York: Harper & Row, 1962.
Daniélou, J. *From Shadows to Reality.* Westminster, Md., 1960.
_____. *Origène.* Paris, France, 1948.
Danker, W.F. "The Anonymous Christian and Christology: A Response," *Missiology* 6 (1978).
D'Aragon, Jean-Louis, "The Apocalypse." In: *The Jerome Biblical Commentary* II, (eds. Joseph A. Fitzmyer and Raymond E. Brown). Englewood Cliffs, N.J.: Prentice-Hall, Inc., 1968.
Davey, F.M. "The Gospel According to St. John and the Christian Mission." In: *The Theology of the Christian Mission*, (ed. Gerald H. Anderson). New York: Abingdon, 1961.
Davies, W. D. *Paul and the Salvation of Mankind.* London: S.P.C.K., 1965.
_____. *The Setting of the Sermon on the Mount.* Cambridge: University Press, 1964.
de Faye, E. *Origène, sa vie, son oeuvre, sa pensée.* (Paris, 1928).
De Jonge, M. "Signs and Works in the Fourth Gospel," [Supplement] *Novum Testamentum* 48 (1978).
Perez, A. del Agua. "A proposito de la obra de Maneschg sobre la tradicion derasica de la serpiente de bronce (Nm 21)," *EstBib* 42 (1984).
Delcor, M. "Un roman d'amour d'origine thérapeute: Le Livre de Joseph et Asénath," *Bulletin de litterature ecclesiastique* 63 (1962).
Delling, G. "Die Kunst des Gestaltens in 'Joseph und Aseneth,' " *Novum Testamentum* 26 (1984).
de Moor, J. "Some Remarks on U 5 V, No. 7 and 8 (KTU 1.100 and 1.107), " *UF* 9 (1977).
Dennison, W.D. "Miracles as Signs: Their Significance for Apologetics," *Biblical Theology Bulletin* 6 (1976).
De Ridder, Richard R. *Discipling the Nations.* Grand Rapids: Baker, 1975.
_____. "Old Testament Roots of Mission." In: *Exploring Church Growth*, (ed. W.R. Shenk). Grand Rapids: Eerdmans, 1983.
de Vaulx, J. *Les Nombres.* SB: Paris, 1972.
de Vries, S. "The Origin of the Murmuring Tradition," *Journal of Biblical Literature* 87 (1968).
de Wette, Wilhelm M.L. and Lucke, Friedrich. *Synopsis evangeliorum Matthaei, Marci, et Lucae cum parallelis Joannis pericopis.* (Berlin, 1818).

Dick, Michael Brennan, *Introduction to the Hebrew Bible: An Inductive Reading of the Old Testament*. Englewood Cliffs, N.J.: Prentice Hall, 1988.

Dietrich, M., (et al.). "Bemerkungen zur Schlangenbeschwörung," *UF* 7 (1975).

Dodd, C.H. *The Interpretation of the Fourth Gospel*. Cambridge: Cambridge University Press, 1968.

——————————. *The Parables of the Kingdom*. New York: Scribner's, 1961.

Drakeford, John. *Psychology in Search of a Soul*. Nashville: Broadman, 1964.

Duke, P. *Irony in the Fourth Gospel*. Atlanta: John Knox, 1985.

Durant, Will. *Caesar and Christ* [The Story of Civilization: Part III]. New York: Simon and Schuster, 1944.

Eichrodt, W. *Old Testament Theology*, III. Philadelphia: Westminster, 1967.

Ellison, H.L. "Pharisees." In: *New Bible Dictionary* (eds. J.D. Douglas, F.F. Bruce, J.I. Packer R.V.G. Tasker, and D.J. Wiseman). Grand Rapids: Eerdmans, 1962.

English, Horace B. and English, Ava C. *A Comprehensive Dictionary of Psychological Terms*. New York: David McKay Co., Inc., 1985.

Etheridge, J. *The Targums of Onkelos and Jonathan ben Uzziel on the Pentateuch*. New York: KTAV, 1968.

Ferguson, Everett. *Demonology of the Early Christian World*. New York: Edwin Mellen Press, 1984.

——————————. "Divine Pedagogy: Origen's Use of the Imagery of Education." In: *Christian Teaching: Studies in Honor of LeMoine G. Lewis*. Abilene: Texas, 1981.

——————————. "The Demons According to Justin Martyr." In: *The Man of the Messianic Reign and Other Essays: A Festschrift in Honor of Dr. Elza Huffard*, (ed. Wil C. Goodheer). Wichita Falls: Western Christian Foundation, 1980.

Fichtner, J. *"ophis,"* *TDNT* 5 (1967).

Fiorenza, Elisabeth Schüssler, "Apocalyptic and Gnosis in the Book of Revelation and Paul," *Journal of Biblical Literature* 92 (1973).

——————————. "Revelation, Book of." In: *The Interpreter's Dictionary of the Bible*, [Supp. Vol.], (eds. Keith Crim, Lloyd Richard Bailer, Sr., Victor Paul Furnish, and Emory Stevens Bucke). Nashville: Abingdon, 1962.

Fitzmyer, J. "The Use of Explicit Old Testament Quotations in Qumran Literature and the New Testament," *New Testament Studies* 7 (1961). Reprinted in: *Essays on the Semitic Background of the New Testament*. Missoula, Mt.: Scholars Press, 1971.

Ford, J. Massyngberde, *Revelation*, [Anchor Bible 38], (eds. William Foxwell Albright and David Noel Freedman). Garden City, New York: Doubleday & Co., Inc., 1975.

Fortna, Robert T. "Source and Redaction in the Fourth Gospel's Portrayal," *Journal of Biblical Literature* 89 (1970).

_____. *The Gospel of Signs*, [SNTSMS 11]. Cambridge, Cambridge University Press, 1970.

Frankl, Viktor. *Man's Search for Meaning*. New York: Simon and Schuster, Inc., 1984.

Frayne, D. "Naram-Suen and the Mušḫuššu Serpents," *JAOS* 102 (1982).

Freed, Edwin D. *Old Testament Quotations in the Gospel of John*. Leiden: Brill, 1965.

Fretheim, T. "Life in the Wilderness," *Dialog* 17 (1978).

Freud, Sigmund. "Obsessive Actions and Religious Practices," (1907), "Totem and Taboo," (1913), "The Future of an Illusion," (1927). In: *The Standard edition of the Complete Psychological Words of Sigmund Freud*, 9, 13, 21, (ed. and trans. James Strachey). London: Hogarth, 1959.

Fritz, V. *Israel in der Wuste*. Marburg: N.G. Elwert, 1970.

Gager, John G. "The Attainment of Millennial Bliss Through Myth: The Book of Revelation." In: *Visionaries and Their Apocalypses* [Issues in Religion and Theology, No. 2], (ed. Paul D. Hanson). Philadelphia: Fortress, 1983.

Gärtner, B. *John 6 and the Jewish Passover*. Lund: Gleerup, 1959.

Gaster, T. "Sharper than a Serpent's Tooth: A Canaanite Charm against Snakebite," *JANES* 7 (1975).

_____. The Ugaritic Charm against Snakebite: An Additional Note," *JANES* 12 (1980).

Geffcken, J. *Zwei griechische Apologeten*. Leipzig: Germany, 1907.

Geva, H. "Excavations in the Citadel of Jerusalem, 1979-1980," *Israel Exploration Journal* 33 (1983).

Gilmore, MacLean S. "The Revelation of John." In: *The Interpreter's One-Volume Commentary on the Bible*, (ed. Charles M. Laymon). London: William Collins Sons & Co., Ltd., 1972.

Ginzburg, L. *The Legends of the Jews*, Vol. 5, (trans. H. Szold, et al.). Philadelphia: Jewish Publication Society, 1910-38.

Girad, Marc, "La Composition structurelle des sept 'signes' dans le quartieme evangile," *Studies in Religion* 9 (1980).

Glassar, William. *Reality Therapy*. New York: Harper & Row, 1965.

Glasson, T.F. *Moses in the Fourth Gospel* [Studies in Biblical Theology 40]. Naperville, Ill.: Allenson, 1963.

_____. "What Is Apocalyptic?" *New Testament Studies* 27:1 (Oct., 1980).

Gonzalez, Justo L. *A History of Christian Thought*. Nashville/New York: Abingdon, 1975.

Goppelt, L. *Typos. The Typological Interpretation of the OT in the New*. Grand Rapids: Eerdmans, 1982.

Grassi, A. "Eating Jesus' Flesh and Drinking His Blood: The Centrality and Meaning of John 6:51-58," *Biblical Theology Bulletin* 17 (1987).

_____. "The Wedding at Cana (John II 1-11): A Pentecostal Meditation?" *Novum Testamentum* 14 (1972).
Gray, G. *Numbers* [International Critical Commentary]. New York: Scribner's, 1903.
Gray, J. *Numbers* [Old Testament Library]. Philadelphia: Westminster, 1964.
Griffiths, D.R. "Deutero-Isaiah and the Fourth Gospel," *Expository Times* 65 (1953).
Grogan, G.W. "The New Testament Interpretation of the Old Testament," *Tyndale Bulletin* 18 (1967).
Grundmann, Walter, "The Understanding of Christ in the Johannine Writings." In: *Theological Dictionary of the New Testament*, (ed. Gerhard Friedrich; trans. and ed. G.W. Bromiley). Grand Rapids: Eerdmans, 1974.
Guilding, A. *The Fourth Gospel and Jewish Worship: A Study of the Relation of St. John's Gospel to the Ancient Jewish Lectionary System.* Oxford: Clarendon, 1960.
Gunkel, Hermann. *Schöpfung und Choas in Urzeit und Endzeit.* Göttingen: Vandenhoeck & Ruprecht, 1895.
Guthrie, Donald, "The Importance of Signs in the Fourth Gospel," *Vox Evangelica* 5 (1967).
_____. *New Testament Introduction.* Downer's Grove: InterVarsity, 1965.
Haenchen, Ernst. *John* [Hermeneia]. Philadelphia: Fortress, 1984.
Hall, D.R, "Annas." In: *New Bible Dictionary*, (eds. J.D. Douglas, F.F. Bruce, J.I. Packer, R.V.G. Tasker, and D.J. Wiseman). Grand Rapids: Eerdmans, 1962.
_____. "Caiaphas." In: *New Bible Dictionary*, (J.D. Douglas, F.F. Bruce, J.I. Packer, R.V.G. Tasker, and D.J. Wiseman). Grand Rapids: Eerdmans, 1962.
Hanson, A.T. *The Wrath of the Lamb.* London: S.P.C.K., 1957.
Hanson, Paul D. "Apocalypticism." In: *Interpreter's Dictionary of the Bible*, [Supp. Vol.]. Nashville: Abingdon, 1962.
_____. "Biblical Apocalypticism: The Theological Dimension," *Horizons in Biblical Theology* 7 (Dec., 1985).
_____. *Old Testament Apocalyptic* [Interpreting Biblical Texts], (eds. Lloyd R. Bailey, Sr., and Victor P. Furnish). Nashville: Abingdon, 1987.
_____. "Old Testament Apocalyptic Reexamined," *Interpretation* 25 (1971). Now in: *Visionaries and Their Apocalypses* [Issues in Religion and Theology, No. 2], (ed. Paul D. Hanson). Philadelphia: Fortress, 1983.
_____. *The Dawn of Apocalyptic.* Philadelphia: Fortress, 1975.
Harding, Thomas, (ed.). *The Decades of Henry Bullinger* [For the Parker Society]. Cambridge: Cambridge University Press, 1849.
Harnack, Adolf. *The Mission and Expansion of Christianity.* New York: 1962.

Harrelson, W. "Guidance in the Wilderness," *Interpretation* 13 (1959).

Hartman, Louis F. and Di Lella, A. *The Book of Daniel* [Anchor Bible 23]. Garden City, New York: Doubleday, 1978.

Hellholm, David, "The Problem of Apocalyptic Genre and the Apocalypse of John," *Semeia* 36 *Early Christian Apocalypticism: Genre and Social Setting*, (ed. Adela Yarbro Collins). SBL, Decatur, Ga.: Scholars Press, 1986.

Hengel, Martin. *Judentum and Hellenismus*, (2nd rev. & enlarged ed), Tübingen: Mohr [Paul Siebeck], 1973. *Judaism and Hellenism* (trans. John Bowden). Philadelphia: Fortress, 1974.

Hiltner, Seward. *The Counselor in Counseling*. New York: Abingdon-Cokesbury, 1952.

Hoenig, S.B. "Oil and Pagan Defilement," *Jewish Quarterly Review* 61 (1970-71).

Hollander, Edwin P. and Hunt, Raymond G. *Current Perspectives in Social Psychology* (3rd ed.). New York: Oxford University Press, 1975.

Holtz, T. "Christliche Interpolationen in 'Joseph und Aseneth,' " *New Testament Studies* 14 (1968).

Hoskyns, Edwyn and Davey, Noel. *The Riddle of the New Testament*. London: Faber and Faber, 1931.

Jackson, B.D. "Sources of Origen's Doctrine of Freedom," *Church History* 35 (1966).

Jacobson, D.M. "Plan of Haram el-Khalil, Hebron," *Palestine Exploration Quarterly* 111 (1981).

Jeremias, Joachim. *Jerusalem in the Time of Jesus*. Philadelphia: Fortress, 1969.

_____. "The Last Supper," *Expository Times* 64 (1952).

Jewett, P.K. *Man as Male and Female*. Grand Rapids: Eerdmans, 1975.

Johns, C.N. "The Citadel, Jerusalem," *Quarterly of the Department of Antiquities of Palestine* 14 (1950).

Johnson, Alan, *Hebrews-Revelation* [Expositor's Bible Commentary, Vol. 12], (eds. Frank E. Gaebelein and J.D. Douglas). Grand Rapids: Eerdmans, 1981.

Joines, K. *Serpent Symbolism in the Old Testament*. N.J.: Haddonfield, 1974.

_____. "The Bronze Serpent in the Israelite Cult," *Journal of Biblical Literature* 87 (1968).

Jung, Carl G. *Psychology and Religion*. New Haven: Yale University Press, 1938.

_____. "Psychotherapists or the Clergy," *Pastoral Psychology* 7:67 (1956).

Kant, Immanuel. *Die Religion innerhalb der Grenzen der blossen Vernunft* (1793). (trans T.M. Green & H. Hudson), *Religion Within the Limits of Reason Alone*. New York: Harper, 1960.

Käsemann, Ernest, "Die Anfänge Christlicher Theologie," *Zeitschrift für Theologie und Kirche* 57 (1960), (trans. James W. Leitch), "The Beginnings of Christian Theology," *Journal for Theology and the Church* 6 (1969).

_____. *The Testament of Jesus*, (trans. G. Krodel). Philadelphia: Fortress, 1968.

Kautzch, E. *Die Apokryphen und Pseudepigraphen des Alten Testaments*, 2 vols. Tübingen: Mohr, 1900.

Kee, H.C. "The Socio-Cultural Setting of Joseph and Aseneth," *New Testament Studies* 29 (1983).

Kilmartin, E.J. "Liturgical Influence on John 6," *Catholic Biblical Quarterly* 22 (1960).

Kilpatrick, G.D. "The Last Supper," *Expository Times* 64 (1952).

Kittle, Gerhard, (ed.). *Theological Dictionary of the New Testament*, vol. 1, (trans. and ed. Geoffrey W. Bromiley). Grand Rapids: Eerdmans, 1964.

Kittel, Gerhard and Friedrich, Gerhard, (eds.). *Theological Dictionary of the New Testament*, vol. 5, (Grand Rapids: Eerdmans, 1968.)

Klassen, W. "Vengeance in the Apocalypse of John," *Catholic Biblical Quarterly* 28 (1966).

Klauser, T. (ed.). "Geister (Dämonen), *Reallexikon für Antike und Christentum* IX (Stuttgart, 1976).

Klausner, Joseph. *The Messianic Idea in Israel*. (trans. W.F. Stinespring). London: George Allen and Unwin, 1956.

Knox W.L. "Jewish Liturgical Exorcism," *Harvard Theological Review* 31 (1938).

Koch, H. *Pronoia and Paideusis*. (Berlin, 1932).

Koch, Klaus, "What Is Apocalyptic? An Attempt at a Preliminary Definition." In: *Visionaries and Their Apocalypses* [Issues in Religion and Theology, No. 2], (ed. Paul D. Hanson). Philadelphia: Fortress, 1983.

Kohler, K. "Demonology." In: *The Jewish Encyclopedia*, vol. IV. New York, 1910).

Kottsieper, I. "KTU 1.100 — Versuch einter Deutung," *UF* 16 (1984).

Kuhn, K.G. "The Lord's Supper and the Communal Meal at Qumran," *The Scrolls and the New Testament*, (ed. K. Stendahl). New York: Harper and Brothers, 1957.

Kümmel, W.G. "Futurische and praesentlische Eschatologie in ältesten Urchristentum," *New Testament Studies* 5 (January, 1959).

_____. *Promise and Fulfillment: The Eschatological Message of Jesus*, (trans. D.M. Barton) [Studies in Biblical Theology 23]. London: SCM Press Ltd, 1961.

Kysar, Robert. *John*. Minneapolis: Augsburg, 1987.

_____. *John the Maverick Gospel*. Atlanta: John Knox, 1976.

_____. *The Fourth Evangelist and His Gospel*. Minneapolis: Augsburg, 1975.

Ladd, George Eldon. *A Commentary on the Revelation of John*. Grand Rapids: Eerdmans, 1972.

_____. *A Theology of the New Testament*. Grand Rapids: Eerdmans, 1974.

_____. "The Place of Apocalyptic in Biblical Religion," *Evangelical Quarterly* XXX (1958).

_____. "The Origin of Apocalyptic in Biblical Religion," *Evangelical Quarterly* XXX (1958).

_____. "The Revelation and Jewish Apocalyptic," *Evangelical Quarterly* XXIX (1957).

_____. "Why Not Prophetic-Apocalyptic?" *Journal of Biblical Literature* 76 (1957).

Lancellotti, Angelo, "L'Antico Testamento nell'Apocalisse," *Rivista Biblica* 14 (1966).

Lederer, Wolfgang, "Some Moral Dilemmas Encountered in Psychotherapy," *Psychiatry* 34:1 (February, 1971).

Lee, C. "Moses' Serpent as a Patristic 'Type,' " *Dialog* 17 (1978).

Légasse, S. "Le pain de la vie," *Bulletin de littérature ecclesiastique* 83 (1982).

Lewis, Jack P. "Topography and Archaeology of the Gospel of John." In: *That Ye May Believe* [Lubbock Christian College Bible Lectures]. Lubbock, Texas: Lubbock Christian College Bookstore, 1976.

Liddell, H.G. and Scott, R. *Greek-English Lexicon*, (9th ed.). Oxford: Clarendon Press, 1940.

Lindars, B. " 'Joseph and Asenath' and the Eucharist," *Scripture: Meaning and Method. Essays Presented to A.T. Hanson for His Seventieth Birthday*, (ed. B.P. Thompson). Hull: Hull University Press, 1987.

_____. *The Gospel of John*. Greenwood, SC: Attic, 1972.

Locher, Gottfried. *Zwingli's Thought: New Perspectives*. Leiden: Brill, 1981.

Loisy, Alfred. *L'Evangile et l'Eglise*, (1903); *The Gospel and the Church*. Philadelphia: Fortress, 1976.

Lows, Malcolm, "Who Were the IOUDAIOI?" *Novum Testamentum* 18 (April, 1967).

Lundberg, P. *La Typologie baptismale dans l'ancienne église*. Uppsala, 1942.

MacGregor, G.H.C. "Principalities and Powers: The Cosmic Background of Paul's Thought," *New Testament Studies* 1 (1954).

MacRae, G. "Theology and Irony in the Fourth Gospel." In: *The Word in the World: Essays in Honor of F.L. Moriarty*, (eds. R. Clifford and G. MacRae). Cambridge: Weston, 1973.

Maddi, Salvatore. *Personality Theories: A Comparative Analysis*. Homewood: Dorsey, 1968.

Malina, B.J. *The Palestinian Manna Tradition: The Manna Tradition in the Palestinian Targums and Its Relationship to the New Testament Writings*. Leiden: Brill, 1968.

Maneschg, H. "Gott, Erzieher, Retter und Heiland seines Volkes," *BZ* 28 (1984).

Manson, T.W. "The Argument from Prophecy," *JTS* 46 (1945).

Marshall, I.H. "John, Gospel of." In: *New Bible Dictionary*, (ed. J.D. Douglas). Grand Rapids: Eerdmans, 1962.

Martyn, J. Louis. *History and Theology in the Fourth Gospel*. New York: Harper & Row, 1969.

——————. "Source Criticism and Religionsgeschichte in the Fourth Gospel," *Perspective* 11 (1970).

Mays, J. *The Books of Leviticus and Numbers* [LBC 4]. Atlanta: John Knox, 1963.

McGavran, Donald A. *Bridges of God*. Friendship Press, 1955.

——————. *Understanding Church Growth*. (rev. ed.). Grand Rapids: Eerdmans, 1980.

McGinn, Bernard, "Early Apocalypticism: The Ongoing Debate," In: *The Apocalypse in English Renaissance Thought and Literature*, (eds. C.A. Patrides and Joseph Wittreich). Ithaca, New York: Cornell University Press, 1984.

McHugh, M.P. "The Demonology of Saint Ambrose in Light of the Tradition," Wiener Studien, *Neue Folge* 12 (1978).

McNamara, M. *The New Testament and the Palestinian Targum to the Pentateuch* [Anchor Bible 27]. Rome: Pontifical Biblical Institute, 1966.

Meeks W.A. " 'Am I a Jew?' Johannine Christianity and Judaism." In: *Christianity, Judaism and Other Greco-Roman Cults*, 4 pts, (ed. J. Neusner). Leiden: Brill, 1975.

——————. "Moses as God and King." In: *Religions in Antiquity*, (ed. J. Neusner). Leiden: Brill, 1968.

——————. "The Man from Heaven in Johannine Sectarianism," *Journal of Biblical Literature* 91 (1972).

——————. *The Prophet-King: Moses Traditions and the Johannine Christology* [Supplements to *Novum Testamentum* 14]. Leiden: Brill, 1967.

Megivern, James J. "Wrestling with Revelation," *Biblical Theology Bulletin* 8:4 (Oct., 1978).

Metzger, Bruce M. *An Introduction to the Apocrypha*. New York: Oxford University Press, 1957.

——————. *A Textual Commentary on the Greek New Testament*. London: United Bible Society, 1971.

Mieses, M. "Hebräische Fragmente aus dem jüdischen Urtext der Apokalypse des hl. Johannes," *Monatschrift für Geschichte und Wissenschaft des Judentums* 74 (1930).

Miller, George. "Psychology as a Means of Promoting Human Welfare," *American Psychologist* 24 (1969).

Minear, Paul S. *New Testament Apocalyptic* [Interpreting Biblical Texts], (eds. Lloyd R. Bailey and Victor P. Furnish). Nashville: Abingdon, 1981.

Moloney, F. *The Johannine Son of Man*. Rome: LAS, 1976.

Moore, George Foot. *Judaism*, vol. 1. Cambridge: Harvard University Press, 1927.

_____. *Judaism in the First Centuries of the Christian Era*, vol. II. Cambridge: Harvard University Press, 1930.

Morris, Leon. *Apocalyptic*. Grand Rapids: Eerdmans, 1972.

_____. *The Revelation of St. John* [Tyndale Commentary], (ed. R.V.G. Tasker). Grand Rapids: Eerdmans, 1969.

_____. *Studies in the Fourth Gospel*. Grand Rapids: Eerdmans, 1969.

Moule, C.F.D. *Birth of the New Testament*. San Francisco: Harper & Row, 1982.

Moulton, J.H. (gen. ed.). *A Grammar of New Testament Greek*, 4 vols. Edinburgh: T. & T. Clark, 1919.

Mounce, Robert H. *The Book of Revelation* [New International Commentary on the New Testament], (ed. F.F. Bruce). Grand Rapids: Eerdmans, 1977.

Mowrer, O.H. *The Crisis in Psychiatry and Religion*. New York: Van Nostrand, 1961.

Nagy, Ivan Boszormenyi- and Krasner, Barbara. *Between Give and Take: A Critical Guide to Contextual Therapy*. New York: Brunner/Mazel, Inc., 1986.

Nauck, W. *Die Tradition und der Charakter des ersten Johannesbriefs*. Wissenschaftliche Untersuchungen zum Neuen Testament 3. Tübingen: Mohr, 1957.

Nevinson, Charles, (ed.). "A Godly Confession and Protestation of the Christian Faith." In: *Later Writings of Bishop Hooper* (London, 1550) [For the Parker Society]. Cambridge University Press, 1842.

Neyrey, J. "John III — A Debate over Johannine Epistemology and Christology," *NT* 23 (1981).

Nicholson, G. *Death as Departure. The Johannine Descent-Ascent Schema* [Society of Biblical Literature Dissertation Series 63]. Chico, CA: Scholars Press, 1983.

Nickelsburg, George W.E. *Jewish Literature Between the Bible and the Mishnah*. Philadelphia: Fortress, 1981.

Noth, M. "Num. 21 als Glied der 'Hexateuch' — Erzahlung," *ZAW* 58 (1940-41).

_____. *Numbers*. [Old Testament Library]. Philadelphia: Westminster, 1968.

Nougayrol, J. (ed.). *Ugaritica V*. Paris, 1968).

Odeberg, H. *The Fourth Gospel*. Amsterdam: B.R. Gruner, 1929.

Osgood, Charles E., Suci, George J., and Tannenbaum, Perch H. *The Measurement of Meaning*. Urbana: University of Illinois Press, 1957.

Pack, Frank. *Revelation*, Part 1. Austin, Tex.: Sweet Publishing Company, 1965.

_____. *The Gospel According to John*, Part 1, Austin, Tex.: Sweet Publishing Company, 1975.

Pancaro, S. *The Law in the Fourth Gospel: The Torah and the Gospel, Moses and Jesus, Judaism and Christianity According to John* [Supplements to *Novum Testamentum* 42]. Leiden: Brill, 1975.

Pannenberg, Wolfhart. *Jesus — God and Man*. Philadelphia: Westminster, 1968.

_____. "Redemptive Event and History." In: *Basic Questions in Theology*, vol. 1, (ed. George H. Kehm). Philadelphia: Fortress, 1970.

Pattison, E.M. "The Role of Clergymen in Community Mental Health Programs." In: *International Psychiatry Clinics* 5:4 (1969).

Pelikan, J. (ed.). *Luther's Works: Sermons on the Gospel of St. John Chapters 1-4*. St. Louis: Concordia Publishing House, 1957.

_____. *Luther's Works: Sermons on the Gospel of St. John Chapters 6-8*. St. Louis: Concordia Publishing House, 1959.

Pelikan, J. *The Christian Tradition: A History of the Development of Doctrine*. Chicago/London: University of Chicago Press, 1984.

Philonenko, M. "Initiation et mystère dans Joseph et Aséneth," *Initiation*, (ed. C.J. Bleeker), [Supplements to Numen, Studies in the History of Religions 10]. Leiden: Brill, 1965.

_____. *Joseph et Aséneth: Introduction, texte critique, traduction et notes*, [Studia post-biblica 13]. Leiden: Brill, 1968.

_____. "Un mystère juif?" *Mystères et syncrétismes*, [Etudes d'histoire des religions 2]. Paris: Geuthner, 1975.

Plotnik, Rod and Mollenauer, Sandra. *Introduction to Psychology*. New York: Random House, 1986.

Potter, G.R. *Zwingli*. Cambridge: Cambridge University Press, 1976.

Potter, R.D. "Topography and Archaeology of the Fourth Gospel." In: *The Gospels Reconsidered*. Oxford: Basil Blackwell, 1960.

Pullias, E.V. *A Search for Understanding*. Dubuque, Iowa: Wm. C. Brown Pub., 1965.

Rainey, A. "Ugaritic Texts in Ugaritica V," *JAOS* 94 (1974).

Redlich, E. Basil. *An Introduction to the Fourth Gospel*. London/New York: Ongmans, Green and Co., 1939.

Reichelt, Karl Ludwig. "The Johannine Approach." In: *The Authority of the Faith*, vol. 1. New York: International Missionary Council, 1939.

Rengstorf, Karl Heinrich, *"apostolos."* In: *Theological Dictionary of the New Testament*, (ed. Gerhard Kittel; trans. and ed. Geoffrey W. Bromiley). Grand Rapids: Eerdmans, 1964.

_____. *"Semeion."* In: *Theological Dictionary of the New Testament*, (eds. Gerhard Kittel and Gerhard Friedrich; trans. Geoffrey W. Bromiley). Grand Rapids, Eerdmans, 1971.

Riga, Peter. "Signs of Glory, The Use of 'Semeion' in St. John's Gospel," *Interpretation* 17 (1963).

Riggs, J.W. "From Gracious Table to Sacramental Elements: the Tradition History of Didache 9 and 10," *Second Century* 4 (1948).

Rist, Martin. "Revelation." In: *The Interpreter's Bible*, vol. 12. (ed. George Arthur Buttrick). New York/Nashville: Abingdon, 1957.

Roberts, J.J.M. "A Christian Perspective on Prophetic Prediction," *Interpretation* XXXIII:3 (July, 1979).

Robinson, J.A.T. "A New Look on the Fourth Gospel." In: *The Gospels Reconsidered*. Oxford: Basil Blackwell, 1960.

_____. "The Destination and Purpose of St. John's Gospel," *New Testament Studies* 6 (January, 1960).

Rothenberg, B. *Timna. Valley of the Biblical Copper Mines*. London: Thames and Hudson, 1972.

Rowland, Christopher. *The Open Heaven: A Study of Apocalyptic in Judaism and Early Christianity*. New York: Crossroad, 1982.

Rowley, H.H. *The Relevance of Apocalyptic*. London: Lutterworth, 1947.

_____. "Zadok and Nehushtan," *Journal of Biblical Literature* 58 (1939).

Rusch, Frederick A. "The Signs and the Discourse — The Rich Theology of John 6," *Currents in Theology and Mission* 5 (1978).

Russell, D.S. *Apocalyptic: Ancient and Modern*. Philadelphia: Fortress, 1978.

_____. *Between the Testaments*. Philadelphia: Fortress, 1960.

_____. *The Method and Message of Jewish Apocalyptic*. Philadelphia: Westminster; London: SCM, 1964.

Saldarini, Anthony J. "Apocalypses and 'Apocalyptic' in Rabbinic Literature and Mysticism," *Semeia* 14 *Apocalypse: The Morphology of a Genre*, (ed. John J. Collins), SBL. Missoula, Mt.: University of Mt. Press, 1979.

Sandmel, Samuel. *A Jewish Understanding of the New Testament*. Cincinnati: Hebrew Union College Press, 1957.

Sang, Barry Ray. *The New Testament Hermeneutical Milieu: The Inheritance and the Heir*. Madison, N.J.: Drew University Press, 1983.

Sänger, D. *Antikes Judentum und die Mysterien: Religionsgeschichtliche Untersuchungen zu Joseph und Aseneth*. Wissenschaftliche Untersuchungen zum Neuen Testament 2.5. Tübingen: Mohr, 1980.

_____. "Bekehrung und Exodus: Traditionshintergrund von 'Joseph und Aseneth,' " *Journal for the Study of Judaism* 10 (1979).

Schlatter, Adolf. *Das Alte Testament in der Johanneischen Apokalypse*. Beiträge zur Förderung Christlicher Theologie XVI 6. Gutersloh: Gutersloher Verlag, 1912.

Schleiermacher, Friedrich D.E. *Das Leben Jesu*. Berlin: Georg Reimer, 1864. (Jack C. Verheyden, ed. and trans.), *The Life of Jesus*. Philadelphia: Fortress, 1975.

_____. *Dialektik*, (ed. Rudolf Odebrecht). Darmstadt: Wissenschaftliche Buchgesellschaft, 1976.

_____. *Der Christliche Glaube*, (ed. Martin Redeker). Berlin: Walter de Gruyter & Co., 1960. (H.R. Mackintosh and J.S. Stewart, trans.), *The Christian Faith*. Edinburgh: T. & T. Clark, 1928.

_____. *Hermeneutik und Kritik mit Besonderer Beziehung auf das Neue Testament*, (ed. F. Lucke). Berlin: G. Reimer, 1838.

_____. *Kurze Darstellung des Theologischen Studiums*, (ed. Heinrich Scholz). Leipzig: 1910; G. Olms Hildesheim, 1961. (T.N. Tice, trans.), *Brief Outline on the Study of Theology*. Richmond: John Knox, 1966.

_____. *On Religion, Speeches to Its Cultured Despisers*, (John Oman, trans.). New York: Harper & Brothers, 1958.

Schlier, H. *Principalities and Powers in the New Testament*. New York: 1961.

Schmithals Walter. *Die Apokalyptik: Einführung und Deutung*. Göttingen: Vandenhoeck & Ruprecht, 1973. (John E. Steely, trans.). *The Apocalyptic Movement: Introduction and Interpretation*. Nashville: Abingdon, 1975.

Schnackenburg, R. "Das Brot des Lebens." In: *Tradition und Glaube: Das frühe Christentum in seiner Umwelt. Festgabe für K.G. Kuhn*, (eds. J. Jeremias, H.W. Kuhn, and H. Stegemann). Göttingen: Vandenhoeck und Ruprecht, 1971.

_____. *Das Johannesevangelium*, 3 vols. [Herders Theologischer Kommentar zum Neuen Testament]. Freiberg: Herder, 1965-75. (K. Smyth et al. trans.). *The Gospel According to St. John*, 3 vols. New York: Seabury Press, 1980-82.

Schneider, Johannes. "*timē*." In: *Theological Dictionary of the New Testament*, (ed. Gerhard Kittel; trans. Geoffrey W. Bromiley). Grand Rapids: Eerdmans, 1972.

Schneiders, Sandra M. "The Face Veil: A Johannine Sign (John 20:1-10)," *Biblical Theology Bulletin* 13 (1983).

Schoeps, H.J. "Die Dämonologie der Pseudoklementinesn." In: *Aus frühchristlicher Zeit*. Tübingen, Mohr, 1950.

Schrage, Wolfgang. "*Aposunagogus*," In: *Theological Dictionary of the New Testament*, (ed. Gerhard Friedrich; trans. and ed. G.W. Bromiley). Grand Rapids: Eerdmans, 1974.

Schreiter, R.J. "The Anonymous Christian and Christology," *Missiology* 6 (1978).

Schulz, S. *Untersuchungen zur Menschensohn-Christologie im Johannesevangelium*. Göttingen: Vandenhoeck & Ruprecht, 1957.

Schürer, Emil. *Geschichte des jüdischen Volkes in Zeitaler Jesu Christi*. Leipzig: J.C. Hinrichs, 1874-1909. (trans. and rev. Matthew Black, Martin Goodman, Fergus Millar, Geza Vermes, and Pamela Vermes), *The History of the Jewish People in the Age of Jesus Christ (175 B.C.-A.D. 135*, 4 vols. Edinburgh: T. & T. Clark, Ltd., 1986.

Schweitzer, Albert. *Von Reimarus zu Wrede: eine Geschichte der Leben-Jesu-Forschung*, 1906. (trans. W. Montgomery). *The Quest of the Historical Jesus*. New York: MacMillan, 1910.

Schweizer, Eduard. *Church Order in the New Testament*, (SBT 32). London: SCM, 1961.

Scott, C. Anderson. *Revelation* [Century Bible]. Edinburgh: T.C. & E.C. Jack, 1902.

Seeberg, Reinhold. *Textbook of the History of Doctrines*, 2 vols. (trans. Charles E. Hay). Grand Rapids: Baker, 1966.

Senior, Donald and Stuhlmueller, Carroll. *The Biblical Foundations for Mission*. Maryknoll: Orbis, 1983.

Sharpe, Eric J. "The 'Johannine' Approach to the Question of Religious Plurality," *Ching Feng* 23:3 (1980).

Shepherd, Jr., Massey H. "The Gospel According to John." In: *The Interpreter's One-Volume Commentary on the Bible*, (ed. Charles M. Laymon). Nashville: Abingdon, 1971.

——————————. "The Jews in the Gospel of John, Another Level of Meaning," *Anglican Theological Review* [Sup. Ser.] 3 (1974).

Simonetti, M. "Due note sul' angelogia origeniana," *Rivista cultura classica e medioevala* 4 (1962).

Sneen, Donald. *Visions of Hope*. Minneapolis: Augsburg, 1978.

Smalley, Stephen S. *John: Evangelist and Interpreter*. Exeter: Paternoster, 1978.

——————————. "Keeping up with Recent Studies, St. John's Gospel," *Expository Times* 97 (1986).

——————————. "The Johannine Son of Man Sayings," *New Testament Studies* 15 (1968/9).

——————————. "The Sign in John XXI," *New Testament Studies* 20 (1974).

Smith, Darrel. "Trends in Counseling and Psychotherapy," *American Psychologist* 37:7 (July, 1982).

Smith, Jonathan Z. "Wisdom and Apocalyptic." In: *Religious Syncretism in Antiquity*, (ed. B.A. Pearson), 1975. Now in: *Visionaries and Their Apocalypses* [Issues in Religion and Theology, No. 2], (ed. Paul D. Hanson). Philadelphia: Fortress, 1983.

Smith, Jr., Moody. "The Use of the Old Testament in the New." In: *The Use of the Old Testament in the New and Other Essays. Studies in Honor of William Franklin Stinespring*, (ed. James M. Efird). Durham, N.C.: Duke University Press, 1972.

Smith, Morton. *Tannaitic Parallels to the Gospels*. Philadelphia: Society of Biblical Literature, 1951.

Snaith, N. "*Numbers*," [PCB]. Berkshire, England: Von Nostrand Reinhold, 1982.

Soury, Guy. *La démonologie de Plutarque*. Paris, 1942.

Sparks, H.F.D. "Joseph and Aseneth: Introduction." In: *The Apocryphal Old Testament*, (ed. H.F.D. Sparks). Oxford: Clarendon Press, 1984.

Spiegler, Gerhard. "Theological Tensions in Schleiermacher's Dialectic." In: *Schleiermacher as Contemporary*, (ed. Robert W. Funk). New York: Herder & Herder, 1970.

Stagg, Frank, "Interpreting the Book of Revelation," *Review and Expositor* LXXII:3 (Summer, 1975).

Stambaugh, John E. and Balch, David L. *The New Testament in Its Social Environment* [Library of Early Christianity], (ed. Wayne A. Meeks). Philadelphia: Westminster, 1986.

Stott, John R.W. *Christian Mission in the Modern World*. Downer's Grove: InterVarsity, 1975.

Strack, H.L. and Billerbeck, Paul. *Kommentar zum Neuen Testament aus Talmud und Midrasch*, 4 vols. Munich: Beck, 1922-28.

Strauss David F. *The Life of Jesus Critically Examined*, (trans. George Eliot). Philadelphia: Fortress, 1972.
Stuart, D. "Michael." In: *The International Standard Bible Encyclopedia*, vol. 3, (rev. gen. ed. Goeffrey W. Bromiley). Grand Rapids: Eerdmans, 1986.
Swete, Henry Barclay. *The Apocalypse of St. John: The Greek Text with Introduction, Notes and Indices*, 3rd ed. London: MacMillan, 1911.
Szasz, Thomas. *The Myth of Psychotherapy*. New York: Anchor Press/Doubleday, 1978.
Tabick, J. "The Snake in the Grass: The Problems of Interpreting a Symbol in the Hebrew Bible and Rabbinic Writings," *Religion* 16 (1986).
Teeple, Howard M. "Qumran and the Origin of the Fourth Gospel," *Novum Testamentum* 4 (October, 1960).
Teichtweier, Georg. *Die Sündenlehre des Origenes*. Regensburg, 1958.
Tenney, Merrill C. "Topics from the Gospel of John, Part II: The Meaning of the Signs," *Bibliotheca Sacra* 132 (1975).
Torrey, C.C. *Our Translated Gospels*. New York/London: Harper & Brothers, 1936.
_____. *The Apocalypse of John*. New Haven, Conn.: Yale University Press, 1958.
_____. *The Four Gospels. A New Translation*. New York/London: Harper and Brothers, 1933.
Tupper, E. Frank, "The Revival of Apocalyptic in Biblical and Theological Studies," *Review and Expositor* LXXII:3 (Summer, 1975).
Tushingham, A.D. *Excavations in Jerusalem, 1961-1967*, vol. I. Toronto: Royal Ontario Museum, 1985.
Tyndale, William. *A Prologue Upon the Gospel of St. John in Doctrinal Treatises and Introductions to Different Portions of the Holy Scriptures*, (ed. Henry Walter) [For the Parker Society]. Cambridge: Cambridge University Press, 1848.
Ubell, Earl. "Has Psycho-Probing Helped Anyone?" In: *Morality and Mental Health*, (ed. O.H. Mowrer). Chicago: Rand-McNalley, 1967.
van der Wall, C. "The Last Book of the Bible and the Jewish Apocalypses," *Neotestamentica* 12 (n.d.).
van Unnik, W.C. "The Purpose of St. John's Gospel." In: *The Gospels Reconsidered*. Oxford: Basil Blackwell, 1960.
Vawter, Bruce. "Some Recent Developments in Johannine Theology," *Biblical Theology Bulletin* 1 (1970).
Verkuyl, J. *Contemporary Missiology: An Introduction*. Grand Rapids: Eerdmans, 1978.
Vincent, L.H. "Le Lithostrotos Evangelique," *Revue Biblique* 59 (1952).
Vine, W.E. *An Expository Dictionary of New Testament Words*. London: Oliphants, Ltd., 1957.
Vitz, Paul. *Psychology as Religion*. Grand Rapids: Eerdmans, 1977.
Völker, W. *Das Vollkommenheitsideal des Origenes*. Tübingen: Mohr, 1931.

von Rad, Gerhard. *Old Testament Theology,* vol. III, (trans. D.M.G. Stalker). New York: Harper & Row, 1965.
Volz, P. *Die Eschatologie der judischen Gemeinde im neutestamentlischen Zeitalter.* Tübingen: Mohr, 1934.
Walvoord, John F. "Revelation" In: *The Bible Knowledge Commentary,* (eds. John F. Walvoord and Roy B. Zuck). Wheaton: Scripture Press, 1983.
Weder, Hans, "Die Menschwerdung Gottes Uberlegungen zur Auslegungsproblematik des Johannesevangeliums am Beispiel von Joh 6," *Zeitschrift für Theologie Und Kirche* 82 (1985).
Weiss, Johannes. *Jesus' Proclamation of the Kingdom of God,* (trans. and eds. Richard H. Hiers and David L. Holland). Philadelphia: Fortress, 1971.
Wendel, Francois. *Calvin: the Origens and Development of His Religious Thought.* London: Wm. Collins, 1963.
Wenham, G. *Numbers* [TOTC]. Intervarsity, 1981.
Westberg, Granger. "The Role of the Clergyman in Mental Health," *Pastoral Psychology* 11:104 (1950).
Westcott, B.F. *The Gospel According to John.* Grand Rapids: Eerdmans, 1908; reprint, 1954.
Wey, H. *Die Funktionen der bösen Geister bei den griechischen Apologeten des zweiten Jahrhunderts nach Christus.* Winterthur, 1957.
Whiting, R. "Six Snake Omens in New Babylonian Script," *JCS* 36 (1984).
Wilkinson, John. *Jerusalem Pilgrims Before the Crusades.* Jerusalem: Ariel Publishing House, 1977.
_____. *The Jerusalem Jesus Knew.* Nashville: Nelson, 1983.
Williamson, Edmond G. and Foley, John G. *Counseling and Discipline.* New York: McGraw-Hill, 1950.
Winn, Albert Curry. *A Sense of Mission: Guidance From the Gospel of John.* Philadelphia: Westminster, 1981.
Winston, D. *The Wisdom of Solomon* [AB 43]. N.J.: Doubleday, 1979.
Woollcott, Jr., Philip. "The Psychiatric Patient's Religion," *Journal of Religion* and *Health* 1:4 (1962).
Wren, Charles G. *Student Personnel Work in College.* New York: Ronald Press Co., 1951.
Yinger, J. Milton. *The Scientific Study of Religion.* New York: Macmillan, 1970.
Young, D. "With Snakes and Dates: A Sacred Marriage Drama at Ugarit," *UF* 9 (1977).
Zwingli, Ulrich. *On Providence and Other Essays,* (ed. William John Hinke). Durham: The Labyrinth Press, 1983.

Scripture Index

Hebrew Scriptures

Genesis	Page
1:ch.	99, 157
1:1	91
1:1-2:1	99
2:ch.	157
2:7	120
2:18f.	77
4:6-7	166
6:1-4	61
28:12	100
40:13	141
40:19	141

Exodus	
6:8	59
7:1	91
13:3	104
15:26	12
16:25	12
16:31	12
16:33	12
19:6	232
19:20	143-144
19:23	143
24:1-2	143
24:9	143
24:9-11	234
24:13	143
32:32-33	234
34:2-4	143
40:34-38	178

Leviticus	
18:6-23	77
18:29	77
20:10	100
3:4	59
7:5	63
10:3	62
11:1-3	135
11:10-33	135
13:7	63
17:5	59
20:ch.	133
20:1	133
20:2-9	133
20:10-13	133
20:14-21	133
20:22-29	133
21:ch.	132, 135-136, 139, 142, 146-147
21:1-3	133
21:4-9	132-136, 138-141, 143, 146-147
21:8	147
21:8-9	138
21:9	143
21:10-20	134
21:21-35	233
22-24:chs.	233
24:25	233
25:1-9	233
31:16	233
23:8	62
27:8	55, 62, 66
35:30	103

Numbers	
21:8 (LXX)	147

Deuteronomy	
6:4	178
6:20-25	134
7:6	103
8:3	13
8:9	134
8:14-16	138
9:18	13
18:18	148
19:15	100, 103
22:22	100
24:1-4	77
26:5-9	134
29:4	219
29:24f.	219
30:11-14	144
30:12f.	210
31:14	103
32:17	55

Judges
4-5:chs.	77
9:23	219

I Samuel
16:14	219
18:10	219
19:19	219

II Samuel
17:14	219
21:6	227

I Kings
12:15	219

II Kings
4:6 (B)	226
18:4	135-136
22:19-23	234

II Chronicles
13:22	209
24:29	209

Nehemiah
9:13-15	13
9:20	13

Esther
2-9:chs.	77

Psalms
2:1-3	233
2:6-8	233
2:9	233
2:9 (LXX)	233
22:ch.	25
25:10	104
33:6	99
33:9	99
36:ch.	63
38:3-8	154
56:8	234
58:6-11	234, 239
68:17	235
68:19	144
69:28	234
75:8	236
78:24f.	13
79:5-7	239
79:6,10,12	234
79:12	239
80:8,13	99
82:6	91
95:5	55
96:5	55
110:1	143
118:26	99
119:103	13
139:19-22	234, 239

Proverbs
9:5	13
30:4	144
31:10f.	77

Ecclesiastes
1:9	12

Isaiah
5:1-7	99
5:26	143
6:1	234
6:1-4	234
6:1-9:7	213
6:2 (LXX)	234
6:3	234
6:9-10	205-207, 215-216, 218-220
11:2	100
11:12	143
13:1-14:23	237
13:2	143
13:19	236
13:47	237
14:ch.	62
14:29	138
18:3	143
21:9	236
24-27:chs.	185
25:8	237
29:9f.	219
30:6	138
34:4	234
40-45:chs.	185
40:11	99
41:4	238
42:1-4	89, 95

44:3	95	15:1f.	99
44:6	237	19:10,14	99
44:23	95	34:1f.	99
45:7	105	37-38:chs.	204
47:7-8	237	37:24	99
47:10-11	237	38:4,11,14	237
49:1-6	89	38-39:chs.	185, 237
48:12	237	40:3,5	235
49:6	95	43:1-5	234
49:10	235	43:13,18	235
50:5-9	89	48:30-35	237
51:21-23	236		
52:13	142-143, 147	**Daniel**	
52:13 (LXX)	143	4:12	124
52:13-53:12	89, 95	7:ch.	233
53:ch.	95, 143	7:3-8	236
53:1 (LXX)	212	7:10	235
53:7-12	99	7:11	187
53:12	166	7:13	143, 233
53:28 (LXX)	217	7:13f.	143, 188
54:5	95	7:13-14	233
55:4-5	95	7:18	233
55:10-11	124	7:19	188
56-66:chs.	185	7:21,25	236
56:8	100	7:27	233
61:6	232	9:ch.	187
62:10	143	9:25-26	104
63:1-6	236	10:12-14,20-21	236
65:17	237	10:20f.	188
66:22	237	12:ch.	188, 236
		12:1	188, 234, 236
Jeremiah		12:2	100
2:21	99	12:3	188
15:16	235	12:11-12	187
23:1-4	99	**Hosea**	
25:15-29	236	8:14 (LXX)	228
31:31-34	129	10:1	99
50-51:chs.	237	**Joel**	
51:7-8	236	2:ch.	185
51:59-64	237	2:1	185
		2:1-11	185
Ezekiel		2:4-6	235
1:ch.	234	2:10-11	234
1:4-5,10,24,26-28	234	2:28	200
2:8-3:3	235	2:31	234
6:4,6 (LXX)	228	3:1	200
10:ch.	234	3:13	236

Amos
3:7	127
5:16-20	185

Micah
5:2	105

Habakkuk
2:15-16	236

Zechariah
1:7-17	234
4:1-6	235
4:11-14	235
6:1-8	234
9-11:chs.	185
12:10	233

Malachi
1:6	93
3:14,16	234
4:6	197

New Testament Scriptures

Matthew
1:23	213
3:1	197
5:38-48	163
7:13-14	167
10:7,32-33	197
10:40	95
11:1	62
11:11	119
12:1-8	90
12:18,40	59
12:46-49	82
13:7	61
13:14-15	207
13:22f.	62
13:23	56
13:24-30	124
16:16-19,28	197
18:10-13	197
18:30	217
19:24	165
20:28	165
22:3	217
22:17-21	70
22:37-39	161
23:24	165
24:ch.	197
24-25:chs.	185
24:6-7,9,29	198
24:30	233
24:34	198
25:40	126
25:44	126
27:19	224
28:8	204
28:16-20	88

Mark
1:15	197
3:15	113
3:17	159
3:19-35	113
4:3-9	124
4:35-6:6	113
4:10-12	207
4:26-29,31-32	124
5:25	204
8:14-21	113
8:18	207
8:22-30	113
8:31	142
8:38	197
9:1,12-13	197
9:31	142
9:37	95
10:30	128
10:32f.	142
10:35-45	165
10:43	128
10:46-52	113
13:ch.	185, 197, 204
13:7-9,24-25	198
15:16	224

Luke
4:38	81
7:28	119
7:46	8

8:1-3	79	1:19-23	70, 97
8:10	207	1:19-25	69
9:27	197	1:19-4:54	216
9:48	95	1:19-12:50	121
9:54	159	1:20	119
10:10	95	1:20-21	102
10:20	234	1:23	89, 99
11:30	140	1:24	101-102, 109
12:8-9	197	1:25	102
13:32	165	1:26	180
15:16	217	1:27	107, 119
15:22	204	1:28	101
15:38	217	1:29	99, 119
17:10	127	1:31,33-34,35-37	119
17:24,26	140	1:35f.	122
21:ch.	197	1:35-39	157
21:5-36	185	1:35-41	176
21:9-12,25-26	198	1:35-51	124
22:20	129	1:36	99, 119
22:24	82	1:37	122
22:24-27	165	1:38	81, 108, 122, 156
22:60	80	1:39	108-109, 122
23:13	224	1:40	122
23:34	163	1:40-42	159

John		1:41	87, 102, 104, 108, 122
1-4:ch.	40	1:42	79, 81, 108
1-12:ch.	89, 217	1:43	81, 122
1:1	50, 103, 105	1:43-51	173
1:1-2	116	1:44	100
1:1-3	174	1:45	99, 102, 122, 179
1:1-18	157, 216	1:46	100-102, 108-109
1:1-51	89	1:47	98, 108, 179
1:2	105	1:48	179
1:4	101, 106	1:49	73, 101, 122, 174
1:5	99, 106, 109	1:51	100, 106, 141, 143-145
1:6-7	119	2-12:chs.	212
1:7	88	2:1	100
1:9	106, 118	2:1-5	176
1:10	109, 130, 180	2:1-10	157
1:11	98, 109	2:1-11	97, 116, 162, 173
1:12	108, 176	2:1-12	100, 173
1:14	17, 43, 50, 91, 106, 108, 116-117, 178, 216	2:1-4:54	173
		2:1-11:57	89
1:16-17	157	2:23-3:36	140
1:17	103-104, 108, 159	2:3-12	82
1:19	98, 101	2:4	78, 116

2:5	176	3:16	86, 93, 109, 118
2:6	97	3:16-21	109, 146
2:7	62	3:17	119, 158
2:11	100, 113, 173, 177-178	3:18	108, 118, 139, 181
2:12	100	3:19	109, 118
2:13	100	3:19-21	140
2:13-17	162, 166	3:20	109
2:17	99	3:20-21	159
2:17 (LXX)	99	3:21	108, 122
2:18	98, 176	3:22-30	140
2:18-20	70	3:23	100
2:18-21	178	3:25	97, 109
2:18-22	174	3:27-28	119
2:19	76, 100, 109	3:29	97, 108, 119
2:21	81	3:30	119, 140
2:23	98, 100, 108, 113, 172-173	3:31	105
2:23-24	217	3:31-36	139-140
2:24	81, 217	3:34	119
2:25	157	3:35	108
3:ch.	132, 139-140, 146	4:ch.	87, 114
3:1	101	4:1	70, 81, 102
3:1-10	140, 168	4:1-42	116
3:1-13	174	4:3	173
3:1-15	72	4:3-26	157
3:1-21	139	4:3-54	100
3:2	113, 139-140, 172, 179	4:4-6	100
3:3	107-109, 113	4:5-10	78
3:4	140	4:6	78, 81
3:6	107	4:6-7	157
3:7	179	4:7-26	78
3:8	109, 140	4:8	97
3:9	140	4:9	67, 103, 179
3:10	109	4:10-19	174
3:10-11	139	4:11	100
3:11	76	4:12	99-100
3:11-21	140	4:13	109
3:12	140-141, 145	4:13-14	168, 175
3:13	43, 141, 143-145	4:16-18	158
3:13f.	140	4:19	102
3:13-14	143	4:20	100, 103
3:13-15	147	4:22	98
3:13-21	139	4:23-24	115
3:14	100, 125, 139, 141, 143-144	4:24	120
1:14f.	139, 142, 144	4:25	87, 101-102, 104, 108
1:14-15	132, 139-141, 146-147, 161	4:27	78
3:15	109, 146-147	4:28-29	179
3:15-16	175		

4:29	78, 101	5:24	95, 109, 118, 120, 178
4:31-34	164	5:24f.	11
4:31-42	124	5:26	122
4:34	95, 118-119, 125	5:26-27	144
4:35	100, 164	5:27	143, 147
4:36	124	5:28-29	167
4:38	90, 119-121	5:29	100
4:39	124, 179	5:30	94, 96, 118-120
4:40	168	5:30-47	95
4:42	101, 179-180	5:33	109
4:43	173	5:33-36	95-96
4:45	172	5:36	95-96, 113, 119, 125, 174, 176
4:46	100		
4:46-54	113, 162	5:36-38	95
4:47	100, 113	5:37	95-96, 119
4:48	88	5:38	96, 119, 180
4:49	100	5:39	99, 101-102, 104, 109
4:50	177	5:39-40	95
4:51	100	5:40	122, 167
4:53	177	5:43	109
4:54	113, 173	5:44	76, 95
5:ch.	84, 90, 94	5:45f.	101
5:1	101	5:45-47	95, 160
5:1-9	89	6:ch.	1, 3, 9-16, 38, 44, 51, 90, 145, 216
5:1-18	113		
5:1-21	90	6-8:chs.	41
5:2	108, 222	6:1	100
5:4	90	6:1-2	156
5:8	90	6:1-14	89, 125, 157
5:9-18	101, 103	6:1-71	100
5:10	98, 103, 113, 180	6:2	122, 172
5:10-16	71	6:3-4	100
5:13	113	6:4-9	177
5:14	158	6:6	180
5:14-15	168	6:10	89
5:15-47	76	6:14	101-102, 180
5:16-30	91	6:15	73, 102, 160
5:17	91-92, 99, 175	6:15-21	156
5:18	91, 98	6:17	100
5:19	92	6:18	180
5:19-20	92	6:18f.	100
5:22-24	92	6:19	100
5:22-29	92	6:22-25	156
5:23	94, 120	6:23-24	100
5:23f.	119	6:25-34	180
5:23-24	95	6:25-59	125

6:26-27	158, 160	7:1-9	100
6:27	11, 125, 144, 168, 180	7:2	101
6:28	101	7:2-10	82
6:29	88, 119, 180-181	7:4	172
6:30	11, 101, 176	7:7	109, 118
6:30f.	104	7:10	101
6:31	99-100, 108	7:10-13	71
6:32f.	12, 14	7:11	157
6:33	14	7:11-13	98
6:35	122, 181	7:13	98
6:37	122, 181	7:15	71, 98
6:38	104, 119-120	7:16	95, 119-120
6:38-39	95	7:17	167
6:38-40	94	7:18	95, 119-120, 164
6:39	109	7:19	103
6:39-40	10	7:20	55
6:40	109, 181	7:22	100
6:41	98	7:22-23	90, 103
6:41-58	76	7:22-24	104
6:42	82	7:23	103
6:44	10, 95 119	7:25-67	71
6:45	99, 109, 122, 169	7:26	102
6:46	143	7:26f.	101
6:47	10	7:27	102
6:47-63	38	7:28	119
6:48-51	12, 14	7:28-29	95
6:49	108	7:29	119
6:50	9	7:31	98, 102, 104, 172
6:51-58	173, 180	7:32	101
6:51-59	15	7:32-35	71
6:52	98	7:32-36	76
6:53	144	7:33	119
6:53-54	109	7:35	97-98
6:54	10, 60	7:37	101, 122
6:57	95, 119-120	7:39	94, 120
6:59	100, 102	7:40	109
6:60-71	125	7:40-43	101
6:62	144	7:40-52	71, 102
6:63	9, 104, 117	7:41-42	102
6:64	81, 180	7:42	99, 105, 108
6:66	122, 125, 180	7:45	101
6:68-69	79, 122, 180	7:47	102
6:69	125	7:48	101-102, 180
6:70	106	7:49	103
7:1	71, 98, 217	7:50-51	72
7:1-5	157	7:51	100, 103

7:52	102, 109	9:1-7	89
8:ch.	90	9:1-14	90
8:1	100	9:1-41	113, 121, 125
8:1f.	100	9:3	113
8:1-11	157-158	9:4	119-120
8:3	101	9:5	106, 118
8:3-11	74	9:6f.	109
8:7,10-11	78	9:7	108
8:11	167	9:7-8	98
8:12	106, 109, 118, 122, 125	9:13f.	102
8:12-10:21	122	9:13-18	102
8:13	102	9:13-29	168
8:14	164	9:13-34	71
8:16	95, 119	9:14	103
8:17	99-100, 103-104	9:16	101, 172
8:18	95, 119	9:17	102
8:21-29	118	9:18	107, 180
8:22	98	9:22	98, 102
8:23	105, 118	9:34	167
8:26	95, 119-120	9:35f.	144
8:26-29	164	9:38	125
8:28	125, 141-142, 144-145, 161	9:39	118
8:29	95, 119-120	9:39-41	118, 125
8:30f.	101	10:1f.	99
8:30-31	89, 98	10:1-15	161
8:30-40	118	10:1-42	122
8:31	98	10:4	122
8:32	159	10:11	164
8:33	68, 108	10:11f.	122
8:34	108-109	10:12-13	164
8:37	108	10:14-16	98
8:39	160	10:16	90, 92, 122, 124
8:41-47	118	10:17-18	161
8:42	105, 119-120	10:18	129
8:44	106, 158	10:19	98
8:44-45	180	10:20f.	55
8:46	160	10:22-23	101
8:48	55, 103	10:22-26	180
8:48-59	71	10:22-38	72, 76
8:49	94	10:24	69, 98, 101
8:52	55	10:25	125
8:54	94	10:27-28	161
8:56	99	10:27-29	181
8:59	98	10:30-36	69
9:1f.	103	10:31	98
9:1-3	167	10:32-33	113

10:33	116	12:1-3	157
10:34	99, 104	12:1-17:26	89
10:36	119	12:3-8	78
10:37-38	125	12:10	101-102
10:40	101	12:10-11	72, 98
11-12:chs.	121	12:13	99, 102, 108
11:1	101	12:13-15	73
11:1-44	89	12:15	99
11:1-57	113	12:19	74, 102, 157
11:5	81	12:20	101, 124
11:7f.	81	12:20f.	97
11:7-8	106	12:20-24	90
11:8	98	12:20-36	95
11:8-10	160	12:21	100, 124
11:8-16	72	12:23	124-125, 144
11:9	118, 159	12:23-26	121-122, 126, 128
11:14	177	12:23-33	218
11:15	88, 177	12:24	124
11:16	108	12:24-25	161
11:17-44	97	12:25	122-123
11:18	101	12:26	94, 113, 118, 123,
11:23-35	78		126, 128, 161
11:24-26	176	12:27	81, 166
11:25	116	12:28	108
11:26	109	12:31	106, 109, 118, 207
11:33	108, 116	12:32	121, 125, 145
11:33-35	162	12:32-33	161
11:33-37	72	12:32-34	141-142, 144
11:34	108-109, 166	12:34	99, 101-102, 125, 144
11:35	81, 116	12:35	106, 109, 159
11:38	81, 108, 166	12:36	106, 108-109, 217
11:42	95, 98, 119-120	12:36-43	216
11:45	98, 180	12:36-50	121
11:45-53	72	12:37	217, 172, 175
11:47	102, 172	12:37f.	212
11:47-48	101	12:38	89, 212, 217
11:48	102	12:38 (LXX)	99
11:48-52	98	12:39	217-218
11:49-51	101	12:39f.	212
11:49-52	74	12:40	89, 99, 113, 205-206,
11:51-52	98		209, 212, 215, 218
11:52	90, 102, 124	12:41	212
11:54	101	12:42	98, 102, 218
11:55	97, 100-101	12:42f.	212
11:57	72, 101-102	12:42-43	74, 160, 180
12:1	101	12:43	218

12:44	95, 218	14:16	156
12:44f.	119	14:17	118
12:44-45	120	14:21	129
12:44-50	125	14:21-24	162
12:46	106, 109, 118	14:24	95, 119-120
12:47-48	118	14:26	119-120, 156
12:49	95, 119-120	14:27	166
12:49f.	129	14:30	106, 109, 118, 175
13:ch.	79	14:31	129
13-17:chs.	129	15:1f.	99
13-21:chs.	121	15:1-8	106
13:1	125, 127, 166	15:1-11	166, 181
13:1-11	114	15:1-17	124, 126
13:2	106, 108	15:2	109
13:3-5	116	15:5,8-17	126
13:3-17	82, 165	15:10	129
13:4-11	127	15:12	106, 126, 129, 162
13:5-11	79	15:12-13	114
13:8	123	15:12-17	82
13:12-20	114, 127	15:13	162
13:13	127	15:15	113, 126-127
13:16	119-121, 127	15:18	116
13:17	113, 126	15:18f.	118
13:18	99	15:18-25	98
13:20	95, 116, 119-121	15:20	116, 127, 161
13:21,23	81	15:21	95, 119
13:24	80	15:21-25	118
13:27	106, 175	15:25	99, 104
13:31	144	15:26	119-120, 156
13:33	98, 128	15:26-16:11	180
13:34-35	82, 106, 114, 126-128, 162	16:1-3	161
		16:2	103, 109
13:35	83, 126	16:5	95, 119
13:36f.	123, 128	16:7	119-120, 156, 166
13:36-38	80	16:8-11	118
13:37	123	16:11	106, 109, 118
13:38	123, 158	16:13	166
14:1-6	166	16:13-15	156
14:2-3	128	16:17	109
14:5	180	16:24	166
14:9	81	16:28	106
14:9-11	116	16:32	124
14:10	113, 175	16:33	106, 118, 166, 175
14:11-12	125	17:ch.	115
14:14	16f.	17:1	125
14:15	129, 162	17:2	108-109

17:3	83, 119	18:29	101
17:4	118, 164	18:29-19:16	73
17:5	118, 143	18:33	101
17:6	108	18:33-37	102
17:7-8	158	18:33-38	77
17:8	95, 109, 119	18:35	98, 101-102
17:10	109	18:36	98, 113, 118
17:11	108-109, 118	18:37	109
17:12	99, 108	18:38	97
17:15	116, 118	19:ch.	223
17:17 (LXX)	99	19:4	95
17:18	90, 96, 119-121	19:6	101-102
17:20	115-116	19:8	102
17:20-21	158, 163	19:10-22	77
17:20-26	83, 181	19:12	102, 109
17:21	95, 119-120	19:12-15	73
17:22	94	19:13	101, 108, 222, 227
17:22-26	162	19:13 (SYR.)	227
17:23	119, 130	19:15	101-102
17:24	94, 118, 143	19:17	101, 108, 222
17:25	95, 118-119	19:19	102
17:26	108	19:20	101
18:ch.	80	19:20-21	98
18-19:chs.	225	19:21	102
18:1	100	19:21-22	73
18:1-20:31	89	19:23f.	99
18:2-13	157	19:24 (LXX)	99
18:3	73, 101-102	19:25	79
18:3-8	166	19:25-27	78, 82
18:9	99	19:26	81
18:10	74	19:28	99
18:10-11	80	19:30	118, 164
18:12	73, 101	19:31	97, 101, 103
18:13-14	101	19:35	88, 99
18:15-18	74, 123	19:36-37	99
18:15-27	80	19:38	98, 101-102
18:17	123, 180	19:39	179
18:18	73, 101	19:39-40	72
18:19	74	19:40	97
18:20	98, 102, 160	19:41	101
18:22	73, 101	19:42	101, 103
18:24	101	20:ch.	80
18:25-27	123, 157	20:1-10	173
18:26	74	20:2-10	81
18:28	97, 101, 116	20:3	124
18:28f.	222	20:10-29	174

20:16	108	10:6f.	210
20:19	98, 123	12:29	83
20:20-21	116	14:10	196
20:21	90, 96, 116, 119, 120-121	15:14	206
20:22	120	**I Corinthians**	
20:24	108	3:13	196
20:27-28	116	7:29,31	196
20:29	174	10:1-4	60, 211
20:30-31	87, 163, 171-172	10:1-6	210
20:31	88, 124, 174, 176-177, 181	10:19-21	55
21:ch.	80, 173-174	15:ch.	185
21:1	100	15:1-2	196
21:1-25	89	15:20	197
21:2	100, 108, 173	15:24-26	196
21:3	198	15:28	64
21:6	198, 200	15:36-38	124
21:7	81	15:50-52	196
21:12	217	15:54-56	210
21:15f.	122, 130	**II Corinthians**	
21:15-17	163	1:5	141
21:15-19	93, 115	4:4	217
21:15-22	123	4:16-5:10	196
21:19	94, 123	5:5,8,10	196
21:20,25	81	5:17	197
		6:2	210
Acts		**Galatians**	
2:7	173	4:7	127
2:17f.	200	4:22-31	211
2:33	141	**Ephesians**	
3:14-17	163	1-2:chs.	201
4:13-21	70	4:8-11	210
5:31	141	6:11	66
7:56	143	6:12	62
12:7	203	**Philippians**	
19:30	217	1:1	201
20:35	165	2:ch.	40
28:26f.	207	2:5-11	39
		3:10-11	201
Romans		4:3	234
1:1	127	**Colossians**	
1:1-4,16-17	115	2:15	59
1:20	91	**I Thessalonians**	
1:21-23	93	4-5:chs.	185
3:21-22	115	4:13-18	195
8:29-30	196		
9:11:chs.	216		
9:7f.	210		

4:15-18	196	1:16	204
5:1-11	196	2-3:chs.	174
II Thessalonians		2:6	233
2:1-8	196	2:10	203
2:1-12	185, 201	2:12	204
2:2	196	2:14-15	233
3:10	112	2:16	204
		2:25	203
Hebrews		2:27	233-234
2:6-9	210	3:3	203
2:14-18	157	3:5	234
3:1	120	3:8	232
3:7-19	210	3:11	203-204
7:ch.	210	4:ch.	234
10:5-10	210	4-5:chs.	188
12:1-3	161	4-11:chs.	200
12:23	234	4:1-8:5	193
		4:2-3, 5-8	234
James		5:1-8:5	174
1:1	201	5:10	232
I Peter		6:1-8	234
2:9-10	232	6:2-7:1	198
2:21-25	99	6:5	234
		6:9-10	238
II Peter		6:12-14	234
3:1-15	201	7:16-17	235
3:9	167	7:17	237
I John		8:2-11:19	193
2:1	156	9:1,3-11	235
2:3-6	162	9:6	232, 235
2:11	207	9:7,9,16	235
		7:20	55
Jude		10:6	203
:1	201	10:8-11	235
:9	236	11:1-7	235
Revelation		11:18	237
1:1	195, 201-203	12:1-15:4	194
1:1-8	193	12:5	233-234
1:3	193, 202	12:7	232
1:4	195	12:7-9,14	236
1:4-8	193	13:1-7	236
1:6	232	13:8	234
1:7	202, 233	14:8	236
1:8	202, 238	14:9-20	237
1:9	195, 201	14:13	202
1:9-3:22	193	14:14-20	236

15:1-16:20	194
16:5-7	238
16:14	57, 188
16:15	202
17:1-19:10	194
17:8	234
17:9-12	193
18:ch.	236-238
18:7,18,21	237
19:5	234
19:9	202
19:11	204
19:11-21:8	194
19:13	204
19:15	204, 233, 236
20:4-22:5	204
20:6	202, 233
20:6f.	187
20:7-10	237
20:11	188
20:12,15	234
21:ch.	187
21:1f.	188
21:1,4	237
21:6	238
21:9-22:5	194
21:12-14	237
21:18-21	202
21:27	234
22:6	203
22:6-21	194
22:7	193, 195, 202-204
22:8-9	195
22:10	193, 195, 202, 204
22:10-21	193
22:12	203-204
22:13	184, 238
22:14	202
22:18-19	193, 195
22:20	187, 202-204

Ancient Writings Index

Apocrypha

Tobit
4:6	109
13:6	109
13:16-17	202

I Macc.
1:41	191
4:46	191

Wisd. of Sol.
9:6-18	144
11-19:chs.	139
16:5-7	139
16:20-23,26	13

Sirach
15:3	13
24:21-23	13
48:22-25	214

Baruch
3:29	144

Jewish Ancient Writings

Abraham, Apoc. of   185
10:17-18	188
10:29	187
29:17	188

Abraham, Test. of   144

Asher, Test. of
6:5	55

Barnabas
18	63

Baruch, Apoc. of
29:3-30:1	104

II Baruch   12
6:8f.	188
27:ch.	187
29:8	12
30:1	188
32:4	188
50:ch.f.	188
70:8	187
73:1	188
85:10	187

IV Baruch
2:1-8	144

Benjamin, Test. of
3:3f.	55

Elijah, Book of   185

I Enoch
I Eno.	185
6:ch.	61
15:ch.	61
22:51	188
48:ch.f.	188
50:1	188
51:4	188
71:ch.	144
85:ch.	187
89:59f.	188
93:ch.	187

Esdras, Apoc. of   185
4:5	187
7:32-33	188
8:52-55	188

Isaiah, Ascension of   185

Isaiah, Martyrdom of
2:9	144
3:7-10	144

Jubilees
1:11	55

Judah, Testament of
16:ch.	63

Joseph and Aseneth   1-9, 11-16
7:1	5, 8
8:5	3, 6
8:5-7	3-5
8:9	3-4, 11
8:11	3

11:17	14	**Mekilta**	
12:1f.	11	Ex. 13:3	104
12:2-4	14	Ex. 15:26	12
14:12-15:2	10	Ex. 16:25,33	12
14-17:chs.	6	Ex. 19:20	144
15:4	3,10	**Midrash Psalms**	
15:5	3-4, 11	Ps. 25:10	104
15:7	11		
15:10	10	**Midrash Rabbah**	
15:12	11	Ex. 31:3	103
16:ch.	5-6, 12	Lev. 4:6	103
16:14	6, 9-10, 12	Eccl. 1:4	105
16:15f.	5, 12	Eccl. 1:8	103, 105
16:16	3-4, 6-7, 10	Eccl. 1:9	12
18:9-11	10		
18:10f.	10	**Mishnah**	
18:12f.	10	Abod. Zar. 3:4	103
19:4	10	Pir. Ab. 2:6	104
19:5	3-4, 7	Pir. Ab. 7:6	104
19:10f.	7	Sanh. 3:5	97
20:6f.	10	Sotah 3:4	78
20:7	11	Ros. Hash. 3:8	135, 139
21:5	3	**Moses, Apoc. of**	185
21:13f.	6		
21:21	3-4, 6	**Moses, Assumpt. of**	185
22:13	11	10:2	188
27:10	11	**Codex Neofiti I**	12
Josephus		**Oracles, Sibylline**	12
Ant. III.1, 6	12	frag. 3:34f.	12
Ant. VIII.46-49	60	frag. 3:46-49	12
Ant. XVI.6.2 [163]	101	4:24-30	8
Ant. XVII.254f.	98		
Life. 346	98	**Patri., Test. of 12**	185
War 1:403	228		
War 2.8.4 [124]	107	**Pesiqta 102f.**	104
War 2.175-176	223	**Philo**	12, 209
War 2.301	223-224, 228	Ouis Rerum	
War 2.305	228	Divinarum Heres 39	13
War 2.308	223	Delegation to	
War 2.429	229	Gaius 38	223
War 2.438-440	224		
War 4.156-181	224	**Prophets, Lives of**	214
War 5.467	223	**Pseudo-Philo**	
War 5.51	227	Liber Antiquitatum	
War 7.2	229	Biblicarum 19:5	13

Qumran

Dead Sea Scrolls	199, 210, 212-214
CD 2:5,15	106
CD 3:16	109
CD 6:19f.	106
CD 8:16	106
CD 8:22	109
Damascus Document	210
Habbakuk Commentary	210
1QH 1:20	105
1QH 10:9	105
1QM 1:1f.	106
1QM 15:9	109
1QS 1:3-4	106
1QS 1:5	109
1QS 1:7-8,10,18	106
1QS 1:20	109
1QS 1:24	106
1QS 2:4-5	106
1QS 2:7,10,18	109
1QS 2:20-23	106
1QS 3:2	106
1QS 3:15,25	105
1QS 4:2	106
1QS 4:12	109
1QS 5:3	109
1QS 5:11,25	106
1QS 6:4-23	106
1QS 7-1f.	106
1QS 8:2,6	109
1QS 9:17-18	106
1QS 10:18	106
1QS 11:1	106
1QS 11:11	105
War Scroll	185, 199

Recension A 10-15   144

Recension B 8-12   144

Reuben, Test. of
2:ch.	55
2-3:chs.	63

Siphre
Num. 35:30	103
Deut. 31:14	103

Solomon, Psa. of   185
17:36	104
17:23-36	105
18:6-8	105

Babylonian Talmud
Yoma 75b	13
Yoma 85a-b	104

Palestinian Talmud
Ned. 38b	104

Targums
Jonathan	135
Isaiah 6:1	212
Onkelos	135

Palestinian Targums
Deut. 30:11-14	144
Psa. 68:19	144
Psa. 78:25	13
Micah 5:1	102

Ps. Jonathan   139

Tos. Shab. 15-16   104

Zodakite Doc. 9:10   104

Non-Jewish Ancient Writings

Acta. Pet.
11	61

Acta. Thom.
42-49,73-81	61

Mary, Apoc. of   185

Paul, Apoc. of   185

Peter, Apoc. of   185

Apuleius
De Deo Socratis	56
De idol. 9	57

Aristotle
Politics I, 2:12	78

Athanasius
Life of Antony — 55

Athenagoras
Leg. 24f. — 61
Leg. 26f. — 56

Clement of Alex.
Protrep. II. 40-41 — 58
Strom. II. 20:113 — 55
Strom. VI.3 — 58
Exc. Theod. 51-52 — 55
Ecl. proph. 20:1 — 55
Ecl. proph. 46 — 64

Cyprian
Ep. 75:15 — 60

Didache
9-10:chs. — 8
18:5f.chs. — 8

Felix, Minucius
Octavius 26f. — 55, 57

Hermas
Mandates
  2:3 — 55
  5:2-7 — 55
  6:2 — 63
  8:3-7 — 55
  10:1 — 55
Similitudes
  6:2 — 55
  9:22-23 — 55

Hippocrates
Sacred Disease 1-3 — 55

Hippolytus
Ref. omn. haer. IV. 28 — 57
Ref. omn. haer. IV. 35 — 57
Ref. omn. haer. VI. 2 — 58

Ignatius
Eph. 19 — 59

Irenaeus
Adv. haer. II.32.4 — 61

Justin (Martyr)
Apol.I.5 — 58
Apol.I.12 — 56
Apol.I.26 — 58
Apol.I.49.5 — 102
Apol.I.56-58 — 58
Apol.II.1 — 58
Apol.II.5 — 56, 59-62
Apol.II.6 — 60
Apol.II.7-8 — 58
Apol.II.8 — 60
Apol.II.12 — 58
Dial. 8:3 — 105
Dial. 18 — 58
Dial. 30 — 60
Dial. 45 — 59
Dial. 49:1 — 105
Dial. 76 — 60
Dial. 78 — 59
Dial. 76, 85 — 60
Dial. 95:4 — 103
Dial. 131 — 58
Dial. 133:6 — 103
Mar. of Polycarp 13:1 — 103

Lactantius
Div. inst. II.17 — 57
Div. inst. IV.15 — 57

Laertius, Diogenes
VIII.32 — 56

Lucian
Jup. Trag. 15,22 — 56
Icaromenippus 26f. — 56
Philopseudes 16 — 60

Origen
Comm. Cant. III.15 — 64
Comm. in Joh. 11,7 — 62
Comm. in Joh. VI.54 — 60
Comm. in Matt. XI.1 — 62

Comm. in Matt. XII.18	59	VIII.41	59
Comm. in Matt. XII.40	59	VIII.43	57, 59
Comm. in Matt. XIII.7	61	VIII.44	60
Comm. in Matt. XIII.22f.	62	VIII.58	60
Comm. in Matt. XIII.23	56	VIII.61	61-63
Contra Celsum	55	VIII.62	56
I.6	57, 60	VIII.65	58
I.31	58	VIII.69	59
I.46	61	De princ. pref. 6	61
I.60	59	De princ. I.5.3	61
I.67-68	57	De princ.I.5.4f.	62
I.68	60	De princ.I.5.5	62
II.49	60	De princ.I.8.1	56
II.51	57	De princ.I.8.3	62
III.26f.	56-57	De princ.III.2.1-2	62-63
III.29	59	De princ.III.2.3-4	64
III.37	56, 58	De princ.III.2.4-5	63
IV.32	56-57	De princ.III.3.2-3	58-59
IV.33	60	De princ.III.5.7-8	65
IV.92, 93f.	56	Exh. to Mart. 43	60
V.5	58, 62	Exh. to Mart. 45	56
V.54-55	61	Hom. in Jesu Nave I.6, 7	63
VI.8	58	Hom. in Jesu Nave II.8	63
VI.41	58-59		
VI.45	57, 62	Hom. in Jesu Nave VIII.2	63
VI.80	57		
VII.3	56	Hom. in Jesu Nave VIII.3	59
VII.4	61		
VII.5-6	56	Hom. in Jesu Nave VIII.7	63
VII.6	56		
VII.7, 9	58	Hom. in Jesu Nave IX.10	59
VII.35	56		
VII.64	55-56	Hom. in Jesu Nave XII.1-2	63
VII.65	55		
VII-67	60	Hom. in Jesu Nave XIII.3	64
VII.69	55, 57-58, 62		
VII.70	62	Hom. in Jesu Nave XIII.4	59, 62
VIII.13	55, 62		
VIII.24f.	56	Hom. in Jesu Nave XIV.1	59
VIII.27	59		
VIII.29f.	56	Hom. in Jesu Nave XV.4-5	64
VIII.31	58, 62		
VIII.33	62	Hom. in Jesu Nave XV.5	59, 62, 64
VIII.34	59, 66		
VIII.36	59, 64	Hom. in Jesu Nave XV.6	63, 65
VIII.39	58-59		

Hom. in Jesu Nave XX.1	61
Hom. in Jesu Nave XXIV.1	60
Hom. Luc.34.4	63
Hom. Num.III.4	59
Hom. Ex.V.5	60
Hom. Ex.VI.3	60
Hom. Ex.VI.8	59
Hom. Num.VII.5	63
Hom. Num.X.3	62
Hom. Num.XIII.7	63
Hom. Num.XVII.5	59
Hom. Num.XVII.8	55, 62
Hom. Num.XXVII.8	66
Sel. in Ps. 36	63

Philastratus
Vita Apoll. IV.20   60

Plato
Symposium 202 E-203A	56
Epinomis 984D-985B	56
Timaeus 91A	78

Plutarch
Lives 309	55
Moralia 415A-418D	56

Porphyry
De abstinentia 2.34   56

Ps. Clement
De Virg. I.12   61

Tatian
Or. 14   62

Sophia of Jesus Christ   185

Tertullian
Apol. 22	57-58, 62
Apol. 23	57, 60
Apol. 27	60
Apol. 32	58
Apol. 35	57
Adv. Marc. II.10	62

Ugarit RS 24.244   137

Key Word, Subject, Place Index

Adultry, 54, 74, 76, 78, 100, 158, 167
Aelia Captiolina, 230
Alexandria, 223
Alloeosis, 45-46
Alpha, 238
Amen, 108-109
American, 93
Anabaptist, 38, 43, 49, 51
Angels, 6, 10, 13-14, 59, 61-63, 144, 187 188, 203, 232, 235-236
Anger (Wrath), 64, 100, 106
Anthropology, 86
Antiochus IV Epiphanes, 236
Anti-trinitarian, 36
Apocalypse, 182-195, 198-199, 201-204
Apocalyptic, 10, 182-183, 185-190, 192, 193-197, 199-203, 235, 238
Apocalyptic Scholarship . . . , 182-204
Apocalypticism, 183, 187, 189, 200
Apocalyptist, 186-188, 190
Apollinarist, 43, 50
Apostle, 29, 34, 39, 42, 48, 79, 120, 122, 159, 163-164, 176, 194-195, 197-198, 200, 216, 227
Arab, 92-93, 227
Arad, 133
Aramaic, 107-109, 141, 159, 215, 222, 227, 230-231
Archaeology . . . , 221-230
Arianism, 42
Armenian Garden, 224-225
Ascension, 26, 44, 52, 141-142, 144, 188, 195, 200
Asia, 84
Asia Minor, 194, 201

Baal, 233
Baal-peor, 233
Babylon, 191, 199, 235-237
Baptism, 59-60, 81, 89, 101, 114, 119
Bar Kochba Revolt, 223
Bashan, 134
Bear, 236
Bee, 7

Belial, 106
Bema, 223-224, 227-228
Bethany, 101
Bethany, Beyond Jordan, 101
Bethesda, Pool of, 90, 100, 108, 168, 222
Bethlehem, 23-24, 102, 105
Bible, 39, 47, 94, 112, 123, 130, 148-149, 157, 165, 196, 199, 215, 218, 220
Birth, New, 107
Birth, Virgin, 27, 41
Blasphemy, 72, 116
Bodmer II ($^P66$), 88
Body, 37, 43-44, 61, 79, 116, 196
Bread, Cup, Ointment, 3, 5, 7-8, 10, 16
Bread from Heaven, 14
Bread of Life, 1, 5-7, 9-16, 44, 98, 117, 122, 125
Buddhist, 84-86
Byzantines, 223, 229-230

Caesar, 73, 75, 162
Caesarea Maritima, 223
Cana, 82, 100, 173, 176, 178
Canaan, 133, 228
Canon, 24, 34-35, 172, 195
Capernaum, 82, 100
Chariot, 235
China, 84-85
Christian, 2-3, 13, 15-16, 18, 26, 31, 33, 34-35, 55-60, 62-63, 66, 85-87, 92, 95, 105, 110, 115, 124, 126, 130, 132, 148, 156, 167-168, 182, 185, 192-194, 196, 199-201, 205, 208-209, 212, 214-215, 220, 222, 226, 230, 232-235, 237
Christianity, 31-32, 34, 46, 54, 62, 65, 84, 200-201, 208, 216
Christmas, 52
Christology, 9, 18, 22, 25-29, 33, 35, 37-38, 40-42, 45-46, 48-50, 52-53, 85, 87, 89, 115-116, 119, 132
Christology, Johannine . . . , 36-53

287

Church, 18, 21, 23, 34-35, 38, 42, 51, 61, 67, 79, 86, 89-90, 92, 96, 109, 111-112, 114-115, 117-121, 123-124, 126-131, 146, 153-154, 168-169, 181, 194-196, 200-201, 219, 233, 235, 238-239
Citadel, 224
City, Upper, 228
Commandment, 14, 128-130, 162, 206, 217
Commission, Great, 96, 116, 119
Communicatio Naturarum, 46
Context, Socio-cultural, 67
Convent, Sisters of Zion, 222, 230
Conversion, 4, 6, 11, 66, 86, 88, 124
Council of Chalcedon (Creed), 37-39
Council of Nicea (Creed), 37-39
Counsel, 149, 155-156, 158, 169
Counselee, 149, 164
Counseling, 148-149, 151, 153, 157-158, 163, 165, 168-169
Counseling, Christian, 168-169
Counseling, Christian Psychological, 148, 152
Counseling from John . . . , 148-170
Counseling, Ministerial, 166
Counseling, Psychological, 148, 160-162
Counselor, 148-149, 155-156, 158-160, 162-165, 167, 169, 180
Covenant, 129, 138, 219
Creation, 41, 49, 65, 85-86, 99, 105, 112, 118, 126, 159, 196, 237
Criticism, Historical, 18, 21, 28, 35
Criticism, New Testament, 230
Criticism, Redaction, 10, 22, 171-172, 179
Criticism, Textual, 54
Cross, 37, 40, 44, 89, 128-129, 131, 141-142, 146-147, 161, 163-164, 223
Crusader, 225
Cultic Ritual, Significance of, 6-8
Culture, 67-68, 79, 86, 92, 94, 184

Damascus, 226
Damascus, Great Mosque of, 226
Death, 38-39, 42-43, 65, 70, 72-74, 80, 92, 96, 101, 107, 116, 118, 121-124, 128-129, 131, 133, 135-138, 140, 143-144, 147, 161-165, 174-175, 178, 191, 193, 196-197, 200, 203, 222, 232, 234, 238
Devil, 41-45, 62, 106, 108, 153, 236
Diaspora, 68, 89, 98
Didache, 88
Disciple, 70, 72, 74-76, 78-83, 87, 89, 94, 98, 114-116, 118-131, 155-156, 159, 161-164, 166, 171, 176-179, 197, 216
Docetism, 33, 47
Dualism, 105, 186

Eanon, 100
Easter, 52, 123
Ebionite, 33
Ecce Homo Arch, 223
Edom, 133-134, 236
Education, 65, 155
Egypt, 24, 60, 133, 137-138, 191, 221, 238
Eilat, 137
Election, 42, 95, 107, 121, 186
Emperor, 59
End Time, 186-188, 190-191, 196, 199, 203
Enlightenment, The, 34
Ephesus, 233
Ephraim, 101
Epistemology, 18, 21
Esagila, 137
Eschatology, 10-11, 94, 105-106, 176, 183, 184, 187, 189-192, 196, 199-200, 238
Eschatology, Apocalyptic, 184
Eschatology, Existential, 184
Eschatology, Inaugurated, 184
Eschatology, Prophetic, 184
Eschatology, Realistic, 184
Eschatology, Realized, 184, 196, 201
Eschatology, Thoroughgoing, 184

Essence, 39, 41, 45, 50, 61, 138, 153
Essene, 107
Eternity, 44, 89, 92, 94-95, 104, 117, 122, 124-125, 132, 146-147, 157, 160, 175-176, 181, 192, 234, 237
Ethics, 112, 128, 130, 158, 169, 186
Euphrates, 237
Eutyches, 37, 51
Evangelism, 87-89, 92, 117, 124, 152, 187, 212
Exaltation, 141, 143, 145-147, 193
Execution, 97
Ex Eventu, 186, 193
Exorcism, 60, 113, 175

Faith, 18, 26-27, 35, 41, 44-45, 48, 50-51, 61, 65-66, 71, 87-89, 95, 99, 111-113, 118, 121, 123-128, 131-133, 135, 138, 146-147, 160-161, 166, 169, 171, 174, 176-181, 186-187, 192, 200, 203, 219, 233-235, 238
Filioque, 38
Flesh, 116-119, 126, 154, 196
Fortress of Antonio, 222-224, 230
Fourth Gospel and Christology . . ., 17-35
France, 161
Function, 205, 207, 216

Gabbatha, 101, 108, 221-224, 227-230
Gate, Damascus, 230
Gate, Sheep, 90
Gentile, 4-7, 15, 54-55, 58, 97-98, 100, 124
Gerizim, 100, 103
Gezer, 137
Glory/Honor, 89, 91-94, 117, 120-121, 124, 128, 131, 162, 164, 178, 181, 188, 192-193, 196, 214, 218, 234, 238
Gnosticism, 98, 105
God-consciousness, 26, 31-34
Godhead, 44-45
God-man, 47

Gog, 237
Golgotha, 101, 108, 222
Gospel, 22, 37, 50, 57, 59, 64-65, 69-70, 74, 79, 81-90, 93-101, 103, 105-118, 122, 124, 126-128, 130-132, 139, 142, 145, 148, 155, 157, 159, 165, 169, 171-172, 174-175, 218, 220
Gospels, Synoptic, 17-19, 22-24, 28-29, 40, 97, 108-110, 112-114, 123, 142-143, 165, 175-176, 197, 207, 213-215, 222, 224, 230
Governor, 59, 75
Grace, 43, 46, 50, 90-91, 104, 108, 135, 138, 157
Greeks, 67-69, 87, 97, 101, 107, 124, 153, 184, 191, 199, 208-209, 221, 225
Greek (Language), 99, 107-109, 148, 153, 159, 208, 215, 227-228, 231-232

Hadrian, 223, 230
Halakah, 14
Hathor, 137
Hazor, 137
Health, Mental, 153-155, 160, 165, 167-168
Heaven(s), 26, 40, 44-49, 58, 64, 94, 105, 144, 146-147, 166, 176, 187-188, 192, 197, 199-200, 202, 234-235, 237
Hebrew (Language), 99, 101, 107, 134, 148, 206, 211, 215, 220, 222, 227, 231-233
Hebron, 226
Hell, 42, 235
Heresy, 54
Hermeneutics, 18-20, 30, 35, 38, 40, 46
Herod, (Palace), 222-230
Herod Agrippa, 225
Heshbon, 134
Hippicus, 224
History, Christian, 18-19
Hittite, 137

Homoousios, 39
Honey, 6, 10, 12
Honeycomb, 5-6, 9-10, 12
Horse, 234-235
Humanism, 46
Humility, 123, 127, 152
Hupostasis, 41, 47, 49-50

Idolatry, 5, 8, 14-15, 55, 58
Immorality, 3, 10-11, 13-14, 45, 48
Incarnation, 49, 84, 106, 112, 115-119, 127-128, 130, 142, 176
Intermarriage, 4-6
Interpersonal Relationships . . . , 67
Iran, 93
Israel, 6, 11, 42, 69, 73, 93, 98, 100, 119, 133-135, 138, 140, 147, 180, 191, 198-200, 219, 227, 232-233, 237-238

Jaffa Gate, 223-224, 226
Jerusalem, 23, 70-71, 74, 76, 81-82, 90, 98, 100-101, 103, 135, 157, 188, 197, 222-224, 226-227, 229-230, 234
Jew, 4-8, 14, 43, 54-55, 60, 68-77, 79, 82, 87, 89-92, 94-95, 98-99, 101-104, 106, 110, 124-125, 132, 137, 153, 160, 177, 179-180, 182, 184-185, 191-193, 195, 197, 199, 208-209, 212-216, 218, 220-224, 228, 230, 234-235
John 3:14-15 . . . , 132-147
Jordan River, 101
Joseph and Aseneth . . . , 1-16
Judaism, 3-4, 6, 13, 15-16, 32, 68, 87, 93, 97, 102, 104, 107, 109-110, 148, 167, 208-209, 221
Judea, 67, 69-70, 72, 81, 98, 101, 191, 199, 222, 233
Judgment, 26-27, 47, 64-65, 71-72, 76-77, 92, 100, 103-104, 114, 118, 125, 144, 146-147, 158, 187, 196, 209, 218, 220, 223-224

Jupiter Damascenus, 226
Justice, 70, 72, 77, 112, 156

Kerygma, 86, 88
Kidron Valley, 100
King, 73, 77, 89, 102, 104, 134, 159, 224, 228, 233, 235
Kingdom of God, 29, 76, 85, 92-93, 113, 140, 165, 168, 176, 186, 188, 191-192, 196-199, 201, 234

Lampstand, 235
Land, Holy, 97, 230
Law, 50, 68, 73-78, 90, 92, 95, 100, 102-105, 121, 144, 157, 160-161
Leopard, 236
Levite, 70, 97, 101
Lion, 234, 236
Lithostroton, 101, 222, 224, 227-228
Locust, 235
Logos, 50, 59, 84-86, 103, 179
Lord's Prayer, 40
Lord's Supper, 37-38, 40, 44-48, 51, 53, 81, 114, 116
Love, 64, 80-83, 92, 95, 104, 106-107, 112, 114-116, 118, 121-122, 125-131, 152, 159, 161-162, 166, 169, 181, 218
Lucifer, 43, 62

Magi, 59
Magic, 54, 57, 60, 134
Magog, 237
Manicheans, 42
Manna, 1, 11-15, 100, 105, 108, 138, 180
Mariamme, 224
Market, Upper, 228
Marriage, 14, 82, 112, 137, 153, 157, 176-178
Martyr, 60, 120, 194, 199
Mediator, 49
Megiddo, 137
Mesopotamia, 191
Messiah, 12, 24-25, 27, 69-70, 72, 76, 87-90, 97-99, 102, 104-108,

122, 130, 157, 175-176, 188, 200, 216
Metaphors and Ministry . . . , 111-131
Michael (angel), 232, 236
Midianites, 137, 233
Midras, 84
Midrash, 209
Ministry, 11, 112-118, 120-122, 126, 128, 130-131, 153-154, 158, 166, 180, 200-201, 215-216, 220
Miracle, 32, 39-40, 57, 102, 104-105, 113, 125, 146, 174-176, 181
Mission(ary), 66, 84, 86-87, 89-92, 95-96, 117, 119, 121, 124-125, 159, 161-162, 164
Missions . . . , 84-96
Moab, 233
Monasticism, 55, 84
Monophysitism, 47, 49, 86
Monotheism, 15, 39, 92, 186
Morality, 68, 70, 74, 77, 112, 128-130, 153, 158, 169
Mount Hor, 133
Muslims, 86, 92, 230
Mystery Religion, 4
Myth(ology), 31, 54, 188

Nag Hammadi, 97
Nature, Divine, 37-38, 41-52, 91-92, 117, 178, 238
Nature, Human, 37-38, 41-52, 117
Nazareth, 23-24, 32-34, 100
Nea Church, 223
Near East, 132, 136-137, 191, 208
Nehushtan, 135
Nero, 199
Nestorius, 37-38, 43, 46, 51
Nicolaitans, 233
Nineveh, 140

Obedience, 115, 123-124, 126, 162
Ointment of Destruction, 5, 11
Ointment of Incorruption, 3, 5-6, 10
Old Testament and Revelation . . . , 231-239

Olives, Mount of, 100
Omega, 238
Omnipresence, 37
Ordinance, 14
Origen's Demonology . . . , 54-66
Orthodoxy, 36-37, 39, 42-43, 46-48

Paganism, 56, 60, 68
Palestine, 68, 93, 97, 100, 105, 107, 110, 137, 209, 221, 226, 237
Papacy, 42
Parable, 207
Paraclete, 85, 120, 123, 156
Paradise, 10, 13-14
Parousia, 62, 182, 195-196, 200-204, 233
Parousia, Delay of, 201-203
Passover, 81, 97, 100-101
Patmos, 194
Pergamum, 233
Persia, 191, 199, 235-236
Pesher, 209-210, 213-214
Pharaoh, 59, 219
Pharisees, 69-74, 81, 101-102, 107, 157, 160
Phasael, 224
Philosophy, Greek, 68, 78
Pluralism, 86
Praetorium, 100, 222-224, 228, 230
Prayer, 58, 61, 96, 115-116, 126, 130, 133-134, 163, 204
Preaching, 26, 65, 113, 124-125, 169, 197, 206-207, 212, 215
Predestination, 187, 196
Priest(s), 70, 72-75, 80, 97, 101-102, 160, 223-224, 228, 232-233
Prophet(s), 42, 71, 79, 86, 89, 97, 99, 102, 105, 148, 166, 175, 186, 189-191, 193, 195, 197, 199-200, 205, 207, 218-219, 235, 238
Protestantism, 40, 44, 52, 153
Pseudonymity, 185, 187, 193
Psychiatry, 153-155, 169, 170
Psychology, 150-155, 162-163, 167, 169, 218-220
Psychology, Pastoral, 154

Psychotherapy, 150-154, 158, 169
Ptolemy, 191

Qumran, 4, 97, 105-107, 109, 214

Rabbi, 78, 103-105, 108, 135, 153, 156, 176, 209, 213, 219-220
Rainbow, 234
Reconciliation, 72
Redeemer, 26, 45
Redemption, 32-34, 43, 45, 49, 96, 147, 164, 197, 199, 200, 219
Reformation, 36, 52-53, 57, 190, 195
Relativity, Historical, 18, 34-35
Religion, 16, 35, 56, 68, 70, 152, 154-155, 157, 168-170, 188, 235
Remnant, 89, 188
Repentance, 106, 168, 197
Resurrection, 25-26, 39, 42, 45, 48, 50, 65, 72, 74-75, 79-80, 90, 94, 96, 98, 100, 116, 121-122, 128, 142, 163, 174, 177, 181, 196, 198, 200, 238
Revelation, 13, 46, 83, 86, 92, 106, 116, 129-130, 146, 178, 182, 187, 192-195, 199, 202, 217, 231-238
Righteousness, 47-48, 107
Rome(an), 67-68, 70-76, 101, 184, 199, 208, 222-224, 228, 230, 235-237

Sabbath, 71, 87, 90, 92, 95, 98, 101, 103, 104
Sacred Meal, 4
Sacrifice, 47, 56, 164
Sadducees, 70, 72, 74-75, 101
Salim, 100
Salvation, 37-39, 41, 43, 47, 49, 65, 89, 98, 120, 125, 127, 146-147, 152, 167, 169, 183, 188, 196, 219
Samaria(tans), 67, 69, 71, 78, 97, 100-101, 103, 116, 124, 168, 178-179
Scholarship, Biblical, 17-18, 21-22, 35, 114

Science, 150-151, 153, 169, 221
Scribes, 69, 74, 101
Scripture, 18, 21, 27-28, 34-35, 39-40, 46, 60, 62, 86, 95, 99, 102, 148, 168, 196, 205, 209, 215-216
Sea, Red (Reed), 59, 133, 238
Sebaste (Samaria), 226, 228
Seleucius, 191
Semitic Backgrounds . . . , 97-110
Senate, 59
Send(ing), 86, 90, 92, 94-96, 112, 115, 116, 119-121, 125-126, 128, 130, 156, 176
Septuagint, 13, 211-212, 215, 219-220
Sepulchar, Church of Holy, 230
Serpent, 100, 132-138, 140, 146-147, 236
Servant(hood), 86, 89-93, 103, 113, 121, 126-128, 130, 142-143, 164-166, 201, 203, 226, 235, 238
Shechem, 100, 137
Signs, 89-90, 98, 102, 104, 113, 122, 125, 140, 160, 171-181, 217
Siloam, 108
Sin, 14, 39, 42-43, 47-48, 51, 55, 60, 62-64, 66, 78, 94, 99, 104, 107, 118, 129, 133, 147, 154, 156, 158, 161, 164, 167, 169, 178, 233
Sinai, 235
Sion, Church of Holy, 230
Society, 16, 68, 83, 93-94, 112, 130, 165, 168-169, 183, 221
Sola Scriptura, 38-39, 46
Soteriology, 11, 13, 45, 49, 85, 187
Soul, 43-44, 61, 64, 153, 161, 168
Source, 205, 207
Source & Function of Isa. 6 . . . , 205-220
Spirit of Life, 9-10
Struthion Pool, 223
St. Sophia (Church), 223
Sychar, 78, 100

Symbolism, 186, 188
Synagogue, 71, 74-75, 102-103
Syncretism, 85
Syria, 137, 191, 226
Syriac, 227

Table Fellowship, 4, 8, 14
Tabernacles, Feast of, 71, 101
Tambaram, 84
Tao, 85
Teacher, 73, 76, 78, 80-83, 102, 120, 122, 140, 156, 160, 164, 167, 169, 194, 197-198, 200-201
Telos, 184, 190
Temenos, 227-228
Temple, 25, 55, 72, 76, 90, 92, 99-102, 104, 157, 197, 225-228, 234-235
Temple Mount, 222-223, 226, 230
Temptation, 63, 92
Tenth Roman Legion, 226, 229-230
Testimony Book, 212
Theocracy, 29
Theology, Alexandrian, 38
Theology, Biblical, 21, 35, 171, 174
Theology, Christian, 19, 22, 31, 200
Theology, Historical, 18
Theology of Signs . . . , 171-181
Theology of the Cross, 37-38, 40
Theology, Practical, 111-112, 130-131
Theology, Protestant, 18, 53
Theology, Systematic, 17-18, 21, 112
Theophany, 234
Therapeutae, 4
Therapy, 150-152, 163-164, 168-169
Therapy, Logo, 155, 160
Therapy, Reality, 154, 161
Throne, 234
Thyatira, 233
Tiberias, 100
Timna, 137
Tradition, 7-9, 12, 15, 68, 71, 85, 92, 99, 109, 215, 220-221
Tradition, Oral, 22, 136, 188-189, 214
Tradition, Reformed, 46

Transmission, Oral, 29
Transubstantiation, 47
Trinitarianism, 39, 41, 43, 47-49, 85
Tritheism, 39
Turkish, Citadel, 224-225
Typology, 209-210
Tyropoean Valley, 223, 230

Ubiquity, 45-47, 49, 52
Uppsala, 85

Via Dolorossa, 222-223, 229

War, 54, 104, 106, 187, 229, 232
Will, Free, 29, 61-64, 83, 162, 167
Wine, 7, 117, 162, 177-178, 236
Wisdom, 9, 106
Witnessing, 86, 89-91, 95-96, 100, 102, 109, 113-114, 119, 124-126, 130-131, 176, 216, 235
Word of God, 31, 34-35, 39, 41-43, 45, 50-51, 59, 61, 94, 98-99, 105, 126, 157-158, 235
World, 112, 115-123, 125-126, 128-130, 145, 156-159, 164-166, 180, 184, 187-188, 190, 196-198, 200, 208, 236
Worship, 57, 92, 94, 103, 114, 168, 228, 233

Zion, Mount, 230, 233

Biblical Persons Index

Aaron, 133
Abraham, 38, 60, 68, 71, 98, 160, 180
Adam, 42-43, 49, 51, 149
Andrew, 69, 81, 100, 122, 159, 176
Annas, 25, 74-76, 101
Archelaus, 70, 73
Augustus, 227-228

Balaam, 233

Caiaphas, 69, 74-75, 101, 222
Cephas (Peter), 79, 81, 108, 159
Cornelius, 92
Cyrus, 235

Deborah, 77
David, 75, 104-105, 136, 154, 203

Eleazar, 133
Elijah, 69, 97, 102, 144-145, 197, 200, 235
Esther, 79
Eve, 149

Gog, 237

Herod, 25, 73, 95, 101, 222-228, 230
Hezekiah, 135-136

Issac, 69
Isaiah, 89, 97, 143-144, 155, 166, 206, 214, 218, 220

Jacob, 60, 78, 99-100, 143, 168, 220
Jethro, 149
Joel, 200
John, 23-25, 28-30, 51, 68, 76, 82, 84, 86-89, 92, 95, 98, 100, 102-103, 106-107, 109, 113-114, 116-117, 120, 123, 130, 139, 141-143, 146-147, 157, 159-160, 168, 172, 174-176, 178-180, 192, 194-195, 199, 201-204, 208, 212, 214-216, 218-222, 224, 230, 233
John the Baptist, 42-43, 69-70, 73, 81, 95, 100-102, 119, 122, 140, 156, 197, 200
Joseph, 100

Joseph, Mary's Husband, 28, 82
Joseph of Arimathea, 69, 98, 101
Joshua (Priest), 235
Judas, 64, 69, 73, 76, 99, 180

Lazarus, 69, 72, 74-75, 78, 81, 97, 101, 113, 116, 173, 176-177
Luke, 24-25, 114, 207, 224
Lydia, 92

Malachi, 93
Malchus, 80
Mark, 113-114, 207, 224
Mary, 28, 38, 41, 43-45, 49, 176
Mary Magdalene, 79
Mary (Martha's Sister), 69, 78, 81, 101
Martha, 69, 78, 81
Matthew, 23-24, 207, 224
Miriam, 133
Moses, 68, 74, 76-77, 95, 99, 102-105, 122, 132-136, 138, 140-141, 143-146, 149, 157, 160, 180, 235-236

Nathaniel, 98, 145, 173-174, 176, 178-179
Nicodemus, 72, 76, 132, 140-141, 145, 147, 168, 174, 178-179
Noah, 140

Og, 134

Paul, 37, 41, 60, 92, 111-112, 127, 165, 195-198, 200-201, 204, 216
Peter (Simon), 69, 74, 79-81, 83, 92, 100, 122-124, 127, 130, 159, 163, 176
Philip, 69, 81, 100, 116, 176, 179
Pilate, 25, 69, 73, 75, 77, 101, 222-224, 230

Sihon, 134
Simon (Peter), 69, 74, 79, 122, 159

Thomas, 69, 108, 116, 174

Zerubbabel, 235

Authors

Abbott, Edwin A., 217
Abrahams, Israel, 97, 104
Achtemeier, Paul J., 113, 128, 196
Albright, William Foxwell, 101, 107
Amiran, R., 224-226, 229
Andersen, W.W., 89
Anderson, Ray, 118
Anderson, Ward, 89
Anselm, 39
Apuleius, 56
Aquinas, Thomas, 207
Ard, Robert C., 169
Aristotle, 78, 178
Arius, 42
Ashcraft, Morris, 204
Athanasius, 47, 55, 194
Athenagoras, 56, 61
Attridge, H.W., 56
Augustine, 37-38, 42, 50-51
Aune, David E., 193, 201-202
Avigad, Nahman, 223, 230
Avi-Yonah, Michael, 228

Bahat, D., 224-225
Bailey, K., 93
Balch, David L., 200
Barclay, William, 236
Barnes, A.C., 54
Barr, David L., 201
Barrett, C.K., 14, 108-109, 115, 119-120, 124, 126, 128-130, 172-174, 176, 208-211, 221
Bartelink, G.J.M., 63
Barth, Karl, 17, 20, 22, 117
Batiffol, P., 2, 3
Bauckham, Richard J., 191
Bauer, W., 203
Beasley-Murray, G.R., 87, 91, 95, 203, 208, 235
Beckwith, R.T., 4
Bell, Albert A., 194
Benoit, P., 222, 227
Bernard, 43
Bernard, J.H., 99
Bertram, G., 141, 143
Bettencourt, S., 54, 61, 63
Billerbeck, P., 1, 12-13, 54, 104, 109

Black, M., 108, 207
Blanc, Cecile, 54, 62-63
Blandrata, George, 39
Blauw, J., 89
Blazer, Dan, 155, 168
Bloch, Joshua, 192
Boadt, Lawrence, 188
Boismard, M.C., 10
Bokser, B., 137
Boraas, R., 135
Borchert, Gerald L., 173
Borgen, P., 12, 143-145
Bornhauser, K., 124
Bornkamm, G., 10
Borsch, F., 142-143
Bosch, D.J., 88
Boszormenyi-Nagy, Ivan, 150
Bowman, C., 137
Bowman, J., 146, 184, 212
Bratcher, R.G., 205-206
Brenk, F.E., 54
Bretschneider, Karl, 17, 28
Bright, John, 68
Brown, Raymond E., 13, 87, 89, 91, 105, 107, 110, 114, 121-122, 124, 127, 129, 139, 141-142, 172-176, 212-214
Brown, Schuyler, 107
Browning, Don S., 111-112, 128, 130
Bruce, F.F., 197, 210
Bucer, Martin, 36
Budd, P., 136
Buis, P., 133
Bull, R.J., 100
Bullinger, Heinrich, 36, 38-39, 52
Burchard, C., 3-4
Burkitt, F.C., 189
Burney, C.F., 107-108

Caird, G.B., 59, 195, 233, 235
Calvin, John, 36-40, 46, 48-52
Cambier, J., 239
Carson, D.A., 88, 124
Celsus, 55-56, 58, 60
Chadwick, Henry, 57
Charles, R.H., 2, 189, 231-232, 234-235

Charlesworth, James H., 187, 192, 194-195, 200
Chesnutt, Randall D., 1, 3-4, 6
Ciholas, Paul, 174
Clark, Kenneth, 152
Clark, W. Royce, 17
Clement of Alexandria, 55, 58, 64, 194
Clinebell, Howard, 153, 168
Coats, G., 134-136
Cohen, Shaye J.D., 189, 210
Collins, Adela Yarbro, 185, 194, 202
Collins, John J. 3-4, 6, 8, 183-184, 190-193, 196, 208
Collins, R.F., 173, 177
Colwell, E.C., 107
Conder, Claude R., 100
Conn, H.M., 86
Conzelmann, Hans, 174
Coppens, J., 143
Coote, R., 137
Cowen, Emory L., 163
Cranfield, C.E.B., 113
Cranmer, Thomas, 53
Crouzel, H., 56
Crowfeet, J.W., 227
Cullmann, Oscar, 10, 184
Cyprian, 60, 212
Cyril of Jerusalem, 207

Dahl, N.A., 102
Daniélou, J., 59-61
Danker, W.F., 86
Danner, Dan G., 36
Davey, Noel, 108
Davies, W.D., 68, 214
D'Aragon, Jean-Louis, 231, 236
de Faye, E., 61, 65
De Jonge, M., 173-174
Delcor, M., 4
Delling, G., 7, 208
de Moor, J., 137
Denck, Hans, 38
Dennison, W.D., 174, 177
De Ridder, R.R., 91, 95
de Vaulx, J., 135
de Vries, S., 133

de Vaard, J., 210
de Sette, Wilhelm M.L., 23
Dick, Michael Brennan, 195
Dietrich, M., 137
Di Lella, Alexander A., 233
Dionysius, 194
Dittmar, W., 205
Dobson, James, 168
Dodd, C.H. 89, 103-104, 108, 139, 175, 184, 213, 218
Dominic, 42
Drakeford, John, 153
Duke, P., 142
Dulles, Avery, 123, 125
Dunn, J.D.G., 208, 211
Durant, Will, 162

Eck, John, 46-47
Eichrodt, W., 135, 218
Eitan, A., 224-226, 229
Ellis, E.E., 207, 209, 211, 213
Ellison, H.L., 70
English, Ava C., 149-150
English, Horace B., 149-150
Etheridge, J., 135
Eutyches, 51
Evans, Craig, 207

Farrar, F.W., 209
Faulkner, Paul, 168
Felix, Minucius, 55, 57
Ferguson, Everett, 54, 65, 208-209
Fichtner, J., 136
Fiorenza, Elisabeth Schüssler, 198-199
Fitzmyer, J.A., 140, 214
Fleming, B.C.E., 86
Foley, John G., 149
Ford, J. Massyngberde, 196, 200, 235
Fortna, Robert, 172, 174
Francis, 42
Frankl, Viktor, 155, 160, 165, 168
Frayne, D., 137
Free, John C., 67
Freed, Edwin D., 99, 205
Fretheim, T., 133, 138

Freud, Sigmund, 150, 152, 154
Fritz, V., 135-136
Funk, Robert, 207

Gadamer, Hans Georg, 19, 22
Gager, John G., 202
Gardner, Stephen, 53
Gartner, B., 12
Gaster, T., 137
Geffcken, J., 56
Geva, H., 224, 229
Griffiths, D.R., 89, 95
Gildersleeve, B.L., 217
Gilmore, S. MacLean, 236
Ginzburg, L., 13
Girad, Marc, 173
Glassar, William, 154-155
Glasson, T.F., 14, 146, 183
Gonzalez, Justo L., 46, 49
Goodenough, E.R., 4
Goodwin, Charles, 212
Grassi, Joseph A., 173, 180
Gray, G., 135-136
Gray, J., 136
Grogan, G.W., 239
Gross, Martin, 151
Gruenwald, Ithamar, 185, 191
Grundmann, Walter, 102
Gundry, R., 213, 215
Gunkel, Hermann, 188
Guthrie, Donald, 88, 173-174

Haenchen, Ernst, 114, 139, 177
Hall, D.R., 74-75
Hanson, A.T., 239
Hanson, Paul D., 183, 185, 200
Hanson, R.P.C., 211
Harnack, Adolf, 66
Harrelson, W., 133
Harris, J. Rendel, 212-213
Hartman, Louis F., 233
Hegel, Georg W.F., 19-20, 31
Hellholm, David, 193
Hengel, Martin, 187, 208
Hermas, 63
Hiltner, Seward, 111, 149
Hippocrates, 55, 57

Hippolytus, 58, 194
Hoenig, S.B., 8
Hollander, Edwin P., 68
Holtz, T., 3-4
Homer, 210
Hooker, Morna, 216
Hooper, John, 52
Hoskyns, Edwyn, 108, 124, 212, 216
Howard, W.F., 108
Hubmaier, Balthasar, 38
Huffard, Evertt W., 84
Hunt, Raymond G., 68

Ignatius, 59
Irenaeus, 61

Jackson, B.D., 61
Jacobson, D.M., 226
Jeremias, J., 4, 8, 74, 77-78, 216
Jewett, P.K., 79
Johns, C.N., 224-225, 229
Johnson, Alan, 194
Joines, K., 135-138
Jung, Carl G., 154, 168
Justyn (Martyr), 54, 56, 58-62, 194

Kant, Immanuel, 19, 21
Käsemann, E., 10, 189, 200-201
Kautzch, E., 2
Kee, H.C., 4
Kenyon, I., 227
Kierkegaard, S., 20
Kilmartin, E.J., 12
Kilpatrick, G.D., 2, 4
Kilpatrick, William Kirk, 151
Klassen, W., 239
Klausner, Joseph, 104
Knox, W.L., 60
Koch, H., 61
Koch, Klaus, 182-183, 188
Kuhn, K.G., 4
Kümmel, W.G., 10
Küng, Hans, 17-18, 20
Kraemar, Hendrick, 84-85, 91
Kraft, C.H., 86
Krasner, Barbara, 150
Kysar, R., 143, 146, 171-173, 175-180

Lactantius, 57
Ladd, G.E., 87-88, 94, 184, 190, 192, 237
Laertius, Diogenes, 56
Lancellotti, Angelo, 231-232
Latimer, Hugh, 52
Lederer, Wolfgang, 169
Légasse, S., 2
Lenski, Gerhard, 111
Lenski, Jean, 111
Lewis, Jack P., 97, 101
Lindars, B., 16, 142, 203
Locher, Gottfried W., 46-47, 49, 52
Loisy, Alfred, 17-18, 20
Longenecker, Richard, 208, 211
Lows, Malcolm, 98
Lucian, 56, 60
Lucke, Friedrich, 23
Lundberg, P., 60
Luther, Martin, 18, 36-49, 52, 195

Maddi, Salvatore, 68
Malina, B.J., 13
Maneschg, H., 132
Manson, T.W., 139, 213, 215
Marrs, Rick R., 132
Marshall, I.H., 67
Martyn, J. Louis, 114, 141, 144, 146, 171-172
(Martyr) Justin, 54, 56, 58-62, 194
Matson, David Lertis, 119-120
Mays, J., 134, 138, 147
Meeks, W.A., 14, 110, 143, 145-146
Megivern, James J., 198
Melanchthon, Philip, 36
Metzger, Bruce M., 88, 90, 186, 202
Mieses, M., 231
Miller, George, 152
Miller, M., 209
Minear, Paul S., 202
Mitchell, Carl, 148
Mollenauer, Sandra, 151-152
Moloney, F., 140, 142-143, 146, 173, 176
Moore, G.F., 68
Morris, Jenny, 209

Morris, Leon, 99, 186, 194
Moule, C.F.D., 88
Mowrer, O.H. 153-154, 168
Mussies, G., 195

MacGregor, G.H.C., 59
MacRae, G., 142

McGavran, Donald, 68, 88-89
McGinn, Bernard, 193
McHugh, M.P., 54
McNamara, M., 141, 209, 212

Nauck, W., 4
Neibuhr, H. Richard, 117-118
Neitzsche, F., 160
Nestorius, 43
Neusner, Jacob, 210
Newman, Barclay, 216
Neyrey, J., 140
Nicholson, G., 142, 145
Nickels, P., 209
Nickelsburg, George W.E., 191
Noth, M., 134, 136
Nougayrol, J., 137
Nygren, Anders, 129

Odeberg, H., 13, 144
Oecolampadius, Johannes, 36-37
Olbricht, Thomas, H. 171
Origen, 54-66, 194
Osborne, G.R., 210
Osgood, Charles E., 158
Osiander, Andreas, 49

Pack, Della, 84
Pack, Frank, 1, 54, 84, 92-93, 132, 202, 231
Painter, John, 206
Pancaro, S., 14, 115
Pannenberg, Wolfhart, 17, 26, 189
Pattison, E.M., 153
Peliken, Jaroslav, 37
Perez, A. del Agua, 132
Philipsz, Dirk, 38
Philo, 209, 223
Philostratus, 60
Plato, 56, 78

Plotnik, Rod, 151-152
Plutarch, 55-56
Porphyry, 56
Porton, G., 210
Potter, G.R., 46-47
Potter, R.D., 101
Priest, James E., 182
Pullias, E.V., 155

Rahner, Karl, 17, 20
Rainey, A., 137
Redlich, E. Basil, 101
Reichelt, Karl Ludvig, 84-85
Rengstorf, K.H., 95-96, 120, 175-176
Riga, Peter, 174, 179-180
Riggs, J.W., 8
Rist, Martin, 202
Roberts, J.J.M., 204
Robertson, A.T., 217
Robinson, J.A.T., 87-88, 98, 105, 124, 199
Robinson, John Thomas, 184
Rogers, Carl, 155
Rothenberg, B., 137-138
Rowland, Christopher, 183-184
Rowley, H.H., 136, 189
Rusch, Frederick A., 180
Russell, D.S., 186, 189, 200

Sabellius, 50
Saldarini, Anthony J., 195
Sanday, W., 207
Sanders, E.P., 210
Sandmel, Samuel, 70-71
Sang, Barry Ray, 183
Sanger, D., 4, 6
Sayers, Dorothy, 79
Schillebeeckx, Edward, 17-18, 20, 115
Schlatter, Adolf, 239
Schleiermacher, Friedrich, 17-35
Schlier, H., 59
Schnackenburg, R., 2, 4, 87, 90-91, 109-110, 116, 119, 123-124, 139-140, 144, 146, 171-172, 174, 181, 219
Schneider, J., 94

Schneiders, Sandra M., 173
Schneweis, E., 54
Schmidt, Johann M., 183
Schmithals, Walter, 197
Schoeps, H.J., 54
Schrage, Wolfgang, 103
Schreiter, R.J., 86
Sharpe, Eric J., 85-86
Schulz, S., 143
Schürer, Emil, 192, 208-210
Schweitzer, Albert, 184, 189
Schweizer, Eduard, 115
Schwenkfeld, Kasper, 42
Scott, C. Anderson, 236
Seeberg, Reinhold, 45-46
Senior, D., 87
Servetus, Michael, 39, 49-51
Shenk, W.R., 89, 91
Shepherd, Jr., Massey H., 98, 171, 173
Sidebottom, E., 143
Simonetti, M., 63
Simons, Menno, 36, 38, 49
Smalley, S.S., 88-89, 143, 171-174
Smith, Darrel, 150
Smith, Jonathan Z., 189
Smith, Jr., D. Moody, 111, 113-116, 125, 216, 239
Smith, Morton, 109
Snaith, N., 134
Sneen, Donald, 198
Socinus, Faustus, 36, 39-40
Socrates, 58
Soderlund, S.K., 211
Soury, Guy, 54
Sparks, H.F.D., 3-4
Spiegler, Gerhard, 34
Stagg, Frank, 199
Stambaugh, John E., 200
Stancaro, Francesco, 49
Steinhauser, M.G., 209
Stendahl, K., 210, 213-214
Stott, J.R.W., 96
Strack, H., 1, 12-13, 54, 104, 109
Strauss, D.F., 19, 27, 33
Stuart D., 236

Stuhmueller, C., 87
Suci, George J., 158
Sukenik, E.L., 227
Sundberg, A.C., 213
Swete, Henry Barclay, 231
Szasz, Thomas, 151, 153

Tabick, J., 136-137
Talbert, Charles H., 113-114
Tannenbaum, Percy H., 158
Tatian, 62
Teeple, Howard M., 106-107
Teichtweier, Georg, 61-62
Tenney, Merrill C., 173
Tertullian, 57-58, 60, 62
Thielicke, Helmut, 118
Tillich, Paul, 17, 19-20
Torrance, T.F., 117
Torrey, C.C., 99, 107-108, 231
Tov, Emanuel, 221
Toy, C.H., 205
Turner, N., 108-109
Turpie, D.M., 205
Tushingham, A.D., 224-225, 229
Tyler, Ronald L., 205
Tyndale, William, 52

Ubell, Earl, 151

van der Wall, C., 199
van Unnik, W.C., 87-88, 102, 124
Vawter, Bruce, 172
Verkuyl, J., 88
Vincent, L.H., 222
Vine, W.E., 156
Vitz, Paul, 152
Volker, W., 60-61, 63-64
Volz, P., 102
von Harnack, Adolph, 17
von Rad, Gerhard, 125, 189, 218-220

Walvoord, John F., 203
Weder, Hans, 180
Weiss, Johannes, 189
Wendel, Francois, 49, 52
Wenham, G., 138
Westberg, Granger, 154

Westcott, B.F., 216, 221
Wey, H., 54, 56
Whiting, R., 137
Wilkinson, John, 226, 230
Williams, Daniel Day, 111
Williamson, Edmond G., 149
Willis, John T., 231
Wilson, John F., 221
Winn, A.C., 88, 95, 120
Wren, Charles G., 149
Wright, G.E., 125
Woollcott, Jr., Philip, 154

Yinger, J. Milton, 68
Young, D., 137
Young, F.W., 214

Zerwick, Maximilian, 217
Zwingli, Huldrich, 36-38, 40, 44-49, 51-52

Editors

Achtemeier, Paul J., 128, 196
Ackroyd, P.R., 208
Aland, K., 205, 207
Albright, William Foxwell, 196, 200
Anderson, Ray S., 117
Arndt, William F., 203
Avi-Yonah, Michael, 228

Bailer, Sr., Lloyd Richard, 199-200, 202
Black, Matthew, 192, 204, 208-209
Bleeker, C.J., 4
Bromiley, G.W., 96, 102, 204, 207
Brown, Raymond, 212, 231
Bruce, F.F., 204
Bucke, Emory Stevens, 199
Burchard, C., 3-7
Busse, Ulric, 114
Buttrick, George Arthur, 202

Charlesworth, J.H., 3, 187
Clifford, R., 142
Collins, Adela Yarbro, 193
Collins, John J., 184-185, 195
Corrie, George Elwes, 52
Cox, John Edmund, 53
Crim, Keith, 199
Cross, Frank, 205

Daube, David, 101
Davies, W.D., 101
Donaldson, J., 212
Douglas, J.D, 67, 194
Dudley, Carl S., 111

Efird, James M., 239
Elliger, K., 205
Evans, G.F., 208

Fitzmyer, J., 212, 231
Freedman, David Noel, 196, 200
Friedrich, Gerhard, 102-103, 156, 175, 211
Funk, Robert W., 34, 114
Furnish, Victor Paul, 199-200, 202

Gaebelein, Frank E., 194
Gingrich, F. Wilbur, 203
Goodheer, Wil C., 54

Goodman, Martin, 192, 208-209
Guthrie, Donald, 203

Haase, Wolfgang, 185
Hanson, Paul D., 182-183, 188-189, 202
Harding, Thomas, 52
Hellholm, David, 194
Hinke, William John, 48

Jeremias, Joachim, 2

Kehm, George H., 189
Kimmerle, Heinz, 18
Kittel, Gerhard, 94, 96, 120, 156, 175, 204, 211
Klauser, Th., 54
Klassen, William, 102
Knight, Douglas A., 183
Kohler, K., 54
Kraft, Robert A., 192, 212
Kuhn, H.W., 2

Laymon, Charles M., 171, 236
Liddell, H.G., 228
Lucke, F., 30

Meeks, Wayne A., 189, 193, 200
Miller, Fergus, 192, 208-209
Motyer, J.A., 203
Moulton, J.H., 108
Mowrer, O.H., 151
Murphy, R., 212

MacRae, G., 142

McCord, James I., 113, 117
McNeill, John T., 37

Nestle, E., 205
Neusner, J., 110, 146
Nevinson, Charles, 52
Nickelsburg, George W.E., 192, 212

Odebricht, Rudolf, 19

Parker, T.H.L., 113, 117
Patrides, C.A., 193
Pelikan, J., 40-41, 45
Person, B.A., 189
Philonenko, M., 3-4

Rahlfs, A., 205
Redeker, Martin, 21
Roberts, A., 212
Rowley, H.H., 204
Rudolph, W., 205

Scholz, Heinrich, 21
Scott, R., 228
Shelp, Earl E., 111
Snider, Graydon F., 102
Sparks, H.F.D., 2
Stegemann, H., 2
Stendahl, K., 4
Stibbs, A.M., 203
Strachey, James, 152
Sunderland, Ronald, 111

Talbert, Charles H., 113
Talmon, S., 205
Tasker, R.V.G., 194
Temporini, H., 208
Thompson, B.P., 16
Tucker, Gene M., 183

Vermes, Geza, 192, 208-209
Vermes, Pamela, 192

Walter, Henry, 52
Walvoord, John F., 203
Wiseman, D.J., 203
Wittreich, Joseph, 193
Wolfgang, H., 208

Yadin, Y., 222, 225

Zuck, Roy B., 203

Translators

Arndt, William F., 203
Barton, D.M., 10
Battles, Ford Lewis, 37
Beasley-Murray, G.R., 10, 108, 117, 171
Bowden, John, 187
Bromiley, G.W., 94, 96, 102-103, 120, 175, 204, 236
Brooks, E.W., 2
Bury, R.G., 78
Butterworth, G.W., 62

Chadwick, Henry, 55-56
Cozens, Brian, 22

Eliot, George, 33

Filson, F.V., 10
Funk, Robert W., 114

Gingrich, F. Wilbur, 203
Green, T.M., 21
Grobel, K., 10

Hay, Charles E., 45
Hiers, Richard H., 189
Holland, David L., 189
Hudson, H., 21

Kohl, M., 188
Krodel, G., 10

Leitch, James W., 200

Mackintosh, H.R., 21
Madvig, D., 210
Montgomery, W., 184, 189
McLusky, F., 10
McLusky, I., 10

Orman, John, 32

Philonenko, M., 3
Pringle, William, 50

Rackam, H., 78
Robinson, J.M., 10

Smyth, Kevin, 2, 110, 116
Sowers, S.G., 10, 184
Stalker, D.M.G., 189
Steely, John E., 197

Stewart, J.S., 21
Stinespring, W.F., 104
Strachey, James, 152
Szold, H., 13

Thackeray, H. St. J., 228
Tice, John, 21

Verheyden, Jack C., 22

Winston, D., 139

Others

Alexander, 190
Antiochus IV Epiphanes, 236
Aseneth, 5-7, 10-12, 14

Bugenhagen, Johannes, 36, 40-41

Cerinthus, 41

Florus, 223, 228
Francis I., 47

Hadrian, 223, 230
Hitler, 165
Hyrcanus, John, 199

Joseph, 5-7, 16

Naram-suen, 137
Neriglissar, 137
Nero, 199